THE SCHEME OF REDEMPTION

ROBERT MILLIGAN

Gospel Advocate Company
P.O. Box 150
Nashville, Tennessee 37202

EXPOSITION AND DEFENSE

OF THE

Scheme of Redemption

AS IT IS REVEALED AND TAUGHT IN
THE HOLY SCRIPTURES.

By R. MILLIGAN,
President of the College of Bible in Kentucky University.

"I am not ashamed of the Gospel of Christ; for it is the power of God for salvation to every one that believeth." Romans i. 16

The Scheme of Redemption
Gospel Advocate Reprint Library Edition, 2001

First Published 1868

Published by Gospel Advocate Co.
P.O. Box 150, Nashville, TN 37202
www.gospeladvocate.com

ISBN: 0-89225-476-9

GENERAL CONTENTS.

Book Second.

PART I.

CHAPTER I.

CHAPTER II.

CHAPTER III.

PART II.

CHAPTER I.

CHAPTER II.

CHAPTER III.

CHAPTER IV.

CHAPTER V.

CHAPTER VI.

CHAPTER VII.

PART III.

CHAPTER I.

CHAPTER II.

PART IV.

CHAPTER I.

CHAPTER II.

CHAPTER III.

PART V.

CHAPTER I

CHAPTER II.

CHAPTER III.

BOOK THIRD.

PART I.

CHAPTER I.

CHAPTER II.

CHAPTER III.

CHAPTER IV.

CHAPTER V.

CHAPTER VI.

PART II.

CHAPTER I.

CHAPTER II.

CHAPTER III.

CHAPTER IV.

CHAPTER V.

CHAPTER VI.

CHAPTER VII.

PART III.

CHAPTER I.

CHAPTER II.

CHAPTER III.

CHAPTER IV.

PART IV.

CHAPTER I.

CHAPTER II.

PART V.

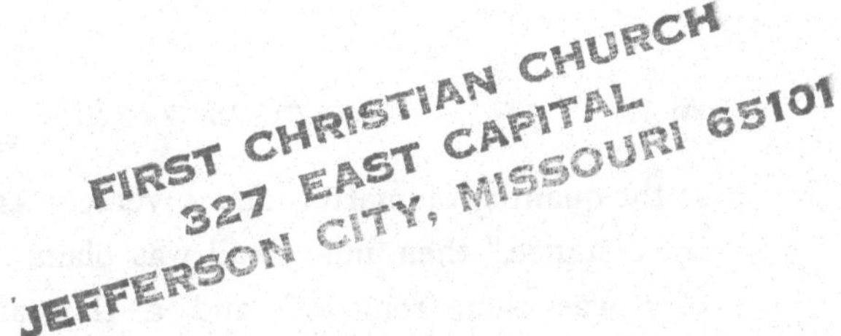

INTRODUCTION.

IN order to understand *fully* and *perfectly* any one part or element of a system, it is necessary to have, in the first place, a general and comprehensive knowledge of the whole. The several elements must be viewed and considered in their *relations* to each other and to the whole scheme or system of which they are the component and constituent parts. Nothing exists in a perfectly independent and isolated state. The universe is a unit—a vast system of means, agencies, and instrumentalities—all the parts of which have a mutual dependence on each other, and none of which can be comprehended *perfectly* without some knowledge of the whole. Before the laws of universal gravitation were discovered by Sir Isaac Newton, the whole physical universe was a series of mysteries; the laws of falling bodies, the weight of materials, the tides of the ocean, the motions of the several planets, and a thousand other terrestrial and celestial phenomena were all inexplicable even to the natural philosopher. But as soon as it was discovered that "every body in the universe, whether great or small, tends toward every other body, with a force which is as directly as the quantity of matter, and inversely as the square of the distance," then, indeed, all was plain, the vail of mystery was then removed, and a thousand subordinate questions were answered by the solution of this one great universal problem.

And just so it is with respect to the Bible. It, too, is a unit. Its primary, general, and ultimate object is to develop one great and glorious System of Divine wisdom, justice, goodness, mercy, and love, through Jesus Christ, for the redemption of fallen man. But, nevertheless, like nature, it has its parts; its subordinate ends and purposes; its wheels within wheels; and its systems within systems—all of which, to be perfectly understood, must be considered in their relations to each other, and to the whole system of which they are but parts.

The neglect or failure to do this has ever been a source of much error in the religious world. Owing, perhaps, to man's limited capacity, as well as to his waywardness, rashness, pride, conceit, and indisposition to toil and labor, system-makers have always been prone to be satisfied with narrow, contracted, one-sided, and imperfect views of the great schemes and purposes of Jehovah. And hence it is that the *common error* of all humanly constructed systems of religion, as well as of medicine, education, philosophy, etc., consists in substituting a part for the whole. One system-maker, for instance, gives undue relative prominence to the grace of God; another to the blood of Christ; another to the influence of the Spirit; another to faith; and another to works. All such systems contain some truth mixed with some error; but none of them contains the whole truth. Pelagianism is about as one-sided as Augustinism, and Arminianism is about as defective and erroneous as Calvinism.

In this work there is no attempt made to construct a system of any kind. This has already been done, and done perfectly, by that Spirit which searches all things, yea, even the deep counsels and purposes of Jehovah. And whatever serves to draw away the minds and hearts of the people from the constant, earnest, and prayerful study of this Divine system, whether it be in the form of a Catechism, a Creed, a Periodical, or a Newspaper, I can not but regard as an unqualified curse to our race. But whatever, on the other hand, serves to clear away the rubbish, the mists and fogs which human traditions and speculations have thrown over and around this system; whatever serves to lead and to incline the people to study it more earnestly, comprehend it more fully, love it more ardently, and reverence it more profoundly, I can not but regard as a great blessing to our race.

To accomplish this end, in some degree, is my sole object in the following work. My former work on "*Reason and Revelation*" was written for the purpose of making the reader *feel* and *realize* that the Bible as a whole, and in all its several parts, is the inspired Word of God. *This work is written for the purpose of helping him to comprehend its sublime and gracious contents, by leading and inducing him to study it by day and meditate on it by night.* And hence I have not attempted to *exhaust* any subject, but merely to give to the reader such hints, suggestions, illustrations, and explanations as will enable and encourage him to study the Bible for himself, and thus to satisfy his hungry and thirsty soul at the original, unwasting, and inexhaustible fountain of God's everlasting grace and love. Many thousand pages would of course be necessary to give any thing like a full exposition and defense of the Scheme of Redemption as it is presented to us in the Holy Scriptures. But I flatter myself that in the following pages I have given to the student of the Bible something that is really more valuable. Of this, others of course must judge. I can only say that the work has cost me much labor and hard thinking, and as much for the sake of brevity as for any thing else.

Primarily, this work, in connection with "*Reason and Revelation*," is designed to serve, *in part*, as a substitute for such a course of preliminary lectures as are found to be necessary in all Colleges and Seminaries of learning in which the Bible is properly taught and studied as a regular Text-Book. In this way I hope it will be of great assistance both to Teachers and to their pupils. It will, I trust, relieve the former from the necessity of delivering so full a Course of Lectures as would be absolutely necessary without it; and it will save the latter from the labor and toil of taking so full and copious notes as would otherwise be necessary.

But the work is also intended to serve as a help to the study and comprehension of the Bible in the Family, in the Sunday School, and in the Bible-Class. And hence it is written in the plainest and simplest style possible. All technicalities are avoided, and no foreign words are introduced into the text that can serve in any way to perplex the English reader. The few Greek and Hebrew words used for the benefit and satisfaction of the classical student may, without embarrassment, be passed over by all who are not acquainted with the original.

In quoting from the Scriptures I have generally used the common English version unchanged. But wherever the meaning of the text is obscure, or the words are either obsolete or barbarous, I have either used other translations, or modified the English text, or made a new translation from the original Greek or Hebrew.

It is due to my brethren to say that no one is responsible for any thing contained in this work but myself. To my friend and *true yoke-fellow*, Prof. J. W. McGarvey especially, I am indebted for many valuable suggestions. But I have in all cases recorded what, after due consideration, seemed to myself to be most consistent with the oracles of God.

And now, dear reader, if this volume serves to draw you nearer to God and to the Word of his grace, which is able to build you up and give you an inheritance among all the sanctified in Christ Jesus, my object will be accomplished. And "to Him who has loved us, and washed us from our sins in his own blood, and has made us kings and priests unto God," even his and our Father, to him be all the honor, and the glory forever and ever. Amen!

R. MILLIGAN.

KENTUCKY UNIVERSITY,
May 19, 1868.

SCHEME OF REDEMPTION.

BOOK FIRST.

PRELIMINARIES.

MY theme is the Scheme of Redemption. I wish to trace it from its origin, throughout all its subsequent phases and developments, till it finally results in the complete and eternal salvation of the Redeemed in God's everlasting kingdom.

Subject of the Treatise.

Like its Divine Author, it is, of course, infinitely perfect. We have nothing, therefore, to add to it, and nothing to subtract from it. Our purpose is simply to ascertain what it is, and what it requires of man.

Perfection of the Scheme.

In this attempt the Bible will, of course, be our chief guide and instructor. The Scheme of Redemption is no part of the original system of nature. It is a subsequent development. And for a knowledge of it, we must of course look to what God has himself said and taught concerning it, in the Living Oracles. In these it is given as the *Mystery revealed.*

Where taught and illustrated.

But first of all, the mind naturally dwells on God himself, as its infinitely glorious and perfect Author. And I will therefore now submit, for the consideration of the reader, a few thoughts on the Theology of the Bible.

First Topic suggested.

CHAPTER I.

GOD.

In speaking of God, we must be very careful not to be wise above what is written. For "*no man knoweth the Son but the Father; neither knoweth any man the Father, save the Son, and he to whomsoever the Son will reveal him.*" Matt. xi, 27.

God properly revealed only in and through the Bible.

True, indeed, it may be said, that "Something is; and therefore something eternally was." For as the ancients taught: "*Ex nihilo, nihil fit*"—from nothing, nothing comes. And hence it follows of necessity, that *something* must have existed from eternity.

Cudworth's argument from philosophical necessity.

But whether this was the Lord God of the Bible, as Moses teaches, or whether it was the Cosmos—the adorned and perfectly arranged universe, as Aristotle supposed, is a question which can perhaps never be satisfactorily decided by the dim light of nature.

Unsatisfactory for two reasons.

And even if we should arrive at the conclusion that the Cosmos is an effect, a creation of something else, it would still be a question what that preexisting something is—whether it is one or many; whether Monotheism,

Dualism, or Polytheism, is the true theology of the universe. The Persians worshiped two supposed coeternal divinities. The Greeks sometimes spoke of the one Supreme God; but they nevertheless worshiped their 30,000 imaginary created and uncreated deities; and the Hindoos still continue to adore about 333,000,000. And hence it is evident, that under the present sin-perverted light of nature, the tendency of the human mind is to Polytheism.

Tendency of the mind to Polytheism.

When, therefore, it is said, "The heavens declare the glory of God; and the firmament showeth his handywork," Psa. xix, 1; and again, "The invisible things of him, since the creation of the world, are clearly seen, being understood by the things that are made, even his eternal power and Godhood," Rom. i, 20—in all such passages, nothing more is intended than that such is the testimony of nature to him, to whom God has revealed himself, and whose mind is not blinded and perverted by sin.

Meaning of Psa. xix, 1, and Rom. i, 20.

To the Bible, then, we must look primarily and chiefly for a knowledge of the being, character, and attributes of God. In it we are taught all things that it is really necessary we should know concerning him, in order to our present and eternal well-being. Such, for example, are the following particulars:

What the Bible teaches concerning God.

I. *That God is one.* "Hear, O Israel, Jehovah our God is one Jehovah." Deut. vi, 4.

His Unity.

II. *That in this sublime and incomprehensible unity there is also embraced a threefold personality.* This is evident from such passages as the following:

His threefold Personality proved.

1. From Genesis i, 1. It is true that in this verse

the verb *created* (בָּרָא) is singular; but the name *God* (אֱלֹהִים) is plural. And hence it seems that the Holy Spirit labors even here, as it often does elsewhere, to guard the readers of the Bible against the extremes of both Polytheism and Unitarianism.

From Gen. i, 1.

Evidence from Genesis i, 26.

2. A still more striking instance of this plurality in the Divine Unity occurs in Genesis i, 26: "And God said, Let US make man in OUR image; after OUR likeness." Here the name *Eloheim*, the pronouns *us* and *our*, and the verb *make*, (נַעֲשֶׂה,) all serve to reveal and to express the plurality of our Creator in some sense.

Hypotheses with regard to this address.

I know it is alleged by some that this language is used merely in imitation of the *majestic style* of kings; and by others, that this address was delivered to angels.

Why neither of these is satisfactory.

But in reply to the first of these hypotheses, it is enough to say that no such majestic style was then in being. And with regard to the second, I need only remind the reader that angels are not *creators*, but simply *creatures*. God himself is the only Creator revealed to us in the Living Oracles.

Conclusion.

And hence we are constrained, by a fair and rational exegesis of this passage, to regard these words of the Holy Spirit as an expression of plurality in the Divine unity.

Evidence from Matt. xxviii, 19.

3. Another very remarkable example of this Trinity is given in the formula of Christian Baptism. "Baptize them," said our Redeemer, "into the name of the Father, and of the Son, and of the Holy Spirit." Here there is clearly but one Divinity, and yet a threefold personality.

4. Each of these three persons is called *God* in the Holy Scriptures. See 1 Cor. viii, 6; John i, 1; and Acts v, 3, 4.

Evidence from the word God, (Θεος.)

I need not multiply examples and illustrations. The *Divine Unity* in one sense, and the *Divine Plurality* in some other and different sense, are both as clearly revealed in the Bible as any thing else. And for us who believe in the plenary inspiration of the Holy Scriptures, this is of course sufficient. To reconcile fully these two attri butes of the Divine nature and character, and to explain satisfactorily in what they severally consist, may, for aught we know, be above the capacity of the Archangel. Indeed, to do this may require a perfect knowledge of the Divine nature. But, of course, the finite can not comprehend the Infinite. Job xi, 7. Let us, then, not attempt to be wise beyond or above what is written; but let us humbly and gratefully receive this sublime truth as a matter of faith, just as we are compelled to receive many other things that are clearly revealed in the three great volumes of creation, providence, and redemption.

Conclusion with regard to the Divine Unity and the Divine Plurality.

III. *It is also clearly taught in the Holy Bible, that God is* SPIRIT, John iv, 24; and, moreover that a spirit has not flesh and bones as we find in the human body. Luke xxiv, 39. And hence it is only by a figure of speech (anthropomorphism) that we ascribe any form of material organization to God.

God's essence is spirit, not matter.

IV. *That he is omniscient—a being of infinite knowledge.* This is proved,

Proof of his Omniscience.

1. By his works. He has weighed the mountains in scales, and the hills in a balance.

2. By prophecy. None but a being of infinite knowledge could have foretold what the Bible reveals to us.

3. By the direct testimony of the Scriptures. Isa. xl, 9, 10; Acts xv, 18; Romans xvi, 27. Finite knowledge is *nothing* compared with that which is infinite.

His Omnipotence.

V. *That he is omnipotent.* This is proved,

1. By his works. Psalms viii and xix.

2. By direct testimony. Genesis xvii, 1; and Revelation iv, 8.

His Omnipresence.

VI. *That he is omnipresent.* 1 Kings viii, 27; Psa. cxxxix, 7–10; Jeremiah xxiii, 23, 24; Acts xvii, 27, 28.

His Justice.

VII. *That he is infinitely just.* This is beautifully illustrated by Psa. lxxxix, 14: "Justice and judgment are the habitation of thy throne." And hence the death of Christ was necessary in order to the justification of the believer. Rom. iii, 25; Luke xxiv, 46.

His Holiness.

VIII. *That he is infinite in holiness.* Isa. vi, 3; and Rev. iv, 8; xv, 4.

His Goodness.

IX. *That he is infinite in goodness;* i. e., that in all cases he acts for the greatest good of the whole creation. Psalm cxlv, 9; and Matthew xix, 17.

His Eternity.

X. *That he is eternal;* without beginning of days or end of life. Psalm xc, 2; and 1 Timothy i, 17.

His Immutability.

XI. *That he is unchangeable.* "With him is no variableness, not even the shadow of turning." James i, 17.

The Source of all things.

XII. *That he is the Creator of all things.* Prov. xvi, 4; Rom. xi, 33–36; Rev. iv, 11.

INFERENCES.

From these premises it follows:

I. *That God makes no experiments;* that he never repents as man repents, (1 Samuel xv, 29,) and that he is never disappointed in any issue or contingency that can possibly arise. And hence it follows, that when God is said to repent, it is only by a figure, (anthropopathy,) in condescension to our imperfections. See Genesis vi, 6.

He is never disappointed.

II. *That his own nature is the Constitution of the universe;* according to which all things were created, and all laws enacted.

His Nature, the Constitution of the Universe.

III. *That his will is the only proper standard of rectitude.* John iv, 34; and 1 Cor. vi, 20.

Standard of Rectitude.

CHAPTER II.

CREATION.

SECTION I.—The Pre-Adamic Earth.

How long Jehovah existed alone, or at what epoch his creative voice first broke the silence of eternity, we have no means of knowing with absolute certainty. But it is probable that things material were first created, and afterward such beings as are purely spiritual or of a mixed constitution.

First epoch of *spiritual* creation.

Be this as it may, it seems pretty evident from Genesis i, 1, that in the beginning, perhaps in an instant, in the twinkling of an eye, all the *matter* of the entire universe was at once

Epoch and extent of *material* creation

launched into being by a single and almighty fiat of Jehovah. No subsequent readjustment of forces was necessary. At the simple command of the Great Architect, suns, and moons, and stars, and systems sprang into existence. And though they were perhaps at first in a chaotic state, they immediately commenced their march sublime under the laws and forces of universal gravitation. "He spake, and it was done; He commanded, and it stood fast."

Meaning of the word create in Genesis i, 1.

That this was an absolute *creation* of matter, and not a mere renovation of something previously existing, is evident,

I. From the context. For,

Proof of this.

1. A mere change or renovation is ordinarily expressed by the word *ahsah*, and not by the word *bahrah*.

2. The beginning of the Adamic renovation is evidently described in the third verse of this chapter.

3. In Genesis ii, 3, both the words *bahrah* and *ahsah* are used: the former to describe creation absolute, as in Genesis i, 1, and the latter to describe the Adamic renovation, as it is given and explained in Genesis i, 3–31.

II. From parallel passages.

1. John i, 1–3. In these words we are assured that "all things *began to be* (ἐγένετο) through the Word."

2. Heb. xi, 3. Here the apostle clearly distinguishes this primary and absolute creation of matter from all subsequent changes and renovations of the same by the statement that "*the things which are now seen were not made out of things which do appear.*"

Epoch of creation, and revelations of geology.

When this beginning was, or how long it occurred before the Adamic epoch, we have no means of ascertaining with any high degree of certainty. But geology makes it quite probable, if not indeed absolutely certain, that it occurred many ages previous to the historic period; and, moreover, that during these intervening ages, many distinct orders of vegetables and animals were created and destroyed at the beginning and close of each geological formation.

Why Moses passes over in silence these intervening ages.

But these matters have no direct connection with the Scheme of Redemption. And hence it is that Moses passes over them all in silence, and simply notices, in the second verse of his narrative, the chaotic state of the earth after the last great cataclysm that occurred shortly before the first day of the Adamic era. "The earth," he says, "was wasteness and emptiness, and darkness was on the face of the abyss; and the Spirit of God brooded on the face of the waters." *

Era of the second verse of Genesis.

Modes of reconciling geology and Genesis.

* Several other modes of reconciling the known facts of geology with the Mosaic cosmogony have been proposed; the most plausible and popular of which is the one supported by Hugh Miller, Profs. Silliman, Dana, etc., and which, for the sake of distinction, may be called "*The Hypothesis of Seven Successive and Indefinite Periods*," as the one which we have adopted has been very properly called "*The Hypothesis of Intervening Periods*." According to the hypothesis of seven successive and indefinite periods, each of the six days of creation represents a period of indefinite length; the first of which commenced with the epoch of creation, and the last of which ended with the creation of man. This theory is now advocated by many able interpreters of both Nature and Revelation. But to my mind there are some weighty objections against it. Such, for instance, as the following:

Objections to the hypothesis of seven indefinite periods.

I. There seems to be no valid reason for using the word *day*, as it occurs in the first chapter of Genesis in a figurative sense. Compare Exodus xx, 9–11.

II. This hypothesis does not harmonize well with the fact that no rain had fallen on the earth before the third day. See Genesis ii, 5.

III. It does not account for the appearance of animals even as low down as the Silurian formation. This, according to Hugh Miller, was the product of the second day. But, according to Moses, no animals were created before the fifth day.

SECTION II.—The Adamic Renovation, or First Week of the Historic Period.

Chronology of the third verse of Genesis.

The third verse of Genesis evidently records the commencement of the historic period. It is very remarkable that Moses introduces the work of each of the six days of creation by means of the same simple but expressive formula, "*And God said.*" At the beginning of the first day God said: "Let there be light, and there was light."

Imperfect state of optical science.

In order that we may clearly and fully comprehend the meaning of this beautiful and sublime oracle, it is necessary that we shall first understand the true nature and philosophy of light. But to do this in the present imperfect state of physical science is, perhaps, impossible. No man can be perfectly sure that we yet understand what light is.

The probably correct, or now most commonly received theory.

It seems quite probable, however, from recent discoveries in optics, that light is not an emanation from the sun and other luminous bodies, as Sir Isaac Newton supposed; but that it is simply an effect in the sensorium, produced through the medium of the optic nerve, by the inconceivably rapid *vibrations* of an extremely subtile fluid,

IV. The number of these geological formations is not yet well defined. Some of our ablest geologists make as many as ten or twelve.

The Bible depends on no hypothesis.

On the whole, then, I much prefer the hypothesis of intervening periods. It seems to harmonize better both with the facts of geology and the cosmogony of Moses. But let it be distinctly understood that we do not suspend the truth of the Mosaic narrative on either of these hypotheses. It is sustained by better and stronger evidence than the recent developments of a science which is even yet but imperfectly understood. But nevertheless it is a satisfaction to know that, so far as we do understand the Book of Nature, it is in perfect harmony with the Mosaic history of creation. This can not be truthfully said of any other system of ancient cosmogony.

commonly called the Luminiferous Ether; just as sound is produced through the medium of the auditory nerve, by the vibrations of the atmosphere. It seems, moreover, that it is the peculiar property of the Sun and other luminous bodies to set this fluid in motion, and to cause it to vibrate.

On this hypothesis, then, it is evident that both the Sun and the Luminiferous Ether are essential to the production of light. Let this Ether, as it now surrounds the Earth, be destroyed, or in any way absorbed by the agency of other matter, and the whole world would be at once enveloped in absolute darkness. The Sun might exist in the Heavens, and the eye might exist here on Earth, but without this medium of connection between the Sun and the eye all here would be dark as Erebus.

The Sun and Ether both essential to Light.

It is probable, therefore, that the darkness immediately antecedent to the Adamic epoch was produced in this way, i. e., by the absorption of the previously existing Luminiferous Ether; for that there was light long before the Adamic era is evident from the fact that animals having eyes lived during even the Carboniferous, Devonian, and Silurian periods. But the existence of an eye implies the existence of light, and the existence of light, according to the present generally received theory of Optics, implies the existence of a Luminiferous Ether.

How the pre-Adamic darkness was produced.

But this primordial Luminiferous Ether was, in all probability, not adapted to the wants of man and other living species; and hence, like the primitive atmosphere, it was absorbed, or otherwise destroyed; and darkness was an immediate and necessary consequence. But as soon as it was reproduced, on

Why the primordial Luminiferous Ether was destroyed.

the first day, the whole hemisphere of the Earth next to the Sun was instantly illuminated. This was probably done after the Sun had crossed the meridian of Paradise; and hence the evening occurred before the morning.

How the Light of the present era was produced.

Work of the second day.

On the second day God made the atmosphere. Something similar to this had doubtless existed during the pre-Adamic ages. It was absolutely necessary to the life and growth of both the animals and the plants that then existed; but, like the primordial Luminiferous Ether, it was not adapted to the wants of men and other existing species.

Evidence of a pre-existing atmosphere.

Why it was destroyed.

Our present atmosphere contains about $\frac{1}{5}$ part of Oxygen; nearly $\frac{4}{5}$ of Nitrogen; $\frac{1}{2500}$ part of Carbonic Acid; about the same amount of Carbureted Hydrogen, and a very small portion of ammonia.

Composition of our atmosphere.

But De Sausure and other naturalists have rendered it very probable that, during at least the age of the Carboniferous Formation, the atmosphere contained a much larger proportion of Carbonic Acid. They have proved by experiments that vegetables under the full influence of the Sun's heat and light, attain to their maximum growth in an atmosphere that contains about $\frac{1}{12}$ part of Carbonic Acid. Such an atmosphere was, therefore, well adapted to the immense growth of vegetables out of which the Coal of the Earth was formed; but it would soon prove destructive to the life and health of most living animals; and hence it was, in all probability, that the primitive atmosphere was caused to pass away as a scroll, and another was produced that is more in harmony with the wants and constitution of existing species.

Experiments of De Sausure.

On the third day God collected the waters on the surface of the earth into one place, and covered the land surface with grass and other living species of vegetables.

Work of the third day.

These all seem to have sprung up instantly, in a state of perfection, at the command of God. Islands and continents, which, on the subsiding of the waters, seemed naked and barren as the flinty rock, were now in an instant covered and adorned with all manner of trees, and fruits, and flowers. This is another fine illustration of the sublime and beautiful.

Perfect state of these primitive plants.

On the fourth day God caused the Sun, and the Moon, and the stars to appear in the heavens, and *made* (*ahsah*) them our time-keepers.

Work of the fourth day.

There is nothing in the text that implies that they were just then *created*. They had doubtless existed in some state, as had the Earth, from the beginning. But on the fourth day the clouds were most likely dispersed, the atmosphere became perfectly transparent, and these luminaries then became visible from the Earth; and hence this was the most suitable time that could have been selected *for making them our Chronometers*.

No evidence of creation on that day.

On the fifth day God said, "Let the waters bring forth abundantly the creeping creature that hath life, and let fowls fly above the Earth in the open firmament of Heaven."

Work of the fifth day.

The bodies of the marine animals were most likely made out of the water; and from Genesis ii, 19, we learn that the bodies of the birds were formed as the body of man, out of the ground. But the souls, or living principles of both, were no doubt a primary creation.

Partly a formation, and partly an absolute creation.

On the sixth day, God first created, in like manner, all terrestrial animals. And then he said, "Let us make man in our image, after our likeness, and let them have dominion over the fish of the sea, and over the fowls of the air, and over the cattle, and over all the Earth, and over every creeping thing that creepeth on the Earth. So God created man in his own image, in the image of God created he him: a male and a female created he them. And God blessed them; and God said unto them, Be fruitful, and multiply, and replenish the Earth, and subdue it; and have dominion over the fish of the sea, and over the fowls of the air, and over every thing that moveth upon the Earth. And God said, Behold I have given you every herb bearing seed, which is upon the face of all the Earth, and every tree in which is the fruit of a tree yielding seed: to you it shall be given for food."

Work of the sixth day.

In the second chapter, which is but an amplification of some of the leading thoughts of the first, we learn that man is a compound being, consisting partly of matter and partly of spirit. See Genesis ii, 7.

Complex nature of man.

An analysis of his body shows that it consists of sixteen material elements; eight of which are metallic and eight non-metallic. The metallic are Potassium, Sodium, Calcium, Magnesium, Aluminum, Iron, Manganese, and Copper; and the non-metallic are Oxygen, Hydrogen, Carbon, Nitrogen, Silicium, Phosphorus, Sulphur, Chlorine, and *traces* of a few others.

Composition of his body.

This was the most perfect piece of machinery ever formed. But it was not till God breathed into it the breath (נְשָׁמָה, from נָשַׁם, to breathe) of lives (חַיִּים, plural of חַי, life, from חָיָה, to live) that man became a living soul.

Perfection of its workmanship.

Origin of the human spirit.

As this passage (Genesis ii, 7) is often quoted to prove Materialism—to prove that the human soul is but a very subtile and attenuated form of matter, it may be well to pause here for a moment, and consider this subject with some particularity. Be it observed, then,

This oracle claimed by Materialists.

Fallacy and refutation of this assumption.

I. That all our knowledge comes primarily from sensation. By this I do not mean, as Aristotle and his followers have taught, that "*Nihil in intellectu, quod non prius in sensu:*" "there is nothing in the intellect which was not first in sensation." This is a most pernicious maxim, and leads of necessity to gross Materialism.

1. Origin of our ideas.

But, nevertheless, it must be conceded,

1. That all our mental faculties are first awakened and excited, directly or indirectly, by sensation.

Explanations.

2. That our first acquired ideas have, therefore, all reference to sensible objects.

3. That these primary ideas become the *occasion* or antecedents of other ideas and emotions derived from our higher rational and moral nature.

II. From these premises it follows that it is natural, and in many cases necessary, to describe spiritual things analogically by applying to them the names and attributes of material objects. And hence it is,

Hence the law of the mind, to describe the spiritual by the material.

1. That God, who is *spirit*, is so often represented in the Bible as if he were clothed with flesh and blood.

Illustrations.

2. That the *Holy Spirit* is designated in most languages by names that are equivalent to the English

word *wind*, or *breath*. Thus in Hebrew it is called *ruahh*; in Greek it is called *pneuma*; and in Latin *Spiritus*.

3. Hence, too, the philosophy and the propriety of all the Levitical and the Christian ordinances.

4. And hence it is that all the inspired writings, and especially the discourses of Christ, abound so much in metaphors, similes, parables, and allegories.

There is, therefore, an antecedent probability that the word *breath* is in this connection used metaphorically. But,

Evidence that the soul of man is not material.

III. That the spirit of man is essentially different from any and all forms of matter, may be proved from its properties and its attributes.

1. The essential properties of matter are extension and impenetrability.

2. The essential attributes and characteristics of the human spirit are thought, feeling, and volition.

They differ essentially in their properties; and hence they differ essentially in their substance and essence.

Evidence that the soul survives all the wrecks and changes of matter.

IV. But is the soul of man dependent for its existence, life, and activity on the body, or on any other forms of matter? Is it, like its clay tenement, mortal? or, like its Creator, is it immortal? These are questions which can be answered with clearness and certainty only from the living oracles. The following passages are full and satis factory on these points: Exodus iii, 6; Daniel xii, 13 Matt. x, 28; Luke xvi, 19–31; 2 Cor. v, 1–9, xii, 1–3 Phil. i, 21–23; Rev. iv.

Conclusions respecting the soul.

From these Scriptures it is perfectly evident that the Soul of man must forever exist in a state of either happiness or misery.

A few words respecting the creation of woman will suffice for this chapter. Woman!

Milton's eulogy on woman.

> "The fairest of creation; last and best
> Of all God's work; creature in whom excelled
> Whatever can to sight or thought be formed;
> Holy, divine, good, amiable, or sweet."

Meaning of the phrase, helpmeet for man.

Man is a social being, and needs society. And God resolved to supply his wants in this respect. "I will," said he, "make him a helpmeet for him;" or rather, "corresponding to him;" his counterpart. (כְּנֶגְדּוֹ, from נֶגֶד, front.) The Septuagint has κατά αὐτόν, according to himself.

Woman's rank and dignity.

This, then, forever settles the question concerning the rank and dignity of woman. If she were either man's inferior or his superior, she would not be his counterpart, nor be according to him.

In what respect she is man's inferior and superior.

But it does not follow that woman must be just equal to man in every respect. She is evidently, as Peter says, (1 Peter iii, 7,) the weaker vessel. Physically and intellectually, she may be man's inferior. But if man has the strongest head, it is very evident that woman has the greatest heart. Both are divinely qualified for their respective spheres of action and influence. We must not forget that man is the lord of the world. And hence a woman is not allowed even to teach, whenever this would imply the usurpation of authority over the man. See 1 Cor. xiv, 34; 1 Tim. ii, 12. But, nevertheless, it is evident that woman has a sphere as wide, as important, and as influential as that of man.

To what extent woman is forbidden to teach.

It seems to have been God's will and purpose that Adam should feel his need of a companion before he would supply this want of his nature. And for this purpose he first caused all the beasts and birds to pass before Adam, probably ***in pairs***, the male and his female. At the same time he so ***in-spired*** Adam as to enable him both to comprehend their nature, and to name them according to their attributes and differentia.

Why the beasts and birds were made to pass before Adam.

By the time that Adam had accomplished this work, he no doubt felt deeply his need of a companion, bearing like himself the image of God. And hence God immediately brought on him a deep sleep, and took one of his ribs, out of which he made a woman, and brought her to Adam as his wife. Thus marriage was instituted in Eden. Fit emblem of the relation between Christ and his Church. Ephesians v, 22, 23.

Of what woman was formed.

Marriage a Type.

Adam awoke and beheld his bride in all her virgin beauty and loveliness. And, no doubt, while still under the influence of that inspiration by which he had named all the animals, he called his wife's name ***eeshshah***, (אִשָּׁה,) because she was taken out of ***eesh***, (אִישׁ.)

What Adam called his wife.

Here, then, ends the work of the sixth day. The order was,

Order of events on the sixth day.

1. The creation of land animals.
2. The creation of man.
3. The naming of the animal tribes.
4. The creation of woman.

CHAPTER III.

MAN'S PRIMITIVE STATE.

SEVERAL things in the preceding narrative clearly indicate that it was God's will and purpose that man should be very happy, and that he should occupy a very high, and honorable, and influential position in the scale of creation. This is evident,

God's will and purpose concerning man.

I. *From the fact that he was made in the image and likeness of his Creator.* No higher honor could be bestowed on any creature than this.

Proved and indicated *first* by his being made in the image of God.

But in what did this image and likeness consist? Not in any thing physical, for God is Spirit, but evidently in those God-like attributes of man's intellectual and moral nature that so eminently qualified him to act as God's vicegerent in the government of this world. See Ephesians iv, 23, 24; and Colossians iii, 10.

In what this image consisted.

II. *The extent of man's dominion is also an evidence of his God-like nature, and of God's purposes of benevolence and grace concerning him.* God never errs in his appointments. He always uses the best means for accomplishing all his ends and purposes. Whom he calls and appoints to any work, him he also qualifies for its performance. Thus it was with Noah, Abraham, Moses, Bezaleel, Aholiab, Joshua, David, Solomon, Nebuchadnezzar, Cyrus, Paul, Luther, and Washington; and thus it evidently was with Adam and Eve. When God said unto them, Have dominion over

Secondly, in the extent of his dominion.

Illustrations.

the Earth, and the Air, and the Seas, he fully qualified and prepared them physically, intellectually, and morally for the work. They were divinely qualified to govern and to enjoy the world, with all its fullness, and to bring out of it a constant revenue of glory to their Creator.

Thirdly, in the rich patrimony of which he was made heir.

III. *God's favor to man is further manifested in the fact, that for his special benefit the whole earth, with all its rich treasures of mineral, vegetable, and animal wealth, was provided.* For him, all the matter of the Earth was created in the beginning. For him, all the gold, and silver, and copper, and iron, and granite, and marble, and coal, and salt, and other precious minerals and fossils, were treasured up, during the many ages that intervened between the epoch of Creation and the beginning of the Historic Period. For him, the light and the atmosphere were produced. For him, the world was clothed with grass, and fruits, and flowers. For him, the Sun rose and set in the firmament, and the stars performed their apparent daily and yearly revolutions. For him, the sea and the land were filled with living creatures, and the air was made vocal with the sweet voices of birds. All these things were provided for the good and happiness of man; and then he was himself created to enjoy them. And thus it happened, that what was first in design was really last in execution.

Fourthly, in the special provisions of Eden.

IV. *But it is, perhaps, in and through the special provisions of Paradise, that God's benevolence is most fully and particularly displayed, and man's primitive happiness indicated.*

Man's primitive abode.

When God created man, we are told that he placed him in a garden, eastward in Eden, (עֵדֶן, pleasantness.)

The site or location of Eden is uncertain. The only

data that we have from which to determine this matter are the four rivers and the direction of the garden from Moses' stand-point, or place of writing. Some think that the four rivers are the Ganges, the Nile, the Tigris, and the Euphrates. Others again think that they are the Phasis, the Araxes, the Tigris, and the Euphrates. But it is most probable that subsequent Geological changes have destroyed even the site of Eden. See Hitchcock's Religion of Geology, page 138.

Site of Eden.

Be this as it may, it was evidently designed merely as a temporary abode for man in a state of innocence. God does nothing in vain; and foreseeing that man certainly would fall, he fitted and prepared the world at large for fallen man; and the Garden of Eden particularly and especially for our first parents. This was wise, and just, and good.

God's object in providing this Garden.

This Garden was of course exceedingly lovely and beautiful. It contained,

What it contained.

1. All that was pleasant to the eye, to the ear, to the smell, to the touch, and to the taste of man. There bloomed the most fragrant and beautiful of all flowers. There were all kinds of delicious fruits, and every thing else that could possibly delight and regale the senses.

All that is pleasant to the senses.

2. There, too, was the Tree of Life; the fruit of which was designed to perpetuate our physical or animal life; to renew and preserve our youth, just as ordinary food is designed to renew and preserve our physical strength. Genesis iii, 22. Fit emblem of the food of the Redeemed in Paradise restored. Rev. xxii, 2.

The Tree of Life.

3. And there, also, was the Tree of Knowledge of Good and Evil. It was so called, because till man ate of it he could not fully appreciate

The Tree of Knowledge.

either the good or the evil. Experience is a dear school, but, nevertheless, it is the only one in which we can learn any thing perfectly. See John vii, 17, and Romans xii, 2.

Test of Man's Loyalty.

On the eating or not eating of the fruit of this Tree were suspended the issues of life and death.

Objection to this arrangement.

To some persons this arrangement has seemed to be wholly inconsistent with infinite wisdom and goodness. "Why," they have sneeringly asked, "why suspend the destiny of the world on so trivial a circumstance as the eating of an apple?"

Answer to this objection.

But such a question indicates very great mental imbecility, as well as an entire ignorance of the whole subject. For observe,

Importance of knowing ourselves.

1. That it is a matter of very great importance to know ourselves, and especially to know whether our hearts are strictly loyal to God or not.

Difficulty of this.

2. That it is exceedingly difficult to do this. Millions of the human race are still ignorant of themselves, notwithstanding all that God has done to reveal the secrets of the human heart.

Fitness of this Ordinance as a test of Man's Loyalty.

3. That no better test of man's loyalty could have been given than that which, according to Moses, God ordained and appointed for this purpose. For,

Its intelligibility.

(1.) It was easily understood by all. No rational and accountable being could possibly mistake what was required by this command.

Its simple and uncomplex character.

(2.) Any violation of this precept must, therefore, proceed from a spirit of pure disloyalty. Like every other *positive* ordinance, its binding obligation depended wholly and solely on the command and authority of the Lawgiver.

(3.) But the obligation of a moral precept or ordinance has its foundation in the nature of things. God commands children to honor their parents, because this is right by virtue of the constitution that God has given to society. In other words, God has, in the ordinances of creation, made it natural for children to love their parents, and for parents to love their children. And such, moreover, is the origin and foundation of every other natural and moral institution. And hence it is obvious, that no moral precept could have been so perfect a test of man's loyalty to God as was the positive precept which was originally given to Adam for this purpose. The parent and the child, the husband and the wife, the king and the subject, might have mutually loved each other, and, nevertheless, been at heart disloyal to their Creator.

Difference between Moral and Positive Precepts.

Why the Positive was preferable in this case.

(4.) But the *spirit* of disloyalty cherished in the heart will as certainly lead to a man's condemnation and final ruin as will the open and overt transgressions of any law, whether it be moral or positive. See Matt. v, 22, 28.

Disloyalty not dependent on an outward act.

(5.) And hence it follows that this positive precept, originally given to man as a test of his loyalty, was in no sense the *cause* of his disloyalty. It was simply the occasion and proof of it. It was the means of clearly and unmistakably revealing to Adam and Eve their true and proper character, and standing before God after they had mentally yielded to the temptation. To know this is

The Tree of Knowledge not the *cause* but the *test* of disloyalty.

always a blessing to any man who is still within the limits of God's pardoning mercy.

Conclusion in reference to this Positive Ordinance.

And hence we conclude that the Tree of Knowledge of Good and Evil, as well as the Tree of Life, was given to man for his good, and in the true spirit of Divine benevolence.

Tendency of all other primitive Institutions.

Such, too, was evidently the object of man's original occupation, of the institution of marriage, of the Sabbath, and of all the other ordinances of Paradise. They were all designed to promote man's comfort and happiness. Nothing was wanting in that "Golden Age" to consummate his felicity but his own submission to the will of his Creator. So long as he was obedient, so long nothing inconsistent with perfect bliss was known in Eden.

CHAPTER IV.

MAN'S FALL.

SECTION I.—Origin of Evil.

Philosophical Theories of the Origin of Evil.

We have, in Genesis iii, 1–6, an account of the origin of evil in this world. This, to the philosopher, has always been a question of great difficulty. Most of the ancient heathen philosophers either denied the existence of evil altogether, or else resolved it into a principle of eternal necessity, over which they supposed that neither men nor gods have any agency or control. But even the infidel Voltaire concedes that none of their theories are satisfactory.

Nor is it to be expected that a subject like this should be free from all philosophical difficulties. It is too broad and too comprehensive for finite minds. And hence with us it is not a question of *philosophy* but of *fact.* Our first business, at least, is to fully ascertain the facts of the case; and after we shall have done this, we may then proceed to explain and apply them so far as the Holy Scriptures, properly interpreted, will enable us to do so.

Difficulty of this Problem.

Proper Rule in all such cases.

Proceeding, then, according to this rule, we find,

Principal facts as given by Moses

I. That Adam and Eve were both created holy and happy; and that they were also furnished with all things pertaining to life and godliness.

II. That they fell by disobedience—how soon after their creation we are not informed.

III. That they were led to disobey God by the seducing power and influence of the Serpent; or rather, as it is in the Hebrew, the *hisser,* (נָחָשׁ from נָחַשׁ, to hiss.) Nothing is said about the form and habits of this creature. Some think that it was of that species which, in Numbers xxi, 6–9, is called a *Fiery* or *Seraph Serpent,* (שָׂרַף, to burn;) and in Isaiah xiv, 29, it is called a *Fiery Flying Serpent.*

IV. It seems, also, that this creature had, at the time of the temptation, the gift of speech.

These are the main facts of the case. And we may now proceed, according to our rule, to the consideration of their meaning. And,

The Power of Speech not a natural endowment of the Serpent

I. It may be well to inquire more particularly what is implied in this gift of speech. Was it a natural endowment of the serpent? or was it a mere accident depending on the agency of a superior intelligence? The latter is, I think, evidently the correct view of the matter. Balaam's ass once spoke in articulate words; but it was evidently by a Divine impulse. Numbers xxii, 28, and 2 Peter ii, 16. And so it was in the case under consideration; the serpent was evidently but an *instrument* through which a far more cunning and diabolical agent spoke and acted. On any other hypothesis the serpent was evidently Eve's superior, as the sequel shows. But this is inconsistent with the dominion given to man. See Genesis i, 28.

The principal Agent in this Tragedy.

II. Who, then, was this principal agent? This, I think, will appear evident if we take into consideration the following particulars:

Proof.

1. That he was the *first of liars.* He told to Eve the first falsehood that was ever uttered on Earth.

2. That he was the *first of murderers.* In the one victory that he gained over our first parents he has murdered our whole race.

3. That in John viii, 44, Christ teaches that Satan is both the first liar and the first murderer. "He was a murderer," says he, "from the beginning, and abode not in the truth. When he speaks a lie he speaks from what is his own; for he is a liar and the father of it."

Since, then, this Agent was the first of liars and the first of murderers, and since the same is also true of Satan, it clearly and necessarily follows that Satan himself was the Agent that used the serpent as the mere instrument of his power in this sad and eventful tragedy. And hence he is called, in Revelation xii, 9, and xx, 2, the Old Serpent.

It may serve to confirm this conclusion if we look a

little more particularly into the character of this Fiend in serpentine form. Observe, then,

Evidence of his Diabolical Malice.

I. His diabolical *malice.* Who but Satan could have ever molested that innocent and happy pair, and brought such a degree and extent of ruin on our whole race?

Evidence of his Diabolical Cunning.

II. Notice, also, his diabolical *cunning.*

1. He seems to have attacked the woman when she was by herself, and unsupported by her husband.

2. His first and chief aim was to weaken her faith in the word of God. And in order to give the more force and plausibility to his infidel insinuations, he seems to have presented his own case as a real and veritable proof and illustration of the good and marvelous effects of that forbidden tree. For "when the woman *saw*"—saw what? What could she see but the Serpent eating that same fruit, while he was ascribing to its virtues his own wonderful elevation and superior knowledge?*

* The hypothesis of a twofold agency and instrumentality is evidently, therefore, the only one that is consistent with the facts of the case. For let us suppose,

Hypothesis that Satan had no agency in the first Temptation.

I. That the literal serpent was the only agent employed in this tragical affair. Then how shall we account,

1. For its speech, its reason, its diabolical cunning and falsehood, and its malicious and murderous intention? *Is it presumable that God would have endowed the serpent or any other creature with such diabolical and hellish propensities?*

2. How does it happen that Satan is called the Old Serpent, and the first of liars and murderers. Or,

Hypothesis that there was no literal and real Serpent engaged in it.

II. Suppose, on the other hand, that Satan was the only agent, and that there was really no literal serpent engaged in this sad affair. Then, on this hypothesis, how shall we account,

1. For what Moses says of the serpent in the first verse of the third chapter? He evidently speaks of it as a well-known creature of Eden—a creature that possessed more cunning and craftiness than any of the behemoth or cattle.

The case of Adam was different. See 1 Timothy ii, 14. He seems to have transgressed merely through sympathy with his fallen bride, and with at least some knowledge of the sad consequences of his disobedience.

The Case of Adam.

Such, then, is the account that Moses has given us of the introduction of sin into this world.* To say that

2. How shall we account for the consequent degradation of the literal serpent, as we find it recorded in Genesis iii, 14?

3. How shall we account for the proverbial cunning of the serpent? See Matthew x, 16.

4. How shall we account for the natural and instinctive enmity that every-where exists between mankind and the serpent kind?

Evidently both of these hypotheses are inadequate to explain several of the most important facts and phenomena of this very complicated problem. But,

Hypothesis of a twofold agency.

III. On the hypothesis that there was in this first temptation a twofold agency; that Satan spoke through a literal serpent, just as Demons, in the time of Christ, spoke through real men and women; on this hypothesis, I say, all is plain, simple, and natural. It is, then, easy to account for all the facts of this eventful case; and especially to see how it was that the woman, being at length *deceivea* and overcome by the hellish malice and diabolical cunning and artifice of the Serpent, stretched forth her hand, and plucked, and ate

> "Of that forbidden tree, whose mortal taste
> Brought death into the world, and all our woe."

Origin of evil in Heaven.

* This, however, was not the first act of disloyalty known to the universe. Evil originated not in Paradise, but in Heaven. Perhaps the clearest Scripture reference to this event is that given by Paul in 1 Timothy iii, 6. He here admonishes Timothy not to appoint a new convert to the high and responsible office of an Elder or Bishop, lest, being puffed up with pride, he should fall into the condemnation of the Devil; that is, lest he should fall, as Satan himself fell, by becoming proud. The Devil (διάβολου) is not here the genitive of the *subject* or agent, but of the *object*. It is not the Devil's but Christ's province to condemn. Romans viii, 34. But all transgressors are, like Satan, subject to condemnation.

Probable origin of Satan's pride.

How pride got possession of Satan's heart it may be difficult for us to conceive. But it seems probable, from the statement of Paul in Timothy, that it was in some way owing to his elevation above those around him. He may have once been the Archangel, superior to even Michael. But in an evil hour we do not fully comprehend the whole matter is, perhaps, but to concede that our knowledge is not infinite.

In opposition to this inspired account of the origin of evil, the Infidel has vauntingly and contemptuously asked, "Why did God make man *capable* of falling?"

First Infidel objection.

In reply to this question, it may be sufficient to ask another. How, we may very justly and reasonably demand—how could God make MAN incapable of falling? If he is to be a subject of moral government, he must be free; and if he is free, he must have liberty to choose; and if he is at liberty to choose, then indeed, however high or low he may be in the scale of being, he must of necessity be liable to err, and of course to fall.

Answer to this objection.

But, says the objector, "Be it so, that liberty is essential to virtue; and that the enjoyment of liberty implies the possibility of falling, still the question occurs, Why did not God interpose, when he saw that man was in danger? Why did he permit Satan to gain such a victory over man?"

Second objection.

This is a plausible objection; and it is, therefore, proper that we should consider it. But, nevertheless, it is very doubtful whether any finite intelligence is capable of comprehending all that

Reply to this objection.

his eye was turned from his Creator to himself as the highest, the most gifted, and the most influential of all the creatures of God. His heart swelled with pride; ambition took possession of his soul; and rebellion was then seen in Heaven.

But justice and judgment are the dwelling-place of God's throne. Psalm lxxxix, 14. He reigns in the midst of the most perfect righteousness, and no sin can be tolerated for a moment in his presence. And hence he had but to speak the word, and Satan, with all his rebel hosts that kept not their first estate, were instantly cast out of Heaven and bound in "eternal chains under darkness to the judgment of the Great Day." Jude v, 6.

His Condemnation.

is involved in such a question. But the following considerations are sufficient to satisfy every honest mind:

I. The fact that God did not interpose in this case is the best possible evidence that he should not.

II. Had God interposed in this case, consistency, at least, would require that he should, in like manner, interpose in all similar cases. But this would be, in effect, to set aside the established natural order of things, and to govern the moral universe by force.

III. It is worthy of very serious consideration whether, on the whole, *greater good* has not resulted to man himself, as well as to other orders of responsible beings, by the course that has been adopted. Until we can trace and fully estimate all the effects of man's Fall and recovery from sin, on the entire moral universe, we should at least be very modest in our objections to the present order of things. But this much no sane man professes to understand. And hence it is idle and presumptuous to object to a scheme of which we know comparatively nothing.*

Two sources of Infidelity.

* The two main sources of infidelity are *ignorance* and *dishonesty;* an uninstructed and darkened *understanding*, and a dishonest and wicked *heart.*

One class of Infidels convertible; the other not.

Infidels and skeptics of the first class may often be convinced and converted by fair and honorable argument; but those of the second class are beyond the reach and influence of all logical argumentation. The trouble with them is that they do not *like* to retain God in their knowledge; they *love* the darkness rather than the light, because their deeds are evil. And hence it is that nothing but the judgments of God on such men can bring them to repentance. It is useless to attempt to answer all their cavils and frivolous objections.

Their common error.

It is too much the practice of both classes, however, and especially of the latter, to deal with matters which they do not, and which they can not understand. They are like persons who would persuade us to reject all the plain, simple, and practical rules of Arithmetic, Algebra, and Geometry, because, forsooth, we may not be able to fully comprehend the highest

Illustrations.

The principal events of this section are matters of almost universal tradition. Thus, for instance, Hesiod speaks of the first, or Golden Age, of the world, before sin was born:

Testimony of Tradition to the truth of this Narrative.

"When Gods alike and mortals rose to birth,
A golden race the Immortals formed on Earth;
Like Gods they lived, with calm, untroubled mind,
Free from the toil and anguish of our kind."

Hesiod's account of the Golden Age.

The same poet thus afterward describes the introduction of evil into the world, through the agency and curiosity of woman:

"The woman's hands an ample casket bear,
She lifts the lid, she scatters ills in air!
Hope sole remained within, nor took her flight,
Beneath the casket's verge concealed from sight.
With ills the land is rife, with ills the sea;
Diseases haunt our frail mortality."

His account of the origin of evil.

The agency of the Serpent in this tragic affair is also a matter of tradition. The following is from the *Zendavesta* of Zoroaster, the Persian philosopher. He says: "The world was created in six different periods of time; in the last of which man was formed by the immediate hand of God. Much happiness for a time prevailed; but Ahriman, the Evil One, after having dared to visit Heaven, descended to the Earth, *assumed the form of a Serpent,* and brought along with him a number of wicked demons. The whole world was then corrupted and thrown into confusion,

Zoroaster's account of the origin of evil.

and most complex generalizations of the Calculus. Or they may otherwise be compared to the combatant who has more confidence in his aquatic *dexterity* than in his own native strength, and who, therefore, contrives to decoy his opponent into water so very deep that neither of them can touch the bottom. In such a case the contest is not one of strength, but of dexterity. Let the battle be always fought on *terra firma.*

until it was necessary to bring on a Deluge of waters to purify it."

I need only remind the reader that every counterfeit implies a reality.

SECTION II.—Extension of the Penalty.

Question as to the extension of the Penalty.

It has long been a question of interest, How far the penalty of death inflicted for the sin of Adam was *extended.* Was it confined simply to our first parents, or did it also include their posterity? Or did it extend even further, so as to embrace within its limits all the various tribes and races of animals?

First hypothesis based on Romans v, 12, &c.

From such passages as Romans v, 12; vi, 23; and 1 Corinthians xv, 21, some have inferred that the death not only of all men, but also of all animals, is the legitimate and necessary consequence of Adam's first transgression.

Lessons taught by Geology and Physiology.

But from Geology we learn that death was in the world long before the sin, or even the creation of man. And, moreover, it is evident from Physiology that death is now a natural and necessary consequence of all animal organization.

Alleged discrepancy.

Here, then, it is supposed by some there is a discrepancy between Science and Revelation. But is it real, or is it only imaginary? Let us inquire.

Proof that it is not *real.*

Logical Principle involved.

Be it remembered, then, that it is a fundamental principle of Logic that the conclusion of an argument can legitimately comprehend nothing more than the premises from which it is drawn. If they are limited and particular, it must also of necessity be limited and particular.

In this principle, then, we have a satisfactory solution of the whole difficulty. From the context of the aforesaid passages of Scripture it is evident,

What we learn from its application to these passages.

I. That they embrace the whole human race; and that all men, therefore, die in consequence of Adam's first transgression. But,

II. It is just as evident that the meaning of these Scriptures extends no further. There is not in Paul's premises, as given in any of these passages, the slightest reference to brutes or other inferior animals; and hence there can be none in his conclusion. And hence, moreover, there is no discrepancy between these passages and the revelations of Natural Science.

That there is, however, *some connection* between the Adamic transgression and all the pains and agonies of this present world, seems evident from such passages as the following: Genesis iii, 17 and 19; and Romans viii, 18–23. Milton then expresses a great truth, when he says that, as a consequence of Eve's eating the for bidden fruit:

Scriptures implying a connection between Adam's sin and all animal suffering.

> "Earth felt the wound! and Nature from her seat
> Sighing through all her works, gave signs of woe,
> That all was lost!" *Book* ix, 780.

But what is the precise nature of this connection between sin and all the sufferings of this present world, and how is this connection to be accounted for?

Best mode of solving this Problem.

Here it is best to fall back on elementary principles. The following will serve to throw light on this difficult subject:

I. It is obvious that the scheme of the whole universe

was known to God from eternity; and that every act of creation was but a part of the one predetermined and harmonious plan. Acts xv, 18.

Statement of Elementary Principles.

II. That the whole Earth, with all its varied tenantry, was created, and from the beginning arranged with special reference to the wants of man.

III. But to make a world free from all decay, suffering, and death—that is, such a world as would have been adapted to the constitution, wants, and condition of man had he never fallen, when at the same time God foresaw that he would soon sin and become mortal—to do so would have been very inconsistent with Infinite Wisdom and Infinite Benevolence. Even erring man would not act so unwisely.

IV. And hence we find that the world in general was from the beginning constituted and arranged with reference to man as he *is*, and not as he *was*, in Eden. Paradise was a mere *temporary* abode for him, during the few days of his primeval innocence.

Conclusions from all the Premises.

From these premises, then, we conclude,

I. That, as before stated, the death of all men is an immediate consequence of Adam's disobedience. Rom. v, 12, 18, 19, and 1 Cor. xv, 21.

II. That the whole irrational creation has, to some extent, suffered from the same cause, but that no other species than man has suffered unto death, mortality being a *natural* and necessary condition of the present constitution of all other earthly species of organized beings. But,

III. That it is, nevertheless, highly probable that this arrangement was made from the beginning with special reference to man's foreseen condition; that is, that the world was from the beginning differently constituted from what it would have been had not man's death been foreseen as a certainty. And hence it follows that, though man's sin was not the *cause* of all death, it was, nevertheless, the REASON why all other animals were made mortal. And hence, moreover, it seems that God has made the very groans and sighs of the brute creation an impressive demonstration of the exceeding sinfulness of sin.

Objection to this Theory.

If it be objected that this theory connects too much suffering with the sin of man, our answer is,

Reply to it.

I. That we are but poorly qualified to determine and decide the question, How much suffering should be connected with any sin?

II. That this suffering is not a chimera or a phantom, but a sad and terrible reality, for the introducing of which God had certainly a good and sufficient reason.

III. That the reason assigned is, on the whole, so far as we can judge, most consistent with the general scheme of both Creation and Redemption.

Question of the existence and condition of Brutes in a Future State.

Whether there will be any brutes in the New Heavens and the New Earth may be a question. I am inclined to think there will be none, chiefly for two reasons:

I. Because they were all created and now exist simply for the good of man. But when this mortal shall have put on immortality, it is not probable that we will have any more need of such helps as the cow and the horse.

II. Because this seems to be implied in Ecclesiastes iii, 21. The words of the inspired writer are as follows: "Who knoweth the spirit (רוּחַ) of man that goeth upward, and the spirit (רוּחַ) of the beast that goeth downward to the earth?" Here it seems to be pretty clearly implied that there is a very marked and essential difference between the state of the brute and that of man after death; that while the brute has no other than a lower earthly life, man has a life which at death "goeth upward."

For these and other like reasons I am of the opinion that there will be no resurrection of the various Departments, Classes, Orders, Families, Genera, and species of the Animal Kingdom, and that none such will be found in the New Heavens and the New Earth. But if there should be any they will most likely be immortal.

SECTION III.—Comprehension of the Penalty.

Scope of Section Third.

Having settled the question respecting the extension of the Penalty threatened and executed on account of man's first disobedience, it now only remains for us to consider its proper Comprehension; or, if you please, to inquire what God meant when he said, "*On the day thou eatest thereof thou shalt surely die.*" Genesis ii, 17.

Mysterious import of the words *Life* and *Death*.

The words *life* and *death* are both representatives of very profound and mysterious realities. And hence it is not a matter of surprise that men of a visionary and speculative turn and habit of mind should have formed some very strange and absurd notions and theories concerning them.

False Theories of Life and Death.

Some, for example, suppose that life is equivalent to mere existence, and that death is equivalent to annihilation; but this is absurd.

I. Because there is existence where there is no life. Minerals exist, but they have no life.

II. Because there is also death where there is no evidence of annihilation, as in the case of trees, flowers, etc. Indeed, there is no satisfactory evidence that any substance is ever annihilated, whether it be material or immaterial.

It is evident, therefore, that life is not mere existence and that death is not annihilation. But it is easier to say what they are not than to define what they are. Some of the necessary *conditions* of life, however, are very obvious. And it is probable that a knowledge of these is the nearest approach that we can now make to an understanding of the thing itself, just as our knowledge of mind and matter is of necessity confined to their phenomena.

Our knowledge of Life limited to its Conditions.

Be it observed, then, that one of the essential conditions of life is *union,* and that one of the essential conditions of death is *separation.* There is no life in atoms, and there can be no death without a separation from some living substance.

Essential Conditions of Life and Death.

But it is not all union that gives life. The particles of rocks are united, but they have no life. Nor is it all separation that causes death. Some vegetables and even animals may be separated into parts, and still each part will retain its vitality.

To give life, then, to any substance it must be *properly united to some living and life-imparting agent. And to work death in any substance it must be separated from said agent by the destruction of its organization or otherwise.* Thus, for example, the carbon of the atmosphere is vivified by being united to living vegetables and animals, and by being separated from these life-imparting agents it again loses its vitality.

The number of living and life-giving agents is, of course, very great. God has made every vegetable and every animal a depository of life.

Number of life-giving Agents.

But, nevertheless, he is himself the only original, unwasting, and ever-enduring fountain of life. See Psalm xxxvi, 9; John v, 26; and 1 Timothy vi, 16.

Union with God essential to Life.

And hence it follows that *union with God in some way and by some means is essential to all life, and that separation from him is always death.* "He gives to all life, and breath, and all things." Acts xvi, 25.

How union with God is supported.

This union with God is maintained through that system of means and instrumentalities that we call nature and Christianity, or the old and the new creation. The links of connection seem to be numerous and various. And hence it is that we have different kinds of both life and death; such, for example, are vegetable life, and animal life, and spiritual life. The branch separated from the vine dies, because the vine is a link, and also, to some extent, a depository of life, between the branch and God.

Metaphorical meanings of the words Life and Death.

Here, then, we have the proper philosophy of all life and of all death. It is true that these words are also used tropically in different senses; as for instance, when we say of a man that he is dead to sin, dead to the law, etc. In all such cases the meaning of the word is analogical.

Complicity of man's union with God.

Whether inanimate objects are united to God in more than one way may be a question. But that man's union with his Maker is supported by various chains or systems of instrumentalities, seems very certain. Through one system of means, for example, is supported his mere existence. Hebrews i 3. Through another his animal life is continued, with an immense train of physical enjoyments; and through still another is maintained his higher spiritual life his union, communion, and fellowship with God, as the ever-enduring and only satisfying portion of his soul. Psalm lxxiii, 25, 26. And hence it follows that there are also different kinds of death, and that a man may be alive in one sense and dead in another. See Matthew viii, 22; John v, 24; Ephesians ii, 1–7; 1 Timothy v, 6.

What, then, was the kind of death involved in the threatened penalty? Was it animal death alone, or was it spiritual death alone? Or was it both of these combined? Or was it both of these and something more?

Kind of death threatened in the Penalty.

That it was animal death alone, or a mere separation of soul and body, is a favorite hypothesis with many. This most affects the senses, and makes the deepest impression on our social and sympathetic nature. And hence it is, perhaps, that many have long regarded it as being at least the chief and primary element of the threatened penalty.*

Why animal Death is by some regarded as the chief and primary element.

* It is often said, that nothing more than mere physical or animal death could be implied in this penalty; because, it is alleged, that in no other sense could Adam have understood it on the day of his creation. But this hypothesis rests on two unwarranted assumptions:

Further allegation grounded on Adam's incapacity to understand the meaning of the word.

I. That Adam had gained by his own observation a knowledge of what is commonly called physical or animal death, previous to the enactment of this positive law. But it would perhaps be difficult to prove that there was any such death in Eden before the Fall of man; and still more difficult to prove that Adam had witnessed any of its sad effects, before he received from God the law and penalty in question.

Two undue assumptions in this allegation.

II. It is assumed that he had no other means of understanding the true and proper import of this penalty than his own observation and experience. But it is certainly very evident from the context, as well as from the nature of the case, that Adam was an inspired man; that by the immediate and direct aid of the Holy Spirit he was enabled *to converse with God, and to name understandingly the various species of animals in Eden, on the same day on which he was created.* And hence there is no room left for any reasonable

But that *spiritual death*, or a separation of the soul from God, is the chief and fundamental element of this penalty, is evident from several considerations.

Reasons for regarding Spiritual Death as the Primary and Chief element.

I. *In no other sense did Adam and Eve die on the same day that they sinned.* But in a spiritual sense they certainly did die at the very time indicated. Genesis iii, 8. They then, by a common law of our nature, became enemies to God by their own wicked works. Colossians i, 21.

II. *Spiritual death seems, a priori, to be the root of all evils; the fruitful source of all our calamities and misfortunes.* Reunion with God implies every blessing, and separation from him implies the loss of every thing. And hence we find that this kind of life and death is always spoken of in the Bible as that which is chief and paramount. See Matthew x, 28, and John xi, 26.

III. *This is further evident from the fact that the first and chief object of the Gospel is to unite man to God spiritually.* It first gives life to the soul and then to the body. It first repairs those losses that are fundamental, and afterward those that are of secondary importance.

IV. *It seems that by eating of the fruit of the Tree of Life, Adam might still have escaped physical or animal death.* Genesis iii, 22. But surely this could not have saved him from all, nor even from the chief consequences of his disobedience.

doubt that by means of the supernatural aid of the same Spirit, he was also able to comprehend the meaning of the word *death* as it is used in the seventeenth verse of the second chapter of Genesis. And hence it is wholly unwarrantable to speak of the death of the body as literal, and the death of the soul as figurative. The literal meaning of the word is its true and proper meaning as given by God and as understood by Adam in the beginning.

Literal meaning of the word *death*.

V. *The Second Death will consist in an eternal separation from God, and not in the separation of the soul and the body.* Revelation xx, 14.

From these premises the following conclusions seem to be fully warranted:

Conclusions from the premises submitted.

I. That spiritual death, or a separation of the soul from God with the loss of its original holiness, was the primary and chief element of the threatened penalty.

II. That fear, remorse, anger, strife, etc., were its necessary, immediate, and implied consequences.

III. That our physical relations being also very greatly disturbed, animal death followed also as a necessary and implied consequence; and, moreover, that it would in all probability have also followed as an *immediate* consequence of sin, had not God mercifully suspended it for a time for wise and benevolent purposes. Romans ii, 3–16.

IV. That in all pain and suffering there is implied a threefold agency; namely, the Satanic, the human, and the Divine. Satan tempts, man voluntarily transgresses, and God himself inflicts the penalty of the violated law. Isaiah xlv, 5–7, and Amos iii, 6.

V. And as the consequences of Adam's first transgression have extended to his entire posterity, as we have shown in the second section of this chapter, it seems to follow of necessity that all men are, by virtue of their connection with Adam, diseased in their spiritual as well as in their physical constitution. And this inference is abundantly sustained by such passages of Scripture as Genesis v, 3; Psalm li, 5; John iii, 6; Rom. v, 12, 18, 19; Ephes. ii, 1–3, etc.

The precise *degree* of this spiritual derangement or

hereditary sinfulness is no where clearly and logically defined in the Holy Scriptures. But that it is only of the positive or comparative and not of the superlative grade is evident,

Evidence that our derived sinfulness is not of the superlative degree.

I. *From our own daily experience and observation.* Nothing is more common than to see wicked men growing worse and worse under the influence of their own personal transgressions. But if all men were as bad by nature as sin can make them, there could, of course, be no progress in human depravity.

II. *This is further proved by the testimony of nearly all the inspired writers.* See, for instance, Genesis vi, 12; Romans i, 21–32; iii, 9–18; 2 Timothy iii, 13.

III. *From the fact that all responsible adults who have the disposition or moral purity of little children are, in the estimation of Christ, fit for the Kingdom of Heaven.* Matt. xviii, 3; xix, 14; Mark x, 14; Luke xviii, 17. The change wrought by the Gospel on the heart of the sinner extends no further at present than simply to the removal of his own personal guilt. No man can ever in his present state become purer than he was in his infancy.

IV. *From the fact that the presumptuous sin committed against the Holy Spirit is a personal sin, and that it is this and this only which fills up a man's cup of iniquity and makes him totally depraved.* See Matt. xii, 31, 32; Hebrews vi, 4–16; x, 28, 29, etc.

As the extremes of Augustinism and Pelagianism*

History of Pelagius.

* Pelagius was an English monk who flourished about the beginning of the fifth century. He went to Rome in A. D. 409, and while there he became disgusted with the doctrine then prevalent in the Latin Church, *which makes man a mere passive instrument of Divine grace.* He then resolved, no doubt with pious intentions, to work a reformation. But one extreme generally leads to another, and

are still prevalent in many parts of Christendom, I have thought it proper and even necessary to make these few remarks on this confessedly difficult and intricate subject. But I wish now, in conclusion, to caution all young persons, and especially all young preachers, against the danger of being led into public controversy on this speculative subject. Such discussions can never result in much good, and they may result in

Why any reference to hereditary depravity is now necessary.

Caution to young Preachers.

to this law of our fallen nature Pelagianism is not an exception. If Augustinism degrades human ability and human character below their proper level, Pelagianism, on the other hand, too highly exalts and elevates them.

In 411 Pelagius went to Palestine, where he was violently opposed by Jerome. His chief opponent in the West was Augustine, the famous Bishop of Hippo, in Northern Africa.

The principal tenets of Pelagius were as follows: He maintained

His principal tenets.

I. That the soul of Adam was neither holy nor unholy by creation, but that it was a mere *carte-blanche* on which he was left free to write his own character.

II. That his body was made mortal by creation, and not by sin.

III. That the fall of Adam had no influence whatever on either the souls or the bodies of his posterity, but that every man when born into the world is just what Adam was when he was created—his body is mortal *per se*, and his soul is wholly without character.

IV. That eternal death is the only punishment for sin, all temporal or physical death being purely natural.

V. That the general prevalence of sin in the world is owing solely to the power of *temptation* and the influence of bad *examples*. And hence that it is possible for all men to live and die without the slightest defilement from sin; that many, in fact, have so lived even among the heathen.

VI. That Christ became a man in order that by his perfect *teaching* and *example* he might offer to us the strongest motives and inducements to self-government, and thereby redeem us. As we have been *imitators* of Adam in sin, so also we are to be *imitators* of Christ in virtue.

VII. That all mankind, infants as well as adults, may therefore enjoy eternal blessedness without baptism, but that it is, nevertheless, an essential condition of entering into the Kingdom of Heaven. He held that there is a threefold state after death; namely, *damnation* for sinners, *eternal life* for the virtuous unbaptized, and the *Kingdom of Heaven* for all baptized children, and also for all baptized adults, who lead a pure and holy life. *Shedd's History of Christian Doctrine, Vol. II, Chapter IV. Mosheim's Ecclesiastical History, Vol. I, pp.* 370–374, *Murdock's Edition.*

much evil. For however good men may differ in their views of hereditary depravity or derived sinfulness, one thing is very certain; namely, *that whatever mankind have lost through the first Adam, they will regain unconditionally through the second Adam.* If through the first all men die, so likewise through the second all will be made alive. 1 Cor. xv, 22. If by one man's disobedience the many were made *sinners*, even so by the obedience of one the many will, *to the same extent*, be made *righteous*. Rom. v, 18, 19.

Why the question of hereditary depravity is in itself a matter of no *practical* consequence.

No man need, therefore, feel any concern or anxiety about the sin of Adam and its effects on his posterity. To remove all the bitter fruits and consequences of this first transgression is the peculiar and exclusive work of the second Adam. What ought now to concern us is the great and important practical question, How we may severally be saved from the effects and consequences of our own personal transgressions. And hence, when you go out as Missionaries of the Cross, it is enough for you to remember,

Points to be kept in memory.

I. That all men, save the redeemed, are now dead in trespasses and in sins. You need not ordinarily stop to inquire *how* this has come to pass.

II. That the Gospel is the remedy—the only and all-sufficient remedy—provided by God and committed to your trust for the salvation of sinners.

III. That its power to save men, however, depends on its being received into their hearts, and made the rule and guide of their lives.

IV. That God has made you the honored instruments in his hand of persuading sinners to be reconciled to him; and that your reward is great in Heaven, if you continue faithful as the Ministers of his word. Remember that "they who are wise shall shine as the brightness of the firmament; and they that turn many to righteousness shall shine as the stars for ever and ever." Daniel xii, 3.

V. And besides all this, it may be well, also, to remember, that while many so-called preachers of the Gospel are wrangling about theories and questions that serve to gender strife and malice rather than practical godliness, *thousands for whom Christ died are going to perdition.* Think of these things, and then let the love of Christ constrain you to do as Paul and the other Apostles did. 2 Corinthians v, 11–15.

BOOK SECOND.

SCHEME OF REDEMPTION IN PROCESS OF DEVELOPMENT.

PART I.

DEVELOPMENTS FROM ADAM TO MOSES.

CHAPTER I.

THE WOMAN'S SEED.

THAT was a sad and sorrowful day to our first parents, when they were driven out of Eden. The great Milton has, no doubt, well described, in the following lines, the feelings of our mother Eve as she cast a last, long, lingering look on the groves and flowers of Paradise lost:

Impressions of Adam and Eve on leaving Paradise.

> "O unexpected stroke, worse than of death!
> Must I thus leave thee, Paradise! thus leave
> Thee, native soil, these happy walks and shades,
> Fit haunt for gods! where I had hoped to spend
> Quiet, though sad, the respite of that day,
> Which must be mortal to us both! O flowers
> That never will in other climate grow,
> My early visitation and my last
> At ev'n, which I bred up with tender hand,
> From your first opening buds, and gave you names,
> Who now will rear you to the Sun, or rank
> Your tribes, and water from the ambrosial fount!"
>
> BOOK II, 268.

But the separation of Adam and Eve from Eden was a necessity. "So God drove out the man; and he placed at the east of the garden of Eden, Cherubim and a flaming sword which turned every way, to keep the way of the Tree of Life." Gen. iii, 24.

Why they were cast out of it.

But even in that dark and trying hour the unhappy pair were not allowed to mourn as those that have no hope. God had, long before their creation, foreseen their fall, and provided the remedy. Of this we have clear and unmistakable evidence in many such passages as the following: Romans viii, 28–30; Ephesians i, 4, (πρὸ καταβολῆς κόσμου); 2 Thess ii, 13; 2 Tim. i, 9, (πρὸ χρόνων αἰωνίων.) And hence it is evident that the Scheme of Redemption was no afterthought on the part of Jehovah. It was perfect and complete in the Divine mind before the foundation of the world or the beginning of the ages.

God's preordained scheme of mercy.

Previous, however, to the fall of man, no creature had, so far as we know, any knowledge of it. The first recorded reference to it is found in the sentence that God pronounced on the Serpent: "And the Lord God said unto the Serpent, Because thou hast done this, thou art cursed above all cattle, and above every beast of the field; upon thy belly shalt thou go, and dust shalt thou eat all the days of thy life. And I will put enmity between thee and the woman, and between thy seed and her Seed; it shall bruise thy head, and thou shalt bruise his heel." Genesis iii, 14, 15.

First intimation of this scheme.

In this very mysterious and sublime oracle we have evidently a double reference:

Double reference of this oracle.

I. To the natural enmity that has ever existed between mankind and the serpent kind.

II. To the warfare that is still carried on between Christ, who is in the highest and most appropriate sense the Seed of the woman, and Satan, who is here symbolically represented by the serpent.

All this is clearly implied,

1. In the fact that the serpent and Satan were both *united* in the temptation; and hence it is but just and right that they should both be included in the sentence. To suppose that the whole penalty should rest on the head of the real and literal serpent, when Satan was the chief and responsible agent in the temptation, would of course be very absurd.*

Evidence of this.

2. The awful solemnity of the occasion is utterly at variance with the assumption that the sentence was pronounced simply and exclusively on the literal serpent. Such a thought is exceedingly degrading to Jehovah, as well as to the Spirit of inspiration. But when it is understood that the higher powers of the spiritual universe are embraced in this marvelous Revelation, we have then an occasion that is worthy of the interposition of God, and we have, also, an oracle that is in all respects worthy

* It has often been objected that it was cruel, and inconsistent with the known character of God, to inflict punishment on the literal serpent; as it seems to have been nothing more than an irrational instrument in the temptation and fall of man.

Objection to this arrangement.

But be it remembered,

I. That the design of all this was *for the good of man.* It was done no doubt for the purpose of impressing on his mind, and perhaps, also, on the minds of all the intelligent universe, the exceeding sinfulness and balefulness of sin. See an analogous case in Exodus xxxii, 20.

Reply to it.

II. That God has a right to give to any creature whatever rank he sees fit; and that this is not to be regarded in the light of a punishment.

III. That it was nothing more than becoming and right to make the degradation of the instrument a type of the final and greater degradation of the principal Agent.

of the very prominent place that it occupies in the Holy Bible.

Conclusion.

By the Serpent, then, in this connection, is chiefly meant the Old Serpent, and by the Seed of the woman is meant the Immanuel who was to be born of the virgin. And here we have, therefore, the first recorded promise of mercy to fallen man. Here began that mighty conflict which is symbolically represented by the enmity that exists between mankind and the serpent kind, but which will not be fully consummated till Christ, the mystical Seed of the woman, shall have completely vanquished Satan and all his host of rebel followers. "O, the depth of the riches, and of the wisdom, and of the knowledge of God! How unsearchable are his judgments, and his ways past finding out! For who hath known the mind of the Lord? or who hath been his counselor? or who hath given to him, and it shall be recompensed to him again? For of him, and through him, and to him are all things; to whom be glory forever. Amen!" Romans xi, 33-36.

CHAPTER II.

INSTITUTION OF SACRIFICE.

SECTION I.—Divine Origin of Sacrifice.

Second reference to the Remedial System.

The second reference to the Remedial System is found in the institution of sacrifice. Genesis iv, 3, 4.

That this institution was of Divine origin is evident from several considerations.

I We learn from Hebrews xi, 4, that Abel offered his sacrifice in faith. But in Romans x, 17, we are told that "faith cometh by hearing, and hearing by the Word of God." And hence it follows that Abel could not have offered in faith without a command from God. *"No testimony, no faith"* is an oracle of the Scriptures as well as of common, sense.

Evidence that Sacrifice is of Divine Origin.

II. It could not have been a human invention, because Reason can perceive no connection between the means and the end. It is evidently a *positive* and not a moral or natural institution.

III. Its universality is another proof of its Divine origin. Mr. Faber says that "throughout the whole world there is a notion prevalent that the gods can be appeased only by bloody sacrifices. There is no heathen people," he adds, "that can specify a time when they were without sacrifice. All have had it from a time which is not reached by their genuine records. Tradition alone can be brought forward to account for its origin."

IV. The distinction between clean and unclean beasts, even in the time of Noah, (Genesis vii, 2,) proves also the Divine origin of sacrifice. This is a distinction which is altogether *positive*, and which has no foundation in either reason or philosophy.

These reasons are, I think, abundantly sufficient to warrant the conclusion that sacrifice is of Divine origin

SECTION II.—DESIGN OF SACRIFICE AND OTHER TYPES.

Our next inquiry has reference to the object or design of sacrifice. For what purpose was it instituted?

Object of Sacrifice.

In order that we may understand this question aright we must first consider briefly the nature and object of types and symbols in general.

Previous Question.

The word *type* (τύπος, from τύπτω, to strike) means,

Different meanings of the word Type.

I. A stroke, or a blow.

II. The impression or print produced by a blow. *E. g.*, in John xx, 25, Thomas says. "Unless I shall see in his hands *the print of the nails*, [τόν τύπον τῶν ἥλων,] and put my finger into *the print of the nails*, and thrust my hand into his side, I will not believe."

III. It denotes the model set before us for our imitation. *E. g.*, the Apostles are said, in Philippians iii, 17, to be an example or a *type* for all Christians. See, also, Hebrews viii, 5; and 1 Thess. i, 7.

IV. In Natural History it is that which most strikingly possesses the principal characteristics of the class. *E. g.*, the eagle is taken as the type of birds, and the lion as the type of beasts.

V. In medicine it denotes the particular *form* or *phase* of a disease under given circumstances. Galen wrote a special work on diseases, called περὶ τῶν τύπων.

VI. In printing it means that which makes the impress or mark.

VII. In a theological or religious sense it is simply a *shadow* of things to come, and generally of good things to come. *E. g.*, in Colossians ii, 16, 17, Paul says, "Let no man judge you in meat or in drink, or in respect of a holy day, or of the new moon, or of the Sabbath days, which are a *shadow* of things to come, but the body [σῶμα] is of Christ." And again, in Hebrews x, 1, he says, "For the law having a *shadow* of good things to come, and not the very image of the things, can never with those sacrifices which they offer year by year continually make the comers thereunto perfect."

From these passages it is evident that at least most of the religious rites and ceremonies of the Old Testament were mere *shadows* relating to Christianity as their substance. But in 1 Corinthians x, 6, 11, the word type is evidently used in the same sense, and to represent many things of the same category. And hence it follows that in a religious sense *a type is a mere shadow or faint outline-picture of something pertaining to the future.*

Meaning of *Antitype* and *Archetype.*

The word *antitype* (ἀντί, *against, over against,* and τύπος, *type*) denotes the substance, or that which is prefigured by the type. *E. g.*, the paschal lamb was the type of which Christ was the Antitype. The word *archetype* (ἀρχή, *beginning,* and τύπος, *pattern*) is used in nearly the same sense. It simply means the *original pattern* or *model,* according to which all the types were constructed.

Several things are implied in these definitions.

Things implied in these definitions.

I. *That there is always some resemblance or analogy existing between the type and the antitype.* *E. g.*, Moses resembled Christ as a deliverer and mediator.

II. *That the likeness is but partial,* and that care should, therefore, be taken not to press it beyond its proper limits. *E. g.*, Canaan was a type of Heaven, or of the New Earth, though the resemblance was but slight. Adam was a type of Christ, but the points of difference were far more numerous than the points of resemblance.

III. *That the points of resemblance were designed and*

preordained. *E. g.*, it was ordained concerning the paschal lamb,

1. That it should be without blemish.
2. That a bone of it should not be broken.
3. That it should be killed between the two evenings, etc.

IV. *That every type is a sort of prophecy.* They all relate to the future. *E. g.*, the sacrifices all pointed to Christ, but as soon as Christ came they were abolished.

Three kinds of Types.

There are three kinds of types; viz., the Historical, the Legal, and the Prophetic.

Historical Types.

I. *Historical types consist in such real events or series of real events as were, by the arrangements and predetermination of God, made to represent some other series of future events.* *E. g.*, such was the history of Sarah and Hagar, Galatians iv, 21–31; such was the history of the Israelites under Moses, 1 Corinthians x, 1–12; and such seems to have been their restoration from their Babylonish captivity under Zerubbabel, Isa. xl–lxvi.

Legal Types.

II. *Legal types consist in such positive ordinances as were, by God's foreknowledge and authority, made to represent, adumbrate, and illustrate the unrevealed glorious realities of the New Institution.* *E. g.* such were all the sacrifices of the Patriarchal and Jewish ages; and such, also, was the Tabernacle with all its furniture and services.

Prophetic Types.

III. *Prophetic types consist in such special symbolical signs and arrangements as were, by God's appointment, used to represent to and through the ancient prophets some important future event.* Thus for example, the rottenness of Jeremiah's girdle, concealed for a short time on the banks of the Euphrates, indicated the speedy ruin of Israel, Jeremiah xiii, 1–7. See also Ezekiel xxxvii, 1–14.

From all this it is obvious that the design of all types is twofold:

Design of Types.

I. *To give a pictorial and outline representation of something in the future, and especially of the Scheme of Redemption.* Such, for example, was evidently the primary object of all the sacrifices that were offered during both the Patriarchal and the Jewish age. See Hebrews ix, x, 18.

II. *The second object of God in giving to his ancient people such a typical system was in order that the type might serve as a proof and demonstration of the Divine origin of the antitype.* This is evident from Heb. iii, 5.

The testimony furnished in this way respecting the truth of Christianity is very strong and convincing. For observe,

Strength of the evidence thus furnished.

1. That these types must have all been ordained by one who perfectly understood the corresponding antitypes. But God alone could have had this knowledge; and, consequently, they are all of God.

2. We see that the Jews were all their lives engaged in setting up types and printing documents that they themselves could neither read nor understand. Hence they never could have invented their own system of religion; and hence, moreover, the Bible is all of God.

With these given explanations, it will now be an easy matter to distinguish between types, and emblems, and symbols. An *emblem* (ἐμβάλλω) is neither preordained, nor does it relate to the future. *It is merely a material or tangible object of some kind, that is used to represent a moral or spiritual quality or attribute, on account of some well-known preëxisting*

Difference between a Type and an Emblem.

analogy between them. E. g., the dove is an emblem of meekness, and a bee-hive of industry.

Types, then, are faint *pictures;* but emblems are characteristic *marks.* A horn is an emblem of power, but it is not a type of power. See Psalm xcii, 10, and Habakkuk iii, 4.

The word *symbol* is generic. It comprehends all types, emblems, parables, allegories, fables, enigmas, hieroglyphics, etc. It is from συμβάλλω, to compare.

What are comprehended under Symbols.

And hence it is obvious that symbols are generally used for the sake of perspicuity; for the sake of presenting more clearly to the understanding the spiritual and abstract qualities of things, by means of outward signs and pictures addressed to the senses. Sometimes, however, they are also used for the sake of energy and ornament; and occasionally they are used, also, for the sake of obscurity. It was for this last purpose that Christ sometimes spoke to the people in parables. Matthew xiii, 10–17.

Use of Symbols in writing.

CHAPTER III.

CALL OF ABRAHAM AND HIS POSTERITY.

SECTION I.—Delay of the Remedial System.

The question is often asked, Why was the full development of the Scheme of Redemption so long delayed? Why did not Christ come and suffer for mankind immediately after the Fall? And why was not the Kingdom of Heaven established.

Query concerning the Delay of the Remedial System.

with all its provisions and in all its fullness, immediately after man's expulsion from Paradise?

A full and explicit answer to this question would require a very lengthy discussion, and would involve the consideration of many very grave and complicated problems. But it may be said, in general, that *some time was necessary in order to prepare Christianity for mankind, and mankind for the reception and enjoyment of Christianity.* Sundry matters had first to be practically demonstrated before the Gospel could be fully and properly revealed to mankind as the power of God for the salvation of every true believer. Such, for example, were the following:

Reply to it.

I. *The inadequacy of the provisions and light of nature to meet and supply the wants of our fallen race.*

Preliminary Problems.

II. *Our present incapacity to save ourselves by works of law;* or, in other words, to render to the Divine law that perfect obedience which justice requires.

III. *The exceeding sinfulness of sin.*

IV. *The necessity of holiness.*

V. *The necessity of a new religious nomenclature;* or of inventing some more perfect medium of communicating spiritual ideas than the ordinary forms of human speech.

Even now, under the present reign of favor and the full-orbed glories of the Remedial System, there is a constant proneness on the part of many to ignore the Gospel, and to trust in self and the laws and ordinances of nature, as the only necessary means and sources of happiness. This is evidently an Adamic weakness. It is a universal proclivity of our fallen race. And hence it was eminently right and proper that all such vain hopes and false refuges should be taken out of the way, and that mankind should be made to feel their need of Divine help, of a Revelation and scheme of justification from God himself, before the Gospel should be revealed as his power for the salvation of every one who would receive and obey it.

Work assigned to the Gentiles.

To demonstrate this problem was the work of the Gentiles, and especially of the Greeks and the Romans. This they did chiefly in two ways:

I. By their numerous failures in theoretical and practical morality.

II. By their failures in theoretical and practical Religion. (See Leland on the Advantage and Necessity of the Christian Revelation.) And hence we find that after the lapse of near four thousand years, during which Platonism, Aristotelianism, Stoicism, Epicureanism, and every other conceivable scheme of philosophy had been unsuccessfully tried, we find that even then mankind were still sighing and groaning under the burdens of sin, and earnestly longing for some hitherto undiscovered remedy that would be adequate to the wants of their entire nature.

Work assigned to the Hebrews.

The solution of other problems was reserved chiefly for Abraham and his posterity. While the Gentiles were proving the inadequacy of the provisions and ordinances of nature to meet and to satisfy the wants of mankind, the Israelites were earnestly engaged in inventing a new religious nomenclature—in demonstrating the awful malignity and hatefulness of sin—the beauty and the necessity of holiness—the impossibility of attaining to justification, sanctification, and redemption, by complying with the requirements of a Divine law; and hence the necessity of a scheme of salvation by grace, through faith, that would enable God to be just in justifving penitent believers.

All this and much more will become more and more obvious as we proceed with the history of Abraham and his seed.

SECTION II.—God's Promises to Abraham.

When God called Abraham out of Ur of Chaldea, he said to him, "Get thee out of thy country, and from thy kindred, and from thy father's house, unto a land that I will show thee. *And I will make of thee a great nation, and I will bless thee, and make thy name great; and thou shalt be a blessing. And I will bless them that bless thee, and curse him that curseth thee; and in thee shall all the families of the earth be blessed.*" (Gen. xii, 1–3.)

Promise made to Abraham, when called out of Ur of Chaldea.

The same promise variously amplified was afterward repeated, as we find in Gen. xiii, 14–17; xv, 1–21; xvii, 1–27; xxii, 15–19, etc.

The Promise repeated and amplified.

From a careful examination and analysis of these passages, it is evident that we have given here what may be regarded as four distinct elementary promises. These are (1) That Abraham should have a numerous offspring (Gen. xiii, 16; xv, 3–5; xvii, 2, 4; xxii, 17); (2) That God would be a God to him and to his seed after him (Gen. xvii, 1–8); (3) That he would give to Abraham and to his seed, an everlasting possession (Gen. xii. 7; xiii, 15; xv, 18–21; xvii, 8); and (4) That he would bless all the nations of the earth through him and his seed (Gen. xii, 3; xxii, 18). But nevertheless they may all in harmony with Scripture usage be regarded as but elementary parts of one and the same promise, made to Abraham and his seed (Acts ii, 39; xiii. 23. 32; xxvi, 6; Rom. iv, 14, 16; Gal. iii, 18,

Four elementary Promises given to Abraham in these passages.

Unity of these Promises.

22, 29, etc.); each part having however a double reference; that is, looking to both the typical and the antitypical side of the Divine economy. The first element, for instance, was a pledge to Abraham that he would have a numerous family, first, according to the flesh; and secondly, according to the Spirit; the second, that God would be a God to both of these families, though in a far higher sense to the latter than to the former; the third, that each of these families would become heirs to an inheritance; and the fourth, that through each of them the world would be blessed.

Their twofold reference.

For awhile the spiritual side or element of this promise was almost wholly concealed behind the carnal or typical side; which from time to time was made more and more prominent by sundry new developments, the most important of these was the Covenant of circumcision.

The typical or carnal side of the Promise, for a time most prominent.

At length, just four hundred and thirty years after the twofold promise was given to Abraham, the carnal or typical element of it was fully developed into the Sinaitic or Old Covenant.* In this were of course embraced many various and distinct elements, such as the laws and ordinances relating to the different kinds of sacrifices, the consecration of the Levites, the cov-

Carnal element of the Abrahamic Promise, developed into the Sinaitic Covenant.

* The word *covenant* (Fr. *convenant*) is of Latin origin. It is derived from the two words *con*, *together*, and *venio*, *to come*. And hence it means literally, *a coming together*. The corresponding Hebrew word is *b'reeth* (בְּרִית); but it is of very different etymology. It comes from the Hebrew word *barah* (בָּרָה) which means *to cut*, *to eat*, and it is therefore now generally supposed that this word has reference to the *cutting asunder* of the victims which were sacrificed at the making of a covenant. See Genesis xv, 9–17 and Jeremiah xxxiv, 18, 19. But some derive the name from the second meaning of *barah*, *to eat;* because when

Derivation of the word *covenant*.

Corresponding Hebrew and Greek words.

enant of the Priesthood, etc.—all serving to illustrate in some way the glorious realities embraced in the spiritual element of the Abrahamic promise, which in due time was about to be developed into a far more glorious Institution than the Sinaitic. In the meantime, the carnal was the stay and support of the spiritual; while the spiritual served also to sanctify the carnal. They were united, but not blended together. For "the law is not of faith," says Paul (Gal. iii, 12).

So matters stood until Christ came "made of a woman, made under the law, to redeem them that were under the law" (Gal. iv, 5, 6). For about three and a half years, he instructed the people, and by his own personal ministry developed to a wonderful extent the beauties, riches, and superlative excellencies of the spiritual and antitypical element of the Abrahamic promise. But nevertheless it was still in but an imperfect state, not yet having received its full and complete development, as a separate and distinct In-

Effect of Christ's personal ministry.

the Orientals made a covenant with each other, it was their custom to partake of the slain victims. And hence it came to pass, that to eat with any one, was commonly regarded in many eastern countries as almost equivalent to making a covenant with him. The Greeks had two words for *covenant*, viz., *suntheke* (συνθήκη) and *diatheke* (διαθήκη). The former was used to denote a solemn agreement made between equals; and the latter, to denote any arrangement made by a superior for the acceptance and observance of an inferior. And hence it is, that all of God's covenants are expressed in Greek by the word *diatheke*. The word *suntheke* is not found in the New Testament; but *diatheke* occurs in it 33 times; and *b'reeth* is used 267 times in the Old Testament.

Three things are implied in every covenant, viz., The covenanter, the covenantee, and the various stipulations which are made and entered into by the parties. In the Adamic covenant, for instance, God is the Covenanter; Adam and his entire posterity are the covenantees; and the conditions of life, health, and happiness are the things stipulated.

Three things implied in every covenant.

stitution. Nor could this be done in fact while the first Institution was standing. The Old Sinaitic Covenant had to be taken out of the way, before the New Covenant could be fully inaugurated as a separate and independent Institution. This was done at the death of Christ (Col. ii, 14). Henceforth it was no longer binding on any one as a *religious* Institution; though it was through the forbearance of God allowed to remain as a *civil* and *social* Institution, for about thirty-six years longer, until Jerusalem was destroyed by the Romans in A. D. 70.

When the Old Covenant was abrogated as a *religious* and also as a *civil* Institution.

In the meantime, the spiritual element of the Abrahamic promise, the covenant concerning Christ (εἰς χριστὸν, Gal. iii, 17), was, according to Jeremiah xxxi, 31, fully developed in the Church of Christ, which was set up as a distinct organization, on the day of Pentecost, which next followed after his death, burial, and resurrection. Then for the first time he was publicly proclaimed to the world as the anointed Sovereign of the universe (Acts ii, 36); and then also believing penitents were first commanded to be baptized by his authority into the name of the Father, and of the Son, and of the Holy Spirit. (Compare Acts ii, 38 with Matth. xxviii, 19.) From that time the Church of Christ is spoken of repeatedly as an existing reality, and its members are said to partake of the many blessings and benefits of the New Covenant. See, for instance, Acts ii, 47; v, 11; viii, 1, 3; ix, 31; xi, 15; and Col. i, 13.

Inauguration of the New Covenant.

The following diagram may assist the reader in his endeavors to form a just conception of the gradual development and intimate relations of these two Covenants, based on the two distinctive elements of the Abrahamic promise.

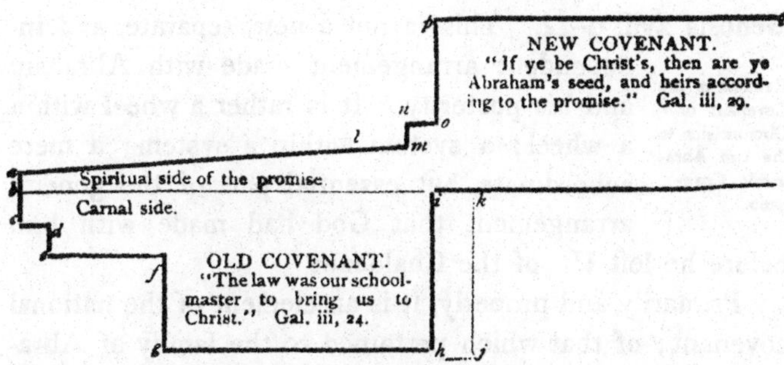

EXPLANATIONS.—*a c* Promise made to Abraham 1921 B. C.; *d e* Circumcision ordained 1892 B. C.; *f g* Inauguration of the Old Covenant 1491 B. C.; *h i* The Law abrogated, A. D. 34; *j k* Jerusalem destroyed A. D. 70; *l* Birth of Christ; *m n* Baptism of Christ; *o p* Inauguration of the New Covenant fifty days after the death of Christ, A. D. 34.

For points of difference between the Old and New Covenants, see particularly 2 Cor. iii, 2–18; Gal. iv, 19–31; and Heb. viii, 6–13. Those given in Gal. iv, may be briefly summed up as follows:

1. The Old Covenant is here represented as a slave; but the New as a free woman.

2. The subjects of the former are also represented as slaves; but those of the latter, as freemen.

3. The birth of the former subjects was natural, according to the flesh; but that of the latter is supernatural.

4. The former differ from the latter in character, as Ishmael differed from Isaac.

5. So also they differ in their fortunes.

SECTION III.—COVENANT OF CIRCUMCISION.

The fullest and most striking development of the Abrahamic covenants previous to the giving of the Law from Mount Sinai is the Covenant of Circumcision.

Genesis xvii, 9–14. This is not a new, separate, and independent arrangement made with Abraham and his posterity. It is rather a wheel within a wheel; a system within a system; a mere subordinate, but essential part of the general arrangement that God had made with him before he left Ur, of the Chaldeans

Relation of the Covenant of Circumcision to the two Abrahamic Covenants.

Primarily and properly, it is an element of the national covenant; of that which pertained to the family of Abraham according to the flesh. But, like most of the other provisions of that covenant, it had also a typical reference to the covenant concerning Christ, and, of course, to the whole family of the faithful.

Its Provisions.

The provisions of this covenant were as follows:

I. That every male child of the seed of Abraham should be circumcised.

II. That this should be done on the eighth day after its birth.

III. That all servants purchased with money, either by himself or by any of his posterity, should, in like manner, be circumcised.

IV. That it should be an everlasting covenant; that is, that, like the covenant of the Levitical Priesthood, it should continue as long as the general and more comprehensive covenant, of which it was but an element, should endure.

V. And, finally, that death should be the penalty for the neglect or violation of this covenant.

The design of Circumcision was twofold:

The first design of Circumcision.

I. *To separate Abraham and his posterity, according to the flesh, from the rest of mankind, and thus to serve as a sign, seal, and token of the Old, or National Covenant.* And hence it was a pledge,

1. That God would bless Abraham himself, as it was also to him a seal of his justification by faith. Romans iv, 11.

2. That God would bless all his natural posterity, whether by Hagar, Sarah, or Katurah.

3. That of his seed according to the flesh (*i. e.*, of a part of it) God would make a great nation, and give them the land of Canaan for an everlasting possession.

4. That through him and his seed God would in some way bless all the nations and families of the Earth.

So far, then, Circumcision was a sort of carnal, national, and political ordinance. But,

Second design of Circumcision.

II. It had, also, a purely religious meaning. *It was made typical of the cutting off of the body of sin from the soul, and the subsequent sealing of it by the Holy Spirit.* This is clearly proved by the following passages:

Evidence of this.

1. Romans ii, 28, 29: "For he is not a Jew who is one outwardly, neither is that circumcision which is outward in the flesh; but he is a Jew who is one inwardly, and circumcision is that of the heart, in the spirit, and not in the letter—whose praise is not of men, but of God."

2. Philippians iii, 3: "For we are the circumcision who worship God in the spirit, and rejoice in Christ Jesus, and have no confidence in the flesh."

3. Colossians ii, 9–12: "For in him (Christ) dwelleth all the fullness of the Godhead bodily. And ye are complete in him, who is the head of all principality and power; *in whom, also, ye are circumcised with the circumcision made without hands, in putting off the body of the sins of the flesh by the circumcision of Christ;* buried with him in baptism; wherein, also, ye are risen with him,

through the faith of the operation of God, who hath raised him from the dead."

4. Ephesians i, 13, 14: "In whom (Christ) ye also trusted, after that ye heard the word of truth, the Gospel of your salvation; *in whom, also, after that ye believed, ye were sealed with that Holy Spirit of promise, which is the earnest of our inheritance,* until the redemption of the purchased possession, unto the praise of his glory."

From these passages of Scripture it is evident,

Lessons taught by these passages.

I. That the man who was a Jew outwardly stood to him who was a Jew inwardly, in the relation of the shadow to the substance, or of the type to the antitype. See also Romans ix, 6, and Galatians vi, 16, etc.

II. That the circumcision of the flesh was a type of the circumcision of the spirit; and that in this, in fact, consisted its chief value.

III. That the circumcision of the heart, or spirit, consists in cutting off from it the body of sin.

IV. That this is done through the agency of the Holy Spirit, in the baptism of every true believer. See also Acts ii, 38; Romans vi, 1–3; and Galatians iii, 27.

V. That the Holy Spirit itself, as it dwells in the heart of the Christian, is the seal of his circumcision.

VI. That it is also to him an earnest of the purchased possession, or a sure pledge that in due time he will enter into the full possession and enjoyment of the eternal inheritance.

PART II.

DEVELOPMENTS FROM THE BIRTH OF MOSES TO THE DEATH OF JOSHUA.

CHAPTER I.

DESIGN OF THE LAW.

THE reader is now prepared to understand Paul's answer to the question, "What, then, was the purpose of the Law? It was added," he says, "on account of transgressions, till the Seed should come, to whom the promise was made."

Purposes for which the Law was given.

This is a very comprehensive oracle, and seems to imply the following particulars:

I. *That the Law was given to the Jews for all the purposes of a civil government.* The Jews were a nation, and as such they needed a code of civil and political regulations. "The Law," says Paul, "was made for the lawless," 1 Tim. i, 9.

First, for the civil government of the Israelites.

In this respect it was well adapted to the development, discipline, and happiness of the individual and the family, as well as the tribe and the nation. But, nevertheless, on account of the hardness of the hearts of the people, Moses was under the necessity of permitting some things *politically* which are not in perfect harmony with the essential principles of morality and virtue. See, for instance, Matthew xix, 8.

Its adaptation to this end.

Perfection of civil government.

This, however, is not to be regarded as an imperfection in the law of Moses. The perfection of civil government consists in its *adaptation* to the capacity, habits, education, and circumstances of the people. And if Solon could truthfully say that he had framed the best code of laws that could be made for the *Athenians,* no doubt we may, also, safely affirm that Moses framed the very best code of laws that could be made for the *Israelites.*

Second, to convict man of sin.

II. *It was added to convince and to convict men of sin, by giving to them a perfect standard and code of morality.* It is true that without a written Revelation from God all men would have some knowledge of right and wrong. But it was only by and through the Law that Paul himself was enabled to understand the exceeding sinfulness of sin. Romans vii, 7–25.

Third, to support true Religion in the world.

III. *The third object of the Law was to prevent the universal spread of idolatry, by preserving among men both the knowledge and the practice of true religion, till Christ should come.* True, indeed, the two schemes of justification by faith and by works of law were as different and as distinct then as they are now. "The Law is not of faith," says Paul, Galatians iii, 12. But, nevertheless, the Law was a *supporter* of true religion. It served to preserve and to sustain in the world the then imperfectly developed scheme of justification by faith; so that, no doubt, hundreds and thousands of Jews were saved through its influence and instrumentality who would have otherwise sunk into the basest idolatry.

Fourth, a pictorial outline of Christianity.

IV. *The fourth and last object of the Law was to give to the world a suitable religious nomenclature, and a sort of pictorial outline of the Scheme of*

Redemption, by means of certain types and symbols, rites and ceremonies, addressed to their senses.

As a logical proposition, this fourth item has already been demonstrated with sufficient clearness and fullness in the previous sections of Part First. But the subject itself has been but barely introduced; and it is, therefore, to its consideration and development that I now invite the attention of the reader in the following chapters. We will begin with the Mission of Moses.

CHAPTER II

THE MISSION OF MOSES.

THE bondage of the Israelites in Egypt is one of the most remarkable events of history. That God should select a people from among all the nations of the Earth, give them laws and ordinances, as well as many other special tokens of his favor, and then allow them to become the most abject slaves of a foreign and wicked despot, is hard for us to reconcile with our limited sense of propriety.

Bondage of the Israelites in Egypt.

But God's thoughts are not as our thoughts, nor are his ways as our ways. In treating of this subject we must never lose sight of the fact that the seed of Abraham, according to the flesh, were made typical of his seed according to the Spirit, and that the history of the former must, therefore, of necessity, be made to correspond with that of the latter.

Why a necessity.

But, previous to their conversion and regeneration, all men are. by nature and practice. the slaves of sin. And hence the obvious necessity that the Israelites should, in like manner, become the slaves of Pharaoh. Otherwise the shadow would not have been in harmony with the substance, and the fearfully stupefying and enslaving power of sin would have had no corresponding phase in the Historical Types of the Mosaic economy.

Object of the Mission of Moses.

The bondage of the Israelites in Egypt was, therefore, a typological necessity, and so, also, was their emancipation. To effect this Moses was raised up and sent as God's embassador with good news and glad tidings to his enslaved brethren.

His qualifications for the work.

For the accomplishment of this great work he seems to have been eminently qualified. By nature he was a man of great power, energy, wisdom, and prudence, and by education he was at least equal to any of his contemporary sages, having been thoroughly instructed in all the wisdom of the Egyptians. Nor was this all: the power to work miracles was also, of necessity, superadded to all his natural endowments and his varied attainments. Mankind *instinctively* demand the evidence of miracles in attestation of any alleged Divine Commission to establish a new religion; and the justice of this claim is conceded by Christ himself. See John xv, 22–24.

First Miracle wrought by Moses.

And hence, when Pharaoh demanded of Moses and Aaron such evidence of their Divine legation, (Exodus vii, 9,) Aaron, at the bidding of Moses, threw down his rod, and it became a serpent. Exodus vii, 10.

Wonders wrought by the Magicians.

But the Magicians also did so with their enchantments: "for they cast down every man his rod, and it became a serpent. But Aaron's rod swallowed up their rods." Exodus vii, 11, 12

That the rod of Aaron was miraculously converted into a real serpent there can be no reasonable doubt. But with respect to the rods of the Magicians the evidence is not so clear. And hence the ablest critics are still divided in their judgments concerning this matter.

Four Hypotheses concerning them.

I. Some think that these extraordinary phenomena were nothing more than mere feats of jugglery, and that they were performed simply by human skill.

II. Others think that they were feats of jugglery or legerdemain, but that they were performed by the *joint agency* of Satan and the Magicians, just as the temptation of Eve was effected through the joint agency of Satan and the serpent.

III. Others suppose that they were real miracles, wrought by Satan through the instrumentality of the Magicians.

IV. And others, again, think that they were real miracles, wrought by God himself through the instrumentality of the Magicians.

Reasons for preferring the Second Hypothesis.

That the second of these hypotheses is the true one is, I think, probable, for the following reasons:

1. Because these facts seem to be superhuman, and yet not miraculous. If the Magicians could work a *real* miracle in one case, why might they not do so in any other case?

2. Because Satan possesses power far above that of man. See 2 Thess. ii, 9.

3. Because he is ever ready and disposed to exercise his power against God and his servants. He did all that he could to bring discredit on the miracles of Christ, as well as those performed by Moses.

4. He nas actually done many wonderful works,

personally and through the instrumentality of his agents This is proved,

(1.) By the facts of ancient witchcraft. God would not legislate against a mere chimera of the imagination. But see Exodus xxii, 18; Lev. xix, 26, 31; xx, 6, 27, etc.

(2.) By the works of Demons in the time of Christ and his Apostles. See Acts xvi, 16–19.

(3.) By heathen Oracles. Most of these were palpable falsehoods; but some of them, as, for instance, in the case of the damsel last referred to, seem to indicate a degree of sagacity that was far beyond the conceptions of men and women in the flesh.*

(4.) By the superhuman feats of modern conjurers, fortune-tellers, table-rappers, etc.

What the miracle of Moses served to prove.

Be this as it may, one thing is certain, that this miracle, performed in the presence of Pharaoh and his servants, served not only to prove the Divine Legation of Moses, but also to show

Examples illustrative of Heathen Oracles.

*The following example will serve to illustrate the ambiguous nature and character of most of the heathen oracles: "*Aio te Æacida, Romanos vincere posse.*" This may be rendered with equal accuracy, "*I say that you, O, Pyrrhus, (son of Æacus,) can conquer the Romans;*" or, "*That the Romans can conquer you, O, Pyrrhus.*" The Oracle was, therefore, safe, however the war might terminate.

But the following reply of the same Oracle to Crœsus is not to be explained nor set aside by any such ambiguity of terms or construction. Being doubtful of the Oracle, Crœsus resolved that he would first test its superhuman knowledge, and he accordingly sent a messenger to Delphi, with instructions to inquire, at the end of one hundred days from that time, in what business the king was then engaged. The reply of the Oracle was, "*I smell the odor of a lamb boiled with a tortoise, while brass is both above and beneath it.*" And this, it is said, was actually the business in which Crœsus was then employed.

This seems to have satisfied Crœsus that the Oracle was superhuman. And he therefore sent to it again, to inquire whether or not he would be victorious in his contemplated war with the Persians. To which the Oracle replied, "*That he (Crœsus) would overthrow a great empire.*" But not fully the absurdity of the then prevalent system of serpent-worship. For "Aaron's rod swallowed up their rods" This was sufficient evidence that the God of the Hebrews was superior to the serpent gods of the Egyptians.

With regard to the hardening of Pharaoh's heart, it is only necessary to remind the reader that "*what softens wax hardens clay.*" What softens and even melts an honest heart often hardens one that is dishonest. And hence it is that the Gospel itself is represented as being either a savor of life unto life or of death unto death." 2 Corinthians ii, 16.

The hardening of Pharaoh's heart.

Had the evidence of the first miracle been duly regarded, that would, of course, have been an end of the whole matter. No punishment would then have been inflicted on Pharaoh or

Why Plagues were sent on Pharaoh.

comprehending the meaning of this answer, Crœsus sent again to inquire whether his power would ever be diminished. To this the Oracle returned the following ambiguous reply: "*Seek your safety in flight when a mule reigns over the Medes.*" In both cases Crœsus was deceived by the ambiguity of the terms, as the sequel fully proved.

There was evidently, therefore, much craft and cunning employed in framing these oracular responses. But that there was also something more than this, something above and beyond mere human sagacity, is rendered quite probable by the fact that for several centuries these Oracles were consulted and sustained by the most enlightened kings, statesmen, and philosophers of the heathen world.

Evidence of superhuman sagacity in some of these Oracles.

But soon after the commencement of the Christian Era they lost all their authority and influence with the people. So much so that even the poet Juvenal was constrained to say,

Decline of these Oracles.

"Delphis oracula cessant,
Et genus humanum damnat caligo futuri."

This was a great mystery to the learned heathen. They could give no rational nor plausible account of the change that had taken place. Even the infidel Porphyry complains with Juvenal that "since Jesus began to be worshiped, no man has received any public help or benefit from the gods." What a commentary is all this on the words of Jesus, "*I beheld Satan. as lightning, fall from heaven.*" Luke x, 18.

Cause of this.

on any one else. But now the rod begins to smart. A series of plagues follow that are without a parallel in the history of the world.

Double reference of each Plague.

And observe that each of these, like the preceding, has a double reference. While it serves to prove the Divine Legation of Moses, it also serves to show in some way the absurdity of Egyptian idolatry, and the supreme Divinity of Jehovah. See Exodus xii, 12.

The first Plague.

The first Plague consisted in changing the water of the Nile, and all the waters derived from it, into blood. Exodus vii, 14–25.

Its Object.

This was designed to disprove the alleged divinity of the Nile, and that, too, it would seem just at the time when Pharaoh was going out to pay to it his morning devotions. See v, 15.

The second Plague.

The second Plague consisted in bringing up from the Nile, and its various streams and pools, an innumerable multitude of frogs on all the land of Egypt. Exodus viii, 1–15.

Its Object.

This was intended to show the absurdity of reptile worship, for which the Egyptians had long been famous.

The third Plague.

The third Plague consisted in changing the dust into lice throughout all the land of Egypt. Exodus viii, 16–19.

Its Object.

This seems to have been a blow aimed at the entire system of idolatrous worship. During its continuance all worship was necessarily suspended, for no priest was allowed to officiate with such an insect on his person. "To conceive of the severity of this miracle as a judgment on their idolatry," says Stackhouse, "we must recollect their utter abhorrence of all kinds of vermin, and their extreme attention to external purity, above every other people perhaps that ever existed. On this head they were more particularly solicitous when they were about to enter the temples of their gods. For Herodotus informs us that the priests wore linen garments only in order that they might be washed daily. *And every third day they shaved every part of their body, to prevent lice or any kind of impurity from adhering to their persons.*" *

The fourth Plague was the miracle of flies. Exodus viii, 20–32.

The fourth Plague.

This was probably designed to illustrate the absurdty of all animal worship, for these flies were a plague to both man and beast. But there is also reason to think that the Fly itself was worshiped in Egypt. It is known, at least, that a winged Asp was one of the guardian divinities of Lower Egypt.

Its Object.

The fifth Plague was the murrain of their domestic animals. Exodus ix, 1–7.

The fifth Plague.

This, too, was directed against animal worship. The Egyptians regarded the death of even one of their sacred animals as a public calamity. How dreadful, then, must have been their consternation when they saw them perishing by thousands!

Its Object.

The sixth Plague consisted in the miracle of boils and blains. Exodus ix, 8–12.

The sixth Plague.

This miracle was directed against the worship of the idol Typhon. Plutarch, on the authority of Manetho, makes the following statement concerning the ancient mode of worshiping this imaginary divinity in some parts of Egypt. He says: "Formerly, in the city of Idithya, the Egyptians were

Its Object.

* Stackhouse's History of the Bible, Vol. I, p. 473.

wont to burn men alive, giving them the name of *Typhos;* and winnowing their ashes through a sieve, so as to scatter and disperse them into the air." They seem to have done this with the impression that every object on which a particle of these ashes fell was safe from the wrath of Typhon. But now, at the command of Moses, these ashes from the furnace of Typhon, become a plague throughout all the land of Egypt.*

Testimony of Manetho.

The seventh Plague was the miracle of thunder and lightning, mingled with hail and rain. Exodus ix, 13–35.

The Seventh Plague.

This was a scourge on the vegetable idols of Egypt. The Egyptians worshiped the Peachtree, the Pomegranate, the Vine, the Acanthus, the Fig, the Tamarisk, the Onion, the Garlic, the Papyrus, the Ivy, etc.

Its Object.

The eighth Plague was an unprecedented swarm of locusts, that covered the whole land of Egypt. Exodus x, 1–20.

The eighth Plague.

This miracle was the supplement and consummation of the preceding plague on the Egyptian vegetable idols.

Its Object.

The ninth Plague was the miracle of darkness. Exodus x, 21–23.

The ninth Plague.

This miracle was directed against the worship of the Sun, Moon, and Stars.

Its Object.

The tenth Plague consisted in the death of the first-born. Exodus xi, 1–10, and xii, 29–36.

The tenth Plague.

This was directed equally against all the gods of Egypt and their worshipers. But before this

* The Egyptians also sacrificed red bullocks to Typhon. Fairbarn's Typology, Vol. II, p. 382.

plague was sent on them the Passover was instituted. The consideration of this we must reserve for the next chapter.

CHAPTER III.

THE PASSOVER.

THERE is perhaps nothing that is real, and valuable, and susceptible of being imitated, that Satan and his emissaries have not attempted to counterfeit in some way. This is just as true of miracles as it is of money, religion, or any thing else. And hence the necessity of having some tests or criteria by which we may be able to distinguish between true and false miracles.

Why certain Tests or criteria of miracles are necessary.

The four Rules given by Leslie, in his "*Short Method with the Deists*," are well conceived and expressed. They seem to meet and to satisfy all the reasonable demands of a candid mind and an honest heart. They are as follows:

The four Rules of Leslie.

I. *The facts must be such that men's senses can judge of them.*

II. *It is necessary that they be performed publicly, in the presence of witnesses.*

III. *That public Monuments be set up, and public actions be appointed to be performed in memory of them.*

IV. *That these Monuments and actions be established and instituted at the time of the facts, and continued thenceforward without interruption.*

The first two of these conditions are necessary for the satisfaction of persons living at the time the alleged miracles are said to be performed.

Use of these various Tests

And the last two are equally necessary for the faith and satisfaction of subsequent generations. And hence it is that God has connected sundry Monuments, or Commemorative Institutions, with all the miracles, both of Moses and of Christ. The first of these is the Passover; and to this the attention of the reader is now invited. Notice, then,

Monuments connected with the miracles of Moses and of Christ.

I. The name of this institution. It is called the *Passover*, (פֶּסַח, Gr. πάσχα, a passing over, sparing, deliverance,) because the Lord passed over and spared the houses of the Children of Israel, while he smote the Egyptians.

What the name implies.

II. It is used,

1. For the Paschal Lamb. Exodus xii, 21.
2. For the Paschal Supper. Numbers xxxiii, 3.
3. For the Paschal Festival of seven days, from the beginning of the 15th to the close of the 21st of the month Nisan. Luke xxii, 1; John xviii, 28; and Josephus I, 470; II, 25, etc.

Its various uses and applications.

III. The following is the Chronology of the Passover:

Chronology of the Passover.

1. On the 10th day of the month Nisan the father of each family was required to select a Lamb or a Kid (a Lamb was generally taken) from his flock, and to keep it up till the 14th day of the same month. Or, if any were necessarily prevented from celebrating the Passover on the first month, Nisan or Abib, they were permitted to do it on the second month, Ijar or Zif. See Numbers ix, 9–11, and 2 Chronicles xxx, 1–27.

2. On the 14th day of the month, between the two evenings, בֵּין הָעַרְבַּיִם) that is, as the Rabbis generally say, at any time between the decline of the Sun, afternoon,

and sunset,* the Lamb was to be killed by its owner, or by one of the Levites. 2 Chronicles xxx, 17. The usual time, however, of killing the Passover was at three o'clock in the afternoon.

3. On the same day, between the two evenings, they began to eat the Paschal Supper, which seems, however, to have been continued into the 15th. See Lev. xxiii, 5; Numbers xxxiii, 3; Joshua v, 10, 11; Luke xxii, 8; John xiii, 1–30.

4. On the 15th day of the month began the Feast of Unleavened Bread, and continued, ordinarily, seven days. Leviticus xxiii, 4–8. But in one case it lasted fourteen days. 2 Chronicles xxx, 23.

Beginning of the Civil and the Ecclesiastical Year.

IV. But just here it may be asked, What month was Nisan or Abib? When did it commence, and with what part of our year did it correspond?

1. Before the Exodus the year commenced with Tishri, (תִּשְׁרִי,) which was still reckoned as the beginning of the Civil year. But from and ever after that memorable epoch the Ecclesiastical year was reckoned from Nisan, (נִיסָן, probably from נִצ, a flower,) or Abib, (אָבִיב, a green ear,) which was the old Hebrew name for the same month.

Number of Months and Days in the Jewish Year.

2. The year ordinarily consisted of 12 Lunar months, or about 354 days and $8\frac{6}{10}$ hours. But this fell short of the true length of the year by about 10 days and 21 hours. And hence the necessity of an intercalary month, which was always added whenever the Priests saw, at the close of the twelfth month, (אֲדָר, Adar,) that the sheaf of barley

* The Greeks had, in like manner, their δείλη πρωΐα and their δείλη ὀψία; their early and their late afternoon.

required by the Law (Leviticus xxiii, 11) would not be ready for use by the 14th day of the next month.*

Intercalary Month.

3. The Intercalary Month was called Ve-Adar, which means simply *and Adar* (וַאֲדָר.) It was added to the close of the Ecclesiastical year.

V. With regard to the victim to be sacrificed observe,

Kind and qualities of the Victim.

1. That it might be either a Lamb or a Kid of the first year without blemish.

Killing the Victim.

2. Before the Exode it was slain by the fathers of the several families in their respective dwellings. But afterward it was slain, either by the owner or by one of the Levites, in the place where the Lord had recorded his name; *i. e.*, in the Court of the Tabernacle or of the Temple. Leviticus xvii, 4; Deuteronomy xvi, 2; and 2 Chronicles xxxv, 1–11.

The Blood.

3. At the first Passover the blood was sprinkled on the lintel and door-posts. V. 7. But after that it was sprinkled at the foot of the altar by the priests. 2 Chronicles xxx, 16.

The Flesh.

4. The victim was then roasted whole, and was eaten by one or two families, according to the number of persons in each. The Rabbinical rule was that there should not be less than ten nor more than twenty for one lamb.

Persons allowed to partake of it.

5. None but circumcised and clean persons were ordinarily allowed to partake of it. Numbers ix, 1–13. See, however, one exception. 2 Chronicles xxx, 17.

Its Bones.

6. A bone of it was not to be broken. Exodus xii, 46.

VI. The prescribed ceremonies of the Paschal Supper were as follows:

* Jahn's Biblical Archæology, Part I, Chapter iv, Section 103.

Ceremonies of the Paschal Supper.

1. The first Passover was eaten by the Israelites while standing, with their shoes on their feet and their staves in their hands. But after they entered Canaan they reclined around a table, this attitude, as they say, being more in harmony with that *rest* into which they had then entered. See John xiii, 23.

2. It was eaten with unleavened bread and bitter herbs, to remind them of their haste and bondage.*

Mode of celebrating the Passover among the Jews.

* The following was the usual order of celebrating the Passover, according to the best Rabbinical writers:

I. The guests being arranged around the table, they first mingled a cup of wine with water and drank it, after the Master of the family had given thanks for it.

II. They then washed their hands, after which the table was furnished with the Paschal Lamb, bitter herbs, two cakes of unleavened bread, and a thick sauce called *charoseth*, made out of dates, raisins, and several other ingredients. This, they say, represents the clay in which their fathers wrought while in bondage. The remains of the Peace-Offerings sacrificed on the same day (the 14th of Nisan) were also served up at the same time. These Peace-Offerings were wholly voluntary.

III. The Master of the assembly then took a small piece of salad, and having blessed God for creating the fruits of the ground, he ate it. Others then partook of the same.

IV. The dishes were then removed from the table, and the children instructed in the nature of the Feast. The passage of Scripture usually read on the occasion was Deuteronomy xxvi, 5–11.

V. Then replacing the Supper, they partook of a second cup of wine, and sung Psalms cxiv and cxv.

VI. Again they washed their hands, while repeating an ejaculatory prayer. After which the Master of the feast broke a cake of unleavened bread, the half of which he distributed among the guests.

VII. They then ate the other half of the cake with bitter herbs, dipping the bread into the charoseth. John xiii, 26.

VIII. Next they ate the flesh of the Peace-Offerings that had been voluntarily offered on the fourteenth day of the month.

IX. They then ate the flesh of the Paschal Lamb, which was followed by the offering of thanks and the washing of hands.

X. A third cup of wine was then filled, over which they all blessed God. This was called "*The Cup of Blessing.*" See 1 Corinthians x, 16.

XI. A fourth cup of wine was then filled. This was called "*The Cup of Hallel.*" They gave thanks over it, and sung or recited Psalms cxv, cxvi, cxvii, and cxviii. After this the whole ceremony was concluded with prayer.

VII. The ceremonies of the Paschal Festival were as follows:

Ceremonies of the Paschal Festival.

1. On each of the seven days, besides the daily Burnt-Offerings, and Meat-Offerings, and Drink-Offerings, the Children of Israel were required to offer,

The daily Offerings.

(1.) Two young bullocks, one ram, and seven lambs of the first year, without blemish, for a Burnt-Offering.

(2.) An ephah and a half of fine flour mingled with oil for a Meat-Offering.

(3.) One goat for a Sin-Offering. See Numbers xxviii, 1–8, and 16–25.

2. After they entered Canaan, they were also required to offer on the day following the Paschal Sabbath* a sheaf of barley. Leviticus xxiii, 11,

Sheaf of Barley.

*Josephus says that this sheaf of barley was always waved on the 16th day of Nisan, (Antiquities, Vol. I, page 103;) and many learned commentators follow him in their explanation of Leviticus xxiii, 4–14, 16. In this they, of course, assume that the first day of Unleavened Bread was *the Sabbath* of the festival. They do so because it is said in the seventh verse of the chapter that on this day there was to be a holy convocation, and that no servile work was to be done on it. But the very same things are said of the seventh or last day of the festival. See verse 8th. Why, then, make the first rather than the seventh day of the feast *the Sabbath?* Or, as we should rather say, Why make either of them *the Sabbath?* Neither is so called either in the text or in the context. And as one Sabbath prescribed by the fourth precept of the Decalogue would always occur during every Paschal festival, it seems clear to my mind that this seventh day of the week would, in the estimation of every Jew, be regarded as THE SABBATH of the Passover.

Day on which the sheaf was waved according to Josephus and others.

Reasons for fixing this on the first day of the week.

And this corresponds exactly with the facts of the Antitype. Christ, the first-fruits of the Christian harvest, rose not on the 16th, but on the 17th day of Nisan. He ate the Paschal Supper, as did all the Jews, on Thursday evening, the 14th day of the month. On Friday, the 15th, he was crucified and buried. On the 16th, which was the seventh day of the week, or the Jewish Sabbath, he rested in the grave. And on the 17th day of the month, which was the morrow after the Sabbath proper, but the second day after

15. This being done, the products of the year were sanctified, or made fit for use. And just so Christ, having risen on the same day of the week, "the first-fruits of them that slept," has, in like manner, sanctified humanity.

Its Typical Significance.

"This is the day the first ripe sheaf
Before the Lord was waved;
And Christ, first-fruits of them that slept,
Was from the dead received."

3. Besides all this many voluntary offerings were sometimes added. See, for example, 2 Chronicles xxx, 23–26, and xxxv, 7–9.

Voluntary Offerings.

VIII. The object of the Passover seems to have been threefold; viz., *commemorative, disciplinary*, and *typical*.

1. *Its primary object was, doubtless, to commemorate the Lord's passing over and sparing the Children of Israel while he slew the first-born of the Egyptians*, and thus to hand down to posterity the most palpable and indubitable evidence of the Divine authenticity of all the facts and miracles connected with the emancipation of the Israelites from Egyptian bondage. Had the miracles not been wrought, no such institution as the Passover could have ever been established and imposed on the people. Without the most reliable evidence of its Divine origin and also of all the miracles that resulted in their final deliverance,

Its influence and importance as a Commemorative Institution.

the first day of the festival, he rose from the dead, the first-fruits of them that slept. This, I think, is strong evidence that by *the Sabbath* of the Paschal festival was always meant the seventh day of the week, whether it occurred on the 15th, 16th, 17th, 18th, 19th, 20th, or 21st day of Nisan.

It is worthy of note, also, that the Boëthusians and the Sadducees, in the time of the second Temple, (Mishna, Menachoth x, 3,) took the word Sabbath, in Leviticus xxiii, 15, in its ordinary sense, as denoting the seventh day of the week. And since the eighth century the Karaites have interpreted it in the same way. *Alexander's Kitto's Bibl. Cyc., Art. Pentecost.*

they could never have been induced to leave their wives, their children, and their homes exposed to their enemies while they went up to Jerusalem every year to celebrate this ordinance. But concede the reality of all the miracles recorded, and then every thing that followed in the early history of this people is plain, simple, and natural.

How it also served as a means of education.

2. *The Passover was also a divinely ordained means for educating the people.* For,

(1.) It provided for the instruction of the children. Verses 26–28.

(2.) By bringing together all the males once every year, to commemorate their deliverance from bondage, it served very greatly to cultivate their sympathies for each other and their reverence for Jehovah.

In what respects it was typical of Christ.

3. *The Paschal Lamb was in several respects typical of Christ.* 1 Corinthians v, 7.

(1.) It was without blemish, and so was he. 1 Peter i, 19.

(2.) It was killed between the two evenings, and so was he. Matthew xxvii, 45–50.

(3.) Its blood procured salvation and deliverance, and so did his. 1 Peter i, 18, 19.

(4.) Not a bone of it was broken, nor was one of his. John xix, 36.

(5.) It was eaten without leaven; and just so we are all required to partake of Christ, without the leaven of malice and hypocrisy. 1 Corinthians v, 7, 8.

There may, perhaps, be other points of intended resemblance; but those given are sufficient for our present purpose. Dr. Godwin enumerates 13 points of resemblance; Dr. Lightfoot gives 17; and Dr. Keach 19. This is, no doubt, pressing the analogy beyond its true and proper typical limits.

Names of the Hebrew Months.

NOTE.—The Hebrew months, called יְרָחִים, (יֶרַח, a month, from יָרֵחַ, the moon, from יָרַח, to be pale,) and sometimes חֳדָשִׁים, (חֹדֶשׁ, a new moon, from חָדַשׁ, to be new,) had anciently no separate names, except the *first*, which was called Abib, (אָבִיב, a green ear.) Exodus xiii, 4, etc. But during the captivity the Hebrews adopted the Babylonian names. They were as follows:

I. Nisan, (נִיסָן), reckoned from the new moon of March or April. Neh. ii, 1.

II. Ziv or Zif, (זִיו,) reckoned from the new moon of April or May. 1 Kings vi, 1.

III. Sivan, (סִיוָן,) reckoned from the new moon of May or June. Esther viii, 9.

IV. Tammuz, (תַּמּוּז,) reckoned from the new moon of June or July.

V. Ab, (אָב,) reckoned from the new moon of July or August.

VI. Elul, (אֱלוּל,) reckoned from the new moon of August or September, Neh. vi, 15.

VII. Tishri, (תִּשְׁרִי,) reckoned from the new moon of September or October. 1 Kings viii, 2.

VIII. Bul or Marcheshvan, (בּוּל or מַרְחֶשְׁוָן,) reckoned from the new moon of October or November. 1 Kings vi, 38.

IX. Kislev, (כִּסְלֵו,) reckoned from the new moon of November or December. Neh. i, 1.

X. Tebeth, (טֵבֵת,) reckoned from the new moon of December or January. Esther ii, 16.

XI. Shebat, (שְׁבָט,) reckoned from the new moon of January or February. Zech. i, 7.

XII. Adar, (אֲדָר,) reckoned from the new moon of February or March. Esther iii, 17.

The intercalary month was also called Adar or וְאָדָר, and-Adar. See Jahn's Bib. Arch., p. 112.

That the year originally began with the month Tishri is proved,

I. From the fact that Tishri is derived from a root which signifies *to begin*, (שָׁרָא,) to begin.

II. From the testimony of the best Jewish authority. See Josephus, Book I, chap. III, 3.

CHAPTER IV.

THE EXODUS, ETC.

WHEN all the necessary arrangements had been made, just at the hour of midnight, the Lord went out and smote the first-born of the Egyptians, both of man and beast.* And there was a great cry throughout all the land of Egypt.

Slaying of the First-Born.

This was enough. The haughty monarch could endure no more. He and all his people rose up, and urged the Israelites to leave Egypt immediately; "for," said they, "*We be all dead men.*" And in order to encourage and hasten their departure, the Egyptians freely gave them all that they *asked.*† So the Israelites left Rameses and came to Succoth.

Its effect on Pharaoh and his subjects.

* This was most likely done through the instrumentality of an angel. See Exodus xii, 23. But this style is common in all languages, and is often applied to persons in authority, on the principle that, "*Qui facit per alium, facit per se.*" What a man does by another, he does by or through himself.

† The original word used here is *shahal,* (שָׁאַל.) It occurs 169 times in the Hebrew Bible; and is the word commonly used for *to ask, to request, etc.* Very seldom is it used with the intention or implied obligation of returning; and that this is not its meaning in this connection is evident from the context and all the circumstances of the case.

Meaning of the word שָׁאַל in Exodus xii, 35, etc.

The Hebrew word most commonly used to express the idea of *borrowing* is *lavah,* (לָוָה.) It is used 26 times in the Bible, and generally in this sense. The word *ahvat,* (עָבַט,) *to exchange,* is, also, sometimes used in the same sense. It occurs 6 times in the Bible.

While the Israelites were at Succoth another commemorative Ordinance was passed. All the first-born of males, both of man and beast, were sanctified to the Lord. Exodus xiii, 2, and 11–16.

Sanctification of the First-Born.

The Levites and their cattle were afterward substituted for the first-born of all the tribes. See Numbers iii, 40–51. The number of the first-born of all the tribes, from a month old and upward, was 22,273; and the number of the Levites, from a month old and upward, was as follows: The Kohathites were 8,600; the Merarites, 6,200; and the Gershonites, 7,500; making, in all, 22,300. Numbers iii, 14–39. But of these only 22,000 were exchanged for the first-born. The remaining 300 were, no doubt, the first-born of the Levites, and belonged to the Lord by virtue of the original ordinance passed at Succoth. Exodus xiii. The 273 supernumeraries of the first-born were redeemed at the rate of five shekels apiece. Numbers iii, 46–48.

Substitution of the Levites for the First-Born.

The long continuance of this ordinance is another proof of the Divine authenticity of the Mosaic history.

Evidence derived from this ordinance.

From Succoth the Children of Israel went to Etham; thence to Pihahiroth; thence to the Red Sea, where they were baptized into Moses by the cloud and by the sea. 1 Corinthians x, 2. Thence they went to Marah, where the bitter waters were made sweet; thence to Elim, where there were 12 fountains of water and 70 Palm trees; thence to the borders of the Red Sea; and thence to the Wilderness of Sin, just one month after their departure from Rameses. Here it was that quails and manna were miraculously supplied.

Journey from Succoth to the Wilderness of Sin.

With respect to this manna the following matters should be carefully noted and considered:

The Manna.

I. The name. Its etymology is somewhat uncertain. But from Exodus xvi, 15, it seems pretty evident that it is composed of the interrogative pronoun מָה, *what*, changed into מָן, for the sake of euphony; and the personal pronoun הוּא, *he*, *she*, or *it*. If this is its true derivation, the word *manna* simply means *What* (*is*) *it*. But some think that it means *a portion*, and that it is derived from מָנָה, *to distribute*.

Etymology of the word.

II. In appearance it was like coriander seed, consisting of small white particles. Exodus xvi, 31.

Its Appearance.

III. Its taste was like that of honeyed wafers. Verse 31.

Its Taste.

IV. It fell on every day of the week, except the Sabbath, for forty years. Verse 35. See, also, Joshua v, 12.

When and how long supplied.

V. The following were the principal directions given concerning it. See Exodus xvi.

Directions concerning it.

1. That an *omer** should be gathered for each one's daily allowance.

2. That it should be gathered every day except on the Sabbath; and that that day's ration should be gathered and prepared on Friday.

3. That none of it should be kept over night, except for the Sabbath.

4. That an omer of it should be put in a vase, (צִנְצֶנֶת Gr., *στάμνος*,) and laid up as a memorial for future generations.

***An omer (עֹמֶר) is the tenth part of an ephah, Exodus xvi, 36; which, according to Gesenius, is 7 pints. Others make it equal to but 5.1 pints. See Jahn's Bibl. Arch., p. 131.**

From the wilderness of Sin the Children of Israel took their journey and came to Dophka; thence to Alush; and thence to Rephidim, near the base of Mount Horeb. While they remained at Rephidim, three events occurred that are worthy of special notice.

Journey to Rephidim.

I. The first was the bringing of a large stream of water out of a rock on Horeb. This rock, says Paul, was Christ; that is, it was a type of Christ. 1 Corinthians x, 4. The stream from this rock must have been very large. For about a year, at least, it supplied between two and three millions of people and their numerous flocks and herds with an abundance of pure, running water. How very copious, then, must be the stream of grace that ever flows from the pierced side of our adorable Redeemer!

Miraculous supply of water.

II. The second event was Israel's victory over the Amalekites. Exodus xvii, 8–16. This passage beautifully illustrates our dependence on the outstretched arm of our glorious and victorious Immanuel.

Victory over the Amalekites.

III. Here, also, Jethro visited the camp of Israel, and advised Moses to choose "*able men, such as fear God, men of truth, hating covetousness*, and to make them rulers over thousands, rulers over hundreds, rulers over fifties, and rulers over tens." This was done evidently with God's approval. Exodus xviii, 23. See, also, Deuteronomy i, 9–18.*

Jethro's Visit and Advice to Moses.

On the third month, (Sivan,) that is, according to

*Thomas Jefferson's test of official competency was expressed by the three following questions: "Is he honest? Is he capable? Is he faithful?" If to these we add *piety*, they are very nearly equivalent to the qualifications required by Moses.

Hebrew usage, on the first day of the month, the Israelites left Rephidim and came to Mount Sinai, which seems to have been a peak of the mountainous region then called Horeb.* Here they remained till the 20th day of the second month of the second year after their departure from Egypt; that is, one year lacking ten days. Numbers x, 11.

Period of their Encampment at Sinai.

In the mean time there occurred on this dreary and desolate mountain, and in its vicinity, some of the most awfully sublime and thrillingly interesting events that are to be found in the annals of the world. The most important of these we will now endeavor to notice in order.

Events of this Period.

CHAPTER V.

THE DECALOGUE.

SOON after the people arrived at Sinai, probably, as tradition says, on the second day of the month, (Sivan,) Moses was called up into the mountain and received from God the following message to the Children of Israel:

Moses called up into the Mount.

"*Ye have seen what I did unto the Egyptians, and*

* "The mountain from which the Law was given is denominated Horeb in Deuteronomy i, 6; iv, 10, 15; v, 2; and xviii, 16. In other books of the Pentateuch it is called Sinai. In the time of Moses Horeb seems to have been the generic name of the group, and Sinai the name of a single mountain. But at a later period Sinai also became a general name. Acts vii, 30–38. As specific names, they are now applied to two opposite summits of an isolated, oblong, central ridge, about two miles in length from north to south, in the midst of a confused group of mountain summits." *Coleman's Biblical Geography, p.* 50

how I bore you on eagles' wings, and brought you unto myself. Now, therefore, if ye will obey my voice indeed, and keep my covenant, then you shall be a peculiar treasure unto me above all people; for all the Earth is mine; and ye shall be unto me a kingdom of priests and a holy nation." Exodus xix, 4–6.

God's proposition through him to the Israelites.

Moses then came down and submitted this proposition to the Elders, and through them to all the people. "And all the people answered together and said, *All that the Lord hath spoken we will do.*" Verse 8.

Their Reply.

Here, then, we have given, in all probability, the first instance of the free exercise of the popular will in accepting a form of civil government. All other Oriental governments were founded by and through force, and this only *with the consent of the governed.*

First instance of popular Representation in Civil Government.

The people were then directed to wash their clothes, to sanctify themselves, and, in a word, to make all the necessary preparations to meet God on the third day following. This should teach us also the necessity of *preparing* to meet God, and not to rush into his presence as the horse rushes into battle. Jeremiah viii, 6; and Job xv, 26.

Preparations to meet God.

On the third day, that is, on the day of Pentecost, o fiftieth day after the Paschal Sabbath, Moses brought forth the people out of the camp to meet God.* And while they were standing at the foot

God's Descent on Mount Sinai

* According to the uniform tradition of the Jews, Moses went up into Mount Sinai on the second day of Sivan; on the third he received the answer of the people; reascended the mountain on the fourth, having first commanded the people to sanctify themselves for three days; viz., on the fourth, fifth, and sixth; and on the sixth the Decalogue was orally proclaimed from the top of Sinai. This was

Chronology of the Decalogue

of Sinai, God himself descended to its summit, in fire, with thunderings and lightnings and the sound of a trumpet. At length God spoke out of the midst of the fire, and said in the audience of all the people:

Preamble to the Decalogue.

"*I am the Lord thy God who brought thee out of the land of Egypt, and out of the house of bondage.*

First Precept.

"*Thou shalt have no other gods before me,* (עַל־פָּנָי, *before my face.*)

Second Precept.

"*Thou shalt not make unto thee any graven image; nor any likeness of any thing that is in Heaven above or in the earth beneath, or that is in the water under the Earth; thou shalt not bow down thyself to them, nor serve them: for I the Lord thy God am a jealous God, visiting the iniquity of the fathers upon the children, unto the third and fourth generations of them that hate me; and showing mercy unto thousands of them that love me and keep my commandments.*

Third Precept.

"*Thou shalt not take the name of the Lord thy God in vain; for the Lord will not hold him guiltless that taketh his name in vain.*

on the fiftieth day after the first Paschal Sabbath, or the fifteenth of Nisan, as appears from the following reckoning: Each month being Lunar, would, of course, consist of 29 1-2 days; or, more exactly, of 29 days, 12 hours, 44 m., 2.8 sec.; and hence, after the fifteenth of Nisan, there would remain of that month 14 1-2 days. And these added to the 29 1-2 days of Ziv, and the first six of Sivan, would make just 50 days. And hence it is that the Jews have always observed Pentecost as commemorative of the giving of the Law from Mount Sinai. (*Alexander Kitto's Biblical Cyclopœdia.*)

The Exodus was on the Sabbath.

It appears from this reckoning, as well as from Deuteronomy v, 15, that the day on which the Children of Israel left Egypt was the Sabbath; that their slavery ceased on the sixth day of the week; and that on the seventh they commenced their march of freedom. For it is obvious from the passage cited that to commemorate their emancipation from bondage was one of the objects for which they were required to keep the Sabbath. But God always connects his commemorative Institutions with the events which they are designed to celebrate.

"Remember the Sabbath day to keep it holy. Six days shalt thou labor and do all thy work; but the seventh day is the Sabbath of the Lord thy God; in it thou shalt not do any work; thou, nor thy son, nor thy daughter, thy man-servant, nor thy maid-servant, nor thy cattle, nor the stranger that is within thy gates; for in six days the Lord made Heaven and Earth, the sea, and all that in them is; and rested the seventh day; wherefore the Lord blessed the Sabbath day and hallowed it.

Fourth Precept

"Honor thy father and thy mother, that thy days may be long in the land which the Lord thy God giveth thee.

Fifth Precept.

"Thou shalt not kill.

Sixth Precept.

"Thou shalt not commit adultery.

Seventh Precept.

"Thou shalt not steal.

Eighth Precept

"Thou shalt not bear false witness against thy neighbor.

Ninth Precept

"Thou shalt not covet thy neighbor's house; thou shalt not covet thy neighbor's wife; nor his man-servant, nor his maid-servant, nor his ox, nor his ass, nor any thing that is thy neighbor's." Exodus xx, 2–17.

Tenth Precept.

This is the only part of the Law that was spoken in an audible voice to all the people. After it was delivered to them they retired from the foot of the mountain and requested that God would henceforth speak unto them through Moses. Their request was granted, and these ten commandments were also afterward written on two tablets of stone by the finger of God, and delivered to the Israelites through Moses as their Fundamental Law and Magna Charta. Exodus xxxi, 18; xxxiv, 1, 28; and Deuteronomy ix, 10.

Effect of this Address on the people.

This Constitution or Organic Law of the Hebrews is

Origin of the name Decalogue.

commonly called the Decalogue, because it consists of ten separate and distinct precepts. (Hebrew, עֲשֶׂרֶת הַדְּבָרִים; Sept., *οι δέκα λόγοι* and *τα δέκα ῥήματα*; Vulgate, *decem verba, the ten words.* Exodus xxxiv, 28; Deut. iv, 13; and x, 4.) The numerical division is not given in the Scriptures, and hence it is that different modes of dividing and classifying them have long prevailed among both Jews and Christians.* The following are the principal of these divisions:

Various Divisions of it.

I. *The Origenian.* This is that which was supported by Origen, and which is still in use in the Greek Church, and in all the Protestant Churches except the Lutheran. It is the same, also, as that which is given by Josephus and Philo, and which I have followed on the preceding pages.

II. *The Talmudical.* This is the division which is given in the Talmud, and that which is generally received by the modern Jews. According to this, the preamble of the Decalogue, as it is given by Origen, is the first Commandment. The second embraces both the first and the second of Origen; and the remaining eight are the same as those of the Origenian, or Greek division.

III. *The first Masoretic Division.* According to this division, which is founded on the order and arrangement

Division of the Bible into Chapters and Verses.

*This diversity of opinion shows how little reliance is to be placed on mere human authority in such matters. And the same thing may be illustrated by the divisions of the whole Bible into chapters and verses. In these the most palpable errors are often manifest, though the work was performed by men of very high reputation for their attainments in Biblical Literature. The division of the whole Bible into chapters was made about A. D. 1240, by Hugo de Sancto Caro, a Roman Catholic Cardinal. And the Old and New Testaments were afterward divided into verses, the former by Rabbi Mordecai Nathan, a learned Jewish Doctor, about A. D. 1445, and the latter by Robert Stevens, in A. D. 1551.

of words given in the twentieth chapter of Exodus, the first Commandment embraces both the first and second of the Origenian. The second corresponds with the third of Origen; and so on, till we come to the ninth, which, according to the Masoretic text, is, "Thou shalt not covet thy neighbor's house;" and the tenth consists of what remains of the tenth of Origen, "Thou shalt not covet thy neighbor's wife," etc. This is the division which was followed by Luther, and also by the Council of Trent.

IV. *The second Masoretic Division,* sometimes called "*The Augustinian,*" is the same as the first made by the Masorites, except that it divides the tenth precept of the Origenian according to the order of words given in Deuteronomy v, 21. And hence the ninth precept of this division is, "*Thou shalt not covet thy neighbor's wife;*" and the tenth is, "*Thou shalt not covet thy neighbor's house,*" etc.

The correct division of the Decalogue.

The Origenian is, I think, evidently the correct division, and I will, therefore, make it the basis of the few remarks that I have to submit with regard to this wonderful document. Let us then notice, as briefly as possible, simply the main scope and bearing of the several precepts in order.

I. The first implies two things:

Scope of the first Precept.

1. That all men should worship and serve Jehovah.

2. That they should worship nothing else.

This precept, then, is opposed to both Atheism and Polytheism, and contains within itself the only sure and firm basis of all religion and morality; and, I may add, of all political, civil, and social order.

II. The second relates to the proper *mode* of worship, and implies three things.

1. That God should be worshiped in spirit and in truth, according to his own prescribed ordinances.

Scope of the second Precept.

2. That it is sinful to attempt to worship him under any material forms or images. All such attempts are idolatry.

3. That God can not and will not suffer any of his glory to be given to any thing else. On this so-called Divine jealousy rests the security of the universe.

III. The third Commandment also implies three things.

Scope of the third Precept.

1. That all men should speak of God with the most profound reverence.

2. That any vain or irreverent use of any of God's names or titles is very sinful.

3. That God is jealous of his name, as he is also of his person.

Learn hence that sacred things are not to be trifled with.

IV. The fourth Commandment implies,

Scope of the fourth Precept.

1. The propriety and necessity of sanctifying to the Lord a portion of our time.

2. That this should be such as God has himself appointed.

3. That all under our authority should be encouraged and required to do likewise.

V. The fifth Commandment implies,

Scope of the fifth Precept.

1. That our parents and all in authority over us should be honored and respected.

2. That the Lord will reward and bless all who do this.

VI. The sixth Commandment requires,

Scope of the sixth Precept.

1. That we should use all lawful means to preserve the lives, the health, and the happiness of all men.

2. That we should avoid every thing of an opposite tendency, such as anger, wrath, malice, etc. Matthew v, 21–26; 1 John iii, 15.

VII. The seventh Commandment requires,

1. That all our thoughts, words, and actions should be holy, pure, and temperate.

Scope of the seventh Precept.

2. That we should avoid every thing that may serve to create within us any impure thoughts or feelings. Matthew v, 27–32.

VIII. The eighth Commandment requires,

1. That we should use all lawful means to preserve the property of other persons.

Scope of the eighth Precept.

2. That we should avoid all theft, unjust dealing, and whatever else may serve to destroy or injure the property of others.

IX. The ninth Commandment requires,

1. That we should use all lawful means to promote the reputation and the good name of other persons.

Scope of the ninth Precept.

2. That we should avoid every thing of a contrary and opposite tendency, and which may serve in any way to injure the character of others.

X. The tenth Commandment requires,

1. That we should be satisfied with such things as we have and as we may lawfully acquire.

Scope of the tenth Precept.

2. That we should avoid all inordinate desires concerning any thing and every thing that is our neighbor's.

What think you, then, courteous reader, of this very short but comprehensive political, moral, and religious Constitution of the Hebrew Theocracy? Have you ever found any thing else in all antiquity that will compare with it?

Depth, comprehensiveness, and purity of the Decalogue.

In the 321st Tract of the American Tract Society there is an account given of a distinguished English lawyer who was for a while skeptical on the subject of religion, and who commenced the study of the Old Testament with the view of satisfying himself with regard to the inspiration of the Bible. When he came to the Decalogue, and had studied it profoundly, he was constrained to exclaim, "*Where did Moses get that law?*" Soon after this he became an earnest advocate of the Divine origin of the Holy Scriptures.

Case of the English lawyer.

In this case there is nothing strange or unaccountable. The conversion of this lawyer was but the natural consequence of his enlarged intelligence and more profound acquaintance with the Oracles of God. Compare the precepts of the Decalogue with the maxims of the most illustrious of all the heathen philosophers, and mark the contrast. In Egypt, Babylonia, Persia, Phœnicia, Carthage, Greece, and Rome were tolerated, and in many cases licensed, theft, piracy, adultery, sodomy, incest, exposure of infants, human sacrifices, and many other crimes equally shocking and detestable. Where, then, we may well exclaim with the skeptical lawyer, "*where did Moses get that law?*"

Contrast between the Decalogue and heathen Codes.

I need scarcely add that nearly all the *principles* of the Decalogue are immutable and of perpetual obligation. As the Constitution of the Jewish Theocracy, it has, of course, been abolished. See 2 Corinthians iii, 6–18; Gal. iv, 21–31; and Heb. viii, 6–13. But this does not destroy nor in any way impair the moral principles that underlie it, and that are expressed by it and through it. The Old Constitution of Kentucky, as such, was abrogated several years ago; but most of its principles have reappeared in the

Perpetuity of the Principles of the Decalogue.

New Constitution. And just so it is with the Decalogue. The great moral principles of this wonderful document have their foundation and origin in the nature of God; and this, as I have shown in Book I, Chapter i, is itself the Constitution of the universe. And hence it follows that these principles are as immutable as the nature of God, and as enduring as his eternal throne.

Subordinate Moral and Civil Precepts.

These fundamental principles of the Decalogue were afterward developed and illustrated by a great variety of subordinate rules and regulations, enacted chiefly for the moral and civil government of the nation, all of which serve to maintain the worship of Jehovah; to discourage idolatry;* to preserve pure and holy the names and

Their general scope.

* It has been often urged as an objection by infidels against the Divine origin of the Pentateuch that "the Laws of Moses contain many things that are puerile, frivolous, and utterly unworthy of the wisdom and majesty of God." Such, for example, are supposed to be the laws against cutting the hair and the beard in a particular way, Leviticus xix, 27; against boiling a kid in its mother's milk, Exodus xxiii, 19; against the use of certain kinds of animal food, Leviticus xi; against wearing garments made of linen and woolen mixed together, Leviticus xix, 19; against the sowing of mixed seeds, Leviticus xix, 19; against the interchange of male and female attire, Deut. xxii, 5; against worshiping in groves and high places, Exodus xxxiv, 13, etc.

Alleged objection against the Mosaic Code.

In reply to this objection, I wish to say,

I. That nothing should be regarded as trivial or frivolous which may serve to prevent in any way and to any extent the heinous sin of idolatry.

Reply to this objection.

II. That most of the laws objected to, as such, have reference to some of the Idolatrous customs and practices of other nations. For instance,

1. Herodotus says, Book III, Chapter viii, that the Arabs cut their hair round in honor of Bacchus, who, they say, had his hair cut in this way.

Illustrations.

2. Dr. Cudworth says (quoting from a Karaite Jew) that "it was a custom of many ancient heathen when they had gathered in all their fruits, to take a kid and boil it in the milk of its dam, and then in a magical way to go about and besprinkle with it all their trees, and fields, and gardens, and orchards, thinking by these means to make them more fruitful, so that

titles of the one living and true God; to sanctify the Sabbath; to honor parents and all others in authority; to preserve human life; to encourage and promote chastity; to preserve and defend the right of property; to prevent all slander and evil speaking; and to make every one content with the lot which God has assigned to him in his providence. These laws are contained in the twenty-first, twenty-second, and twenty-third chapters of Exodus, and sundry other portions of the Pentateuch, and should be carefully studied by every scholar, and especially by every teacher, preacher, lawyer, moralist, and statesman. But their full discussion does not properly fall within our prescribed limits. And we must, therefore, now pass on to the consideration of the Legal Types. These have a more direct and intimate connection with the Scheme of Redemption, and will constitute the subject of the next chapter.

Should be studed by all.

they might bring forth more abundantly the following year." *See Cudworth on the Lord's Supper.*

3. The learned Maimonides, who carefully examined the whole history of idolatry, says "it was the custom of many Gentile priests to wear garments made out of both vegetable and animal products, hoping thereby to secure the beneficial influence of the planets on their sheep and flax."

4. The same author informs us that "it was the custom of both men and women to exchange garments in the worship of several of their gods."

Conclusion.

From such facts, the number of which might be greatly multiplied, we see the wisdom and benevolence of God in forbidding many things which are in themselves perfectly harmless, but which, under the then existing circumstances, were liable to lead many into the sin of idolatry. For a similar reason, Christians are forbidden to do any thing by means of which a weak brother may be caused to stumble. See Romans xiv.

CHAPTER VI.

LEGAL TYPES.

THE Bible represents God as being omnipresent "If I ascend into Heaven," says David, "thou art there. If I make my bed in Hades, behold thou art there. If I take the wings of the morning, and dwell in the uttermost parts of the sea, even there shall thy hand lead me; and thy right hand shall hold me." Psalm cxxxix, 8, 9.

God is Omnipresent.

But as the author of this beautiful and heart-searching ode says in the same connection, "Such knowledge is too wonderful for us." The finite can not comprehend the Infinite. And hence it is that the human heart has always desired, if not a local Deity, at least some local manifestation of his presence. "O, that I knew," says Job, xxiii, 3, "*where* I might find him, that I might come even to his seat!"

The natural desire of the human heart with respect to God.

To gratify this desire of the human heart was, therefore, evidently one of the benevolent objects for which both the Tabernacle and the Temple were erected. God's primary design in both cases was simply to furnish a *House* in which his presence, and his power, and his glory might be manifested to his people, and where they might all seek and find him. See Exodus xxv, 8; xxix, 45; 1 Kings vi, 11–13; 2 Corinthians vi, 16; Hebrews iii, 6; and Revelation xxi, 3.

God's first object in building the Tabernacle and Temple.

No wonder, then, that the Tabernacle and Temple

were objects of so much interest to the Israelites. There was the place where Jehovah had recorded his name; there were the symbols of his presence, and of his power, and of his glory; and there he had promised to meet with them.

Why they were objects of so much interest to the Jews.

But be it remembered that these things were also written for *our* instruction and *our* comfort. Romans xv, 4. In the Legal Types we have as I before said,

Reasons why the Legal Types should be studied by all.

I. *A beautiful pictorial outline of the Christian System*

II. *A most conclusive proof of the Divine origin of the whole Bible.*

These two reasons alone are sufficient to make the study of the Legal Types a matter of profound interest to all who desire to understand the Holy Bible; and to their consideration I therefore now invite the attention of the reader. We will begin with the Tabernacle.

SECTION I.—THE TABERNACLE.

It is variously designated in the Bible as *the Tent* (אֹהֶל,)* Exodus xxvi, 36; *the Tabernacle of the congregation,* (that is, the Tabernacle of the appointed season for the meeting of the

Names applied to the Tabernacle.

* The word *ohel* (אֹהֶל) occurs 326 times in the Bible, and is variously applied,

Applications of the Hebrew words *ohel* and *mishkan*.

1. To any movable dwelling. E. g., "Abraham pitched his tent," (אֹהֶל.) Genesis xii, 8.

2. To the Tabernacle erected by Moses. E. g., "And Aaron and his sons thou shalt bring to the door of the Tabernacle of the congregation," (אֹהֶל מוֹעֵד.) Exodus xxix, 4.

3. To the covering of the Tabernacle, made of goats' hair. E. g., "Thou shalt make curtains of goats' hair to be a covering (*a tent,* אֹהֶל) upon the Tabernacle," (מִשְׁכָּן.) Exodus xxvi, 7. See, also, verses 9, 11, 12, 13, 14, etc.

The word *mishkan* (מִשְׁכָּן) occurs 135 times in the Bible, and is used,

1. For the whole Tabernacle erected by Moses. E. g., "Let them make

congregation, אֹהֶל מוֹעֵד,) Exodus xxvii, 21, etc.; *the Tabernacle of the precept or witness,* (מִשְׁכַּן עֵדוּת; Sept., σκηνὴ τοῦ μαρτύριου; Vulg., *tabernaculum testimonii,*) Numbers i, 50, 53, (and אֹהֶל עֵדוּת,) Numbers ix, 15, etc.; *the House of the Lord,* (בֵּית יְהוָֹה,) Deut. xxiii, 18; *the Sanctuary,* (מִקְדָּשׁ,) Exodus xxv, 8; Lev. xii, 4; xxi, 12, etc.; *the Holy,* (קֹדֶשׁ,) Exodus xxxv, 19; and *the Temple of Jehovah,* (הֵיכַל יְהוָֹה,) 1 Samuel i, 9; iii, 3, etc.

The materials of the Tabernacle were all free-will offerings, (Exodus xxv, 2,) and were of divers sorts; viz., of gold, silver, and copper, with blue, and purple, and scarlet fabrics, fine linen, goats' hair, rams' skins dyed red, tachash skins,* acacia

Materials for the Tabernacle.

me a Sanctuary, (מִקְדָּשׁ,) that I may dwell among them. According to all that I shew thee, the pattern of the Tabernacle, (מִשְׁכָּן,) and the pattern of all the instruments thereof, even so shall ye make it." Exodus xxv, 8, 9. See, also, Numbers iv, 25, etc.

2. For the linen curtains of the Tabernacle. E. g., "Moreover, thou shalt make the Tabernacle (מִשְׁכָּן) ten curtains of fine twined linen." Exodus xxvi, 1. See, also, verses 7, 12, and 13; and Exodus xl, 19, etc.

3. For any movable dwelling. Job xviii, 21.

* The meaning of the word *tachash* (תַּחַשׁ) is uncertain. The ancient interpreters generally understood by it a certain *color* given to the leather. Thus, the Septuagint has ὑακινθα, *purple;* Aquila and Symmachus have ἰανθινα, *violet-colored;* and the Chaldee and Syriac versions have words signifying *red.* But the Talmudists and other Hebrew interpreters take *tachash* to be a species of animal, the skins of which were used for covering the Tabernacle, and also for shoes and sandals. See Exodus xxv, 5; xxvi, 14; xxxv, 23; xxxix, 34; Numbers iv, 6, 8, 10, 11, 12, 14, 25; and Ezekiel xvi, 10. This is also the view that is now adopted by most Christian writers. But they are not agreed as to the kind of animal that was represented by it. According to Rashi, Luther, Gesenius, etc., it was the *badger* or the *seal.* Others suppose that it was a species of the antelope. The word occurs only 14 times in the Bible, and in the Common English Version it is always translated by the word *badger.* The badger, however, is not found so far south as Egypt, Arabia, or even Palestine. It lives chiefly in northern Europe and Asia, and a species of it, called the *ground-hog,* is found in North America. The seal is found in Arabia. On the whole, I am not prepared to translate this word, (תְּחָשִׁים,) and I therefore transfer it.

Opinions concerning the Hebrew word *tachash.*

wood,* oil for the lights, spices for anointing oil and for sweet incense, onyx stones, and stones for the Ephod. Exodus xxv, 1–8.

Cost of the materials.

The cost of all these materials is estimated by Dr. John Kitto at about £250,000 sterling, or $1,111,100.

Walls of the Tabernacle.

The walls of the Tabernacle were composed of boards, or rather of planks made of the acacia wood, and covered with gold. Each plank was ten cubits long, and a cubit and a half broad. The thickness of these planks is not given in the text; but, according to Jewish tradition, each plank was one cubit thick. And hence the Hebrew word *kehresh,* (קֶרֶשׁ,) is in the Septuagint translated στύλος, *pillar.* Exodus xxvi, 15–25.

Dimensions of the Tabernacle.

On this hypothesis, the *internal* dimensions of the Tabernacle were thirty cubits in length, ten in breadth, and ten in hight; and the *external* dimensions were thirty-one cubits in length, twelve in breadth, and ten in hight.

Its Foundations and Bars.

The foundations of the walls were ninety-six sockets (אֶדֶן) of silver; each socket being equal to one talent, or about 93 3–4 lbs. avoirdupois.† See Exodus xxxviii, 27. The walls were also supported by five bars, made of acacia wood and covered with gold. Exodus xxvi, 26–29; and xxxvi, 31–34.

Shittim wood.

* "The acacia," (שִׁטָּה, plur., שִׁטִּים,) says Gesenius, "is a large tree growing in Egypt and Arabia, from which the Gum Arabic is obtained. The wood is exceedingly hard, and when old it resembles ebony."

† Dr. Arbuthnot estimates the weight of the Hebrew shekel, (שֶׁקֶל,) at 9 pennyweights and 2 4–7 grains, Troy weight, which is about half an ounce avoirdupois; and hence, according to the Doctor's estimate, a shekel of silver is worth about 50 cents.

And from Exodus xxxviii, 25, 26, we learn that a talent is equal to 3,000 shekels, which, according to the preceding data, are equal to 93 3–4 lbs. avoirdupois, or nearly 114 lbs. Troy weight. On the same estimate, a talent

Coverings of the Tabernacle.

The coverings of the Tabernacle were four. The first (מִשְׁכָּן) was composed of ten curtains of fine twined linen. Each thread, according to the Rabbis, was six double; and the whole covering was beautifully variegated with colors of blue, and purple, and scarlet, and curiously embroidered all over with figures of Cherubim.

Structure and Dimensions of the first curtain.

Each of these curtains was twenty-eight cubits long and four cubits broad, and the ten were formed into two separate hangings of five curtains each, permanently joined together. And these again were united, when necessary, by fifty taches or clasps of gold, placed in fifty loops of blue tape, attached to the selvedges of the fifth and sixth curtains. This covering was, therefore, forty cubits long and twenty-eight cubits broad. Exodus xxvi, 1–6; and xxxvi, 8–13.

Its Position.

This inner curtain is generally supposed to have been spread *over* the frame-work of the Tabernacle. But on the whole, I am inclined to think with Bähr, Fairbairn, and some others, that it was suspended *within* the frame-work by means of hooks and eyes, so as to form the interior lining of the whole Tabernacle. See 1 Kings vi, 29.

Materials, Dimensions, and Position of the second curtain.

The second covering (אֹהֶל) was composed of eleven curtains of goats' hair, each curtain being thirty cubits in length and four in breadth. These were also joined together in two

of silver is worth about $1,500, and a talent of gold $24,000. Later writers, however, estimate the value of the shekel at about 60 cents.

It is worthy of remark just here that the relative and commercial value of silver and gold was anciently much greater than it is at present, owing to their greater scarcity. It has been estimated that their value in the fourth century before Christ, was to its value in England in the year 1780 in the ratio of ten to one. See Jahn's Bib. Arch., p. 129.

The Euboic and Attic talent is commonly estimated at $1,179.75.

hangings: the one on the east consisted of six curtains, and the one on the west of but five. The two were united together by fifty brazen clasps. The first curtain in front was doubled. Exodus xxvi, 7–13, and xxxvi, 14–18.

Third and fourth coverings.

The third covering was of rams' skins dyed red; and the fourth of tachash skins. Their dimensions are not given. Exodus xxvi, 14; xxxvi, 19.

The Partition Vail.

The whole tabernacle was divided into two east and west rooms by a partition vail, (פָּרֹכֶת; Gr., καταπέτασμα.) It was made of the same kind of material as the inmost curtain, and was figured and embroidered in like manner. It was suspended directly under the golden clasps of the linen curtains, from golden hooks attached to four pillars of acacia wood, resting on four sockets of silver, of one talent each. Exodus xxvi, 31–34; xxxvi, 35, 36; and xxxviii, 27.

The Entrance Vail.

The doorway, or entrance of the Tabernacle, was closed by a vail or hanging, (מָסָךְ covering,) of the same kind of material as the partition vail. But it was not so highly ornamented. The Rabbis say that in the partition vail and inmost curtain the figures were made to appear on both sides; but that they only appeared on the inside of the entrance vail. It was suspended from golden hooks, attached to five pillars, which rested on five sockets of brass. Exodus xxvi, 36, 37; xxxvi, 37, 38.

Symbolical meaning of the Tabernacle.

The primary design of the Tabernacle, as before said, was to furnish *a house for God*. But as God dwells both in Heaven and also among his people on Earth, it was fit that the Tabernacle should be divided into two rooms or apartments.

each having its own proper furniture. And accordingly we find,

I. That the Most Holy Place of both the Tabernacle and Temple was a type of Heaven. Hebrews vi, 19, 20; ix, 8 and 24.

The Most Holy Place.

II. The Holy Place was a type of the Christian Church. Acts xv, 16, 17; 1 Corinthians iii, 16; 1 Timothy iii, 15, etc.

The Holy Place.

III. The partition vail was a type of Christ's body. Hebrews x, 20. And hence, when his body was pierced, the vail was rent. Matthew xxvii, 51.

The Vail.

IV. The gold, the silver, and the fine linen, seem to denote merely the great value and purity of all that is in God's presence. See Revelation xxi and xxii.

The Gold, etc.

V. The Cherubim were symbolical of the presence and ministration of angels. See Ezekiel i, and x; also, Hebrews i, 14, etc.

The Cherubim.

Before we bring this section to a close, it may be well to notice a few points of resemblance and contrast between the Tabernacle and the Temple. And,

Points of Resemblance and Contrast between the Tabernacle and the Temple.

I. We find that the walls of the Temple were built of stone, and wainscoted with cedar boards covered with gold; and the whole was covered all over with figures of cherubim, palm trees, and open flowers. 1 Kings vi, and 2 Chronicles iii.

The Walls.

II. The ceiling was also made of cedar boards, covered with gold, and ornamented with cherubim.

The Ceiling.

III. The floor was of boards. covered with gold. 1 Kings vi, 30.

The Floor.

IV. The dimensions of the Temple were sixty cubits long, twenty broad, and thirty high. But the Most Holy Place was a complete cube of twenty cubits. And here it is worthy of remark that a cube was used among the ancients as a symbol of perfection.

The Dimensions.

V. The general design of the Tabernacle and the Temple was the same. Compare Exodus xxv, 8, with 1 Kings vi, 13.

Design of the Temple.

VI. And hence we may legitimately infer that all matters in which the Tabernacle and the Temple differed were *circumstantial* and not *essential*.

Inference.

SECTION II.—Furniture of the Tabernacle.

The next thing that requires our attention is the *symbolical furniture* of the Tabernacle. In the Most Holy Place we find the Ark of the Covenant, the Tables of the Testimony, the Mercy-Seat the Cherubim, the Golden Censer, the Urn of Manna, and Aaron's Rod that budded. And in the Holy Place were the Altar of Incense, the Table of the Presence-Bread, and the Golden Candelabrum. Of these we will now speak in order

Furniture of the Tabernacle.

FURNITURE OF THE MOST HOLY PLACE.

I. The Ark of the Covenant.

The Ark (אָרוֹן) was a sort of chest, (Latin, *arca*,) two and a half cubits long, a cubit and a half broad, and a cubit and a half high. It was made out of acacia-wood, and overlaid both within and without with pure gold. Around the upper edge was a rim or cornice of pure gold, and on each side

Materials and Construction of the Ark.

were two rings of gold, through which were passed two staves of acacia-wood covered with gold, for the purpose of bearing the Ark. Exodus xxv, 10–16; xxxvii, 1–5.

Contents of the Ark.

In the Ark were placed the Tables of the Testimony, the Urn of Manna, and Aaron's Rod. Heb. ix, 4. But it seems from 1 Kings viii, 9, that the Urn of Manna and Aaron's Rod had both been removed and probably lost before the building of the Temple, which was about four hundred and eighty-six years after the building of the Tabernacle.

II. The Mercy-Seat.

Construction and Material of the Mercy-Seat.

On the Ark was placed the Mercy-Seat, (כַּפֹּרֶת; Septuagint, ἱλαστήριον; Vulgate, *propitiatorium.*) It was composed wholly of pure gold, and was two and a half cubits long, and one and a half broad. Exodus xxv, 17; xxxvii, 6.

III. The Two Cherubim.

Construction and Position of the Cherubim.

On the ends of the Mercy-Seat, and out of the same piece of solid bullion, were formed two Cherubim (כְּרוּבִים) with extended wings, and having their faces turned toward the Mercy-Seat. Exodus xxv, 18–22; xxxvii, 7–9.

Colossal Cherubim in Solomon's Temple.

In Solomon's Temple, besides the two Cherubim which stood on the ends of the Mercy-Seat, there were two others of colossal size, each one of which was ten cubits high, and had wings extending ten cubits. 1 Kings vi, 23–27.

IV. The Shekinah.

Between the two Cherubim, and on the Mercy-Seat, was the *Shekinah,* (שְׁכִינָה,) or symbol of God's presence

The word is not used in the Hebrew Scriptures, but it is common in the Targums and Jewish literature. It is derived from the Hebrew word שָׁכַן, *to dwell*, and hence primarily means simply a *dwelling*. But as it seems to have been always bright and luminous, it came also to signify the Divine glory, by means of which the Most Holy Place of the Tabernacle and Temple was illuminated. To this Paul refers in Romans ix, 4, when, speaking of the Israelites, he says, "To whom pertained the adoption, and the *glory*, (ἡ δόξα,) and the covenants, and the giving of the law, and the service of God, and the promises." It was also the Oracle from which audible responses were given to the High Priest. Compare Exodus xxviii, 30, with Numbers xxvii, 21, etc.

Meaning and Place of the Shekinah.

V. The Golden Censer.

The censers used for burning the daily incense on the Golden Altar were made of brass, Numbers xvi, 39; and they were severally called by the Hebrews either a *miktereth*, (מִקְטֶרֶת, from מִקְטָר, *incense*, 2 Chronicles xxvi, 19; Ezekiel viii, 2;) or a *machtah* (מַחְתָּה, that is, a *fire-pan*, from חָתָה, *to take coals*, Leviticus x, 1; and Numbers iv, 14.) But the Censer used for burning incense in the Most Holy Place was, according to the Talmud, made of gold. And this seems to be in harmony with the testimony of Paul in Heb. ix, 4, where he speaks of the Most Holy Place as having a golden censer (χρυσοῦν ἔχουσα θυματήριον—by some rendered, *a golden altar*), as well as the Ark of the Covenant.

Two kinds of Censers and their uses.

The design of all these things was partly commemorative, partly typical, partly for the sake of ornament, and partly to impress on each

Fourfold Design of these arrangements

successive generation, by means of sensible signs and symbols, suitable ideas of God and of his government. Thus, for instance,

I. The Urn of Manna commemorated the miraculous supply of food furnished to the Children of Israel during the forty years of their sojourn in the wilderness.

Design of the Pot of Manna.

II. The Rod of Aaron commemorated the rebellion of Korah and God's choice of Aaron's family for the priesthood. Numbers xvii, 1–13.

Of Aaron's Rod.

III. The Ark or chest on which the Shekinah rested was a symbol of God's throne, Hebrews iv, 16; Jeremiah iii, 16, 17; and its containing the Law indicated that said throne contains within itself the eternal principles of justice and righteousness. Psalm lxxxix, 14.

Of the Ark.

IV. But these Tables of the Testimony needed a propitiatory covering, or otherwise they would ever be *openly testifying* for God and against Israel. And hence the great symbolic beauty and fitness of the Mercy-Seat, which, being sprinkled with the blood of atonement, Leviticus xvi, 14, 19, *covered* the Tables of the Testimony as Christ now covers all the testimony and demands of law and justice against his people. See Romans iii, 25, 26.

Of the Mercy Seat.

V. The Cherubim evidently represent angels, who have ever looked with intense interest and wonder into the unfolding mysteries of redemption. 1 Peter i, 12.

Of the Cherubim.

How clearly, then, and how forcibly all this serves to prove the Divine origin of the Bible! Hebrews iii, 5. If it be said that the Egyptians, the Greeks, and the Romans had their Adyta,

Bearing of all this on the Divine Origin of the Bible.

their Penetralia, and their Arks, we need only reply that all counterfeits imply a reality.

FURNITURE OF THE HOLY PLACE.

Let us now pass through the Partition Vail and notice briefly and in order the furniture of the Holy Place.

I. The Altar of Incense.

First in order, and directly before the vail, stood the Altar of Incense, (מִזְבַּח קְטֹרֶת.) It was made of acacia-wood, overlaid with gold, and was two cubits in hight, one in length, and one in breadth.

Structure of the Altar of Incense.

Like the Ark and the table, it had a crown, or rather a rim or cornice of gold around its upper edge. It had also four rings of gold, through which were placed two staves of acacia-wood covered with gold, by means of which it was carried by the Kohathites. Numbers iv, 4–15. It had also four horns, or projecting corners, covered with gold, on which the High Priest made an atonement once a year. Exodus xxx, 1–10; xxxvii, 25–29; Leviticus xvi, 18.

Its Cornice, Rings, Staves, and Horns.

On this altar, also, the Priests every evening and every morning offered sweet Incense (קְטֹרֶת) made out of equal weights of stacte, onycha, galbanum, and pure frankincense. Exodus xxx, 34–38.

Offerings made on it.

The Altar itself seems to have had no further symbolical import than simply to denote that God has an *appointed place*, where he will meet with his people and receive their vows and their offerings. The Incense was typical of the prayers of the saints. See Psalm cxli, 2; Luke i, 9, 10; and Revelation v, 8, and viii, 3, 4.

II. The Table of Shew-Bread.

Materials and Construction of the Table and its Furniture.

Next in order, and situated at the north side of the Tabernacle, was the Table of shew-bread, or more literally, *Table of the presence-bread, or bread of the face,* (שֻׁלְחַן לֶחֶם פָּנִים,) so called, no doubt, because it stood in the presence or before the face of Jehovah. This was also made of acacia-wood, overlaid with gold. It was two cubits in length, one in breadth, and one and a half in hight; and like the Ark and the golden Altar, it had four rings, two staves, and a cornice of pure gold. Its dishes (קְעָרוֹת) for the cakes, its cups (כַּפּוֹת) for the frankincense, its wine cups, (קְשָׂוֹת,) and its libation cups (מְנַקִּיּוֹת) were also all of gold. Exodus xxv, 23–30; xxxvii, 10–16.

The Presence-Bread and Frankincense.

On this Table were placed every Sabbath by the High Priest twelve cakes (חַלּוֹת) of fine flour, six in a row, and on each row a cup of frankincense. The cakes were eaten by the priests, and the frankincense was burned. Leviticus xxiv, 5–9.*

Their Symbolical meaning

The symbolic meaning of these cakes is easily understood from their relation to the Tabernacle as *God's house.* A well-furnished house always implies a table of provisions. It is evident, therefore, that these twelve cakes were symbolical of the spiritual food of Christians, who are all priests to God. 1 Peter

Quantity of flour in each Cake.

* According to the statement made here in Leviticus, each cake (חַלָּה) was to contain two-tenth deals or parts (שְׁנֵי עֶשְׂרֹנִים) of fine flour. And from Numbers xxviii, 5, it seems that the ephah, consisting, according to Gesenius, of thirty-five quarts, was in all such cases the standard measure among the Hebrews. If so, the two-tenth deals of flour would be equal to seven quarts. If this estimate is true, which seems most probable, these cakes must have been of mense size.

ii, 5, 9. The frankincense seems to have been emblematical of praise and thanksgiving. Revelation v, 8.

III. The Candelabrum.

The Candelabrum (מְנוֹרָה; Sept., λυχνία) stood on the south side of the Tabernacle, over against the Table on the north. It was wrought or beaten out of a talent of pure gold, and consisted of one upright shaft, (the Rabbis say four cubits high,) and six branches, all ornamented with "bowls, knops, and flowers." On the top of the main stem and each branch there was a lamp, (נֵר; Sept., λύχνος.) Its snuffers and its snuff-dishes were also of gold. See Exodus xxv, 31–40; xxxvii, 17–24.

Structure and Position of the Candelabrum.

In these lamps (נֵרוֹת) was burned pure olive oil continually. Exodus xxvii, 20, 21; Leviticus xxiv, 1–4.

Oil for the Lamps.

The symbolical meaning of the Candelabrum is very obvious. It was simply a type of the Christian Church *as God's appointed means for preserving and dispensing the light of the Gospel.* This is evident from such passages as the following: Zechariah iv, 1–14; Revelation i, 20, etc. And hence it follows that every Christian Congregation should be a *light-dispenser.* See 1 Timothy iii, 15.

Symbolical meaning of the Candelabrum.

But observe that the Candelabrum was only a dispenser of light. It was the oil that produced it. And oil, throughout the whole Bible, is used as the common and appropriate symbol of the Holy Spirit. This will be made clear by a consideration of the following passages: Isaiah lxi, 1; Acts x, 38; Hebrews i. 9; 1 John ii, 20, 27.

Of the Oil.

Of the seven Lamps.

The *seven* lamps of the Candelabrum are symbolical of *perfect* light. See Revelation iv, 5, etc.

Candelabra of the Temple.

In Solomon's Temple there were ten golden Candlesticks or Candelabra.

How beautifully, then, all this harmonizes with the *realities* of the New Institution! Who that understands this lesson can doubt that Moses made all these things according to the pattern that was showed to him in the Mount?

SECTION III.—The Court and its Furniture.

Dimensions and Curtains of the Court.

Passing through the Entrance Vail or Hanging of the door eastward, we next come into the Court (חָצֵר, an inclosure) of the Tabernacle. This was simply an inclosure of one hundred cubits long and fifty broad, surrounded by curtains of fine twined linen five cubits high.

Its Gate.

The Gate on the east was a hanging of twenty cubits long and five cubits high, made of blue, and purple, and scarlet, and fine twined linen, wrought with needle-work.

Its Pillars.

These curtains were suspended on sixty pillars of brass, twenty on the north side, twenty on the south, ten on the east, and ten on the west. The pillars rested on sixty sockets of brass, and were joined or coupled together above by means of sixty silver rods, which passed through the same number of silver hooks. Exodus xxvii, 9–19; xxxviii, 9–20.

Design of the Court.

The object of this inclosure was merely to separate between the *holy* and the *profane.* It seemed to say to the unsanctified, as in the case of the Eleusinian mysteries, "*Procul, O procul este profani, totoque absistite luco.*" Retire, far hence retire, ye profane, and quit entirely the sacred grove! None but Israelites had a right to enter this Court. It is much to be regretted, therefore, that in modern times this wall of separation between the sacred and the profane, between the Church and the world, has been in a great measure broken down, and in many cases even almost obliterated.

Connected with Solomon's Temple there were two Courts.

Courts of Solomon's Temple.

I. The Inner Court, or Court of the Priests. 1 Kings vi, 36.

II. The Outer, or Great Court. 2 Chronicles iv, 9.

The Courts of Herod's Temple were as follows:

Courts of Herod's Temple.

I. The Court of the Priests. This very nearly corresponded with the Court of the Tabernacle and the Inner Court of Solomon's Temple.

II. The Court of the Israelites. This completely surrounded the Court of the Priests.

III. The Court of the Women lay directly east of the Court of the Israelites.

IV. The Court of the Gentiles. This was one stadium, or nearly one furlong, in length and the same in breadth. It completely surrounded all the other Courts, but the greater portion of it lay to the south. From this Court Christ drove the money-changers, etc. Matthew xxi, 11. This is also the Court to which reference is made in Revelation xi, 2.

The chief articles of furniture in the Court of the Tabernacle were the Laver and the Altar of Sacrifice.

Furniture of the Court.

THE LAVER.

The shape and dimensions of the Laver are not given in the Scriptures. But it is generally supposed to have been a circular basin of brass, having for its pedestal another shallow basin to receive the waste water. Its Hebrew name is כִּיּוֹר, *a fire-pan,* from כּוּר, *to boil up.* Hence, also כּוּר, *a furnace for smelting metals.* These were both generally of a circular form. The Septuagint has for כִּיּוֹר, λουτήρ, *a bathing-tub,* from λούω, to wash.

Material and Construction of the Laver.

In water taken from this Laver (מִמֶּנּוּ, *from it,*) the Priests were required, under penalty of death, to wash both their *hands* and their *feet* before entering the Tabernacle or ministering at the altar. Exodus xxx, 17–21.

Use of the Laver.

The fundamental idea here symbolized is that of *cleansing*. And hence this washing was a beautiful type of the moral and spiritual purity that is required of all Christians.*

Typical significance of the Washing.

* By some expositors these washings are regarded as typical of Christian Baptism, and the Laver itself as a type of the bath (λουτρόν) of regeneration. But it seems to me that this is an unwarrantable hypothesis, for the following reasons:

These Washings not a Type of Christian Baptism.

I. So far as we know one *Legal* type is never used to represent another. It seems always to point to a *substance* and never to a *shadow*. See Col. ii, 16, 17, and Heb. x, 7.

II. Because this rite was performed daily by and for the same persons But Baptism is to be administered but once to the same person.

III. This ordinance consisted in *washing* merely the *hands* and the *feet* But Baptism consists in the *immersion* of the *whole person.* Romans vi, 4, etc. The Hebrew word used in this connection is רָחַץ, which means simply to wash the body or any part of it. The Hebrew word for *dip* or *immerse* is טָבַל.

IV. This washing was not designed *to make* men priests, but simply to qualify for their daily duties those who had been previously ordained to the sacerdotal office. And hence it never changed the relations of any one. But Christian Baptism is essentially an initiatory ordinance. It is always

Matthew v, 8; Hebrews xii, 14; 1 Peter i, 16. To this David beautifully alludes in Psalm xxiv, 4, 5, when, in answer to the question, "*Who shall ascend into the hill of Jehovah? or who shall stand in his holy place?*" the reply is, "*He that hath clean hands and a pure heart; who hath not lifted up his soul unto vanity, nor sworn deceit*

designed to change the relations of the person baptized; to transfer him from the kingdom of darkness into the Kingdom of God's dear Son. John iii, 5.

That there was some *analogy* between all these sacerdotal washings and Christian Baptism I freely admit. They were all symbolical of *inward purity*, and so also is baptism. This is evident from many such passages as the following:

1. Ephesians v, 26: "Christ loved the Church and gave himself for it, that he might sanctify it, καθαρίσας τῷ λουτρῷ τοῦ ὕδατος ἐν ῥήματι, *having cleansed it by a bath of water through the word.*"

2. Titus iii, 5: "Not by works of righteousness which we have done, but according to his mercy he saved us, διὰ λουτροῦ παλιγγενεσίας, *through a bath of regeneration.*"

3. Hebrews x, 22: "Let us draw near with a true heart, in full assurance of faith, having our hearts sprinkled from an evil conscience, καὶ λελουμένοι τὸ σῶμα ὕδατι καθαρῷ, *and having our body washed with pure water.*"

These and other like passages show very clearly that there is some analogy between the sacerdotal washings of the Law and Christian Baptism. They both alike indicated the necessity of *inward purity*. But it does not hence follow that the former were *types* of the latter. Before this can be rightfully and legitimately inferred it must be shown that the aforesaid analogy was *designed* and *preordained* by the Divine Founder of the Jewish Institution. But here, I think, the evidence is wanting.

If there is an allusion or typical reference to Baptism in any of these washings, it is, I think, to be found in the washing of consecration. Exodus xxix, 4, and Leviticus viii, 6. Between this and the washing of regeneration there are certainly several very direct and striking points of analogy. *E. g.*:

I. In the former the whole body was washed in water, and in the latter the whole body is immersed in water.

II. The former was to be performed but once, and so also is the latter.

III. The former was a part of the ceremony of consecration to the priest's office, and the latter is for a similar purpose. All baptized believers are made kings and priests unto God.

IV. The former was followed by the sprinkling of blood and oil on the person or persons so washed and purified; and it is in and through the latter that believers are brought under the influence of the blood of Christ and are made partakers of the Holy Spirit.

Was this washing of consecration, then, a type of Baptism?

fully. He shall receive a blessing from Jehovah; and righteousness from the God of his salvation."

In the Court of Solomon's Temple there were ten Lavers of brass and one Sea, (יָם.) The Sea was ten cubits in diameter, thirty in circumference, (or more exactly 31.4159,) and five in depth, and contained according to 1 Kings vii, 26, two thousand baths, or about 15,000 gallons; and according to 2 Chronicles iv, 5, and Josephus, it contained three thousand baths, or about 22,500 gallons. The latter estimate *may* refer to the actual capacity of the entire vessel, including the twelve oxen which supported it as a base, and the former *may* simply denote the quantity of water that it usually contained. 1 Kings vii, 23–40.

Lavers and Sea in the Court of Solomon's Temple.

THE ALTAR OF BURNT-OFFERING.

East of the Laver, in the Court of the Tabernacle, stood the Altar of Burnt-Offering, (מִזְבַּח עוֹלָה,) which was also sometimes called the Brazen Altar, (מִזְבַּח נְחֹשֶׁת.) It was made of acacia-wood, overlaid with brass. Its dimensions were five cubits long, five broad, and three high. The Altar of Burnt-Offering in Solomon's Temple was twenty cubits in length and breadth, and ten in hight. 2 Chronicles iv, 1.

Structure and Materials of the Brazen Altar.

The utensils of the Brazen Altar were as follows, and were all made of brass, or most likely of hardened copper:

Its Utensils.

1. *Pans* or urns (סִירוֹת) for receiving and carrying away the ashes that fell through the grating.

2. *Shovels* (יָעִים) for collecting the ashes and cleaning the Altar.

3. *Basins* or skins (מִזְרָקוֹת) for receiving the blood of the victims, and sprinkling it on the Altar.

4. *Flesh-hooks* or large forks (מִזְלָגוֹת) for turning the pieces of flesh or for removing them from the fire.

5. *Censers* or fire-pans (מַחְתּוֹת) for burning incense. Exodus xxvii, 1–8.

The Brazen Network.

Within the boards, and at some distance from the top of the Altar, was suspended a network of brass. On this the sacrifices were consumed, and on this the Sacred Fire was ever kept burning. Leviticus ix, 24; vi, 12, 13; 2 Chronicles vii, 1.

The Sacred Fire.

Heathen rites derived from this Altar.

In imitation of this the Persians, Greeks, Romans, etc., kept fire constantly burning on their altars. The most common word for fire in Hebrew is אֵשׁ, *esh;* from which, it would seem, is derived the Greek 'Εστία, and also the Latin Vesta, the imaginary goddess of fire. And hence, too, we have the Roman "*Vestales Virgines,*" Vestal Virgins, whose duty it was to keep the sacred fire ever burning.

Its Rings, Staves, and Horns.

Like the Golden Altar the Brazen Altar had also four rings, two staves, and four horns.

Design of this Altar.

Primarily, this Altar served merely as *God's appointed place for offering sacrifice.* But as it was always here that God first met with the sinner on terms of reconciliation and pardon, it became an object of most profound interest to every Israelite.

Symbolical meaning of the Horns.

The *horns* of the Altar seem to have been a symbol of power and Divine protection. See Exodus xxi, 14; 1 Kings i, 50; xxii, 11; and Habakkuk iii, 4. And hence it is pretty clearly intimated by the horns on the Golden and Brazen Altars, that it is only by means of prayer and the blood of atonement that the sinner can prevail with God.

The fire on the altar seems to represent God's administrative justice, which accepts the victim in lieu of the sinner. See Hebrews xii, 29, and Genesis xxii, 13.

Of the Fire.

SECTION IV.—Legal Offerings.

Next to the Altar, it is natural and proper that we should consider the principal sacrifices and offerings of the Old Covenant. These were as follows:

I. THE BURNT-OFFERING.

This was the oldest, and in its scope the most comprehensive of all the Legal Sacrifices.* It was offered not only for particular and specific sins, but, also, as in the case of the daily Burnt-Offering, for sins in general.

Its relative age and comprehensiveness.

The victim offered might be a bullock, a ram, a goat, a dove, or a pigeon. But in all cases the law required that it should be a male without blemish.

Kind of Victim required.

Offerings of this kind were both *voluntary* and *required.* In either case the law provided that the person who offered the victim should bring it to the door of the Tabernacle, and there lay his hand on its head and kill it.

What was required of its Owner.

* The difference between an *offering* and a *sacrifice* is simply this: the latter is a species of the former. All sacrifices are offerings; but all offerings are not sacrifices. A sacrifice always implies, of necessity, a real *change* or *destruction* of the thing offered. But every thing presented to God, whether changed or unchanged, was called an offering or oblation. And hence the word most commonly used by the Hebrews to denote a sacrifice is *zehvahh*, (זֶבַח, from זָבַח, *to slaughter.*) The noun occurs 160 times in the Old Testament, and the verb 133 times. The word most frequently used for an *offering* or *oblation* is *minchah*, (מִנְחָה, from the obsolete verb מָנַח, *to give* or to *distribute.*) It occurs 196 times in the Hebrew Scriptures. The word *korban*, (קָרְבָּן,) is also used to denote an offering or oblation.

Difference between a sacrifice and an offering.

The Priest then sprinkled all the blood round about upon the Altar, and burned the whole victim on it, except the skin, which was the Priests' portion. Leviticus viii, 8. And hence the name *olahm*, (עוֹלָם,) *ascension*, was commonly given to this kind of sacrifice, because in its consumption most of it was made to *ascend* toward Heaven. The Greeks called this sacrifice a *holokautoma*, (*ὁλοκαυτωμα*;) and the Latins called it a *holocaustum*, or *whole burnt-offering*.

Disposition made of the Blood, Flesh, and Skin.

Specific name of this Sacrifice.

For the law relating to this Sacrifice see Leviticus i, 1–17; vi, 8–13; Exodus xxix, 38–46.

Law of the Burnt-Offering.

II. THE SIN-OFFERING.

The Law of this Sacrifice is found in Leviticus iv, v, 13, and vi, 24–30.

Law of the Sin-Offering.

This Sacrifice seems to have been unknown before the time of Moses. It is first named in Exodus xxix, 14. And, as its name (חַטָּאת *sin*) implies, it had in all cases a special reference to sin. Something more definite and specific than the Burnt-Offering and the Meat-Offering seems to have been necessary under an Institution that was added on account of *sin* till the Seed should come. Galatians iii, 19. And hence we find that it was generally required on particular occasions and for particular sins. For instance, it was required,

Origin and Scope of the Sin-Offering.

1. Of the Priests at their consecration. See Exodus xxix, 10–14.
2. Of mothers at childbirth. Leviticus xii
3. Of lepers when they were healed. Leviticus xiv, 1–32.

Special Occasions on which it was required.

4. Of Nazarites unexpectedly contaminated. Numbers vi, 1–21.

The kind of victim that was required depended on the rank and ability of the person who was to offer it, and the particular circumstances of the case. It might be a young bullock, a male kid, a female kid, or a lamb, a dove, or a pigeon; and, in cases of extreme poverty, the tenth part of an ephah, or about seven pints of fine flour, was accepted in lieu of two turtle doves or two young pigeons.

Kind of Victim required.

In all cases the sinner was required to lay his hand on the head of the victim, to confess his sins, and then to kill the sacrifice. If the whole congregation had sinned, the Elders were required to act as their representatives.

Part performed by the Sinner.

The High Priest then took the blood, and, if the victim were a bullock for himself or for the congregation, he sprinkled a portion of it seven times before the Inner Vail, put some of it on the horns of the Golden Altar, and then poured out the remainder of it at the foot of the Brazen Altar. In most other cases he first put some of the blood on the horns of the Brazen Altar, and then poured out the rest at its foot.

Disposition made of the Blood.

The fat was then burned on the Altar of Burnt-Offering, and the flesh was either wholly consumed by fire without the camp, or it was eaten by the Priests in the Holy Place. The law required that, if any of the blood of the victim had been taken into the Sanctuary, then the flesh was to be burned without the camp. Hebrews xiii, 11.

Of the Fat and the Flesh.

III. THE TRESPASS-OFFERING.

Law of the Trespass-Offering.

The law of the Trespass-Offering (אָשָׁם, *a fault* or *trespass*) is to be found in Leviticus v, 14–vi, 7, and vii, 6.

Relation of the Trespass-Offering to the Sin-Offering.

This Offering was very nearly related to the Sin-Offering, and was, in fact, a sort of supplement or appendix to it. Like the Sin-Offering, it was required for specific offenses. *But, unlike the Sin-Offering, it had not reference to sin in the absolute, but only in its subordinate and civil relations. And hence it was required only for such sins against God or man as admitted of some estimation or recompense.* Numbers v, 5–8.

The Victim, and other requirements.

The victim required in all cases was a ram or he-lamb without blemish. And, besides this, the transgressor was required to make good to the injured party his entire loss, and to add one-fifth more to it. Leviticus v, 15, 16.

Disposition made of the Blood, Fat, and Flesh.

In all cases the blood of the Trespass-Offering was sprinkled round about upon the Altar, the fat was burned on it, and the flesh was eaten by the Priests in the Holy Place.

IV. THE PEACE-OFFERING.

Law of the Peace-Offering.

For the law of the Peace-Offering (שֶׁלֶם) see Leviticus iii, 1–17; vii, 11–36; and xxii. 21–25.

Why it was called a Peace-Offering.

This was an offering made in token of peace and reconciliation between God and man.

The appointed seasons for these offerings were such as the following:

1. At the consecration of the Priests. Exodus xxix, 1 37, and Leviticus viii–ix.

Its appointed Seasons.

2. At the expiration of the Nazarite's vow. Numbers vi, 13–21.

3. At any solemn dedication; as, for instance, of the Altar. Numbers vii, 10–88.

4. At the Feast of Pentecost. Leviticus xxiii, 19.

5. It was moreover the privilege of the Hebrews to offer Peace-Offerings at any time as voluntary Thank-Offerings, or as an expression of their gratitude to God. Leviticus xix, 5; xxii, 21–25, etc. And this seems to have been their custom at all their festivals. Numbers x, 10.

Kind of Victim required.

The victim offered might be either a male or a female of the herd or of the flocks. But it was required that in all cases it should be without blemish, except when offered as a free-will offering. Leviticus xxii, 21–23.

Kinds of bread used with the Peace-Offering.

With the animal was also brought leavened and unleavened bread. Leviticus vii, 11–21. Of course, the leavened bread was not for sacrifice, but for food; for neither leaven nor honey was allowed to be burned on the Altar. Leviticus ii, 11.

The Blood and Fat.

The owner of the victim killed it as usual, and the Priests, the sons of Aaron, sprinkled the blood on the Altar, and burned all the fat on it.

The Flesh.

The breast and the right shoulder were both con secrated to the Priests as their portion, the former as a Wave-Offering, (תְּנוּפָה,) and the latter as a Heave-Offering, (תְּרוּמָה.) The rest of the sacrifice was eaten by the owner and his friends. Leviticus vii, 28–36. This was the only sacrifice of which the *people* were allowed to partake.

V. THE MEAT-OFFERING.

The law of the specific Meat or Meal-Offering (מִנְחָה) is given in Leviticus ii and vi, 14–23.

Law of the Specific Meat-Offering.

It was a bloodless offering, and consisted of three kinds or varieties, to all of which a portion of *salt* and *oil* was added.

Of what it consisted.

1. The first consisted of fine flour and frankincense.

2. The second of unleavened cakes, prepared either in an oven, (תַּנּוּר,) or in a pan, (מַחֲבַת,) or in a pot, (מַרְחֶשֶׁת.)

3. The third of parched corn and frankincense.

Disposition made of the Meat-Offering.

In all cases the High Priest burned a part of the offering on the Brazen Altar, and the rest was to be eaten by the Priests as a most holy thing.

VI. THE SUBSIDIARY MEAT-OFFERING.

The Minchah of Bloody Sacrifices.

The preceding Minchah or Meat-Offering was specific and coördinate with the Burnt-Offering, the Sin-Offering, the Trespass-Offering, and the Peace-Offering. But usually the Meat-Offering was a mere accompaniment or part of the Burnt-Offering and the Peace-Offering. And the quantity of flour and oil that was used on such occasions was regulated by the kind of victims that were offered.

Quantity of Flour and Oil for each Victim.

To each *bullock* were assigned three-tenths of an ephah (21 pints) of the finest wheat flour,* and half a hin † (5 pints) of oil; to a *ram* two-tenths of

Barley Offerings.

* Offerings of *barley* were required only on a few special occasions as, for instance, on the day after the Paschal Sabbath (Leviticus xxiii, 10–14,) and at the trial of jealousy, (Numbers v, 15.)

† According to Gesenius a hin is equal to nearly 5 quarts.

an ephah (14 pints) of flour, and a third of a hin (3 1-3 pints) of oil; and to a *lamb* a tenth part of an ephah (7 pints) of flour, and a fourth part of a hin (2 1-2 pints) of oii. Numbers xv, 1–16, and xxviii and xxix.

VII. THE DRINK-OFFERING.

Quality and Quantity of the Wine used in the Drink-Offering.

The Drink-Offering (נֶסֶךְ, from נָסַךְ, *to pour out,*) was also a part of the Burnt-Offering and the Peace-Offering. From Exodus xxix, 38–46, Numbers xv, 1–16, and xxviii, 7–29, we learn that the quantity of wine used in all cases was equal to the quantity of oil; that is, half a hin for a bullock, a third of a hin for a ram, and a fourth of a hin for a lamb.

Disposition made of the Wine.

From these passages it is also evident that the wine, as well as the oil and flour, was offered and burned with the victim *on the Brazen Altar.* Josephus says "it was poured out περὶ τὸν βῶμον, *around the Altar.*" But this may simply mean that it was poured out on all parts of the sacrifice as it lay on the altar. And this view is confirmed by Paul's allusion to the Drink-Offering in Phil. ii, 17: "Ἀλλὰ εἰ καὶ σπένδομαι ἐπὶ τῇ θυσίᾳ," etc. "Yea, should I be poured out as a libation *upon the sacrifice* and service of your faith I would be joyful and rejoice with you all.'

VIII. THE WATER OF PURIFICATION.

Removal of the Unclean from the Camp.

In Numbers v, 1–3, we have the following very significant but somewhat oppressive ordinance: "*The Lord spake unto Moses, saying, Command the Children of Israel that they put out of the camp every leper, and every one that hath an issue, and whosoever is defiled by the dead: both male and female shall ye put out: without the camp shall ye put them; that they defile not their camps in the midst whereof I dwell.*"

Object of the Water of Purification.

The number of persons cut off by this regulation would, of course, be very great, especially in the case of those who were defiled by the dead. And hence the necessity of an ordinance for the purpose of removing this species of symbolic defilement. For this purpose the Water of Purification was provided according to the law given in the nineteenth chapter of Numbers. From what is here said concerning this very peculiar and remarkable ordinance, we learn the following particulars:

Specifications of this Ordinance.

1. That the sacrifice was a species of Sin-Offering, (חַטָּאת,) verses 9 and 17; not, however, for sin in the absolute, but only for symbolic defilement.

2. That the victim required was a red or earth-colored heifer, (פָּרָה אֲדֻמָּה,) without a spot of any other color, without a blemish of any kind, and one that had never borne the yoke. Verse 2.

3. That she was to be slain without the camp by a representative of the congregation; a portion of her blood sprinkled seven times toward the front of the Tabernacle by a Priest of high dignity and rank; and that the rest of her blood and her entire carcass, with cedar-wood, and hyssop, and scarlet, were to be burned to ashes without the camp. Verses 3–6.

4. That the officiating Priest and the person who burned the heifer were required to wash their clothes, bathe their flesh in water, and remain out of the camp as unclean persons till evening. Verses 7, 8.

5. That a clean person was required to gather up the ashes, and that they were to be preserved in a clean place without the camp as a means of purification. Verse 9.

6. That he who gathered the ashes was required to wash his clothes and remain out of the camp as unclean till evening. Verse 10.

7. That the Water of Purification was to be prepared by mixing the ashes in living or spring water. Verse 17.

8. That all persons touching the dead, and all persons in a tent where a dead body was laid, as well as the tent itself and all the open vessels in it, were legally unclean. Verses 14–16.

9. That they could be cleansed only by means of this Water of Purification, and that for this purpose it had to be sprinkled on them by a clean person with a bunch of hyssop on the third day and also on the seventh day, after which he who sprinkled the water was himself thereby made unclean, and was required to wash his clothes and remain out of the camp till evening. Verse 21.

10. That the person who willfully neglected this ordinance, and thus by his presence defiled the Sanctuary, was to be cut off from the congregation as a presumptuous sinner. See Numbers xv, 22–31, and 1 Corinthians iii, 17.* †

Punishment of the willful and presumptuous Sinner.

* The *principle* of this punishment was not peculiar to the Law of Moses. It is also revealed in a still more severe and awful form in the New Institution. See Matthew xii, 31, 32; Hebrews vi, 4–6; x, 26–30; and 1 John v, 16. Under the Old Covenant the punishment was temporal death, but under the New it is eternal death.

† Let the reader note still further in this connection the awfully impressive lesson that is taught in this chapter respecting the polluting nature and influence of *sin*, which is here symbolically represented by *death*, which is the wages of sin. Is it any wonder, when we contemplate the subject in the light of this ordinance, that *human nature* has been defiled by its contact with the sin of Adam, and that the whole creation groans and travails in pain till now? But let us rejoice that "as by one man's disobedience the many were made *sinners*, even so by the obedience of one the many shall be made *righteous*." Romans v, 19.

Frequent use of the Water of Purification.

"No mention is made of the frequency of this sacrifice; but it was probably offered whenever a fresh supply of ashes was needed. Some of the ashes are said to have been kept in every town after the settlement of the people in Canaan. They must have been in constant requisition, as it is scarcely possible that a person could die and be buried without some of his family or attendants coming into contact with the body." Annotated Par. Bible.

DESIGN OF THESE OFFERINGS.

Fourfold design of these Offerings.

From the preceding brief account of the principal sacrifices and offerings of the Old Covenant, it is evident that their design was fourfold.

I. They were intended to be expressions of thanksgiving and gratitude to God.

II. They were supplicatory, and designed to procure some favor or benefit from him.

III. They were expiatory. Without the shedding of blood there has never been remission of any kind, under either Law or Gospel. Hebrews x, 22.

IV. But the pardon procured by these offerings was only *relative* and *symbolical.* For it is not possible that the blood of bulls and of goats could take away sins *absolutely.* Hebrews x, 4. And hence it is evident that the main design of these offerings was to adumbrate and illustrate the nature, necessity, and efficacy of the sacrifice of Christ.*

Analogy between Nature and Revelation with regard to Typical Forms.

* In this respect there is a striking analogy between the Book of Nature and the Holy Bible. As all the *types* of the former pointed to the first Adam, so all the *types* of the latter pointed to the second Adam. From Comparative Anatomy, we learn, for example, as Professor Owen eloquently remarks, that "all the parts and organs of man had been sketched out in anticipation, so to speak, in the inferior animals; and the recog

This they did just as the different parables of Christ served to explain and illustrate the nature of his kingdom. Each one was especially and peculiarly adapted to reveal, explain, and illustrate some attribute, characteristic, or qualification of the Great Antitype. The Burnt-Offerings, for instance, being wholly consumed by the fire of God, indicated, perhaps better than any other species of offering could have done, that God had accepted the victim in place of the sinner. The sprinkling of the blood of the Sin-Offering in the Most Holy Place, illustrated most beautifully and impressively the offering that Christ was about to make of his own blood in Heaven itself, for

Why so many Typical Forms were used.

Illustrations.

nition of an ideal exemplar in the vertebrated animals, proves that the knowledge of such a being as man must have existed before man appeared. For the Divine mind which planned the archetype also foreknew all its modifications. The archetypal idea was manifested in the flesh long prior to the creation of man. To what natural laws or second causes the orderly succession and progression of such organic phenomena may have been committed, we are as yet ignorant. But if, without derogation of the Divine power, we may conceive the existence of such ministers, and personify them by the term NATURE, we learn from the past history of our globe that she has advanced with slow and steady steps, guided by the archetypal light amidst the wreck of worlds from the first embodiment of the vertebrate idea under its old ichthyic vestment, until it became arrayed in the glorious garb of the human form."

Remarks of Prof. Owen on the Types and Archetype of the Animal Kingdom.

Compare, for illustration, the foreleg of vertebrate animals with the human arm; and the brain of the lower Vertebrates with the human brain. Concerning the latter, Hugh Miller makes the following appropriate remarks: "Nature," says he, "in constructing this curious organ in man, first lays down a grooved cord, as a carpenter lays down the keel of his vessel; and on this narrow base the perfect brain, as month after month passes by, is gradually built up, like the vessel from the keel. First it grows up into a brain closely resembling that of a *fish;* a few additions more convert it into a brain undistinguishable from that of the *reptile;* a few additions more impart to it the perfect appearance of the brain of a *bird:* it then develops into a brain exceedingly like that of a *mammiferous quadruped*, and finally, expanding atop, and spreading out its deeply corrugated lobes, till they project widely over the base, it assumes its

Illustrations.

the justification and sanctification of all who are Israelites indeed. The law of restitution connected with the Trespass-Offering served well to illustrate a great moral principle of the Divine government, without the observance of which even the Sin-Offering of Christ is of no avail to the sinner. See Matthew v, 23–26. The Love-Feast of the Peace-Offerings beautifully and most appropriately illustrated the peace and joy of all those whose iniquities are pardoned, and whose sins are covered. Acts ii, 41–47. Even the *leavened* bread offered with the sacrifice, though unfit for the Altar, was, nevertheless, a very appropriate and suitable part of the festival. And finally, the Water of Purification sprinkled on the flesh for the removal of symbolical uncleanness, most impressively

unique character as a *human brain.* Radically such at the first, it passes through all the inferior forms, from that of the fish upward, as if each man were in himself not the microcosm of the old fanciful philosopher, but something greatly more wonderful—a compendium of all animated nature, and of kin to every creature that lives. Hence the remark, that man is the sum total of all animals—"the animal equivalent," says Oken, "to the whole animal kingdom."

The Archetype of all the Scripture Types.

"But no sooner," says the same eloquent author, "had the first Adam appeared and fallen than a New School of prophecy began, in which type and symbol were mingled with what had now its first existence on Earth—verbal enunciations—and all pointed to the second Adam, the Lord from Heaven. In him creation and the Creator meet in reality, and not in mere resemblance, as in the first Adam. On the very apex of the finished pyramid of being sits the adorable Monarch of all:—as the Son of Mary—of David—of the first Adam, the created of God, the eternal Creator of the Universe. And these—the two Adams—form the main theme of all prophecy, both natural and revealed. And that type and symbol should have been employed with reference not only to the second, but (as held by men like Agassiz and Owen) to the first Adam, also, exemplifies, we are disposed to think, the unity of the style of Deity, and serves to show that it was He who created the worlds that dictated the Scriptures."

For a full discussion of the subject of Natural Types see Professor Owen on *The Archetype and Homologies of the Vertebrate Skeleton;* Hugh Miller's *Footprints of the Creator;* and Dr. James M'Cosh on *Typical Forms and Special Ends in Creation* illustrated the necessity of a personal application of that blood which alone can purify the conscience. Hebrews ix, 13, 14.

How awfully sublime and impressive, then, are the revealed mysteries of Judaism! To the eye of profane Reason many of the ceremonies of the Old Covenant were, no doubt, somewhat revolting. That so much blood, for instance, should be required in the worship of an infinitely pure and holy God seems indeed to the *natural man* to be something even more than foolishness. But to the man who has been properly instructed by the Spirit of God, and who can, therefore, through these types and symbols perceive the necessity, fitness, fullness, and sufficiency of the Antitype, all is plain, simple, beautiful, and Divine.

Concluding Reflections.

SECTION V.—THE LEVITICAL PRIESTHOOD.

During the Patriarchal Age, so far as we can learn from the record, any one, or at all events the father of every family, might officiate at the altar. See Genesis iv, 3–5; xxxi, 54; and Exodus xxiv, 4–8. But after the erection of the Tabernacle the family of Aaron were made Priests to the exclusion of all others. Exodus xxviii, 1; and Numbers iii, 10. The question of the Priesthood was, indeed, for a time agitated by some aspiring and ambitious men of other tribes and families; but it was finally and forever settled by God's judgments on Korah, Dathan, and Abiram. Numbers xvi–xviii, 7.

Priests of the Patriarchal Age.

Priests of the Jewish Age.

The Hebrew word for *priest* (כֹּהֵן; Sept., Ἱερεύς; Vulg., *sacerdos*;) is of doubtful etymology. The English word is generally supposed to be a contraction of *presbyter*, (πρεσβύτερος;) but there can be no

Etymology of the word *priest*.

reasonable doubt that the native power of this word differs essentially from that of the Hebrew.

Duties of the Priests.

The meaning of the word will, therefore, be best understood from the duties and functions of the office. These were both numerous and various. But to the Priests assisted by the Levites it belonged especially

I. *To offer sacrifice, burn incense, and perform all the other services of the Tabernacle.* See Exodus xxvii, 20, 21; xxx, 1–10. Compare Luke i, 9; Leviticus i, 5–17, etc. Compare Hebrews viii, 4, and x, 11; Numbers iii, 5–10; iv, 4–15; xviii, 1–7, etc.

II. *It was also their duty to instruct the people, and to act in all respects as God's ministers of mercy and benevolence.* Leviticus x, 8–11; Deut. xxiv, 8, 9; xxxiii, 8–11; Nehemiah viii, 1–8; Jeremiah ii, 8; Malachi ii, 1–9; and Luke x, 31, 32.

Holiness required of them.

The proper discharge of all these various functions would, of course, require a very high degree of sanctity on their part. And accordingly we find that *the necessity of purity and holiness is a predominating idea in nearly all the laws and regulations that have reference to the Levitical Priesthood.* This will be sufficiently illustrated by a brief consideration of their *qualifications*, their *clothing*, and their *consecration*.

Illustrations.

QUALIFICATIONS OF THE PRIESTS.

It was required of all the Priests in order that they might minister acceptably at the Altar and in the more solemn services of the Tabernacle,

I. *That they should be at least thirty years of age*

Numbers iv, 1–3. The Priests were all Kohathites, and were therefore most likely included in this regulation. See Exodus vi, 16–25.

Period of their Official Service.

In Numbers viii, 23–26, twenty-five is given as the age when all the Levites, including of course the Priests, should go in *to wait* on the service of the Tabernacle. And from 1 Chronicles xxiii, 24–32, we learn that David fixed the period of their service at from twenty years of age and upward. See also 2 Chronicles xxxi, 17, and Ezra iii, 8. But this preliminary service is to be understood as a sort of *apprenticeship* in the less important matters of the service; and the age of thirty was the time when they entered on the full discharge of all the prescribed duties of the sacerdotal office.

After the age of fifty their services became in a great measure voluntary. They were still allowed and expected to "*minister* with their brethren in the Tabernacle of the congregation," (Numbers viii, 26, and 1 Chronicles xxiii, 27,) but they were relieved from all the more onerous duties of the Priesthood.

Symbolical meaning of this arrangement.

In a symbolical Institution, such as we are now considering, it is not probable that this regulation with regard to the period of the Priests' service would have reference merely to their physical qualifications and comfort. It is most likely that it had also a deeper signification, and that it was, in fact, primarily intended to denote that the spiritual life of every Priest of the Most High God should be one of soundness, vigor, energy, and completeness. And hence, in the Priesthood of the New Covenant, there is no place for *infants*.

II. *It was also required that the Priests should be free from all physical impurities, infirmities, and imperfections*, such, for example, as the leprosy, a running issue, etc. Lev. xxi, 16–24, and xxii, 1–9. And hence a Priest was not permitted to defile himself by the touch of a dead body, except in the case of a very near relative, (Leviticus xxi, 1–6,) and the High Priest was not allowed to defile himself for any one, not even for a father or a mother. Leviticus xxi, 10–12.

Their freedom from physical impurity and imperfection.

Here, again, there is evidently a symbolical meaning implied in all these legal requirements. They were manifestly intended to denote that *spiritual purity* without which no one can, even now, have communion and fellowship with God. 1 Peter i, 16. Comp. Leviticus xi, 44; xix, 2; and xx, 7.

Symbolical import of these restrictions.

III. *It was moreover required of every Priest that he should not marry any person of ill fame, nor any one who had been divorced,* (Leviticus xxi, 7, 8,) *and the High Priest was allowed to marry no one but a virgin of good character and of his own people.* Leviticus xxi, 13–15. The reason of these restrictions is made plain by the subsequent revelations of the New Covenant. As the High Priest was a type of Christ, so also it would seem that his wife was a type of the Church. And hence Paul says, 2 Corinthians xi, 2, "I have espoused you to one husband, that I may present you a *chaste virgin* to Christ."

Law respecting the Marriage of the Priests.

Its typical import.

CLOTHING OF THE PRIESTS.

The garments worn by each and every Priest who officiated at the Altar and in the Tabernacle were a pair of Drawers, a long Coat or Tunic,

Garments of the Priests.

a Girdle, and a Turban. Exodus xxviii, 40–43. These were all made of fine white linen, a kind of material that, in all ages, has been regarded as symbolical of purity. See 2 Chronicles v, 12, and Revelation xix, 8.

Garments of the High Priest.

Besides these the High Priest wore, when in full dress, four golden garments. These were,

The Robe of the Ephod.

I. *The Robe of the Ephod* (מְעִיל הָאֵפוֹד.) It was a long sky-blue robe, without a seam, and worn directly under the Ephod. Around its lower border were tassels made of blue, and purple, and scarlet, in the form of pomegranates, alternating with golden bells. The Rabbis say there were seventy-two of each. Exodus xxviii, 31–35; xxxix, 22–26.

The Ephod.

II. *The Ephod* (אֵפוֹד, from אָפַד, *to bind.*) This was a short coat worn over the Robe, and, with its curious Girdle, was made of gold, and blue, and purple, and scarlet, and fine twined linen, with cunning work. To the shoulder-pieces were attached two onyx stones, on which were engraved the names of the twelve sons of Jacob "according to their birth." Exodus xxviii, 6–14; xxxix, 2–7.

The Pectoral.

III. *The Pectoral, or Breast-plate of Judgment,* (חֹשֶׁן מִשְׁפָּט.) This was a sort of pouch or bag of a span or half a cubit square. It, too, was made of gold, and blue, and purple, and scarlet, and fine twined linen. To each of its four corners was attached a gold ring, by means of which it was fastened to the Ephod. On the inside of its face were four rows of precious stones set in sockets of gold, through which they were externally visible, and on these stones were engraved, most likely "according to their birth," the names of the Twelve

Precious Stones and inscribed Names.

Tribes of the Children of Israel, as follows. See Exodus xxviii, 15–30.

בָּרֶקֶת Carbuncle. לֵוִי Levi.	פִּטְדָה Topaz. שִׁמְעוֹן Simeon.	אֹדֶם Sardius. רְאוּבֵן Reuben.
יַהֲלֹם Diamond. נַפְתָּלִי Naphtali.	סַפִּיר Sapphire. דָּן Dan.	נֹפֶךְ Emerald. יְהוּדָה Judah.
אַחְלָמָה Amethyst. יִשָּׂכָר Issachar.	שְׁבוֹ Agate. אָשֵׁר Asher.	לֶשֶׁם Ligure. גָּד Gad.
יָשְׁפֵה Jasper. בִּנְיָמִין Benjamin.	שֹׁהַם Onyx. יוֹסֵף Joseph.	תַּרְשִׁישׁ Beryl. זְבוּלוּן Zebulon.

Urim and Thummim.

In the Pectoral were placed the Urim and Thummim, (אוּרִים וְתֻמִּים, *Lights and Perfections;* Sept., δήλωσις καὶ ἀλήθεια, *Revelation and Truth;* Vulg., *Doctrina et Veritas, Doctrine and Truth.*) The Hebrew words are both plural, and they are generally supposed to be the *plural of excellence, (plurales excellentiæ,)* meaning simply *light* and *completeness*, or *perfection.* It is also the common opinion of our best critics that the words are used metonymically for the *things* or the *modes* by and through which the light or revelation was given and the truth declared. But what these things were is still a matter of uncertainty. Three principal opinions have long prevailed concerning them:

Three Hypotheses concerning the Urim and Thummim.

Hypothesis of Josephus.

1. That they were identical with the stones of the Pectoral, and that by means of these God, in some way unknown to us, indicated his will to the people through the High Priest as their representative. This is the view maintained by Josephus. In his Antiquities, B. III, Ch. viii, Sec. 9, he says: "God declared beforehand, by these twelve stones which the High Priest bore on his breast, and which were inserted into his Breast-plate, when they should be victorious in battle, for so great a splendor shone forth from them before the army began to march that all the people were sensible of God's being present for their assistance. Whence it came to pass that those Greeks who had a veneration for our laws, because they could not possibly contradict this, called that Breast-plate *the Oracle*. Now, this Breast-plate and this sardonyx (one of the stones on the High Priest's shoulders) left off shining two hundred years before I composed this book, God having been displeased at the transgressions of his laws."

Hypothesis of Philo.

2. The second hypothesis is that "the Urim and Thummim were two small *oracular images*, similar to the Teraphim, personifying *Revelation* and *Truth*, which were placed in the cavity or pouch formed by the folds of the Breastplate, and which uttered oracles by a voice." This is the view maintained by Philo, the learned contemporary of Josephus. See his "Life of Moses," Vol. II, Book III, p. 152, of Mangey's Edition.

Hypothesis of Michaelis.

3. The third hypothesis is that the Urim and Thummim were three precious stones, used for the purpose of casting lots. On one of them, it is alleged, was engraven the word כֵּן, *Yes;* on the second was engraved the word לֹא, *No;* and the third was

left without any inscription. The question proposed was always put in such a way that the answer, if any were given, might be either *Yes* or *No*. These stones were carried in the purse or bag, formed by the lining of the Breastplate. When the question was proposed, if the High Priest drew out the stone which contained *Yes*, the answer was affirmative; if the one which contained *No*, the answer was negative; and if he drew out the one which had no inscription, then no answer was given. See Michaelis on the "Laws of Moses." Art. 304.

Conclusion respecting the Urim and Thummim.

None of these hypotheses seems to be wholly free from objections; and it may now indeed be impossible to ascertain the exact import of these mysterious terms. But this much is evident, that it was in some way, by means of the Urim and Thummim, that God usually responded to the questions of the High Priest in matters of practical importance involving doubt and uncertainty. See Numbers xxvii, 21; Judges xx, 27, 28; 1 Samuel xxiii, 9; xxviii, 6; and Ezra ii, 63.

The Golden Plate.

IV. *The fourth article of the High Priest's golden attire was the Plate of Gold,* (צִ֫יץ זָהָב,) *which was fastened to his Miter or Turban by a blue fillet.* On this plate was inscribed the words, קֹ֫דֶשׁ לַיהוָֹה, HOLINESS TO JEHOVAH. To this inscription there is a beautiful allusion in Zechariah xiv, 20, 21. During the blessed era contemplated by the prophet, every thing will be sanctified to Jehovah, as was the High Priest during the Jewish Age. For a description of this Plate see Exodus xxviii, 36-38, and xxxix, 30. See also Psalm xciii, 5.

CONSECRATION OF THE PRIESTS.

The ceremonies of consecrating Aaron and his sons to the Priesthood are given in Exodus xxix and Leviticus viii and ix, and were as follows:

Ceremonies of the Priest's Consecration.

I. Moses brought Aaron and his sons to the door of the Tabernacle, and washed (רָחַץ) them in water. Lev. viii, 5, 6.

The Washing

II. He clothed them in their proper garments. Verses 7–9, 13.

The Investing.

III. He anointed the Tabernacle and all its furniture; also the Laver and the Altar; and finally Aaron himself. Verses 10–12.

The Anointing

IV. He brought forward the bullock for a sin-offering; caused Aaron and his sons to place their hands on its head, and killed it. He then put some of the blood on the horns of the Brazen Altar; poured out the rest of it at its foot; burned the fat on it; and the skin, flesh, and dung he burned without the camp. Verses 14–17.

The Sin-Offering.

V. He brought the ram for a burnt-offering, and caused Aaron and his sons to place their hands on its head, and killed it. He then sprinkled the blood on the Altar round about, and after cleansing the legs and the entrails, he burned the whole ram on the Altar for a burnt-offering. Verses 18–21.

The Burnt-Offering.

VI. He brought the ram intended for a peace-offering, otherwise called "The Ram of Consecration," and caused Aaron and his sons to lay their hands on its head, and killed it. He then took of the blood and put it on the right ear of Aaron and his sons, to sanctify their ears for hearing;

The Peace-Offering.

Its Blood.

on the thumb of their right hand, to sanctify their hands for serving; and on the great toe of their right foot, to sanctify their feet, for treading God's courts.* The rest of the blood he sprinkled on the Altar. Verses 22–24.

Parts consumed on the Altar.

He then took the fat, rump, kidneys, caul or omentum, and the right shoulder, with one loaf of unleavened bread, one cake of oiled bread, and one wafer anointed with oil, and put them into the hands of Aaron and his sons, and waved them for a wave-offering, and then burned them on the Altar. Verses 25–28.

Moses portion of the Peace-Offering.

The breast he waved and took as his own portion. Verse 29.

The Sprinkling of Blood and Oil.

He then took some of the blood from the Altar, mingling it with oil, and sprinkled it on Aaron and on his sons, and on their garments to sanctify them. Verse 30.

Infidel objection to such applications of Blood, etc.

*It has often been urged against this application of blood, and other similar applications of oil and water, that "*they are utterly beneath the dignity and wisdom of that God who delights only in the homage and worship of the heart.*"

But be it observed,

Reply to it.

I. That holiness of heart is essential to all acceptable worship. Without it all religious pretensions are worse than useless.

II. That the whole world, both Jews and Gentiles, were in a great measure ignorant of this fundamental truth. They had no just and adequate conception of God's holiness, and had, therefore, no proper standard by which to judge of the degree of holiness that is necessary in order to enjoy God.

III. To *create* this conception in the minds of the Hebrews was, therefore, very important, and at the same time extremely difficult. Every thing around them had an unfavorable and contrary tendency.

IV. And hence the necessity that in a religion that was designed to prepare the world for Christianity and Christianity for the world, there should be divers applications of blood, oil, and water in order that through these external signs and symbols the minds of all might be led to perceive more clearly the necessity of the blood of Christ, the renewing of the Holy Spirit, and that inward purity of heart without which no man shall see the Lord.

V. And hence we find, as usual, that this objection has its foundation wholly in the ignorance of him who urges it.

After that he caused Aaron and his sons to boil the remainder of the flesh of the ram of consecration at the door of the Tabernacle of the congregation. There they ate it with unleavened bread. Verses 31, 32.

VII. The same ceremonies, or at least a portion of them, were repeated for seven successive days, in order to indicate that the purification and consecration should be perfect and entire. Verses 33–36; Exodus xxix, 35–37.

Repetition of the same Ceremonies.

VIII. On the eighth day, Aaron having been fully consecrated and set apart to the sacerdotal office, offered sacrifices for himself and also for the people. At the close of his ministrations the glory of Jehovah appeared to the people, and fire came out from him and consumed the flesh that was on the Altar. Leviticus ix.

Aaron's Offerings and the Sacred Fire.

EMOLUMENTS OF THE PRIESTS.

The emoluments and revenues of the Priests were derived chiefly from three sources.

Revenues of the Priests.

I. From the perquisites of the thirteen Levitical cities that were assigned to them by lot. Joshua xxi, 4.

II. From the tithes that they received from the Levites. Numbers xviii, 25–32.

III. From the sacrifices and other offerings of the Sanctuary; such as the skins of the burnt-offerings, Leviticus vii, 8; the flesh of the sin-offerings, Leviticus vi, 25, 26; the flesh of the trespass-offerings, Leviticus vii, 1–6; the peace-offerings of the congregation at Pentecost, Leviticus xxiii, 19, 20; the breast and the right shoulder of all the peace-offerings, Leviticus vii, 31–34; the shew-bread, Leviticus xxiv, 9; the firstling of every clean beast,

Numbers xviii, 15; the first-fruits of oil, wine, wheat, and whatsoever was first ripe in the land, Numbers xvii, 8–19; all devoted things, etc.

RELATION OF THE LEVITICAL PRIESTHOOD TO CHRISTIANITY

Matters of local necessity and convenience in the Levitical Priesthood.

In the laws and ordinances of the Levitical Priesthood there was much that was of a merely local character. Many things of necessity had reference only to the peculiar wants, organization, and circumstances of the Israelites as a people. But, nevertheless, the Levitical Priesthood, like all the religious rites and ceremonies of the Hebrews, was *a shadow* of good things to come. Every thoughtful student of the Bible must see in it abundant evidence that the sacerdotal relations of the Old and the New Covenant were designed and preordained by the Divine Author of both Institutions. It is evident, for instance,

Matters of Typical significance.

The Priests.

I. That the Priests themselves were all types of the citizens of Christ's Kingdom. This is proved by a reference to 1 Peter ii, 5, 9, and Revelation i, 6; v, 10.

Their Garments and Washings.

II. Their pure white garments and their sevenfold washing were typical of the moral purity that is required of all Christians. Revelation xix, 8; and Hebrews ix, 10–14.

The Blood and Oil of their consecration.

III. The repeated applications of blood and oil signified that the aforesaid purity of heart and life can be secured only through the atoning blood of Christ, and the renewing and sanctifying energies of the Holy Spirit. See Hebrews ix, 14; x, 14, 19; Isaiah lxi, 1; Acts x, 38; Hebrews i, 9; 1 John ii, 20, 27.

IV. The closing festival of their consecration was a beautiful symbol of the spiritual repast of those who have been reconciled to God. Revelation iii, 20; Acts ii, 41–47.

The Feast of Peace-Offerings.

V. And the separation of the Levitical Priests from all secular pursuits was evidently intended to denote that the chief business of all Christians is to offer up spiritual sacrifices to God through Christ, and to attend to the concerns and interests of his Kingdom. Matthew vi, 33; Mark x, 28–31; 1 Timothy iv, 8; 1 Peter ii, 5, etc.

Their separation from secular pursuits.

In like manner we see many points of preordained resemblance between Aaron and Christ. Such, for example, as the following:

Points of Typical resemblance between Aaron and Christ.

I. Aaron was called to his sacerdotal office by God; and so was Christ. Hebrews v, 4, 5.

II. Aaron bore on his forehead evident marks of his entire consecration to God; and so also did Christ. Of this his whole life is sufficient evidence.

III. Aaron bore the names of the Twelve Tribes of Israel according to the flesh, both on his shoulders and on his heart; and in like manner Christ bears on his shoulders and on his heart all the promised seed. See Isaiah ix, 6; Hebrews ii, 14–18, etc.

IV. Aaron went once a year in behalf of all Israel into the Most Holy Place; and so Christ has gone, once for all into Heaven itself, in behalf of all his people; and to them that look for him he will appear again without a sin-offering for their salvation. Hebrews ix, 28.

How evident it is, therefore, that the Bible is a UNIT, and that the Old Covenant is but the shadow of the New!

Conclusion.

SECTION VI.—Festivals and other Stated Solemnities

Sacred Seasons appointed by Jehovah.

In Leviticus xxiii, 2, etc., these are called ***moadeem,*** (מוֹעֲדִים,) from יָעַד, *to appoint.* The radical idea conveyed by the original is, therefore, not that of a feast or festival, as in the English Version, but rather that of ***an appointed season,*** or ***a meeting together*** for religious purposes. The most important of these were the weekly Sabbath, the Feast of the New Moon, the Feast of Trumpets, the Day of Atonement, the Feast of the Passover, the Feast of Pentecost, the Feast of Tabernacles, the Sabbatical Year, and the Year of Jubilee.* We will notice each of these briefly in order.

THE SABBATH.

Questions concerning the Sabbath.

Five questions very naturally arise just here concerning this ordinance:

I. When was it instituted?

II. For what purposes was it instituted?

III. Is it, as an Institution, still binding on Christians?

IV. Does it belong to the ***Moral*** or to the ***Positive*** order of institutions?

* Besides these the Jews observed several Post-Exile Festivals; the principal of which were the following:

Post-Exile Festivals.

I. *The Feast of Purim,* (פּוּרִים, *lots.*) It was instituted by Mordecai, and was celebrated on the 14th and 15th days of the twelfth month, (Adar,) in commemoration of the deliverance of the Jews from the destruction that was threatened by the wicked Haman. See Esther iii, 7; and ix, 20–28.

II. *The Feast of Dedication,* (חֲנֻכָּה; N. Test., τὰ ἐγκαίνια.) This was instituted by Judas Maccabæus, B. C. 164, in commemoration of the purification of the Temple, after its profanation by Antiochus Epiphanes. It is still celebrated by the Jews during eight days, commencing on the 25th of the ninth month, (Kishlev.) John x, 22; 1 Maccab. iv, 52–59.

III. *The Feast of Wood-carrying.* This has been celebrated by the Jews on the 15th day of the fifth month, (Ab,) ever since their return from the Babylonish captivity. It commemorates the wood-offering that was every

V. By what sacrifices was it distinguished?

We will consider these questions briefly in order. And, *first*, When was the Sabbath instituted?

Opinion of Paley, etc., with reference to the Origin of the Sabbath.

The opinion has long been entertained, by some able writers, that the Sabbath had its origin in and with the fourth precept of the Decalogue, and that, previous to the giving of the Law from Mount Sinai, there was really no such institution known among men.

Proof that their hypothesis is false.

But that this is an erroneous opinion is, I think, clearly proved by the following passages:

From Genesis ii, 3.

1. "And God blessed the seventh day and sanctified it, because that in it he had rested from all his works which God had created to make." Genesis ii, 3. No one, it seems to me, but a theorist can after a fair examination of this passage, doubt that God rested and blessed the seventh day *immediately* after he had completed the work of the cosmos.

From Genesis xxix, 26–28.

2. "And Laban said, It must not be so done in our country, to give the younger before the first-born. Fulfill her *week*, and I will give thee

year made on this day for the supply of the Temple. Nehemiah x, 34; Josephus, Jewish Wars, Book II, ch. xvii, sec. 6.

IV. *The Feast of Water-drawing.* This was held every year on the last day of the Feast of Tabernacles, which was the 22d of the seventh month, (Tisri.) The origin and design of the custom are both uncertain. John vii, 37; Mishna, Succa iv, 9; v, 1–3.

V. *The Feast of Nicanor.* This was instituted by Judas Maccabæus, and celebrated on the 13th day of the twelfth month, (Adar,) in commemoration of the victory which on that day Judas gained over Nicanor. 1 Maccab. vii, 49; Joseph. Antiq. xii, 10, 5.

VI. *The Feast of Acra.* This was instituted by Simon Maccabæus, B. C. 141. It was annually celebrated on the 23d day of the second month, (Zif,) in commemoration of the recapture and purifying of Acra, the hill that stood north of the Temple, and on which Antiochus Epiphanes built a citadel. Maccab. xiii, 50–52 this also for the service which thou shalt serve with me yet seven other years. And Jacob did so, and fulfilled her *week*; and he gave him Rachel, his daughter, to wife also." Genesis xxix, 26–28. If the Sabbath had not been instituted ere this, how could Laban know any thing about *weeks?* Days, and months, and years are all *Natural Institutions*, but the week is wholly *Positive.*

3. See, also, Exodus xvi, 22–30. The laws and regulations here recorded respecting the Manna were given some time before the Law was delivered from Mount Sinai. But in this passage there is a clear reference to the Sabbath as a previously existing Institution.

From Exodus xvi, 22–30.

4. Exodus xx, 8–11. The Sabbath is here again spoken of, not as a *new*, but as an *old* Institution that was to be remembered.

From Exodus xx, 8–11.

5. Hebrews iv, 3. The argument of the Apostle in this passage is simply this. In Psalm xcv, 11, David, by the Spirit, speaks of a rest that was still in the future; and he admonishes all Israelites to beware lest they should fail to enter into that rest, just as many of those who left Egypt under Moses failed to enter into the rest of Canaan. But this rest, he argues, could not be the *weekly Sabbath*, because, he says, "the works were finished from the foundation of the world," which is equivalent to his saying that the Sabbath had been sanctified and observed from the foundation of the world. For it is a law of all commemorative Institutions, human and Divine, that they should always be established in connection with the events which they are designed to celebrate. This law was strictly observed in the ordinance of the Passover, of the Pentecost, of the Feast of Tabernacles, the Pot of Manna, etc. And hence Paul very logically

From Hebrews iv, 3.

and forcibly argues, in the passage cited, tnat the rest spoken of by David could not be the weekly Sabbath. And for a similar reason he argues still further that it could not be the rest in Canaan. And hence he concludes that there is still a rest remaining for the people of God. Hebrews iv, 9.

6. Finally, we have the testimony of Christ on this subject. In Mark ii, 27, he says: "The Sabbath was made for man, and not man for the Sabbath." From this passage it is evident that the Sabbath was made not merely for the *Israelites*, as Paley and Hengstenberg would have us believe, but for *man*, (הָאָדָם; Gr., ὁ ἄνθρωπος;) that is, for *the race.*

From Mark ii, 27.

Hence we conclude that the Sabbath was sanctified from the beginning, and that it was given to Adam, even in Eden, as one of those primeval institutions that God ordained for the happiness of all men.

Conclusion.

Secondly. For what purposes was the Sabbath instituted? Evidently,

Purposes for which the Sabbath was instituted.

1. To commemorate God's rest after creating and arranging the universe with reference to man. Genesis ii, 3; and Exodus xx, 9–11.

2. That it might be a season of rest for man and beast. Exodus xx, 9–11. The importance of the Sabbath in this respect has often been proved *experimentally.*

3. That it might be a season for mutual instruction and social worship. See Leviticus xxiii, 3; Luke iv, 16; Acts xv, 21.

4. That it might serve as a type of that rest which we enjoy in and through Christ, both here and hereafter.

In Colossians ii, 16, 17, Paul says: "Let no man therefore judge you in meat, or in drink, or in respect of a holyday, or of the new moon, or of the Sabbath days:

which are a shadow of things to come; but the body is of Christ." Here, then, it is evident that the Sabbath was intended to be a *shadow* of something pertaining to Christianity. But what is that substance of which the Sabbath was a shadow? That it includes our rest after death is, I think, sufficiently obvious. But is this all? Does it mean nothing more than the rest that remains for those who die in the Lord? Or does it also comprehend the *partial rest* that we even now enjoy through Christ from the toils and burdens of sin?

That the latter as well as the former is implied in the language of the Apostle, seems to me quite probable, for several reasons:

(1.) It is required by *the law of resemblance* that must always exist between the type and the antitype. But the Israelites *began* to enjoy the promised rest as soon as they put off the yoke of bondage and started on their pilgrimage for Canaan. And just so it is now with all who become the real followers of Christ. All who come to him and take his yoke upon them find rest to their souls. Matthew xi, 28–30.

(2.) The same thing is implied also in *the law of continuity*, or immediate sequence that exists between the type and the antitype. The sacrifices, for instance, were all continued till they were fulfilled in the Great Antitype. Then, and not till then, they all ceased. And just so it was with all the various Sabbaths of the Law. As shadows they must all have continued till the corresponding substance came into view. But from Colossians ii, 14–17, we learn that they were all abrogated and taken out of the way when Christ was nailed to the Cross. And hence we conclude that the rest foreshadowed by the Sabbath is begun here, and that it is perfected hereafter.

5. And, finally, the ordinance of the Sabbath was designed to remind the Jews of their emancipation from Egyptian bondage. "And remember," says Moses, "that thou wast a servant in the land of Egypt, and that the Lord thy God brought thee out thence through a mighty hand and by a stretched-out arm; *therefore the Lord thy God commanded thee to keep the Sabbath day.*" Deut. v, 15.

The Sabbath not binding on Christians.

Thirdly. Is the Sabbath, as it was originally instituted and reënacted in the Law of Moses, still binding on Christians?

A negative answer is given to this question in the passage previously cited from Colossians ii, 14–17. This passage covers all the typical and ceremonial institutions of the Patriarchal Age as well as of the Jewish. Circumcision, for instance, was not of Moses but of the Fathers. John vii, 22. But, nevertheless, it was abolished with all the ordinances of the Law when Christ was crucified. Rom. ii, 25–29; 1 Cor. vii, 19; Gal. v, 6; vi, 15; Phil. iii, 3, etc. And the same may be said of the patriarchal sacrifices, tithes, priesthood, Sabbath, etc. All shadows disappeared when the substance came through Jesus Christ. The covenant made with Noah was of a different character.

Fourthly. Was it a *Moral* or a *Positive* Institution?

Its Positive and Moral Character.

The proper answer to this question is also implied in the same quotation from Colossians. If it was abolished it must have been a Positive Institution, for God never abolishes any thing that is purely *moral* or *natural.* By this I do not mean that the ordinance of the Sabbath did not contain some *moral elements.* Several such elements it certainly did contain, all of which are of perpetual obligation, and, as we shall hereafter see, they have all reappeared in the still more sacred ordinance of the Lord's Day. But as an *Institution* the Sabbath was Positive, just as the Law of Moses and the Old Constitution of Kentucky were Positive; and like them it is no longer of binding obligation on either Jews or Gentiles.

Fifthly. By what sacrifices was the Sabbath distinguished?

In order to answer this question properly, we must first consider the law of the daily sacrifices. This is given in Exodus xxix, 38–46, and Numbers xxviii, 1–8. From these passages we learn that the required daily sacrifices consisted,

The daily Offerings.

1. In two lambs, one of which was offered up in the morning and the other in the afternoon, (generally about 3 o'clock,) for a burnt-offering.

2. In two-tenths of an ephah of flour, (14 pints,) mingled with half a hin of oil, (5 pints,) half of which was offered with each lamb for a meat-offering.

3. In half a hin of wine, (5 pints,) the half of which was offered with each lamb for a drink-offering.

The law of the Sabbatical offerings is given in Numbers xxviii, 9, 10. According to this the sacrifices required on the Sabbath were just twice as many as those that were offered daily.

Offerings required on the Sabbath.

THE NEW MOONS AND FEAST OF TRUMPETS.

The beginning of each month was announced by the sounding of trumpets. Numbers x, 10. But the sound of the trumpet on such occasions seems to have been symbolical of the voice of God. Numbers x, 1–10. And hence we find that the

Solemnities of the New Moons.

first day of every month was distinguished by sundry marks of respect and religious devotion. It is no where in Scripture called a *Sabbath.* But it seems from sundry passages that on that day the people abstained from servile labor, Amos viii, 5, etc., and on it they were required to offer an unusual number of sacrifices. These, as we learn from Numbers xxviii, 11–15, consisted of two young bullocks, one ram, and seven lambs of the first year without spot for a burnt-offering, with their usual meat-offerings and drink-offerings, and one kid of the goats for a sin-offering, besides the daily burnt-offerings.

Solemnities of the Feast of Trumpets.

The first day of the seventh month of the ecclesiastical year, which was also the first day of the civil year, was called a *Sabbath,* and also *the Feast* (מוֹעֵד) *of Trumpets.* Compare Leviticus xxiii, 1, with xxiii, 23–25. On this day the people were required to abstain from all servile labor; to meet together, as on the Sabbath, for religious instruction; and to offer, besides the usual daily and monthly sacrifices, one young bullock, one ram, and seven lambs of the first year without blemish for a burnt-offering, with their usual meat-offerings and drink-offerings; and one kid of the goats for a sin-offering. Numbers xxix, 1–6.

THE DAY OF ATONEMENT.

Sacredness the Day of Atonement.

The Day of Atonement, (יוֹם הַכִּפּוּרִים; Sept., *ἡμέρα ἐξιλασμοῦ,*) occurred annually on the tenth day of the seventh month It is called a *sabbath* in Leviticus xvi, 31; and in some respects it was the most solemn day in the year.

For this reason all the services of the day were performed, or at least superintended, by the High Priest himself. These, so far as we can learn from the Scriptures and Jewish tradition, were conducted as follows:

Order of its solemnities.

I. The High Priest laid aside his ordinary dress, bathed himself in water, and put on his *golden garments*.

II. He went to the Laver, washed his hands and his feet, and proceeded to offer the usual morning oblations.

III. He went into the Holy Place, trimmed the lamps, offered the incense, and came out and blessed the people.

IV. He prepared himself and the people for the more solemn services of the day, by offering the sacrifices prescribed in Numbers xxix, 7–11. These consisted of one young bullock, one ram, and seven lambs of the first year without blemish, for a burnt-offering, with their prescribed meat and drink offerings; and one kid of the goats for a sin-offering.

V. He washed his hands and feet a second time at the Laver; went into the Tabernacle and put off his golden garments; bathed himself a second time in water, and put on his plain white linen garments. Leviticus xvi, 4.

VI. He took the bullock, which had been previously selected as a sin-offering for himself and his family, laid his hands on its head, and uttered the following prayer and confession: "O Lord, I have sinned; done perversely, and transgressed before thee.—I and my house. I beseech thee, O Lord, expiate the sins, perversities, and transgressions whereby I have sinned, done perversely, and transgressed, I and my house; as it is written in the law of Moses thy servant, saying, For in this day he will expiate for you to purge you from all your sins before the Lord, that ye may be clean." Verse 11.

VII. He killed the bullock, and reserved its blood Verse 11.

VIII. He took a censer full of coals from the Brazen Altar, (verse 12. Compare 1 Kings viii, 64,) and his hands full of sweet incense; went into the Most Holy Place, and there burned the incense before the Ark Verses 12, 13.

IX. He took the blood of the slain bullock, entered a second time into the Most Holy Place, and sprinkled the blood seven times on and before the Mercy-Seat. Verse 14.

X. He came out into the Court, cast lots for the two goats, that he might know which was intended for Jehovah, (לַיהוָה,) and which for *Azazel*, or the Scape-Goat.*

* The meaning of the word *azazel*, which occurs four times in this chapter and no where else, is still a matter of uncertainty. The following views are still entertained by able critics:

Hypotheses concerning the Scape-Goat.

I. That the word *azazel* is used here as the name or designation of the goat; and that it is composed of the two words עֵז, *a goat*, and אָזַל, *to depart*.

But it is difficult to see why a buck (שָׂעִיר) should be here represented by עֵז, which properly and usually means a she-goat. And besides, the prefixed preposition לְ seems to designate the object for which the goat was intended. As the first goat was for Jehovah, so the second was for *azazel*. And hence,

II. Some think that it is the name of the place to which the goat was sent.

III. Others suppose that it is the name of Satan, or some other evil demon of the desert; some of them alleging that the goat was a real sacrifice offered to Satan to appease his wrath, just as sacrifices were sometimes offered to Typhon! But others allege that the goat was simply made the bearer of sins to their proper author.

Probable Etymology of the word *azazel*.

IV. Perhaps the most probable view is that the word *azazel* is formed by simply doubling the word עָזַל, *to separate*, in order to express more fully and emphatically the idea of a *complete and final separation*. Hence we have עָזַל-עָזַל; and, by contraction, עֲזַעְזֵל; and by a change of kindred letters, for the sake of euphony, we have finally עֲזָאזֵל. The first goat by his blood covered the sins of the people, and the second bore them away into a state of complete separation and eternal forgetfulness. The first goat was for Jehovah. the second was for an oblivious and eternal separation.

XI. He killed the goat on which the Lord's lot fell; took of its blood into the Most Holy Place, and sprinkled it seven times on and before the Mercy-Seat. Afterward, he made in like manner an atonement for the Holy Place and all that pertained to it. Verses 15–17; Exodus xxx, 10. See also Josephus, Ant. III, 10, 3.

XII. He then went out of the Tabernacle into the Court; took of the blood of the bullock and of the goat; put of the mixture on the horns of the Brazen Altar, and sprinkled it with his finger seven times upon the Altar. Vs. 18, 19.

XIII. When this was done, he next laid his hands on the head of the Scape-Goat, confessed over it the sins of the people, and sent it away by a fit person into a place of separation. Verses 20–22.

XIV. He went into the Tabernacle, put off his linen garments, washed himself in water, and put on again the rich garments peculiar to his office. Verses 23, 24.

XV. He offered one ram as a burnt-offering for himself, and another for the people. Verse 24.

XVI. He burned the fat of the sin-offerings on the Brazen Altar, and caused their flesh, etc., to be burned without the camp. Verse 25.

XVII. Finally, he washed his hands and his feet at the Laver, and proceeded to offer the evening oblations and to trim the lamps.

Lessons taught by these ceremonies.

These ceremonies are of profound significance, and full of the most important practical instruction But the few following hints and reflections are all that I propose to say for the present concerning them:

1. The remembrance on this day of all the sins of the past year, made it a fit season for deep humiliation, fasting, and prayer. Verses 29–31.

2. It proved the inefficacy of all the daily, weekly, and monthly sacrifices that had been previously offered. Hebrews x, 1–4.

3. The sin-offering for Aaron and his family showed the imperfection of the Levitical Priesthood. Hebrews vii, 27. And hence Aaron was required to lay aside his golden garments, and to enter the Most Holy Place as a suppliant.

4. The use of incense with the blood proves that prayer is necessary in connection with the blood of Christ.

5. The *two* goats fitly illustrate the sin-offering of Christ, which both covers our sins and consigns them to oblivion. Hebrews x, 11–17.

6. The sprinkling of the Golden Altar and the *repeated* sacrifices of the day show that even our prayers and our most solemn acts of worship need the sanctifying influence of atoning blood. "We must not repent," says Matthew Henry, "that we have repented, but we must repent that we have not repented better."

7. Finally, we see in many of these ceremonies much of the polluting nature and influence of sin, and the necessity of the Great Sin-Offering.

THE FEAST OF THE PASSOVER.

This very solemn and interesting festival has already been sufficiently explained in Chapter III of Part II, Book Second, and we will, therefore, now pass on to the consideration of

THE FEAST OF PENTECOST.

This festival is called *the Feast of Weeks* (Exodus xxxiv, 22; Deut. xvi, 9, 16; and 2 Chronicles viii, 13) because it was celebrated seven

Names given to this Festival

complete weeks after the Paschal Sabbath. Leviticus xxiii, 15, 16. It is called *the Feast of Harvest* (Exodus xxiii, 16) because on it were presented the first-fruits of the wheat harvest. Exodus xxxiv, 22; Leviticus xxiii, 17; and Numbers xxviii, 26. The name *Pentecost* (חֲמִשִּׁים יוֹם; Gr., Πεντηκοστὴ ἡμέρα) does not occur in the Old Testament, but it is common in the Jewish writings, (Tobit ii, 1; 2 Macab. xii, 32; Josephus, Jewish Wars, B. II, ch. iii, 1, etc.,) and hence it is the name given to this festival in the New Testament. See Acts ii, 1; xx, 16; and 1 Corinthians xvi, 8. It means simply the *fiftieth*, the word *day* being understood. And as it was reckoned from the

Rule for reckoning the time of the Pentecost.

morrow after the Paschal Sabbath, (Leviticus xxiii, 15, 16,) it would, of course, always occur on *the first day of the week*, but not always on the *sixth day of the month Sivan*, as many modern Jewish writers testify.*

The length of time during which this festival was to

Duration of the Pentecostal Festival.

be continued is not definitely given in the Scriptures. The prescribed ceremonies have all reference to the *fiftieth* day after the Paschal Sabbath, but it usually lasted seven days.

By whom celebrated.

To it, as well as to the Passover and the Feast of Tabernacles, all the able-bodied *male*

Probable Origin of the Pharisees' mode of reckoning it.

* This very prevalent error seems to have originated as follows: The first day of the first Paschal Festival fell on the weekly Sabbath. See *note*, page 98. "The morrow after the Sabbath" would, of course, *that year* fall on the sixteenth of Nisan, and the following Pentecost would be on the sixth of Sivan. And hence it happened that in the course of time, when tradition gained the ascendency over the minds of many, the Pharisees made the original day of the *month*, instead of the prescribed day of the *week*, the basis of their reckoning. But the Sadducees, who discarded all traditions, and who professed to follow the strict interpretation of the inspired text, always reckoned the Pentecost from the first day of the week, or the morrow after the Paschal Sabbath. This rule is also still followed by the Karaites. *Alexander's Kitto's Bibl. Cyc.*

members of the Tribes were required to go up,* and none were allowed to go empty. Every one had to take with him a free-will offering according to his ability. Exodus xxiii, 14–17; xxxiv, 18–23; Deut. xvi, 16, 17.

During their absence from home God promised that he would protect their families and their estates, so that no one would even "*desire*" to invade their territory nor to possess their lands. Exodus xxxiv, 24. What a striking illustration we have here given of the doctrine of God's special providence! Without God's protecting and restraining influence how very easy it would have been on such occasions for the surrounding hostile tribes to have captured the homes of these absent Israelites, and to have enslaved their wives and children! But, nevertheless, history has not recorded a single invasion of their territory during their attendance on these festivals! How plain it is that "*the way of duty is the way of safety!*"

The required solemnities and ceremonies of the day were as follows:

Ceremonies of Pentecost.

I. On this day there was to be held a holy convocation of the people, and they were required to abstain from all servile labor. Leviticus xxiii, 21; and Numbers xxviii, 26.

II. A new meat-offering of the first-fruits of the wheat harvest, consisting of two loaves, (שְׁתֵּי לֶחֶם *scil.* בִּכּוּרוֹת) of *leavened* bread, made of fine flour, of two-tenths of an ephah (7 quarts) each. Leviticus xxiii, 17.

III. A special offering in connection with these loaves, consisting of one young bullock, two rams, and seven lambs of the first year, without blemish, for a burnt-

* The Jewish Doctors say that all *superannuated* men, *sick* men, and boys under *thirteen* years of age were exempt from the requirements of this law.

offering, one kid of the goats for a sin-offering, and two lambs for a peace-offering. Verses 18, 19.

IV. The usual offering of the New Moon, and of each day of the Passover, consisting of two young bullocks, one ram, and seven lambs of the first year, without blemish, for a burnt-offering, one kid for a sin-offering, besides the daily burnt-offerings and their required meat-offerings and drink-offerings. Numbers xxviii, 26–31.*

* Some commentators have alleged that the burnt-offering and the sin-offering described in Leviticus xxiii, 18, 19, were designed to be identical with those that are given in Numbers xxviii, 26–31, and that there is, therefore, a real discrepancy in the two statements. But Josephus evidently regards them as distinct sacrifices. He says, in his Antiquities, B. III, ch. x, sec. 6: "On the fiftieth day, which is Pentecost, they bring to God a loaf made of wheat flour, of two-tenth deals, with leaven. And for sacrifices they bring two lambs, and when they have only presented them to God they are made ready to supper for the Priests; nor is it permitted to leave any thing of them till the following day. They also slay three bullocks for a burnt-offering, and two rams and fourteen lambs, with two kids of the goats for sins." His specifying *two* rams instead of *three* is evidently a mistake, for in the Talmud (Menachoth iv, 3) it is said: "The kind of sacrifice prescribed in Numbers xxviii, 27, was offered in the wilderness, and the kind of sacrifice enjoined in Leviticus xxiii, 18, was not offered in the wilderness; but when they (the Israelites) entered the promised land they offered *both* kinds."

Still more specific and definite is the testimony of the learned Maimonides on this subject. He says: "On the fiftieth day, counting from the offering of the omer, is the feast of Pentecost. Now, on this day additional sacrifices are offered like the additional ones for the New Moon, consisting of two bullocks, one ram, and seven lambs, all of them burnt-offerings, and of a goat as a sin-offering. These are sacrifices ordered in Numbers xxviii, 26, 27, 30, and they constitute the addition for the day. Besides this addition, however, a new meat-offering of two loaves is also brought, and with the loaves are also offered one bullock, two rams, and seven lambs, all burnt-offerings, a goat for a sin-offering, and two lambs for a peace-offering. These are the sacrifices ordered in Leviticus xxiii, 18. Hence the sacrifice on this day exceeds the two daily sacrifices by three bullocks, three rams, fourteen lambs, (all these twenty animals being a burnt-offering,) two goats for a sin-offering, which are eaten, and two lambs for a peace-offering, which are not eaten." (*Iad Ha Chezaka Hilchoth Tamidin U-Mosaphin.*) Hence I think that the alleged discrepancy in this case, as in most others, is only apparent, and that both the sacrifices were offered as Josephus, Maimonides, and the authors of the Talmud testify.

The design of this festival, like that of the Passover, seems to have been threefold:

Threefold object of the Feast of Pentecost.

I. *It was a sort of Harvest-Home;* and as such had a very great influence on the moral, social, and religious education of the people, and especially did it serve to cultivate in their hearts sentiments of gratitude to the bountiful giver of the harvest, and, indeed, of every other blessing. Deuteronomy xvi, 9–12.

II. *It is probable that it was also designed to commemorate the giving of the Law from Mount Sinai.* True, indeed, this is no where specially stated in the Bible. But it is according to the testimony of the most distinguished Jewish writers on this subject, as well as of many of the Christian fathers. Maimonides says: "Pentecost is the day on which the Law was given. . . . And because this great manifestation did not last more than one day, therefore we annually commemorate it only one day." More Nebuchim III, 43.

III. But whatever may be thought of its commemorative design, there can, I think, be no doubt that *its main object was typical.* Its definite and specific relations to the Passover, as well as the ceremonies of the day, all seem to mark it out as the day when "the Law of the Spirit of life in Christ Jesus" should be proclaimed in all its fullness from Mount Zion, Isaiah ii, 3; and the first-fruits of the world's great harvest should be presented as a thank-offering to God. Acts ii, 41. And hence the converts of that day are, by Paul in Romans xi, 16, called the first-fruits of the Jewish nation. And from this he argues that as the first-fruits had been offered and accepted, so now the whole mass of the people were in a *legal* sense holy, and might also be converted to Christ and made heirs of the Kingdom of Heaven.

THE FEAST OF TABERNACLES.

Names given to the third Annual Festival.

This festival was so called because during its continuance all the Israelites were commanded to live in booths, tents, or tabernacles. Lev. xxiii, 42, 43. It was also called *the Feast of Ingathering*, Exodus xxiii, 16; Deut. xvi, 13, etc., because it was held after both the harvest and the vintage were completed.

Time of its commencement and duration.

It commenced on the fifteenth day of the seventh month, and continued seven days. The eighth day, called in John vii, 37, "the great day of the Feast," was not, strictly speaking, a part of the festival. It was rather an appendix to it; a *sabbath* designed to be a solemn winding up of the festive season. And hence it became to the Jews one of the most solemn and interesting days of the whole year. See Leviticus xxiii, 33–43; and Deut. xvi, 13–17.

Use made of various kinds of branches.

From Nehemiah viii, 13–17, it seems that the tents were made out of olive branches, pine branches, myrtle branches, palm branches, and branches of thick trees. They were, of course, constructed previous to the fifteenth day of the month, for that day was a *sabbath*, and on it all servile work was forbidden. But on it the people were required to take in their hands boughs of goodly or stately trees, branches of palm-trees, boughs of thick trees or mountain shrubs, and willows of the brook, most likely to symbolize the different kinds of vegetation in the wilderness and in Canaan.

Sacrifices offered during this Festival.

The required sacrifices of this festival were as follows: On the first day there were offered thirteen bullocks, two rams, and fourteen lambs for a burnt-offering, with the usual meat-offerings and drink-offerings, and a kid of the goats for a sin-offering, beside the required daily offerings. On each of the following days the same number of rams, lambs, and kids was offered; but the number of bullocks was reduced by one every day, so that on the seventh only seven bullocks were offered. And hence during the seven days of the festival there were offered 70 bullocks, 14 rams, 98 lambs, and 7 kids, with 33 3-5 ephahs of flour, 64 1-6 hins of oil, and 64 1-6 hins of wine; that is, about 36 3-4 bushels of flour, 80 5-24 gallons of oil, and the same quantity of wine,* beside the usual burnt-offerings and their meat-offerings and drink-offerings.

Offerings of the eighth day.

The offerings of the eighth day were one bullock, one ram, and seven lambs of the first year for a burnt-offering, with the required meat and drink-offerings, and one kid for a sin-offering. Numbers xxix, 12-38.

Later ceremonies of the Festival.

In later times it was customary to pour profusely on the temple courts water drawn from the pool of Siloam, while the people were rejoicing and the Levites were singing Psalms cxiii-cxviii. In the evenings they illuminated the court of the Women and sung Psalms cxx-cxxxvi. To these customs there seems to be an allusion in John vii, 37-39; viii, 12, etc.

Design of the Feast of Tabernacles.

The design of this festival was,

I. *To commemorate Israel's sojourn in the wilderness.* Leviticus xxiii, 43.

II. *To give to them a suitable opportunity for national and social praise and thanksgiving, after all the products of the year had been collected together.* Deut.

* An ephah, according to Gesenius, etc., is equal to 35 quarts, or one bushel and three quarts; others make it equal to but 3 pecks and 3 pints. *Jahn's Bibl. Arch.*, § 131. A hin is equal to 5 quarts nearly.

xvi, 13-15. And hence, like the Feast of the Passover and the Feast of Pentecost, it had a powerful influence on the moral and religious education of the entire nation.

III. *To keep all Christians mindful of the fact that, like the Israelites, we are still dwelling in tents, but that we are traveling to a city which has foundations whose builder and maker is God.* See Zechariah xiv, 16–21.

THE SABBATICAL YEAR.

Names given to the Sabbatical Year.

This Institution is called ***the Sabbath of Sabbatism,*** (שַׁבַּת שַׁבָּתוֹן,) Leviticus xxv, 4; *the Year of Sabbatism,* Leviticus xxv, 5; *the Year of Release,* Deut. xv, 1, 2, 9; *the Seventh Year,* Deut. xv, 9; and in the Hebrew Canons it is called, by way of eminence, simply *the Seventh.*

Time of its commencement.

The time of the commencement of this year is somewhat uncertain. But it is generally thought that it began with the Feast of Trumpets, on the first day of the month Tishri. So Maimonides and other Jewish Doctors testify; though, from Deut. xxxi, 10, it would seem that the month Tishri was rather the *end* than the beginning of the Sabbatical year. The words of Moses are as follows: "At the *end,*" (מִקֵּץ, מִן, *from, in,* or *at,* and קֵץ, *the end,* from קָצַץ, *to cut off;* compare Genesis iv, 3; viii, 6; xvi, 3; xli, 1, etc.) And when it is remembered that this Institution, so far as it respected the Israelites, had reference chiefly to their agricultural interests and employments, I think it worthy of consideration whether the seventh year did not commence with the beginning of their agricultural labors, and end after these were all brought to a close; just as our *collegiate* or *fiscal* year may begin and end at any period of the *civil* year. If so, it may have commenced either immediately after the Feast of Tabernacles or with the beginning of the month following. For in southern Palestine the Israelites commenced preparing the ground for the seed as soon as the autumnal rains had sufficiently mollified it. This generally occurred about the last of Tishri, which on this account was called also Ethanim, (אֵיתָנִים ;) that is, the month of *perpetuities* or of *flowing brooks.* 1 Kings viii, 2. By the end of October, then, or about the beginning of the eighth month, Bul or Marcheshvan, the ground was generally ready to receive the seed ; "and the sowing of wheat continued in different situations through November into December. Barley was not generally sown till January and February." Alex. Kitto's Bibl. Cyc., Art. Agriculture.

The law of the Sabbatical year required,

Things required by the Law of this Institution.

I. That on it all agricultural operations should be suspended. Exodus xxiii, 10, 11 ; Levit. xxv, 2–5.

II. That the spontaneous productions of the year should be free for the use of the poor, the hirelings, the strangers, and the cattle. Ex. xxiii, 11 ; Levit. xxv, 5–7.

III. That at the beginning of the year all debts should be remitted. Deut. xv, 1–3. This release of the debtor was final and absolute. Talmud, Shebiith x, 1–5, etc.

IV. That during the Feast of Tabernacles, at the end of the year, the whole Law should be read to all the people, men, women, and children ; and even to those that were strangers and sojourners in the land. Deut. xxxi, 10–13.

Its Design.

The design of this Institution is not specifically stated in the Holy Scriptures. But from all that is said concerning it, we think it probable that it was intended,

I. *To teach the Israelites that God is the only rightful proprietor of the soil, and that they were but his tenants.*

II. *To teach them to be more trustful in God's providence, and to be more liberal and benevolent to each other as the servants of God.*

III. *To typify and illustrate more fully the "rest that remains for the people of God,"* and to magnify its importance and significance as an element of the Scheme of Redemption.

Neglect of it.

That this Institution was much neglected by the Hebrews, especially before the captivity, is evident from comparing Leviticus xxvi, 27–36, with 2 Chronicles xxxvi, 21. But that it was observed to some extent—sufficiently so to test God's fidelity to his promises—is proved,

Evidence of its observance.

I. *From the implied testimony of the Scriptures themselves.* The Sabbatical years, including the years of Jubilee, from Moses to the captivity, were about one hundred and thirty-seven. And as God charges the Israelites, in the preceding reference, with having neglected but seventy of these years, it is fair to presume that they had faithfully kept the remaining sixty-seven, or nearly one-half of the entire number.

II. *From the first Book of Maccabees*, vi, 49. The author, while speaking of the war between Judas Maccabæus and Antiochus Eupator, the son and successor of Antiochus Epiphanes, says: "Then the King's army went up to Jerusalem to meet them (the Jews;) and the King pitched his tents in Judea and against Mount Zion. But with them of Bethsura he made peace; for they came out of the city, because they had no victuals there to endure the siege, it being *a year of rest to the land.*"

III. *From the testimony of Josephus.* Speaking of

Alexander the Great and of his visit to Jerusalem, he says: "And when the Book of Daniel was showed him, wherein Daniel declared that one of the Greeks would destroy the empire of the Persians, he supposed that he himself was the person intended. And as he was then glad, he dismissed the multitude for the present; but the next day he called them to him, and bid them ask what favors they pleased of him. Whereupon the High Priest desired that they might enjoy the laws of their forefathers, and might pay no tribute *on the seventh year.* He granted all they desired." Antiq., Book XI, ch. viii, sec. 5.

Again, the same author, quoting from the decrees of Julius Cæsar in reference to the Jews, says: "Caius Cæsar, Imperator the second time, has ordained that a. the country of the Jews, excepting Joppa, do pay a tribute yearly for the city of Jerusalem; excepting the *seventh, which they call the Sabbatical year,* because thereon they neither receive the fruits of their trees, nor do they sow their land." Antiquities, Book XIV, ch. x, sec. 6.

IV. *From the testimony of Tacitus.* In Book V, sec. 4, of his History, he writes as follows: "Septimo die otium placuisse ferunt; quia is finem laborum tulerit: dein, blandiente inertiâ, *septimum quoque annum ignaviæ datum.*" "They" (the Jews) "give the seventh day to ease, because it puts an end to labors: moreover, through the allurements of idleness, *the seventh year is also given to inactivity.*"

THE YEAR OF JUBILEE.

Meaning and Etymology of the word Jubilee.

The etymology of the word Jubilee (יוֹבֵל) is somewhat doubtful. In the Targum of Jonathan, the Talmud, and other Rabbinical writings, it is supposed to denote primarily *a ram.* Gesenius calls this "an absurd conjecture," and derives the word from יָבַל, *to shout for joy and triumph.* He thinks that this year was so called because it was introduced on the evening of the Day of Atonement with the sound of a trumpet and shoutings throughout the whole land. See Levit. xxv, 9. This is also the view taken by Dr. Julius Fuerst, and is most likely correct.

The law of this Institution is given in Leviticus xxv, 8–55, and provided,

Laws respecting the Jubilee.

I. That it should be celebrated every fiftieth year, beginning on the tenth day of the seventh month.* Verses 8, 9.

II. That at the beginning of this year all Israelites who, through poverty or otherwise, had become slaves should go free. Verses 10, 39–43.

III. That during this year the land should remain fallow or uncultivated, as it had during the seven preceding Sabbatical years. Verses 11, 12.

IV. That all unredeemed lands, houses in the country and villages, and also the Levitical houses in the cities, should, at the beginning of this year, be restored to their original owners. Verses 23–34.

The design of the Year of Jubilee seems to have been fourfold:

For what purposes it was instituted.

I. *To remind the Jews that God was the only rightful owner and proprietor of their*

* Many Rabbinical writers allege that the year of Jubilee commenced like the Sabbatical year, with the Feast of Trumpets, on the first day of the seventh month. But they say that, from the Feast of Trumpets till the Day of Atonement, the slaves were neither allowed to return to their homes, nor were they used by their masters; but they ate, and drank, and rejoiced, and wore garlands on their heads. On the evening of the Day of Atonement the Judges first blew their trumpets; and this was followed by nine blasts on rams' horns from every Israelite; so that the trumpet was literally sounded throughout the whole land, from Dan to Beersheba. Then the slaves were manumitted, and the lands were set free. Mishna, Maimonides, etc.

lands; and that they, as his tenants, were allowed to hold their estates on certain conditions. Verse 23.

II. *To remind them of their own equality as the sons of Israel and the subjects of Jehovah.* And hence, according to the law of this Institution, no Israelite could be retained in servitude contrary to his own will beyond a limited period.

III. *To cultivate a sense of their dependence on God and of their obligations to him.* For this purpose the extraordinary fruitfulness of the second year preceding the Jubilee was peculiarly well adapted. See verses 20–22.

IV. *The Jubilee served to magnify even more than the Sabbatical Year the great importance of our release from Sin, and of the liberty, rights, and immunities of which we have even now an earnest and a foretaste in and through Christ; but which we can never fully appreciate and enjoy till all the conflicts of life are over, and this whole Earth, purified by fire, shall have been restored to the redeemed as their proper and rightful inheritance.* See Isaiah lxi, 1–3; Romans iv, 13; Hebrews ii, 5–9; Rev. v, 10, and xxi.

Proof from this Institution of the Divine Legation of Moses.

Finally, we have in this Institution, as well as in the Sabbatical Year, the most clear and convincing evidence of the Divine legation of Moses, and also, indeed, of the Divine origin of the whole Bible. For surely no legislator, unless conscious of being Divinely inspired, would have committed himself by enacting such a law as this. And hence we find nothing like it in all the other systems of ancient jurisprudence. "How incredible it is," says Dr. Graves, in his Lectures on the Pentateuch, Vol. I, p. 230, "that any legislator would have ventured to propose such a law as this, except in consequence of the fullest conviction on both sides that

Remarks of Dean Graves on this subject.

peculiar providence would constantly facilitate its execution. When this law, therefore, was proposed and received, such a conviction must have existed in both the Jewish Legislator and the Jewish people. Since, then, nothing could have produced this conviction but the experience or the belief of some such miraculous interposition as the history of the Pentateuch details, the very existence of this law is a standing monument that when it was given the Mosaic miracles were fully believed. Now this law was coeval with the witnesses themselves. If, then, the facts were so plain and public that those who witnessed them could not be mistaken as to their existence and miraculous nature, the reality of the Mosaic miracles is clear and undeniable."

Much more might be said on the subject of Legal Types. But all the main points, principles, and provisions of this part of the Mosaic system have, I think, been sufficiently illustrated for our present purpose, and in the next chapter we shall therefore again take up the subject of Historical Types, as this is illustrated in the further journeyings and pilgrimage of the Israelites.

CHAPTER VII.

FROM THE GIVING OF THE LAW AT MOUNT SINAI TO THE REST IN CANAAN.

SECTION I.—Journey from Sinai to the Jordan.

Scope of the Book of Numbers.

In the Book of Numbers we have an account of the numbering of the Israelites, the order of their march and encampment, and the leading events and incidents of their journey from

Mount Sinai to the banks of the Jordan. To the very brief consideration of these matters I now invite the attention of the reader. We will begin with their numbering and the order of their encampment. The following diagram will furnish to the reader a synopsis of the main points of the narrative contained in the first four chapters:

Number of the several Tribes, and Order of their Encampment.

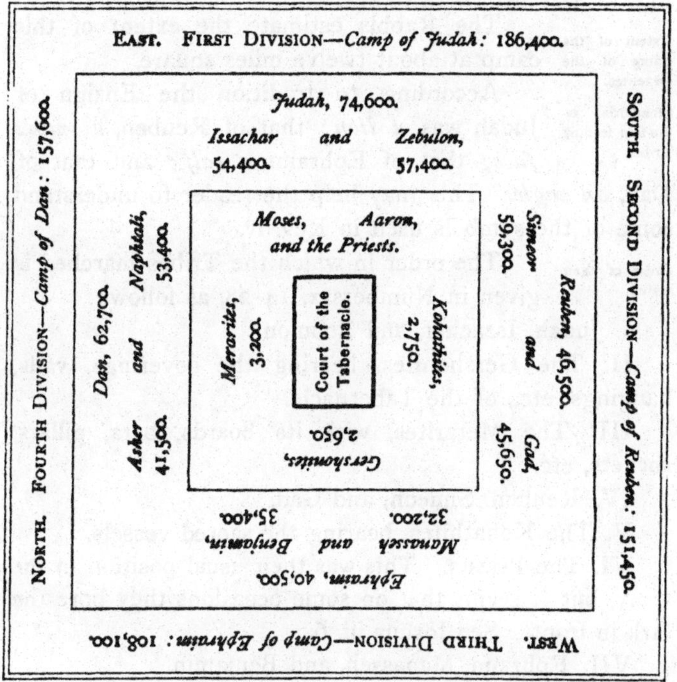

In the preceding estimate the Levites are numbered from thirty to fifty years of age, according to Numbers xiv, 34–45, and the other tribes from twenty to the age when they were free from

Ages to and from which the Tribes were numbered.

military service. The Scriptures no where define this limit, but the Rabbis fix it at the age of sixty.

Reckoned from a month old and upward, the number of the Kohathites, as before stated, was 8,600; the Merarites 6,200; and the Gershonites 7,500; making in all 22,300, 22,000 of whom were exchanged for the first-born, the remaining 300 being, no doubt, the first-born of the Levites.

Extent of the Camp of the Israelites.

The Rabbis estimate the extent of this camp at about twelve miles square.

Standards of the four leading Tribes.

According to tradition the Ensign of Judah was *a lion;* that of Reuben, *a man's face;* that of Ephraim, *a calf;* and that of Dan, *an eagle.* This may help the reader to understand some of the symbols used in Rev. iv.

Order of their march.

The order in which the Tribes marched is given in Numbers x, 14–28, as follows:

I. Judah, Issachar, and Zebulon.

II. The Gershonites, bearing the coverings, vails, hangings, etc., of the Tabernacle.

III. The Merarites, with its boards, bars, pillars, sockets, etc.

IV. Reuben, Simeon, and Gad.

V. The Kohathites, bearing the sacred vessels.

VI. The Priests. This was their usual position in the army, but it seems that on some occasions they bore the Ark in front. See Joshua iii, 6.

VII. Ephraim, Manasseh, and Benjamin.

VIII. Dan, Asher, and Naphtali.

The signal for marching.

The signal for marching was always the removal of the Cloud from the Tabernacle. Numbers ix, 21, 22. The sounding of the silver trumpets (Numbers x, 1–10) was merely to indicate the time when the several divisions were required to move. Thus, for instance, on the sounding of the first alarm the camp of Judah moved forward; on the second, that of Reuben, etc.

Sounding of the two Silver Trumpets.

The people remained at Sinai one year, lacking ten days. Compare Exodus xix, 1, and Numbers x, 11. But, all things having been prepared, the signal for marching was now given. The Cloud was taken up from the Tabernacle, and the people moved forward,

Time spent at Sinai.

Principal stations and events in the order of their march.

I. To Taberah, in the wilderness of Paran. Here the Lord consumed some of them for complaining, and hence the name Taberah, which means *burning*. From Taberah they moved forward,

II. To Kibroth-Hattaavah. Numbers xxxiii, 16. Here we have an account,

1. Of the people's murmuring.

2. Of the appointment of seventy Elders to assist Moses in the general administration of the government, etc. These Elders were chosen from among those who had been previously elected as chiliarchs, centurions, etc. Exodus xviii, 24–26.

3. Of a supply of quails.

4. Of the people's eating to excess.

5. Of the plague sent on them. And hence this place was called Kibroth-Hattaavah, which means *the graves of lust*. Numbers xi, 1–34.

III. To Hazeroth. Numbers xi, 34. Here Aaron and Miriam were guilty of sedition. Numbers xii, 1-15.

IV. To Kadesh Barnea, in the desert of Paran. Numbers xii, 16. Here we have an account,

1. Of the sending out of twelve men to spy out the land of Canaan. Numbers xiii 1–15. In this case

every Tribe had a representative except the Tribe of Levi.

2. Of the evil report brought back by ten of the spies.

3. Of the weeping, murmuring, and rebellion of the people.

4. Of God's purpose to cast them off.

5. Of the intercession of Moses in their behalf.

6. Of God's judgment on all the murmurers over twenty years of age.

7. Of the death, by a plague, of the ten spies that brought back an evil report.

8. Of the purpose and determination of the people to go up and possess the land.

9. Of their rout by the Amalekites and the Canaanites. See Numbers xiii and xiv. Here also, most likely, occurred the events that are recorded in the fifteenth, sixteenth, seventeenth, eighteenth, and nineteenth chapters, for it is said in Deut. i, 46, that the people abode in Kadesh many days.

V. To Rithma. Numbers xxxiii, 18.

VI. To Rimmon-Parez. Numbers xxxiii, 19.

VII. To Libnah. Numbers xxxiii, 20.

VIII. To Rissah. Numbers xxxiii, 21.

IX. To Kehelathah. Numbers xxxiii, 22.

X. To Mount Shapher. Numbers xxxiii, 23.

XI. To Haradah. Numbers xxxiii, 24.

XII. To Mackheloth. Numbers xxxiii, 25.

XIII. To Tahath. Numbers xxxiii, 26.

XIV. To Tarah. Numbers xxxiii, 27.

XV. To Mithcah. Numbers xxxiii, 28.

XVI. To Hashmonah. Numbers xxxiii, 29.

XVII. To Moseroth. Numbers xxxiii, 30.

XVIII. To Bene-jaakan. Numbers xxxiii, 31.

XIX. To Hor-Hagidgad. Numbers xxxiii, 32.

XX. To Jotbathah. Numbers xxxiii, 33.

XXI. To Ebronah. Numbers xxxiii, 34.

XXII. To Ezion-Gaber. Numbers xxxiii, 35.

XXIII. To Kadesh-Barnea again. Numbers xxxiii, 36. Here occurred several events worthy of notice, as we learn from Numbers xx, 1-21.

1. Here Miriam died.

2. The people again murmured for water. Hence the place was called, also, Kadesh Meribah, "because the Children of Israel here *strove* with the Lord."

3. Waters were supplied from the rock.

4. Sentence against Moses and Aaron.

5. Message to the King of Edom, and his reply.

XXIV. To Beeroth. Deuteronomy x, 6.

XXV. To Mount Hor, (Numbers xx, 22,) and encamped at Mosera. Deut. x, 6. Here it was,

1. That Aaron died.

2. That Eleazar was made High Priest.

3. That the Israelites gained a victory over Arad the Canaanite. Numbers xxi, 1–3.

XXVI. To Gudgodah. Deut. x, 7.

XXVII. To Jotbath. Deut. x, 8.

XXVIII. To Elath and Ezion-gaber, by the way of the Red Sea. Numbers xxi, 4, and Deut. ii, 8.

XXIX. To Zalmonah. Numbers xxxiii, 41. Here occurred the Plague of the fiery Serpents. Numbers xxi, 4–9.

XXX. To Punon. Numbers xxxiii, 42.

XXXI. To Oboth. Numbers xxi, 10.

XXXII. To Ije-abarim. Numbers xxi, 11.

XXXIII. To the brook Zered. Numbers xxi, 12.

XXXIV. To the brook Arnon. Numbers xxi, 13.

XXXV. To Dibon-gad. Numbers xxxiii, 45.

XXXVI. To Almon-Diblathaim. Num. xxxiii, 46

XXXVII. To Beer, in the desert. Numbers xxi, 16.

XXXVIII. To Mattanah. Numbers xxi, 18.

XXXIX. To Nahaliel. Numbers xxi, 19.

XL. To Bamoth. Numbers xxi, 21.

XLI. To Mount Pisgah, here put for the range of mountains called Abarim. Numbers xxi, 20, and xxxiii, 47. While here they conquered Sihon, king of the Amorites.

XLII. To the plains of Moab, by the way of Bashan Numbers xxi, 33, and xxii, 1. Here it was,

1. That Balaam prophesied concerning Israel. Numbers xxii–xxiv.

2. That the Israelites fell into idolatry, and 24,000 of them perished by a plague, (Numbers xxv, 9,) 23,000 in one day. 1 Cor. x, 8.

3. That the people were numbered a second time from twenty years of age and upward, showing a decrease in thirty-eight years of 603,550—601,730=1820. Here, also, the Levites were again numbered from a month old and upward, showing an increase over the first census of 23,000—22,273=727 Numbers xxvi, 1–65.

4. Here Moses delivered his great valedictory, consisting of the first thirty-three chapters of the Book of Deuteronomy. Deut. i, 1.

5. Near this, also, Moses died on the top of Pisgah, a peak of Mount Nebo, which is one of the mountains of Abarim. Deut. xxxiv, 5–8.

SECTION II.—THE ISRAELITES UNDER JOSHUA.

First Orders of Joshua.

After the death of Moses, Joshua, at the command of God, took charge of the host of

Israel, (Joshua i, 1–9,) and gave orders for them to prepare to cross the Jordan. Verses 10–15.

Crossing of the Jordan.

"And it came to pass when the people moved from their tents," on the third day, "to pass over Jordan, and the Priests bearing the Ark of the Covenant before the people; *and as they that bare the Ark were come unto Jordan, and the feet of the Priests that bare the Ark were dipped in the brim of the water,* (for Jordan overfloweth all his banks at the time of harvest,) *that the waters which came down from above stood and rose up upon a heap very far from the city Adam, that is beside Zaretan;* and those that came down toward the Sea of the plain, even the Salt Sea, failed and were cut off; and the people passed over right against Jericho. And the Priests that bare the Ark of the Covenant of the Lord stood firm on dry ground in the midst of Jordan, and all the Israelites passed over on dry ground, until all the people were passed clean over Jordan.*" Joshua iii, 14–17. "*For the Priests who bare the Ark stood in the midst of Jordan, until every thing was finished that the Lord commanded Joshua to speak unto the people, according to all that Moses commanded Joshua; and the people hasted and passed over. And it came to pass, when all the people were clean passed over, that the Ark of God passed over, and the Priests, in the presence of the people.*" Joshua iv, 10, 11.

Conquest and Division of Canaan.

Very soon after this the conquest of Canaan was commenced with the fall of Jericho, Josh. v, 13; vi, 24; and in about seven years thirty-one of its kings were subdued, Josh. xii, 24,

* The meaning of this somewhat obscure passage seems to be this: that the waters, being arrested by the passage of the Ark, formed a wall above it, and filled up the channel of the river as far up as Zaretan, supposed to be about thirty miles above the place of crossing.

and the land divided by lot among the twelve Tribes of Israel. Joshua xiii–xix.

Objections urged against this part of Sacred History.

Perhaps no other chapter of the Divine administration has been subject to so much censure and animadversion as that in which we have an account of the conquest of Canaan by Joshua. Infidels of all classes have objected to the extirpation of the Canaanites and the division of their land among the Israelites as "cruel," "unjust," "inhuman," "barbarous," etc. And the ancient Gnostics were wont to refer constantly to this part of Sacred history to prove that the God or Demiurgus of the Old Testament was not the same as the God of the New.

Allegations of some Jewish and Christian writers.

That this objection has not been urged without having some effect on the public mind is evident from the very unsatisfactory manner in which it has been responded to by some Jewish and Christian writers. It has been urged, for instance, most likely from a false interpretation of Deut. xxxii, 8, that the Israelites had a prior claim to the land of Canaan; that it was, in fact, given to them by "the Most High" when he separated the sons of Adam and divided to the nations their inheritance; and, consequently, that in the conquest of Canaan Joshua was but subduing a set of *usurpers*, and vindicating the rights originally guaranteed to the Hebrews by Jehovah himself.

An attempt has also been made to still further soften and justify the apparent severity of the Israelites in this case by asserting that "Joshua sent three letters to the land of the Canaanites before the Israelites invaded it, or rather he proposed three things to them by letters: that those who preferred flight might escape; that those who wished for peace might enter into covenant; and that such as were for war might take up arms."*

But all this is utterly inconsistent with the plain instructions and obvious purpose of Jehovah with regard to these abandoned idolaters. Of this the following passages furnish sufficient evidence: "I will set my bounds from the Red Sea even unto the sea of the Philistines, and from the desert unto the river: for I will deliver the inhabitants of the land into your hand; *and thou shalt drive them out before thee. Thou shalt make no covenant with them, nor with their gods. They shall not dwell in thy land, lest they make thee sin against me:* for if thou serve their gods it will surely be a snare unto thee." Exodus xxiii, 31–33. "And he [God] said, Behold, I make a covenant: before all thy people I will do marvels, such as has not been done in all the Earth: and all the people among whom thou art shall see the work of the Lord: for it is a terrible thing that I will do with thee. *Observe thou that which I command thee this day. Behold, I drive out before thee the Amorite, and the Canaanite, and the Hittite, and the Perizzite, and the Hivite, and the Jebusite. Take heed to thyself, lest thou make a covenant with the inhabitants of the land whither thou goest, lest it be for a snare in the midst of thee. But ye shall destroy their altars, break their images, and cut down their groves:* for thou shalt worship no other God; for the Lord, whose name is Jealous, is a jealous God: lest thou make a covenant with the inhabitants of the land, and they go a whoring after their gods, and do sacrifice unto their gods; and one call thee, and thou eat of his sacrifice; and thou take their daughters unto thy sons, and their daughters

These Allegations not satisfactory. Why?

* Nachman, quoted by Selden de Jure Nat., etc., L. vi, c. 13.

go a whoring after their gods, and make thy sons go a whoring after their gods." Exodus xxxiv, 10–16. "*But of the cities of these people, which the Lord thy God doth give thee for an inheritance, thou shalt save alive nothing that breatheth; but thou shalt utterly destroy them: namely, the Hittites, and the Amorites, the Canaanites, and the Perizzites, the Hivites, and the Jebusites; as the Lord thy God hath commanded thee:* that they teach you not to do after all their abominations, which they have done unto their gods; so should you sin against the Lord your God." Deut. xx, 16–18.

Right of the Amorites, etc., to the Land of Canaan recognized.

It is evident, therefore, that the Hebrews were not allowed to make any covenant or compromise with the Canaanites. Their doom was irrevocably sealed before the Israelites crossed the Jordan, but not till they had first filled up the cup of their iniquity. This they had not done in the time of Abraham. Genesis xv, 16. And hence God did not allow even that distinguished patriarch to possess a foot of their land, save what he bought as a mere burying-place, and for which he gave a fair equivalent. Acts vii, 5; and Genesis xxiii, 3–20.

When and how these claims were forfeited.

But God foresaw that the time would come when the Canaanites, by filling up the cup of their iniquity, would have forfeited all just claims on his bounty, his mercy, and his benevolence; and when they would, in fact, be as ripe for destruction as were the Antediluvians when he swept them away by a deluge; and as were the inhabitants of Sodom and Gomorrah when he rained down on them fire and brimstone from heaven. And that they had actually done this before Joshua crossed the Jordan is evident from Leviticus xviii, and sundry other passages of Scripture.

No unusual severity was therefore ever exercised by Divine authority toward these Canaanites. They were cut off by virtue of *a moral necessity*, and in harmony with a principle of justice that pervades the whole Divine administration. "He that despised Moses' law died without mercy under two or three witnesses." Hebrews x, 28; and Numbers xv, 30, 31. And the same principle is frequently recognized as a law of the New Institution. See, for instance, Proverbs xxix, 1; Matthew xii, 31, 32; Hebrews vi, 4–6; x, 26–29; 1 John v, 16.

Destruction of the Canaanites in harmony with God's general Administration.

There was, moreover, in the case of the Canaanites, *a typical necessity* that they should be destroyed. As we have already said, the Old Institution was in its history, as well as in its laws and ordinances, a type or shadow of the New. 1 Corinthians x, 1–12; and Hebrews, *passim*. The bondage of the Israelites in Egypt seems to have been intended as a type of our bondage in sin previous to our conversion. Their emancipation by Moses was symbolical of our deliverance by Christ. And just so the rest of the Children of Israel in Canaan fitly represented the rest that all the Children of Abraham, by faith, will enjoy on this Earth as their regained Paradise, after that it shall have been dissolved by fire, and thus freed from all its dross and impurities. See Romans iv, 13–16; Hebrews ii, 5–9; Matthew v, 5; Revelation v, 10, and xxi.

Further evidence from Typology.

But in the final conflagration the wicked inhabitants of the Earth will all be destroyed. See 2 Peter iii, 7; and 2 Thessalonians i, 6–10. And hence it seems probable that the destruction of the Canaanites by Joshua was intended to be a type of the baptism in fire which shall befall the wicked when our greater Joshua shall come to be admired by his saints, and to lead them into the possession and enjoyment of the eternal inheritance.

PART III.

HISTORICAL DEVELOPMENTS FROM THE DEATH OF JOSHUA TO THE BIRTH OF CHRIST.

CHAPTER I.

JEWISH DEMONSTRATIONS.

IT has been often said that "*History is but Philosophy teaching by example.*" This remark is certainly true within certain limits; and it explains to us, moreover, why it is that so much of the Bible is taken up with matters of history. Very few persons can ever become philosophers. Their talents and learning are not sufficient to enable them to grasp and comprehend principles in the abstract. But all responsible persons can at least apprehend a fact; and most of them can be made to understand and comprehend it as an *exponent* of some law or principle. In this way the elements of most sciences are taught and illustrated; and hence it pleased God to place the Jews under law, and then to allow them to work out historically certain great problems for the benefit of mankind. The invention of a religious nomenclature was in a great measure completed with the giving of the law. And Moses may be said to have finished this work before he expired on the top of Pisgah. And hence we find that both Prophets and Apostles refer

Why so much of the Bible is taken up with History.

Problems to be demonstrated historically by the Jews.

constantly to the Pentateuch for terms to express their religious ideas. But other questions required more time for their solution. Nothing short of a long series of experiments, made under the most favorable circumstances, could satisfactorily prove to mankind their own utter inability to attain to justification and sanctification by works of law, and to demonstrate in just and adequate terms the exceeding sinfulness of sin, and the necessity of holiness as a condition and means of happiness. These and other like problems, preliminary to the full development of the Scheme of Redemption, were committed to the Jews, and about fifteen hundred years were allowed for their solution.

How the facts of Jewish History are to be regarded.

The history of the Jews during this period is, therefore, a subject of intense interest to every student of human nature, and of the laws and principles of the Divine government. To the enlightened Christian philosopher every fact embraced in it is an exponent of some great principle, just as the fall of an apple was to the mind of Sir Isaac Newton an exponent of the laws of universal gravitation.

Magnitude of this subject.

But on the discussion of this subject we can not now enter. To do it justice would require at least a respectable octavo; and I must, therefore, simply request the reader to study for himself all the historical and prophetical books of the Old Testament, from the beginning of the Book of Judges to the end of Malachi. He will there find developed, under a great variety of circumstances, all the principles and proclivities of the human heart. He will see the actual workings of God's providence and the operations of the Divine government on both the penitent and the impenitent; and, unless he is blinded by prejudice and infatuated through the influence of his own

Conclusions drawn from the historical and prophetical Books.

false philosophy, he will finally conclude, with Paul, that by the deeds of law no flesh living can be justified, and that a system of redemption by grace through faith is indispensable in order to the salvation of mankind. See Paul's Epistles to the Romans and the Galatians, *passim.*

CHAPTER II.

GENTILE DEMONSTRATIONS.

As we before intimated, the Gentiles had also a certain work to accomplish. To them were also committed for solution some very important problems; *and particularly the problem of ascertaining whether or not Natural Religion is adequate to the wants of our fallen race.*

Problems committed to the Gentiles.

To the investigation of this subject the most learned of the heathen world have ever devoted their main energies. But, having all descended from Noah,* the father of the postdiluvian world, it is not probable that any of them, save, perhaps,

Tradition of the One Living and True God.

* The unity of mankind may be proved,

I. From the direct testimony of the Scriptures. In Acts xvii 26, for example, it is said that "God has made of one blood all nations of men to dwell on the face of the Earth, and has determined the times before appointed, and the bounds of their habitation." This, be it remembered, is a part of Paul's speech before an assembly of philosophers, and in opposition to all the systems of caste that were then prevalent. And hence the word "*all*" in this quotation admits of no limitation whatever. See, also, Genesis ix, 18, 19, etc.

Evidence that all mankind are of one species.

II. From the fact that all men are endowed with the same physical, intellectual, moral, and religious faculties. Men differ much in their size, strength, color, etc., but the same powers and susceptibilities belong to all.

III. From the fact that Christ took upon himself the nature of but one species, and yet he is said to have "tasted death for every man." Hebrews ii, some of the most degraded, would ever lose entirely their knowledge of the one only living and true God, received

9; John iii, 16. But if, as some allege, the human race is not a unit, then we would ask, For what species of mankind did Christ die, and whose nature did he assume?

IV. From the fact that God has given to mankind but one moral and religious code or system, and that this has been found to be equally adapted to the wants and happiness of all. See Romans i, 16; Revelation xiv, 6, etc.

V. From the fact that hybrids, such as mules, etc., have not the capacity to propagate their kind. But all the varieties of mankind intermarry and propagate the human species.

VI. From the fact that all mankind were originally of one language. This is the testimony not only of Moses, but also of all the profane ancient historians who treat of this subject.

VII. From the fact that all mankind, save Noah and his family, were destroyed by the Flood. I am aware that the universality of the Noachic Deluge has been denied by many modern writers, and especially by Geologists. But I do not see how this hypothesis can be well reconciled with the language of Moses in Genesis vii, 19–23, and ix, 8–17; and also with the testimony of Peter as it is given in the third chapter of his second epistle. Whatever the Word of God teaches, when fairly interpreted, must be received as true, though it should seem to conflict with all the received dogmas of Natural Science. We are not of that School that would limit the exercise of God's miraculous power by the comparatively feeble instrumentality of second causes.

VIII. From the fact that no satisfactory division of their "*genus homo*" has ever been made by the advocates of a plurality of species. These gentlemen can not agree among themselves either as to the *number* of species that compose the human race, or as to the true and proper *basis* of such a division and classification of mankind. Some, making color alone the ground of their classification, would have us believe that there are three species of the "*genus homo*;" others make five, others ten, and others, again, affirm that there are as many as fifteen, sixteen, or seventeen. It would be well, then, for such vain speculators to agree among themselves touching these points before they call on us to renounce the plain teachings of the Bible for their baseless hypotheses.

IX. From the fact that the unity of the human race is taught in all systems of heathen mythology that treat of the origin of mankind. They all, in effect, testify as follows: That the first parents of the human race, Chronos, or Saturn, and Rhea, were born of Cœlus and Terra, by which is meant that they were made by Cœlus (God) out of Terra, (the Earth,) and that their three sons, Jupiter, Neptune, and Pluto, (Cain, Abel, and Seth,) divided the Earth between them. These were afterward confounded with Noah and his three sons, Shem, Ham, and Japheth, who, under different names, were worshiped, as Sir William Jones has shown in his "*Asiatic Researches*," throughout Europe, Asia, and Africa.

by tradition from their great common ancestor. Such knowledge, once embalmed in the hearts and literature of any people, is not easily obliterated. And hence we find *traces* of it in the history of at least all the most enlightened nations, tribes, and families of the world. In one of the Vedas, or Sacred Books of the Hindoos, for instance, we find the following reference to God as the Creator of all things: "Originally there was soul only. He thought, I will create worlds. So he created worlds. Then, I will create guardians of worlds. He framed out of the water an embodied being, and showed him to the deities whom he had made. They exclaimed, Well done! O, wonderful!" Soon, however, their divinities were multiplied. From Brahm proceeded Brahma the creator, Vishnu the preserver, and Siva the destroyer. And, finally, "every thing that had life, whether animal or vegetable, was supposed to have something of the deity in it, and was worshiped." These imaginary gods, amounting to about 333,000,000, were at length generalized, and Pantheism became the religion of India.

Religion of the Hindoos.

In the Greek and Roman Classics there is frequent reference made to the "Supreme God." But he is generally thrown so far into the background of their theology that he can scarcely be recognized among the immense number of their inferior divinities. Plato, for example, often speaks of "God over all," "the first God," "the greatest God," "the sovereign mind which passes through all things," "who always was, and never was made," etc. But on this point, as well as on the doctrine of Divine providence, and many other matters that have been made plain by the Gospel, he was always in a state of doubt and uncertainty. Indeed, this may be regarded as a common characteristic of

Religion of the Greeks and Romans.

all the religious discussions of the Greek and Roman philosophers. Socrates once said that "the only thing he knew was that he knew nothing." Plato maintained that our most fixed opinions amount at last to nothing more than mere probabilities. In like manner Aristotle complains, that "as the eyes of bats are to the brightness of daylight, so also is the understanding of our souls even toward those things which, by nature, are most manifest to all." Cicero, though a professed advocate of the doctrine of the soul's immortality, thus expressed his doubts on the subject. He says: "A question has been raised whether the soul dies with the body; or whether if surviving, it shall have a perpetual existence or only a temporary one. Which of these opinions is true," he says, "some god must determine." Not long after Cicero, and just about the time when Rome had reached the zenith of her glory, Juvenal uttered the following words of complaint respecting man's future state: "The human race," he says, "is cursed by the darkness which hangs over the future." No wonder, then, that when the Greeks and the Romans abandoned the traditions of their ancestors, they too, notwithstanding all their learning, became polytheists and pantheists. What a commentary is all this on the saying of Paul, that "*the world by wisdom knew not God!*"

Religion of the Egyptians.

While speaking of the theology of the Egyptians, Mr. Hardwic says: "It is the same with the Egyptian as with the Hindoo. A vague idea of the unity of God lingered in the background of his metaphysical system long after it had ceased to have any practical effect. Fascinated by the mysterious powers and processes of nature, he abandoned the ancient faith in God, and bowed down in adoration to the world above him, beneath him, and around him." And to so great an extent did they carry their idolatry that even Plutarch, their friend and apologist, was constrained to say that "the greater part of the Egyptians, by adoring the animals themselves as gods, have filled their ritual with subjects of laughter and opprobrium."

Religion of the North American Indians.

Among the North American Indians we find a fuller, clearer, and more perfect recognition of the One Supreme Being than we find in the history of any other heathen people. Professor Schoolcraft says: "There can be no doubt that, when properly viewed, the Great Spirit of the Indians is a purer deity than that of the Greeks and Romans, with all their refinement." These "philosophers of the woods see their "*Jan*," or "*Great Spirit*," in the thunder, the lightning, and indeed in all the phenomena of nature. But, nevertheless, like all the rest of the heathen, they have multiplied their inferior divinities. It is supposed that in North and South America there are not less than three thousand mounds which the Indians have erected in honor of the Sun, Moon, and Stars, all of which they reverence and worship as inferior deities. They worship, also, an immense number of *Manettos*, by which they mean good and evil spirits who are engaged in doing what the great *Jan* or *Wazatoad* does not care to do.

Religion of the ancient Mexicans.

The ancient Aztecs, or Mexicans, recognized and worshiped *one Supreme God*, under whom they ranked and served thirteen principal deities, and more than three hundred inferior ones. They also believed in an *evil spirit*, who was the enemy of the human race. The chief of the thirteen intermediate gods was the *Mexican Mars*, or god of war; to whom, it is supposed by Prescott and other historians, not less than twenty thousand human victims were offered annually.

Religion of the Peruvians.

According to the most reliable account that we have of the religion of the ancient Peruvians, they too had one supreme Deity, whom they called *Con*. But in process of time the worship of the Sun, Moon, and stars was introduced among them by Mango Capac, supposed to be a Buddhist priest. He was the first of the *Incas*, or Divine Kings of Peru, all of whom claimed divine honors from their subjects. To these were added many other inferior deities, such as the rainbow, thunder, lightning, the Earth, winds, rivers, etc. Indeed, every thing that had life became in time an object of worship; and finally these were all generalized as in India, and Pantheism became the religion of Peru.

Scripture illustrated by these facts.

Many more instances and illustrations to the same effect might be given from the history of other nations. But those already cited are, I think, sufficient for our present purpose. They abundantly demonstrate the truth of what Paul says in Romans i, 21–23, that "*when they* (the Gentiles) *knew God they glorified him not as God, neither were thankful, but became vain* ἐν τοῖς διαλογισμοῖς αὐτῶν *in their speculations, and their foolish heart was darkened. Professing themselves to be wise, they became fools; and changed the glory of the incorruptible God into an image made like to corruptible man, and to birds, and four-footed beasts, and creeping things.*"

Origin and progress of Idolatry; deification of Heroes.

The progress of the Gentiles in idolatry, as in other vices, was *gradual.* Their first step in it was the deification and worship of their ancestors. The learned Sir William Jones has, in a very able article, endeavored to prove that all the principal gods of Europe, Asia, and Africa were identical, being nothing more nor less than Noah and his three sons deified. As Noah begat Shem, Ham, and Japheth, so Saturn was said to have begotten Jupiter, Neptune, and Pluto, and Brahm to have triplicated himself int Brahma, Vishnu, and Siva.

Worship of the heavenly bodies.

Their next step in idolatry was the worship of the heavenly bodies. Sanchoniathon, the oldest Phœnician historian, says that *Chryson* (supposed to be Noah) was the first deified mortal; and that the several members of his family were, after their death, raised to the rank of gods in connection with the heavenly bodies. The Hindoos have a tradition that the *Richis,* who were preserved in the Ark, became after their death the souls of the seven stars of the Great Bear; and that the souls of their wives were, in like manner, transferred to the Pleiades. The ancient Egyptians believed that *Helius,* their first king, had been translated to the Sun. And hence it was that in a short time the opinion became quite prevalent that all the stars and planets were living beings, and proper objects of worship.

Further progress of Error.

Other objects of worship were easily added to these newly created divinities, and very soon all animated nature was deified. In some cases the progress of error stopped with Polytheism; in others it resulted in Pantheism; and in others again there was a reaction of the human mind in favor of general Skepticism. This was the manifest *tendency* of philosophy among all the Gentiles who were not restrained by the traditions of their ancestors. Plato saw and felt all this; and hence his earnest and repeated efforts to cultivate in the minds and hearts of the people a reverence for these traditions. "We ought," he says, "always to believe the ancient and sacred words." But, notwithstanding his earnest appeals to antiquity, and his great zeal for the traditions of his ancestors, the fact is patent in all Greek and Roman history that from the death of Plato to the coming of Christ Skepticism was generally on the increase. Religion was tolerated by the state as a means of controlling and governing the passions of the multitude; but when Pilate contemptuously said to Christ, "*What is truth?*" he expressed the common sentiment of most of the politicians and public men of the empire. How true it is, then, as was well remarked by Mr. Locke, "*that in the time of Christ Philosophy had spent its strength and done its utmost!*"*

Remarks of Prof. Schaff.

* The old world, at the appearance of Christ, had already begun to putrefy, and from directly opposite quarters evinced the absolute necessity of an entirely new principle of life to save it from hopeless ruin. The world had, indeed, been preparing for Christianity in every way, positively and negatively, theoretically and practically, by Grecian culture, Roman dominion, the Old Testament Revelation, the amalgamation of Judaism and Heathenism, the distractions and misery, the longings and hopes of the age; but no tendency of antiquity was able to generate the true religion or satisfy the infinite needs of the human heart. The wants of the world could be met only by an act of God, by a new creation. The mythologies had plainly outlived themselves. The Greek religion, which aimed only to deify earthly existence, could afford no comfort in misfortune, nor ever beget the spirit of martyrdom. The Roman religion was ridiculed and forever stripped of its power by being degraded into a mere tool for political ends, and by the exaltation of worthless despots to the rank of gods. The Jewish religion in Pharisaism had stiffened into a spiritless, self-righteous formalism; in Sadducism had been emptied of all its moral and religious earnestness; and in the system of Philo had gone out of itself and become adulterated with elements entirely foreign to its original genius. . . . The best feature of that age was a religious *yearning* which takes refuge from the turmoil and pain of life in the sanctuary of hope, but, unable to supply its own wants, is compelled to seek salvation entirely beyond itself. Expectations of the coming of a Messiah, in various forms and degrees of clearness, were at that time, by the political, intellectual, and religious contact and collision of the nations, spread over the whole world, and, like the first red streaks upon the horizon, announced the

From our premises, thus briefly stated and illustrated, it is evident, therefore, that Natural Religion is not a religion adequate to the wants and necessities of mankind. For,

Conclusion concerning Natural Religion.

I. It wants the AUTHORITY that is necessary to restrain their evil passions and propensities.

II. It does not beget and cherish in the human heart a consciousness of sin, and a hungering and thirsting after righteousness.

III. It has no sin-offering for the relief of the guilty conscience, no means of cleansing and purifying the human soul from the polluting power and influence of sin.

These problems, then, having been clearly demonstrated by a long and varied series of human experiments, the time had now come for the full revelation and manifestation of God's scheme of philanthropy. And hence the next great event in the Divine administration was the coming of Him of whom the Law and all the Prophets had spoken.

The fullness of time now come.

approach of day. The Persians were looking for their *Sosiosch*, who should conquer *Ahriman* and his kingdom of darkness. The Chinese sage Confucius pointed his disciples to a *Holy One* who should appear in the West. The wise astrologers who came to Jerusalem to worship the new-born King of the Jews we must look upon as the noblest representatives of the Messianic hopes of the Oriental heathens. The western nations, on the contrary, looked toward the East, the land of the rising Sun and of all wisdom. Suetonius and Tacitus speak of a current saying in the Roman Empire that in the East, and more particularly in Judea, a new universal empire would soon be founded. It was probably also the same blind, instinctive impulse toward the East which brought the Galatians from Germany and Gaul into Asia Minor." *History of the Apostolic Church, by Prof. P. Schaff, pp.* 182, 183.

PART IV.

DEVELOPMENTS IN THE LIFE, DEATH, BURIAL, RESURRECTION, ASCENSION, AND CORONATION OF CHRIST.

CHAPTER I.

MINISTRY OF JOHN THE BAPTIST.

Custom of Oriental monarchs.

WE are told by ancient historians, that when Eastern monarchs were about to set out on an important expedition, it was their custom to send harbingers or heralds in advance of their armies, with orders to provide supplies, make bridges, find the best fording-places over streams, level hills, construct causeways, cut down forests, and, in a word, to do whatever might be necessary to prepare the way before them.*

Historical illustrations.

* This is well illustrated by the following account which Diodorus Siculus gives of the march of Queen Semiramis from Babylon into Media and Persia: "On her way," says the historian, "she came to the Zarcean mountain, which, extending many furlongs, and being full of craggy precipices and deep hollows, could not be passed without making a great compass. Being, therefore, desirous of leaving an everlasting memorial of herself, as well as of shortening the way, she ordered the precipices to be digged down and the hollows to be filled up, and, at a great expense, she made a shorter and more expeditious road, which to this day is called from her, '*The way of Semiramis.*' Afterward she went into Persia and all the other countries of Asia subject to her dominion, and wherever she went she ordered the mountains and precipices to be leveled, causeways to be raised in the plain or flat country, and, at a great expense, made the ways passable." *Diod. Sic., B. II.*

To the same effect is also the following passage from Arrian's History

And just so did Christ make his advent into this world, and begin his mighty conflict with Sin and Death. To this the prophet Isaiah evidently refers in the following passage from the fortieth chapter:

Manner of Christ's Advent.

> "The voice of one crying in the wilderness,
> Prepare ye the way of the Lord;
> Make straight in the desert a highway for our God.
> Every valley shall be exalted,
> And every mountain shall be made low;
> And the crooked shall be made straight,
> And the rough places plain;
> And the glory of the Lord shall be revealed,
> And all flesh shall see it together;
> For the mouth of the Lord hath spoken it."

Isaiah's reference to it.

The primary reference of this prophecy is to the Lord's leading Israel from Babylon up again to Jerusalem. This is evident from the context. But that Isaiah refers here, also, to the coming of Christ and the ministry of his Harbinger, John the Baptist, is very obvious from Matt. iii, 3; Mark i, 2, 3; Luke i, 76; iii, 2–6; and John i, 23. See, also, Malachi iii, 1; and iv, 5, 6.

Twofold reference of this prophecy.

Be it observed, however, that the obstacles in the way of Christ's advent were not such as impeded the march of earthly monarchs, nor were they such as even Jehovah himself had to encounter in leading his people up through the great and terrible wilderness that lay between Babylon and Jerusalem. It was not literal mountains and valleys, nor was it the hostility and opposition of semi-barbarous tribes, but it was the infidelity and wickedness of his own kindred and

Nature of the Obstacles in the way of Christ.

of Alexander the Great: "He (Alexander) now proceeded to the River Indus, a company going before which made a way for him, for otherwise there would have been no mode of passing through that region." *B. LIV, Ch. xxx.*

chosen people that Christ had to overcome before he could with propriety set up his kingdom and begin his reign on Earth. As has been stated in a previous chapter, the Jews as well as the Gentiles had at that time almost filled up the cup of their iniquity. And had not God just then used extraordinary means to check the tide of corruption that was threatening to inundate the whole Earth, another flood would no doubt very soon have been necessary to free the world from a population as depraved as were the abandoned antediluvians.

Scope of John's Mission.

To remove these obstacles, then, so far as to prepare the Jews for the coming of the great Hero, was the special work of John the Baptizer. When he was about thirty years of age he appeared in the wilderness of Judea, and with a clarion voice that reëchoed and reverberated throughout its hills and its valleys, and with an earnestness that roused into activity the slumbering energies of the whole nation, he called on the people to repent of their sins, to cease to do evil and learn to do well, and thus to prepare themselves for the approaching reign of Heaven.

Effect of his preaching.

His appeal was not in vain; for we are told that "Jerusalem, and all Judea, and all the region round about the Jordan, went out to him and were baptized by him in the Jordan, confessing their sins." Matt. iii, 5, 6. See also Mark i, 3–8; and Luke iii, 3–18.

Only change required and effected by John's Ministry.

Here, then, we have in a few words the whole scope of John's ministry. It was simply "to prepare a people for the Lord." He neither changed nor abrogated the existing laws and institutions of his country, and he added nothing to them save Baptism, which he himself had received directly from Heaven. Matthew xxi, 23–27. Those who were baptized by him rose from their liquid graves subject in all respects to the laws and institutions of Moses. *The only change in their condition was a death to sin and a resurrection to a life of holiness, preparatory to the coming of their anxiously looked-for Messiah.*

His Death.

In this work of reformation John and his disciples continued to labor, as is generally supposed, for about a year and a half. He was then imprisoned by Herod Antipas in Machærus, a frontier fortress between Peræa and Arabia, about nine miles east of the Dead Sea; and soon after that he was beheaded by Herod, at the request of his stepdaughter Salome. See Matt. xiv, 1–12; Mark vi, 14–29; and Luke ix, 7–9.

CHAPTER II.

CHRIST'S NATURE, CHARACTER, AND PERSONALITY.

Two important Questions.

THE questions, "Who is Christ?" and "What is Christ?" are matters of paramount importance to our entire race. They are matters which have largely occupied the attention and consideration of the whole civilized world for more than eighteen hundred years; and even to-day they are still growing in freshness and in interest.

Various answers given to them.

But as we might anticipate under the present lapsed state of human nature, very different answers have been given to these questions. Some make Christ to be one thing and some another. But all who profess to receive the Bible as the

Word of God, save some of the ancient dreaming, semi-infidel Gnostics,* and a few other ancient sectaries, agree that he was a *man;* not a myth, not a phantom, not a mere creation of

Conclusion as to his Humanity.

* The following brief account of these ancient heretics is from Gibbon's Decline and Fall of the Roman Empire, Vol. VI, p. 6. London Edition. The author says: "The prevailing doctrine of the eternity and inherent pravity of matter infected the primitive Churches of the East. Many among the Gentile proselytes refused to believe that a celestial spirit, an undivided portion of the first essence, had been personally united with a mass of impure and contaminated flesh; and in their zeal for the divinity, they piously abjured the humanity of Christ. While his blood was still recent on Calvary, the *Docetes,* a numerous and learned sect of Asiatics, invented the *fantastic* system, which was afterward propagated by the Marcionites, the Manichæans, and the various names of the Gnostic heresy. They denied the truth and authenticity of the Gospels, so far as they relate to the conception of Mary, the birth of Christ, and the thirty years that preceded the exercise of his ministry. He *first* appeared on the banks of the Jordan in the form of perfect manhood; but it was a *form* only and not a *substance*—a human figure, created by the hand of Omnipotence to imitate the faculties and actions of a man, and to impose a perpetual illusion on the senses of his friends and enemies. Articulate sounds vibrated on the ears of the disciples; but the image which was impressed on their optic nerve eluded the more stubborn evidence of the touch, and they enjoyed the spiritual, not the corporeal, presence of the Son of God. The rage of the Jews was idly wasted against an impassive phantom, and the *mystic* scenes of the passion and death, the resurrection and ascension of Christ, were represented on the theater of Jerusalem for the benefit of mankind."

Views of the ancient Gnostics.

This hypothesis has long since been exploded, and none are now so visionary as to maintain it. Even Dr. David Frederick Strauss, the great champion of the Mythical Hypothesis, concedes, in his Life of Christ that he had a historical existence, and that he was, moreover, a man of great genius, power, and religious influence.

Concessions of Dr. Strauss.

But I wish it to be distinctly understood that in all these discussions I *assume* the Divine origin and plenary inspiration of the Holy Scriptures. For the present I have nothing to do with any of the various rationalistic hypotheses of *Imposture,* or *Self-Deception,* or *Poetic Fiction.* These have all been often tried and refuted. And the only legitimate question, therefore, that is now before us is simply this: *What do the Scriptures, when fairly interpreted, teach us concerning Jesus of Nazareth?* This, when properly ascertained, is to us, at least, an end of all controversy.

The only proper Question in all discussions concerning Christ.

some fruitful imagination, but *a man*—a real person, having a human body and a human soul, and endowed with all the faculties, powers, elements, and susceptibilities of human nature in its primitive sinless state. On no other hypothesis can we possibly account for the facts connected with his birth, his early education, his baptism, his temptation in the wilderness, his public ministry, his crucifixion, his burial, his resurrection, his subsequent interview with his disciples, and his ascension to glory. We shall, therefore, henceforth regard and treat the question of Christ's complete and perfect humanity as a settled matter.

Hypotheses o the subject o Christology.

But what about his Divinity? Was he a mere man having no existence prior to his conception by the virgin Mary, as was taught by the ancient Ebionites, and as is still maintained by the Socinian portion of the modern Unitarians? Or did he exist in any other state of conscious personality previous to that time? If so, to what rank or order of beings did he belong? Was he a *creature* of some angelic or super-angelic order, as Arius and his followers believed, and as some Unitarians still maintain? Or was he an uncreated *Æon,* or emanation from the Deity, as was alleged by the Nominal Trinitarians and some of the ancient Gnostics? Or was he God himself, one with the Father in essence, and endowed with all the attributes of Divinity, but nevertheless having his own separate and distinct personality, as has always been taught by the more learned, pious, and prudent of the Trinitarian School? Or is it true, as the Sabellians and other Patripassians maintained, that there is no distinction of persons in the Godhood, and that Christ was nothing more nor less than the Eternal Father himself, invested with a human body?*

What think you, courteous reader, of these hypotheses? It strikes me that these matters are too high for us, far beyond the reach and grasp of our feeble reason, and that it is therefore folly, if not presumption, in us to attempt to be wise beyond what is written on such subjects. "To the law and to the testimony" must ever be our appeal when we speak of the Infinite.

Not a proper subject for philosophical speculation.

This, however, should neither prevent nor discourage us from making an honest and earnest effort to understand what God has *revealed* to us on such matters. Whatever was written by inspiration was written for our instruction, edification, and encouragement. And surely no theme is more worthy of our constant and most profound consideration than the character and perfections of Him who died for our sins, and who was raised from the dead for our justification.

But so far as *revealed*, to be studied profoundly.

What, then, do the Scriptures teach us concerning Christ? Evidently THAT HE WAS GOD AS WELL AS MAN; *that in some respects he was one with the Father and the Holy Spirit; and that in other respects he was different from them both.*

General Proposition.

As evidence of the truth of this general proposition, I submit the following:

I. *The Scriptures ascribe to Christ, in a great many instances, the proper names of the Deity.* This is evident from the following passages:

Evidence from the Names ascribed to Christ.

1. Isaiah ix, 6: "For unto us a child is

*For a full account of all the various theories and hypotheses on the subject of Christology and the Godhood, I refer the reader to the Ecclesiastical Histories of Neander, Mosheim, Gieseler, and Schaff, and also to Shedd's History of Christian Doctrine.

born, unto us a son is given; and the government shall be upon his shoulder: and his name shall be called Wonderful, Counselor, THE MIGHTY GOD, (אֵל גִּבּוֹר,) The Father of the everlasting age, The Prince of Peace."

2. John i, 1: "In the beginning was the Word, and the Word was with God, and the Word was GOD (θεός)."*

3. Hebrews i, 8: "But unto the Son," (the Father saith,) "Thy throne, O GOD, (ὁ θεός,) is forever and ever; a scepter of righteousness is the scepter of thy kingdom."

Still more conclusive, if possible, is the evidence derived from the use of the name Jehovah. This has always been regarded as the most sacred of all names, and it is claimed by God himself as one that is untransferable. Thus, for instance, it is said in Psalm lxxxiii, 17, 18, "Let them (the enemies of God's people) be confounded and troubled forever; yea, let them be put to shame and perish; that men may know that thou *whose name alone is* JEHOVAH (יְהוָה) art the Most High over all the Earth." And again, in Isaiah, xlii, 8, God himself is represented as saying, "I am JEHOVAH (יְהוָה;) that is MY NAME, and my glory will I not give to another, neither my praise to graven images." But, nevertheless,

*The Greek word λόγος (Logos) is not properly synonymous with either ἔπος, *a word in its grammatical sense*, or with ῥῆμα, *a word spoken or uttered by the living voice*. It comprehends usually both the medium of the communication and the thing communicated, regarded as the reason, design, or object of the communication. In this comprehensive sense it is very happily used by John as the distinctive Title of the Messiah previous to his incarnation. For it is through him that God has made all his communications to fallen man; and not only so, but he is also himself the reason, the subject, and the object of all these communications. He is the way, the truth, the resurrection, and the life—the wisdom of God and the power of God for the salvation of the world.

Meaning of Logos as a Title of Christ.

Christ is often included in this name, as we learn from the following passages:*

(1.) Psalm xcvii, 7: "Confounded be all they that serve graven images, that boast themselves of idols. *Worship* HIM, *all ye gods*." Here the proper antecedent of *Him* is the Jehovah of the first and fifth verses. But in Hebrews i, 6, it is pretty evident that these words are applied to Christ.

(2.) Isaiah xl, 3: "The voice of him that crieth in the wilderness, Prepare ye the way of JEHOVAH (יְהֹוָה;) make straight in the desert a highway for our GOD (אֱלֹהִים)." From Matthew iii, 1–3, it is evident that the Herald here spoken of was John the Baptist, and, consequently, that the names *Jehovah* and *Eloheem* have both reference to Christ. See also Jer. xxiii. 5, 6.

Restricted use of the name Jehovah in the Old Testament.

* It is not true, as some have supposed, that the name Jehovah is the *distinctive* appellation of Christ in the Old Testament. Whenever the Father and the Son are spoken of *in contrast*, the name Jehovah, if used at all, is given to the Father, and the Son is designated by some other name or title, as, for instance, in the second Psalm: "Why do the heathen rage," (says the Psalmist,) "and the people imagine a vain thing? The kings of the Earth set themselves, and the rulers take counsel together against Jehovah (יְהֹוָה) and against his Anointed, (מָשִׁיחַ, Messiah,) saying, Let us break their bands asunder, and cast away their cords from us.

"He that sits in the Heavens shall laugh; the Lord (אֲדֹנָי) shall have them in derision. Then will he speak unto them in his wrath, and vex them in his sore displeasure, saying, Yet have I (Jehovah) set my King (my Son) upon my holy hill of Zion.

"I will declare the decree, (says the Messiah;) Jehovah (יְהֹוָה) hath said unto me, Thou art my Son; this day have I begotten thee. Ask of me and I will give thee the heathen for thine inheritance, and the uttermost parts of the Earth for thy possession. Thou shalt break them with a rod of iron; thou shalt dash them into pieces like a potter's vessel.

"Be wise now, therefore, (says the Psalmist,) O ye kings; be instructed, ye judges of the Earth. Serve Jehovah (יְהֹוָה) with fear, and rejoice with trembling. Kiss the Son, lest he be angry, and ye perish from the way when his wrath is kindled but a little. Blessed are all they that put their trust in Him." See, also, Psalm cx; Isaiah xlii, 1–8; Malachi iii, 1, etc.

(3.) Revelation xxii, 6: "And he said unto me, These sayings are faithful and true, and the LORD GOD of the holy Prophets sent his angel to show unto his servants the things which must shortly be done." Here it is said that the Lord God sent his angel to reveal the future to his servants. But in the sixteenth verse it is said, "I, JESUS, have sent my angel to testify to you these things in the Churches." And hence it follows that the names *Lord God* or *Jehovah Eloheem* are both applicable to HIM who became flesh and dwelt among us.

I grant that in none of these cases is the name *Jehovah* applied to Christ *exclusively*. Nor is this necessary to our argument. It is enough to show that it comprehends the whole Godhood, and that it is, therefore, applied to the Son as well as to the Father and the Holy Spirit. In this comprehensive sense it is generally used in the Old Testament. For other equivalent expressions in the New Testament see John viii, 58; Revelation i, 11, 17, etc.

Evidence from the Powers, Honors, and Prerogatives of Christ.

II. *The Scriptures ascribe to Christ the peculiar and exclusive powers, honors, and prerogatives of the Deity.* For instance,

His creative power.

First. It is universally conceded that God alone has power to create, and that he is, in fact, the Creator of all things. Genesis i, 1; Isaiah xlviii, 12, 13; Rom. xi, 33–36; Rev. iv, 8–11.

But in many other passages of Scripture the same power is ascribed to Christ. *E. g.*,

1. John i, 1–3: "In the beginning was the Word, and the Word was with God, and the Word was God: the same was in the beginning with God. *All things came into being through him; and without him came not one thing into being that is in being.*"

2. Ephesians iii, 8–11: "Unto me, who am less than the least of all saints, is this grace given, that I should preach among the Gentiles the unsearchable riches of Christ; and to make all men see what is the fellowship of the mystery, which from the beginning of the world hath been hid in God, *who created all things by Jesus Christ:* to the intent that now unto the Principalities and Powers in heavenly places might be made known through the Church (διὰ τῆς ἐκκλησίας) the manifold wisdom of God, according to his eternal purpose which he purposed in Christ Jesus our Lord."

3. Colossians i, 16, 17: "*For by Him (the Son) were all things created that are in Heaven and that are in Earth, visible and invisible, whether they be thrones or dominions, or principalities or powers: all things were created by him and for him;* and he is before all things, and by him all things consist."

4. Hebrews i, 10–12: "*And thou Lord in the beginning didst lay the foundation of the Earth; and the Heavens are the works of thy hands.* They shall perish, but thou remainest; and they all shall wax old as doth a garment, and as a vesture shalt thou fold them up, and they shall be changed; but thou art the same, and thy years shall not fail."

Second. God is the only proper object of worship. Deut. vi, 13; Matt. iv, 10; Rev. xix, 10; xxii, 9.

The same kind and degree of homage claimed for the Son as for the Father.

But, nevertheless, this honor is, by divine authority, given to the Son as well as to the Father. For the proof and illustration of this proposition take the following passages:

1. John v, 22, 23: "For the Father judgeth no man, but hath committed all judgment unto the Son: *that all men should honor the Son, even as they honor the Father*

He that honoreth not the Son honoreth not the Father who hath sent him."

2. Hebrews i, 6: "And again, when he bringeth his first-begotten into the world, he saith, *And let all the angels of God worship him.*" Here the highest orders of created intelligence are required to do him homage.

3. Acts vii, 59, 60: "And they stoned Stephen, calling upon God, and saying, *Lord Jesus, receive my spirit.* And he kneeled down and cried with a loud voice, *Lord, lay not this sin to their charge.*" Stephen was an inspired man; and what he did and said on this occasion he did and said, therefore, by the authority of God.

4. Philippians ii, 9–11: "Wherefore God also hath highly exalted him, (Christ Jesus,) and given him a name that is above every name: *that at the name of Jesus every knee should bow of things in Heaven, and things in Earth, and things under the Earth; and that every tongue should confess that Jesus Christ is Lord, to the glory of God the Father.*" Surely, then, we have no need of any further testimony on this point.

His authority to forgive sins.

Third. It is evident, from the general tenor and scope of the whole Bible, that it is God's peculiar and exclusive prerogative to forgive sins; and yet it is just as evident, from sundry passages, that Christ both claimed and exercised this authority, even during his public ministry here on Earth. In Luke v, 20–25, for instance, we read as follows: "And when he (Jesus) saw their faith, he said unto him, (the paralytic,) Man, *thy sins are forgiven thee.* And the Scribes and the Pharisees began to reason, saying, Who can forgive sins but God only? But when Jesus perceived their thoughts, he answered and said unto them, What reason ye in your hearts? Whether is it easier to say, Thy sins be forgiven thee, or to say, Rise up and walk? *But that ye may know that the Son of Man has power on Earth to forgive sins,* (he said unto the sick of the palsy,) I say unto thee, Arise, and take up thy couch, and go into thy house. And immediately he rose up before them, and took up that whereon he lay, and departed to his own house, glorifying God."

Evidence from the coördinate relations of the Father, Son, and Holy Spirit.

III. *The Scriptures frequently represent the Father, the Son, and the Holy Spirit as coördinate agents and authorities in the work of creation, providence, and redemption.* Take for illustration the following passages:

1. Genesis i, 26: "And God (Eloheem in the plural number) said, *Let us make man in our image, after our likeness;* and let them have dominion over the fish of the sea, and over the fowl of the air, and over the cattle, and over all the Earth, and over every creeping thing that creepeth upon the Earth." And in Genesis i, 1, it is said that "in the beginning Eloheem created the Heavens and the Earth."

Now that God the Father was present on these occasions, and had an agency in the work of creation, is evident from Rev. iv, 11. That the Son was there, and exercised his power in the primitive creation, as well as in the Adamic renovation, is proved by John i, 1–3; and Colossians i, 16. And that the Holy Spirit was present and participated in this work is obvious from Genesis i, 2; and Job xxvi, 13. And hence it follows that the Father, Son, and Holy Spirit were coördinate in the work of creation, and that they are all included in the Eloheem of the first chapter of Genesis.*

* I use tne names *Father* and *Son proleptically*, or by anticipation, just as we speak of Abraham before he left Ur of Chaldea, though he was not called

2. The same coördinate relation between the Father, the Son, and the Holy Spirit is beautifully expressed and illustrated by the formula of Christian Baptism, given by Christ himself in Matt. xxviii, 19: "Go ye, therefore," said Christ to his Apostles, "and make disciples of all the nations, *baptizing them into the name of the Father, and of the Son, and of the Holy Spirit.*"

3. In like manner they are often spoken of and repre sented as being *conjointly* the fountain and source from which all our blessings flow to us. Thus, for instance, it is said in 2 Cor. xiii, 14, "*The grace of the Lord Jesus Christ, and the love of God, and the communion of the Holy Spirit be with you all.*" See also Romans i, 7; 1 Cor. i, 3; 2 Cor. i, 2; Ephesians i, 2; Phil. i, 2; Col. i, 2; 1 Thess. i, 1; 2 Thess. i, 2; 1 Tim. i, 2; 2 Tim. i, 2; Titus i, 4; Phil. iii; 2 Peter i, 2; 2 John iii, etc.

IV. *The Scriptures often ascribe to Christ an equality and oneness with the Father.* The following passages are sufficient to prove and illustrate this proposition:

Direct evidence of Christ's oneness and equality with the Father.

1. John v, 17, 18: "But Jesus answered them, My Father worketh hitherto and I work. Therefore the Jews sought the more to kill him, because he not only had broken the Sabbath, but said also that God was his Father, *making himself equal with God.*"

2. John x, 30–33: "*I and my Father are one,* said Christ. Then the Jews took up stones again to stone him. Jesus answered them, Many good works have I showed you from the Father: for which of these works do ye stone me? The Jews answered him saying, For a

Abraham for twenty-nine years afterward. In like manner the Messiah is called *Son* in the second Psalm; though Gabriel said to Mary, "that holy thing that shall be born of thee *shall be called the Son of God.*" Luke i, 35.

good work we stone thee not, but for plasphemy; *and because that thou being a man, makest thyself God.*"

3. John xiv, 8, 9: "Philip said unto him, Lord, show us the Father, and it sufficeth us. Jesus said unto him, *Have I been so long time with you, and yet hast thou not known me, Philip? He that hath seen me hath seen the Father;* and how sayest thou then, Show us the Father?"

4. Phil. ii, 5–8: "Let this mind be in you, which was also in Christ Jesus: *who, being in the form of God, thought it not robbery to be equal with God;* but made himself of no reputation, and took upon him the form of a servant, and was made in the likeness of men; and being found in fashion as a man, he humbled himself, and became obedient unto death, even the death of the cross."

Clearness and fullness of this evidence.

Any attempt here at an explanation of these passages would be wholly superfluous. No language can be plainer than that which the Holy Spirit has itself used to express the relations which exist between the Father and the Son. For if Christ was God, and if he thought it not robbery to be equal with God, it seems to me that this should be an end of the whole controversy.

The Son's inferiority also a matter of Revelation.

I am aware that in some other passages of Scripture the Son's inferiority in some sense is also very clearly stated. But this neither implies a contradiction in the Word of God, nor does it in any respect invalidate our conclusions. For,

To what this may have reference.

I. *The inferiority spoken of may refer simply to the humanity of Christ, and have no reference whatever to his Divinity.* As a man, "he increased in wisdom and in stature." Luke ii, 52. His human nature had need to be educated as well as ours.

Hebrews ii, 10; and v, 9. But his Divine nature was always perfect, as God himself is perfect.

II. *In other cases it may refer merely to his* OFFICIAL *relations.* Two persons may be perfectly equal both by nature and education, but nevertheless the one may be officially subordinate to the other. Nay, more, it often happens that a superior is made officially subordinate to an inferior.

III. *Or, finally, the inferiority of the Son may, in some cases, refer to something in the Godhood that lies wholly beyond the narrow limits of our comprehension.* But it does not hence follow that we should reject as absurd the clearly revealed equality of the Father and the Son in other respects. The tyro in Mathematics does not throw aside his Arithmetic as false and worthless because, forsooth, he does not, and perhaps can not, comprehend the mysteries of the Calculus. No more should we reject as absurd the clearly revealed lessons of Christology because we can not fully understand all the incomprehensible mysteries of the Godhood.

Conclusion.

On the whole, then, I think there is no reason to doubt that the LOGOS who became flesh and dwelt among us was himself God—one with the Father and the Holy Spirit in some respects, and different from them both in other respects. But to define clearly and fully in what these points of difference and identity consist is, in all probability, beyond the capacity of even the Archangel. Job xi, 7–9. Instead, then, of attempting to be wise on this subject beyond what is written, let us rather conclude with Paul that "*great is the mystery of godliness:* GOD WAS MANIFEST IN THE FLESH, *justified in the Spirit, seen of angels, preached unto the Gentiles, believed on in the world, received up into glory*" - Tim. iii, 16.

CHAPTER III.

WHY THE WORD BECAME FLESH.

Question demonstrated in the preceding Chapter.

IN the preceding chapter it has been demonstrated, I hope, to the satisfaction of every thoughtful reader, that Christ is *God* as well as *man*, and that he is *man* as well as *God;* that he combines in his own person perfect humanity and perfect Divinity, and that, in a word, he is himself "God manifest in the flesh."

Question to be considered.

A question, then, of very great interest, and also of very great importance, rises just here: Why did the Word become flesh? Why did he become incarnate and dwell among us? To the earnest and prayerful consideration of this question I now respectfully invite the attention of my readers.

SECTION I.—THE ATONEMENT.

Something due to Law and Justice in all Governments.

That something is always due to offended and violated Justice will, perhaps, be readily conceded by all. The father who never holds his children responsible for any of their misdemeanors will soon have the mortification of seeing all kinds of disorder prevailing in his family. And just so it is in the government of a school, a Church, a state, or a nation. The demands of Justice must be met and the majesty of the law sustained in every human organization, or otherwise the bonds of the association will soon be severed, and anarchy and lawlessness will soon universally prevail. Brutus felt this when he put his own sons to death for conspiring against the laws and constitution of the Roman Republic. Zaleucus, king of Locris, felt this when he divided between himself and his offending son the severe penalty required by the laws of his realm.* Every President and Governor of this Republic feels this when, notwithstanding the petitions of many citizens, and the tears and entreaties of helpless women and children, he refuses to pardon the willful and presumptuous transgressor of the laws of his country. And may I not add, with reverence, God himself felt this when he banished from his presence the angels that kept not their first estate, "reserving them in everlasting chains under darkness unto the judgment of the great day?" Jude 6.

Difficulty of ascertaining her rightful claims even in human Governments.

But what is it that is due to Justice in such a case? What is sufficient to meet and to satisfy the claims of justice on account of transgressions committed in the family, in the school, in the Church, in the state, or in the nation? Can any one now answer this question clearly, definitely, and authoritatively? How many parents are able to decide, with entire satisfaction even to themselves, what they should and what they should not require of their offend-

Case of Zaleucus.

* Zaleucus flourished about 500 years B. C His government over the Locrians was severe but just. In one of his decrees, he forbade the use of wine unless it were prescribed as a medicine; and in another, he ordered that all adulterers should be punished with the loss of both their eyes. When his own son had subjected himself to this penalty, the father, in order to maintain the authority of the laws, and to show at the same time a becoming parental lenity, shared the penalty with his son, by causing to be thrust out one of his own eyes and one of the eyes of his offending son. In this way, the majesty of his government was maintained, and his own character as a just and righteous sovereign was magnified in the eyes of his subjects.

ing children? What King, Governor, or President has ever enjoyed the satisfaction of knowing that he has in all cases exercised the power of pardon for the good of the offender, and also for the best interests of society; that he has never erred in the exercise of this most delicate and embarrassing of all his executive functions? Who has ever heard of such a case? I know of none myself, and I presume that history records none.

Greater complexity of the problem in relation to God's Government.

But, if this problem is so very difficult and embarrassing even in its relations to the small and comparatively unimportant governments of this world, what does it become when it is extended to the vast empire of Jehovah; when it is made to embrace a government *which has for its Constitution the Divine nature itself, and on the proper administration of which depend the order, stability, and well-being of the whole universe?* Who can say on what conditions a sin may and should be pardoned that has been committed against Him who has established his throne in the heavens, and whose kingdom ruleth over all? Psalm ciii, 19.

Probable inference from the fall and destiny of Satan and his angels.

For a long time this was the mystery of all mysteries. And hence it is that the history of Redemption is a history of successive wonders. So far as we know it has no parallel in the Divine administration. When the angels sinned that was the end of their probation. Their hopes then vanished forever. Nothing remained for them but a fearful looking for of judgment and fiery indignation which shall devour the adversary. And it is most likely that when man sinned and fell his case was regarded as equally hopeless by all the higher created intelligences of the universe who were cognizant of the fact. They knew that

God is just, that he is impartial, and that his government must and will be sustained; and hence it is most likely that all the angels, both good and bad, looked upon man as lost—forever lost—the moment that he transgressed in Eden.

With what feelings of surprise, then, must Satan and all his rebel host have heard from the lips of Jehovah the awfully sublime and mysterious oracle, *The Seed of the woman shall bruise the head of the Serpent!* How intensely they must have gazed upon the first lamb that was ever offered in sacrifice! And with what mingled feelings of wonder, astonishment, and disappointment must they have seen the soul of Abel, as it was separated from its clay tenement, borne by angels into the mansions of the blessed!

Wonder excited by God's first dealings with fallen man.

If ever there was a time when any of God's creatures might be supposed to be ready to charge him with partiality and injustice, it seems to me that that was the time. The fact that man had sinned was known in Heaven, Earth, and Hell. And the fact that Justice demanded satisfaction was also known. But when, where, and how had this satisfaction been given? Ah, that was the question. Nothing had yet appeared within the horizon of even the tallest angel in glory that was sufficient to justify such an event as the salvation of a soul that had been defiled by sin. And hence it seems probable that if the charge of partiality and injustice could have been made against God on any conditions it would have been preferred on that occasion.

Charge of partiality impossible.

But no, that was impossible! Even Satan himself would not dare to entertain such a thought! God must and will be just, though the whole created universe should prove false. The

More probable conception of good and bad angels.

conception would therefore more naturally arise that there was something yet undeveloped in the purposes of Jehovah; something which no created eye had yet seen, but the *shadow* of which was even then present on every patriarchal altar.

Confirmed by sundry new developments.

This conception was more or less confirmed by every new development of God's great purpose, whether in type or in prophecy. Such promises as that in the Seed of Abraham all the nations of the Earth should be blessed, and that the scepter should not depart from Judah until Shiloh (שִׁילֹה, tranquilizer or pacificator) should come, would greatly serve to enlist the feelings of all rational beholders.

Interest taken by good men and angels in the Drama of Redemption.

And hence we find that holy Angels became greatly interested in the sublime drama of human redemption. This is indicated not only by their frequent visits to the heirs of salvation, but also, and more particularly, by some of the provisions of that typical system which Moses, at the command of God, constructed for a testimony to the people, and also for the purpose of aiding all men in their honest efforts and attempts to rise to a just conception of the spiritual nature of the scheme and economy of redemption. The inner curtain of the Tabernacle, for example, which was but the typical canopy of the Church, was covered all over with cherubic or angelic figures. So, too, was the Vail that separated the Holy Place from the Most Holy. And from the Mercy-Seat that covered the Ark of the Covenant there rose up two of these same symbolic figures, with their faces turned downward, as if anxious to penetrate the sublime mysteries that then lay concealed in and beneath the golden Propitiatory. To this Peter seems to allude when he says that the angels desired to look into these things. 1 Peter i, 12. And the same Apostle informs us that the ancient Prophets earnestly inquired into these matters, searching what or what manner of time the Spirit of Christ which was in them did signify when it testified beforehand the sufferings of Christ and the glories that should follow. 1 Peter i, 10, 11.

Evidence of Satan's interest in it.

In the mean time, Satan and his emissaries were not idle and indifferent spectators of the scene. He too became a diligent student of the types and prophecies. He was often found among the Sons of God; and no sooner was Jesus introduced to the multitudes on the banks of the Jordan as the Messiah, the Son of God, than he was assailed by this diabolical Tempter with a degree of cunning and sagacity that indicates not only a most profound knowledge of human nature, but also a very special acquaintance with the Scheme of Redemption, so far as it had then been developed.

The Mystery not yet revealed.

But still all was mystery. The Vail of the Temple made without hands had not yet been rent; the way into the true Holy of Holies had not yet been made manifest to any creature; the grave had not yet lost one of its victims, and life and immortality had not yet been fully brought to light by the Gospel. Even the Apostles of Christ were yet ignorant of the fact that their Master must suffer death, be buried, and rise again the third day, according to the Scriptures. See Mark ix, 9–10; Luke xxiv, 45–47; John xx, 9; and Hebrews ix, 8.

The Problem demonstrated.

But in the fullness of time the Great Antitype of all the sacrifices that were ever slain by Divine appointment appeared on the Cross. And as his flesh was torn and mangled for the sins of the world, the vail of the symbolical Temple was rent in twain from the top to the bottom; and the way into the Holiest of all was then typically revealed to the eyes of mortals. Soon after this the bars of Death were broken, and Christ rose from the dead, the first-fruits of them that slept. He spent forty days with his disciples, speaking to them of things pertaining to the Kingdom of God; and then, having ascended to the Heavens as our Great High Priest, not with the blood of bulls and of goats, but with his own blood, HE MADE AN ATONEMENT FOR THE SINS OF THE WORLD. God accepted the offering as being fully adequate to meet and to satisfy all the demands of his government; and thus was solved the greatest moral problem that had ever occupied the attention of men or angels. It was then seen that what the Law could not do in that it was weak through the flesh, God had himself accomplished by and through the death of his own Son, whom he had finally set forth as a propitiatory sacrifice for a demonstration of his administrative justice "in passing by the sins that were formerly committed through the forbearance of God, for a manifestation of his justice at the time then present, SO THAT HE MIGHT BE JUST WHILE HE JUSTIFIES HIM WHO BELIEVES IN JESUS." Romans iii, 25, 26. And, accordingly, soon after that, when the four Living Creatures and the twenty-four Elders fell down before the Lamb to worship him in the Heavens, they were heard to sing "a *new song*, saying, Thou art worthy to take the book and to open the seals thereof; for thou wast slain, and hast redeemed us to God by thy blood, out of every kindred, and tongue, and people, and nation." Revelation v, 8, 9.

Song of the redeemed.

I do not mean to say that the problem of redemption was then fully and perfectly understood. By no means

It is not even yet so understood. And it will, in all probability, require an eternity to trace out and comprehend all the effects of the blood of Christ on the government of God and the interests of humanity. But what I mean to say is simply this: that all that was necessary to be known in order to the salvation of the world was then revealed. All the just and reasonable expectations of the intelligent universe were then fully satisfied. It was then seen, for example,

The Demonstration not yet complete.

Some of the main points elucidated.

I. *That it had never been God's purpose to pass by any sin or transgression of his law without a just and adequate satisfaction.* Had not the Remedial System been in prospect, no doubt Adam and his guilty bride would, like the angels that fell, have been at once banished forever from the presence of the Lord and from the glory of his power. But "known unto God are all his works from eternity." He knew perfectly well that, in the fullness of time, he could and would demonstrate to the whole intelligent universe that he had acted justly in passing by, for the time being, many sins that were committed during the Patriarchal and Jewish ages. And hence it was that he permitted thousands, perhaps, indeed, millions, of the sons and daughters of fallen humanity to enter Paradise very much as those who die in infancy now enter it; that is, without understanding either how or why it was that they were saved. But when the blood of atonement was offered in the Heavens, then it was that all was clear and satisfactory. Justice was then satisfied, and God's eternal government approved and magnified in the eyes of adoring millions. Mercy and Truth then met together, and Righteousness and Peace then embraced each other. Psalm lxxxv. 10

God's purpose from the beginning.

The only ground of pardon.

II. *It was then also very manifest that no sin had ever been pardoned on any other ground than on the merits of Christ's blood.* It was then evident that all the sacrifices that had ever been offered on Patriarchal and Jewish altars had never taken away one sin; that all these were but types or pictures designed to illustrate the merits of the one great sacrifice about to be offered, on which they all depended, and without which they were all as empty and as worthless as a shadow. Hebrews x, 1–4.

Illustration.

And hence it was that, in the Apocalyptic vision to which we have referred, John heard persons *out of all nations*, Jews as well as Gentiles, ascribing their salvation to the blood of the Lamb. And just so it will ever be. When the sea shall give up the dead which are in it, and when Death and Hades shall give up the dead which are in them, the same glorious song will be heard again in the Heavens. And, O my soul, what a song that will be when Abel, and Enoch, and Noah, and Abraham, and Moses, and Job, and Daniel, and all the blood-washed throng out of all the kindreds of the Earth shall tune their harps and join their voices to sing the praises of our Immanuel!

> "O what a sweet, exalted song,
> When every tribe and every tongue,
> Redeemed by blood, with Christ appear,
> And join in one full chorus there!"

Dear reader, would you join that glorious company? Do you desire to unite in that heavenly anthem, and to swell the song of our Immanuel's praises? If so, you must first be purified by his blood; and if you would be purified by his blood, you must first obey his precepts. He has become the Author of eternal salvation to all them, and to them only, who *obey* him. Blessed are they that do his commandments, that they may have a right to the tree of life, and may enter in through the gates into the city. Rev. xxii, 14.

The claims of Justice met and God's law magnified.

III. *It was then evident that the demands of Justice and all the claims of the Divine government had been met and satisfied by the sin-offering of Christ even more fully and more perfectly than if all the penalties of violated law had been directly inflicted on the offending parties.* Do we, then, says Paul, make law void through faith? Nay, verily, but rather we confirm and establish law. Romans iii, 31. And to the same effect is God's own testimony through the prophet Isaiah. While speaking of the services of Christ, he says "he will magnify law [תּוֹרָה] and make it honorable." Isaiah xlii, 21.

Inflexibility of the Divine Law.

This he has certainly done in the eyes of all who have any knowledge and comprehension of this subject. For if nothing short of the blood of Christ could atone for our sins and bring deliverance to the captive, how exceedingly unyielding and inflexible must be the Divine government! How true it is that justice and judgment are the habitation of his throne, and that Heaven and Earth must pass away before any of his laws can be set aside with impunity!

Scope of Christ's prayer in Gethsemane.

Viewed from this stand-point, how very significant are the words of our blessed Savior as in the garden he thus prayed in agony to his Father: "O, my Father, IF IT BE POSSIBLE, let this cup pass from me." That is, if there is any other possible way in which poor sinners can be saved, the claims of Justice satisfied, and the Divine law magnified, then and only then, let this cup of indescribable suffering pass from me. But rich and inexhaustible as are the Divine resources, it seems that there was no other possible remedy. Christ himself had to suffer in order to meet and to satisfy the just and necessary demands of the Divine government, or otherwise the whole human race must perish forever. He saw it! He understood it! He felt it! He no longer hesitated. He accepted the dread alternative. He was borne to the Cross as an innocent lamb was borne to the altar, and his blood was poured out for the sins of the world! See, also, Luke xxiv, 46; Hebrews ii, 10, etc.

Conclusion.

And now, O, sinner, will you reject the rich benefits procured for you through the infinite merits of that blood? Or will you not rather say,

> "Were the whole realm of nature mine,
> That were a present far too small;
> Love so amazing, so Divine,
> Demands my soul, my life, my all?"

SECTION II.—RECONCILIATION THROUGH CHRIST.

First object of the Incarnation and Death of Christ.

Justice is the fundamental principle of the Divine government. "Justice and judgment," says the Psalmist, "are the habitation of his throne." Psalm lxxxix, 14. And hence it is evident *that the first object of the incarnation and death of Christ was to meet and satisfy the claims of Justice against the sinner.* It was to magnify God's law and make it honorable. It was to open up a new and living way through which God's mercy and grace might freely and justly flow to guilty man.

This object accomplished.

But all this has been done. All the demands of Law and Justice have been fully met and fully satisfied by the sin-offering of Christ. And hence it is that God now offers salvation to the whole world on the simple condition of their submitting to a few plain precepts which he has kindly and benevolently given to all men as a test of their loyalty, and also as a means of promoting their own growth in grace and progress in the Divine life.

Query.

A very grave and important question, then, rises just here: *Why are not all men saved?* Why has not every man submitted to rules and conditions which all enlightened reason must approve as but just, and right, and benevolent?

Answer given by Christ.

A very clear and satisfactory answer to this question is found in the inimitably touching address of our Savior to Jerusalem, as he thought of that devoted city and wept over it. "O, Jerusalem, Jerusalem!" said he, "thou that killest the prophets and stonest them that are sent unto thee, how often *would I* have gathered thy children together as a hen doth gather her brood under her wings; and ye *would not!*" Luke xiii, 34. Ah, yes, this is the solution of the whole matter. How often would I, but ye would not!

The consent of two Wills essential to the salvation of every man.

It is evident, therefore, that the cordial consent of two wills is essential to the salvation of any and every man. I speak not now of infants nor of idiots. I refer to such, and to such only, as are responsible for their own actions; to such as have a will to choose or to refuse, to obey or to disobey. Before such a one can be saved there must, of necessity, be a concurrence of the will of God and the will of the sinner. God must first be willing to pardon the sinner, to justify, and sanctify, and save him, or otherwise there can, of course, be no salvation for him.

And it is just as evident that the sinner must also be made willing to receive these favors before it is possible for him to enjoy them. God will compel no man to receive them against his will. He stands at the door of every man's heart who hears his blessed word, and there he earnestly *knocks* for permission to enter it, (Rev. iii, 20,) not being willing that any should perish, but anxious that all should be brought to reformation.

God is willing.

But, strange to say, the sinner is not willing to receive the proffered boon. He has no disposition to receive and to entertain such a guest as the Holy One. His will is controlled by his desires, and his desires are all deranged by sin. His whole moral nature has been greatly perverted, and his whole heart has been filled with enmity to God by wicked works.

But the sinner is not willing.

Now, the second object of our Savior's incarnation and death is to change the disposition of the sinner. It is to take away his hard and stony heart, and to give him a heart of flesh. It is to remove his enmity, and to make him willing to become a child of God and an heir of Heaven. This is evident from the following passage of Scripture: "For it pleased the Father that in him (that is, in his Son) should all fullness dwell; *and having made peace through the blood of his Cross, by him to reconcile all things unto himself; by him, I say, whether they be things in Earth or things in Heaven. And you who were formerly alienated and enemies in your minds by wicked works, yet now has he reconciled, in the body of his flesh through death, to present you holy, and unblamable, and unreprovable in his sight.*" Colossians i, 19–22. See, also, 2 Corinthians v, 18–21.

Second object of the Incarnation and Death of Christ.

But why is it, we are constrained to ask just here, why is it that any man should ever cherish enmity in his heart to his Maker? Why should beings who have been so constituted as to love that which is lovely, and to hate that only which is hateful, ever cherish in their hearts enmity to One who is himself the very essence of all that is lovely and beautiful in the universe?

Query.

The *fact* is patent to all. On no other hypothesis can we explain the spirit of rebellion and disloyalty that we see on every hand. God, for example, commands all men every-where to repent. But very few do repent. God commands all to enter the Church—to become citizens of the Kingdom of his dear Son—through a bath of water and the renewing energies of the Holy Spirit. But the majority of those who hear and understand this plain, benevolent, and most reasonable requisition positively decline and refuse to obey it.

Evidence of the *fact.*

Now, how would such conduct be regarded and treated under any form of human government? Is that youth looked upon as a faithful and dutiful son who habitually neglects the known wishes and commands of his father? Is that man regarded as a friend and lover of his country who habitually disregards its laws and its institutions? Most assuredly not. In every such case neglect of the laws is regarded as evidence of disrespect to the lawgiver. And just so it is, and so it must ever be, under the Divine government. "*They that are not with me,*" says Christ, "*are against me; and he that gathereth not with me scattereth abroad.*" Matthew xii, 30. There is no neutral ground here. It is either loyalty or disloyalty; it is either obedience or it is disobedience; it is either love or it is hatred.

Analogous cases.

But still the question recurs, How came this hatred? Whence arose this preternatural state of enmity in the human heart? Paul says, in the citation made from his letter to the Colossians, that *it came by wicked works;* that is, the evil germ implanted in the soul by temptation was developed and increased by wicked works. And this answer, however strange and paradoxical it may at first appear, is both scriptural and philosophical. It accords with the spirit and tenor of the whole Bible, and it is, moreover, in perfect harmony with our own natural constitution. One of the most clearly defined laws of the human mind is this: *that the injurer always becomes, de facto, an enemy to the injured.* If A, for example, slanders B, he at once becomes B's enemy. If he fraudulently takes B's property, or in any other way trespasses on the rights of B, that moment his heart is filled with resentment.

Paul's answer to the Question.

Law of Human Nature.

And just so it was when man sinned in Paradise. Previous to that he loved God with all his heart, and soul, and mind, and strength. But no sooner did he transgress the commandments of his Maker than his heart was filled with enmity. And hence it was that when he afterward heard the voice of the Lord God in the garden he endeavored to conceal himself from him as from an enemy. How very true, then, and appropriate is the language of Paul to the Colossians: "*Enemies in your minds by wicked works!*"

Origin of man's enmity to God.

But "woe unto him that is at enmity with his Maker." For such a one Earth has no happiness, and Heaven itself has none. Every man who is in this condition may very justly apply to himself the following soliloquy, which Milton puts into

Its removal essential to our happiness.

the mouth of Satan as he lies floating on the burn ing lake:

> "Me miserable! which way shall I fly
> Infinite wrath, infinite despair?
> Which way I fly is Hell; myself am Hell;
> And in the lowest depth, a lower deep
> Still threatening to devour me opens wide,
> To which the Hell I suffer seems a Heaven."

Ah, yes; the flame of torment must be extinguished in the soul, the feeling of enmity must be taken away from the human breast, and the heart must be filled with love, and peace, and joy before any man can be made happy in any part of this wide universe.

But how can this be done? Can it be done by pains and penalties? Can it be effected by punishments of any kind, whether on Earth or in Purgatory, whether in time or in eternity? So many have thought, and so they have taught. And hence the various theories of post-mortem salvation that now abound all over Christendom.

Only way an means of effecting this.

But all such theories and hypotheses are mere vagaries of the imagination. They have not the shadow of a foundation on which to rest, either in philosophy or in fact. All experience shows that the only way to remove the enmity of the human heart is by proper manifestations of love. "If thine enemy hunger, feed him; if he thirst, give him drink; for in so doing thou shalt heap coals of fire on his head." Romans xii, 20. So teaches Paul, and so teaches all sound philosophy and all correct history and experience.

How Punishment becomes an element of reformation and reconciliation.

I am aware that punishment may often become an element of reformation. It is so used in all human governments, and it is also so used in the Divine government. God often providentially compels men to pause and reflect seriously on the solemnities of life, death, judgment, and eternity; and he does this sometimes by his judgment, even when the rich manifestations of his mercy and his love have been ineffectual. He did so in the case of Manasseh, and Nebuchadnezzar, and Saul of Tarsus, and many other persons less known to fame.

But, nevertheless, all that punishment can do in such cases is merely to arrest the attention, to humble the proud heart, and to open up natural channels through which love, and mercy, and benevolence may freely flow into the dried-up fountains of the human soul. No man ever yet loved his fellow-man simply as an avenger of wrong, and no man ever loved God on this account. "*We love God because he first loved us.*" So the beloved John testifies, and so our own experience testifies.

Fullest exhibition of God's love to man.

But in no other conceivable way could the love of God be so fully, so directly, and so efficaciously manifested to us as in the gift of his own Son. True, indeed, to him whom the Lamp of Truth illuminates, all nature is but an index or manifestation of the goodness and benevolence of God, as well as of his wisdom and power. But, nevertheless, there is no converting power in nature. There is nothing in it to warm the human heart and to draw the sinner nearer to God. The very reverse of this is seen in the history of the whole heathen world. They all had, at least for a time, some traditional knowledge of the one only living and true God. But under the dim light of nature the poor blinded heathen saw nothing that was attractive in his character. In all cases the repelling influences predominated. And as time rolled on, we find that all heathen nations were being separated further and further from their Maker.

Defect in the revelations of nature.

But how very different are the tendencies of the Gospel! The man who believes and realizes that "God SO loved the world that he gave his only begotten Son, that whosoever believeth into him should not perish, but have everlasting life," feels a new impulse of life Divine begotten in his soul; and, like the poor prodigal of our Savior's parable, he says, "I will arise and go to my Father, and I will say unto him, Father, I have sinned against Heaven and before thee, and I am no more worthy to be called thy son: make me as one of thy hired servants." Luke xv, 18, 19.

Practical effect of the Gospel on the heart of the sinner.

But before he goes very far, even while he is yet a great way off, his Father meets him and embraces him. He takes away from him his filthy garments and clothes him with the habiliments of a son. And while the Heavens are rejoicing that another poor sinner has been redeemed, he himself feels that he is no longer a slave, but a son—a son of God and an heir of Heaven. He now realizes that God is not the severe, stern, and unfeeling Being that he once supposed; but that as a father pities his children, even so the Lord pities them that fear him. And thus it is that the enmity of his heart is slain, while he himself is by the cords of love drawn into the family of God, and is then made to rejoice with a joy that is unspeakable and full of glory.

And now, in conclusion, let me say to you, poor sinner, whoever you are and wherever you are, that this is your privilege, if you see fit to enjoy it. God now says to every man that thirsteth, Come to the waters and drink. And to him that has no money he says, Come, buy and eat; yea come, buy wine and milk, without money and without price. Isaiah lv, 1

The invitation is to all.

SECTION III.—CHRIST OUR EXEMPLAR.

Another reason why the Word became flesh and dwelt among us *was to show us by his own example how we should all walk and please God.*

Third object of the Word's becoming incarnate.

It is an old and trite, but, nevertheless, true maxim, that "*Example is stronger than precept.*" We are all greatly prone to imitate those that we most love and admire. Thus it is that children follow the example of their parents, pupils that of their most highly esteemed and venerated teachers, and soldiers that of their heroic generals. And hence we see the very great importance of having a correct religious model, after which all may safely mold their character and shape their destiny. This indeed is very important in all the relations of life; but in religion it is paramount. Here its importance can not well be exaggerated.

Importance of such a Model.

But previous to the coming of Christ we look in vain, among all the sons of men, for such a model; and since his ascension from Earth to Heaven we look also in vain. Christ alone is worthy of such a place in our affections. True, indeed, history records many examples of moral greatness and goodness. Abraham, and Isaac, and Jacob, and Moses, and Joshua, and Samuel, and David, and John the Baptist, and Peter, and James, and John, and Paul, and Luther, and Calvin, and Wesley, and a host of other soldiers of the Cross, are all worthy of our admiration, and in some respects of our imitation. But, nevertheless, they were all transgressors of the Divine law, and had themselves to be purified by the blood of Jesus before they were fit for the society of the redeemed, either on Earth or in Heaven. Christ is

Christ the only perfect Model.

the only one of our race who was tempted in all respects as we are, and yet without sin.

Him, therefore, has God presented to us as our only exemplar and leader in the great conflict of life. "Behold," says he, "I have given Him for a *witness* to the people, a *leader* and commander to the people." Isaiah lv, 4. And hence Paul admonishes his Corinthian brethren to be followers of him, *even as he also was a follower of Christ.* 1 Cor. xi, 1. And to the Ephesians he says: "*Be ye therefore followers of God as dear children*, and walk in love, as Christ also has loved us, and given himself for us, an offering and a sacrifice to God for a sweet-smelling savor." Eph. v, 1, 2. And again he says to the Thessalonians: "And ye became followers of us, *and of the Lord*, having received the word in much affliction, with joy of the Holy Spirit." 1 Thess. i, 6. And in like manner he admonishes his Hebrew brethren *to look constantly to Jesus* while they were earnestly running their Christian race. Heb. xii, 2.

Evidence of his appointment as our Guide and Exemplar.

The importance of giving heed to these admonitions will be best understood by considering a few particulars. We will select, merely by way of illustration, a few out of the many lessons that are taught in the life of our blessed and adorable Redeemer.

Practical illustrations.

Be it observed, then, first of all, that *Christ made the will of his Father his supreme rule of conduct.* "My meat," said he, "is to do the will of Him that sent me, and to finish his work." John iv, 34. And to the last moment of his life, even during his agony in the garden, the burden of his prayer still was, "not my will, but thine be done." Luke xxii, 42.

Christ's Rule of Conduct.

Now, who can estimate the advantages and the benefits that would at once accrue to the Church and to the world if all Christians would strictly follow the example of Christ in this one particular? If all, for instance, who are now following the popular party or the multitude to do evil, or who are led away by the sinful promptings of their own lusts, passions, and appetites, would simply ask, as did Christ and Paul, "Lord, what wilt thou have me to do?" how very soon would the Church be purified and the world saved!

Benefits arising from its general adoption.

But in order that we may understand, as far and as fully as we can, the beautiful workings and bearings of this rule of life, let us be still more particular. *It was not merely in what we usually call great and important matters that Christ followed the will of his Father, but also in even the most minute and circumstantial events of his life.* This is well illustrated by the facts of his baptism. John was sent to baptize the people for the remission of their sins, on condition of their faith and repentance. But Christ was not a sinner. He had nothing of which to repent. And hence, so far as this was a ground of consideration, he might have justly declined being baptized by John. But no. He well knew the influence and force of example, and especially of the example of teachers and others in authority. And he knew moreover that God was about to set him forth not only as a propitiatory sacrifice to take away the sins of the world, but also as our Exemplar in all our attempts to serve him. And hence when John hesitated to baptize him on the ground of his well-known personal holiness and purity of life, he simply and modestly replied, "Suffer it to be so now: FOR THUS IT BECOMETH US TO FULFILL ALL RIGHTEOUSNESS." Matt. iii, 15.

Christ's punctilious exactness in doing the will of his Father.

Courteous reader, have you ever comprehended the full import and meaning of these simple words of Christ? If not, let me ask you to ponder them well. Embalm them in your heart. Let them be as frontlets between your eyes, and write them in letters of gold on your doors and on your gates. And whenever you feel inclined to neglect any duty or to commit any wrong, however trivial it may seem to be under your very imperfect angle of vision, remember and apply to yourself these very precious words of our Redeemer, "It becomes us to fulfill ALL RIGHTEOUSNESS." This one rule, properly considered and applied, would soon free society from ten thousand evils, and make the world a temple of God's praise.

Christ's mode of resisting the Evil One.

Another lesson of great practical importance taught and illustrated in the life of Christ is *his manner of meeting and overcoming temptations.* He was in one sense infinite in knowledge. And hence, of course, whenever he was assailed by Satan, he could have easily overcome him and exposed his sophistry by philosophical arguments drawn from the nature and circumstances of the case. But nevertheless, in all his conflicts with the Evil One, his main reliance was on the Holy Scriptures. In every case and under all circumstances his great and chief argument was simply this: "IT IS WRITTEN." When the Tempter came to him and said, "If thou be the Son of God, command that these stones be made bread," Jesus simply replied, "*It is written,* Man shall not live by bread alone, but by every word that proceedeth out of the mouth of God." And when the Devil, having placed him on a pinnacle of the Temple, said unto him, "If thou be the Son of God, cast thyself down: for it is

Illustrations.

written, He shall give his angels charge concerning thee; and in their hands they shall bear thee up, lest at any time thou dash thy foot against a stone," Jesus said to him, "*It is written again,* Thou shalt not tempt the Lord thy God." And again, when the Devil took him up into a very high mountain and showed him all the kingdoms of the world, saying, "All these things will I give thee if thou wilt fall down and worship me," Jesus said to him, "Get thee hence, Satan: *for it is written,* Thou shalt worship the Lord thy God, and him only shalt thou serve." Matt. iv, 1–11.

Aberrations from Christ's example.

Hence it is evident that in all cases and under all circumstances Christ attached the very highest authority to *the written Word of God.* It was with him an end of all controversy. And how happy it would be for the Church, and also for the world, if to-day even all those who profess to receive the Bible as the Word of God would in this respect follow his example! But instead of doing so, how many, alas! exalt the authority of their own weak reason above that of the Holy Scriptures! God says, "He that believes and is baptized shall be saved; and he that believes not shall be damned." But says one, I do n't believe this. God is too good to damn any one. Again, God assures us that this damnation will be eternal; that those who, on account of their own personal disobedience, are condemned at their death and at the judgment, will be condemned forever. He has by his servant John revealed to us, as his own irrevocable decree, that the man who is found to be unjust on the great day when the books shall be opened, and when every man shall be judged for the deeds done in his own body, shall be unjust still; that he who is filthy then shall be filthy still; that he who is righteous then shall be righteous still; and that he who is holy then shall be holy still. Rev. xxii, 11. But, says some weak-minded sophist, that would be unjust. And as I know that God is just as well as merciful, this so-called revelation must be untrue. All men will certainly be saved finally, the Word of God to the contrary notwithstanding. Thousands mistake all this for argument; and thus it is that Hell is now being filled with immortal souls through the sophistries of Satan and their own disregard for God's authority.

Christ's devotion to the service and glory of God.

The last characteristic of Christ that I shall notice for the present is *his entire personal consecration to God.* Whatever he had was at the disposal of his Father. He kept nothing back. Even his own life was finally given for the glory of God and the good of his race.

Effects of following his example in this respect.

Suppose now that all who profess to be the Disciples of Christ would really become his followers in this respect; would ever remember and practically acknowledge that they are not their own, that they have been bought with a price, and that they should therefore no longer live for themselves, but for Him who died for their redemption, what effect would this have on their own happiness, on the welfare and interests of the Church, and also on the salvation of the world? Is it not perfectly evident to every believer in the Word of God that very soon the nations would all beat their swords into plowshares and their spears into pruning-hooks, and that the lion would soon lie down with the lamb and the leopard with the kid?

Our practical delinquencies

But, alas! how far we all come short of this perfect standard! How very imperfectly we realize the extent of our obligations, our privileges, and our birthrights as the sons and the daughters of the Lord God Almighty! In many places the Church is now famishing, and the world is actually perishing for want of that help which God has enabled us to give them if we would; and yet how few, alas! how very few, are willing to come to the rescue, in the spirit of their Master! O, that every one of us had a heart like that of our Redeemer, and that our lives corresponded in all possible respects with his life! Then, indeed, would the wilderness and solitary parts of the Earth soon be made glad, and the deserts would rejoice and blossom as the rose.

SECTION IV.—Destruction of Satan's Works.

"*For this purpose the Son of God was manifested, that he might destroy the works of the Devil.*" 1 John iii, 8. See also Hebrews ii, 14.

Fourth object of Christ's becoming incarnate.

The works of the Devil are both numerous and various. By his subtile artifice and diabolical cunning he first separated man from his Maker, and thus deprived him of his chief good. As an immediate and necessary consequence of this man's faculties were all deranged; all the powers and susceptibilities of his entire nature were, to some extent, perverted; his heart was filled with selfishness, pride, malice, hatred, and every other evil passion; and in his physical constitution were sown the seeds of all manner of diseases. Nor was this enough to satisfy the hellish malice and the diabolical ambition of the Evil One. He became a usurper, took away man's dominion, deprived him of his home, made him his slave, and finally put an end to his earthly existence by hard and cruel bondage. The Earth was

Summary of Satan's works.

converted into a graveyard, and the whole world was filled with groans, and sighs, and tears, and misery and death. This is no fancy sketch. It is a sad reality, which every man constantly sees and feels for himself.

Greatness of Christ's undertaking.

It was no small undertaking, then, that Christ resolved on, when he determined to destroy the works of the Devil. It is no exaggeration to say,

> "'T was great to speak the world from naught,
> 'T was greater to redeem."

Evidence of this.

Of the truth of this we have already had sufficient evidence in what Christ has done to meet and to satisfy the claims of the Divine Government; to remove enmity from the sinner's heart by revealing to him God in his true character; and in illustrating by his own example how all men should honor God and labor for the good of their race. But all this was only preliminary; it was only to prepare the way for he great conflict which was to follow. But a short time, however, intervened between the Cross and the Crown. Soon after his crucifixion our blessed Lord was invested with all authority in the Heavens above and on the Earth beneath. The reins of universal government were given to him, and all the loyal subjects of the vast empire of Jehovah were marshaled for the conflict. On the day of Pentecost, A. D. 34, the battle was begun; and since that ever-memorable epoch every day has witnessed new victories and brought fresh laurels to the crown of our Immanuel. Satan's influence over the world has been greatly curtailed, and a vast multitude of happy spirits redeemed by the blood of the Cross out of every kindred, and tongue, and people, and nation

The Conflict under the Messiah.

now fill the Heavens with their shouts of triumph and their songs of victory.*

The victory not yet complete.

True, indeed, the victory has not yet been fully achieved. More than half the world is still under the dominion of the Wicked One; the bodies of all the dead are still in their graves; mankind have not yet regained their lost dominion over the world;

Query proposed by Skeptics.

* It is often asked, If God is omnipotent, omniscient, and omnipresent, why does he allow this conflict to be so long continued? Why does he not put an end to it at once by annihilating, if need be, both Satan and all those who are under his influence?

Reply to it.

This question is commonly urged as an objection against the fitness and Divine origin of the Bible Scheme of Redemption; but, as usual, the objector makes a false issue; and he is either deceived himself, or he attempts to deceive others by false analogies. If it were a physical contest, or such a one as is often waged by hostile nations for the sake of gratifying their inordinate ambition, or for other purposes of conquest, then indeed there would be some point in the query of the objector. But not so. If Satan and all his emissaries, human and angelic, were annihilated, God's object would not be gained. What he proposes is *the salvation of man in harmony with all the laws and principles of the moral universe.* Justice must be satisfied on the one hand, and the freedom of the human will must be respected on the other. Were man a mere machine, like a clock or a watch, God would of course treat him as such. But as God has endowed him with freedom of will, he will not allow any thing whatever to interfere with its proper exercise. He permits every man to choose or to refuse for himself, and simply holds him responsible for the right exercise of his freedom. If, during the allotted period of his probation, any man chooses to be saved through Christ, by a full and hearty compliance with God's revealed will, it is his blessed privilege to be saved. But if he is not willing to enjoy the great salvation; if, notwithstanding all the pleadings and motives of the Gospel, he still chooses to continue in his sins, then, indeed, by a necessity as profound as the Divine nature itself, and as enduring as the throne of Jehovah, he must and he will be banished with an everlasting destruction from the presence of the Lord and from the glory of his power. This Earth and all that pertains to it must be forever freed from every vestige of the works and the workings of the Devil. This is all that is fairly implied in the words of the inspired writers. The word rendered *destroy* in 1 John iii, 8, is λυω, which means properly *to loose*, *to dissolve*, or *to undo;* and hence *to destroy.* And the word used in Hebrews ii, 14, is καταργεω, (κατα, intensive, α, privative, and ργον work,) which means *to make idle*, *to bring to naught;* and hence *to destroy.* See also 1 Cor. xv, 25.

and even the Earth itself, and the atmosphere around it, are still polluted by the touch and the breath of sin.

But as Paul, in his letter to the Hebrews, reasons with respect to man's dominion over the world, even so may we also reason with regard to every thing that comes within the scope of Christ's mission to the Earth. "We do not yet," says he, "see all things put under him, (man;) but we see Jesus, who was made a little lower than the angels, on account of the suffering of death, that by the grace of God he might taste death for every man—we see him crowned with glory and honor." Hebrews ii, 8, 9. This, in Paul's estimation, was sufficient to insure the due fulfillment of the promise that the whole world would yet be rescued from the power of the usurper and placed under the dominion and government of Abraham and his seed, according to the promise." Romans iv, 13. O yes! this is enough. To see Jesus crowned Lord of all is a sufficient guarantee that all is well; that in due time all the effects of Adam's first transgression will be fully and forever canceled, the spirits of the faithful redeemed, the bodies of all raised from the dead, the Earth and its surroundings purified from the defilements of sin, Satan and his emissaries removed hence and cast into the lake of fire, and the redeemed made forever happy in the new Heavens and the new Earth, where there will be fullness of joy and pleasures forevermore. For all this and much more we may now look forward with as much certainty as we look for the rising of the Sun to-morrow.

Guarantee that all will be accomplished in due time.

And now, dear reader, where do you stand in this mighty conflict? Are you on the side of Jesus? Have you enlisted under the banner of our glorious Immanuel? If so, maintain your position.

Appeal to the Reader.

Put on the whole armor of God, and fight on; yes, living or dying, fight on, and soon your part of the victory at least will be won.

But remember that in this warfare there is no neutral ground. "He that is not with me," says Christ, "is against me, and he that gathereth not with me scattereth abroad." Matthew xii, 30. If, then, you are not with Christ, you are certainly still on the side of Satan. And, if so, let me ask you, with all tenderness and affection, what motives or encouragements have you to serve him? What has he done for you, or for any of your friends, that you should still continue in his ranks, and promote his cause by your influence? What does he yet propose to do for you? Do you want to meet Death alone? Do you want to stand on the last day at the left hand of your Judge? Do you want to hear from his pure and sacred lips the dreadful words, "Depart ye cursed into everlasting fire, prepared for the Devil and his angels!" Matthew xxv, 41. Do you want to dwell forever with Satan and his angels in everlasting burnings? If not, fly to Jesus, and fly *now*. "Behold *now* is the accepted time; behold *now* is the day of salvation." 2 Corinthians vi, 2.

SECTION V.—Conservative Influence of Christ's Mediation.

The Atonement made only for mankind.

We have no reason to think that Christ died to make an atonement for any others than the human race. He took not on him the nature of angels, but the nature of the Seed of Abraham; or, more generically, of the human race. Hebrews ii, 16; John i, 14, etc. And hence we infer with a good degree of probability, if not, indeed, with absolute certainty, that it was for mankind, and for mankind alone, that he bled, and died, and made reconciliation.

But is the moral effect of his incarnation and death confined to this little planet that we call the Earth? Or has it also a conservative influence on beings that inhabit other worlds and systems?

Whether its conservative influence extends to other worlds.

Whatever may be the truth on this subject, it is not probable that it would be made known to man by any *direct* revelation. The Bible was not given to us for the purpose of gratifying our curiosity, but to instruct us in the way of life and holiness. It was designed to teach us what God has done for *our* salvation, and what he requires of *us* in order that we may enjoy it. Every thing beyond this is a matter of inference, about which we may or we may not be mistaken, the conclusion in all such cases depending on the kind and degree of the evidence submitted.

Why not a matter of *direct* revelation.

While, therefore, I would not affirm positively that the atonement of Christ was designed by God to have a conservative influence over the whole moral universe, I am nevertheless constrained to think that this is quite probable, for several reasons.

Probabilities of the case.

I. *It seems to be implied in the fact that Christ's mediatorial reign is universal.* That his reign is universal is evident from many such passages of Scripture as the following:

Argument from the universality of Christ's reign.

1. Matthew xxviii, 18: "And Jesus came and spake unto them, (the eleven disciples,) saying, *All authority in Heaven and on Earth is given to me.*" The words *Heaven* and *Earth* are commonly used in the Bible to denote the whole universe, and this, I think, is their obvious meaning in this passage.

2. John iii, 35: "The Father loveth the Son, *and hath given all things into his hand.*" The phrase "*all things*" seems to be used here without any other limitation or exception than God himself.

3. 1 Corinthians xv, 24–27: "Then cometh the end, when he (Christ) shall have delivered up the kingdom to God, even the Father; when he shall have put down all rule, and all authority and power. For he must reign till he hath put all enemies under his feet. The last enemy, Death, shall be destroyed. *For he* (God) *hath put all things under his* (Christ's) *feet.* But when he saith, All things are put under him, it is manifest that he is excepted, who did put all things under him." Here again, as in the preceding citation, we are assured that the Father himself is the only being in the whole universe who is not now put under Christ.

4. Ephesians i, 9, 10: "Having made known unto us the mystery of his (God's) will according to his good pleasure which he had purposed in himself: that in the dispensation of the fullness of times (that is, under Christ's mediatorial reign) *he might gather together in one all things in Christ, both which are in Heaven and which are on Earth.*"

5. Ephesians i, 18–23: "The eyes of your understanding being enlightened, that ye may know what is the hope of his (God's) calling, and what the riches of the glory of his inheritance in the saints, and what is the exceeding greatness of his power toward us who believe, according to the working of his mighty power which he wrought in Christ, when he raised him from the dead, and set him at his own right hand in the heavenly places, *far above every Princedom, and Authority, and Power, and Lordship, and every name that is named not only in this age, but also in*

that which is to come; and put all things under his feet, and gave him as a head over all things to the Church, which is his body, the fullness of him that filleth all in all."

6. Philippians ii, 9–11: "Wherefore God has highly exalted him, (Christ,) and given him a name which is above every name; *that at the name of Jesus every knee should bow, of things in Heaven, and things in Earth, and things under the Earth: and that every tongue should confess that Jesus Christ is Lord to the glory of God the Father.*"

7. I Peter iii, 22: "Who (Christ) is gone into Heaven, and is on the right hand of God; *angels, and authorities, and powers being made subject to him.*"

What is implied in the passages quoted.

In these passages it is evidently implied not only that the reign of Christ is over all worlds and systems of worlds, but also that this fact is well understood by their intelligent, moral, and responsible inhabitants,* all of whom are required to do him homage, and to receive him as their rightful Sovereign. But why make such an arrangement—why extend the scepter of the Lord Jesus over the whole

Tenantry of other Worlds.

* I affirm nothing here positively touching the question whether the other planets of the Solar System and the ten thousand times ten thousand other worlds of the vast empire of Jehovah are inhabited or not. If, however, the purpose of God, so far as it respects this little earth, was wholly incomplete till man was created in the image of his Maker and placed over it as its viceroy and governor, it is certainly nothing more than reasonable to suppose that all other worlds were created for a similar purpose. And the probabilities are, therefore, all in favor of the hypothesis now generally received by the learned that said worlds were made to be occupied by intelligent, moral, and accountable beings like men and angels. But whether this hypothesis be true or false, one thing is certain: viz., *that said worlds, with all their varied tenantry, are now placed under the supervision and government of the Lord Jesus.* Does not this fact furnish additional evidence that they are under God's *moral* government, and therefore inhabited by *moral* and *responsible* agents?

universe if the influence of his incarnation, death, and atonement is to be confined wholly and exclusively to the human race? On the assumption that it extends, like the force of gravitation, to the utmost limits of Jehovah's empire, all is plain and intelligible; but on any other hypothesis the whole subject is, to us at least, involved in mystery.

Argument from the probable wants and circumstances of other worlds.

II. Another argument in favor of the aforesaid extended conservative influence of the incarnation, death, and atonement of the Lord Jesus Christ may be drawn *from the probable wants and circumstances of the moral and responsible inhabitants of the heavenly regions.* Whatever may be their rank in the scale of creation, they must all have been endowed, like men and angels, with freedom of will, with power to choose or to refuse, to obey or to disobey; and this, of course, implies the possibility of falling. At any rate, there was no way in which this could be consistently prevented except by the presentation of proper motives addressed to the heart through the medium of the understanding.

Motives the only means of preventing moral agents from sinning.

No adequate motives known previous to the death of Christ.

But it seems that previous to the incarnation and death of Christ there were found no motives adequate to this end. Angels fell, and so did man, though they were, no doubt, both placed under the very strongest moral influences then known to induce them to remain loyal to their sovereign Lord and Lawgiver.

But the Redeemed can sin no more. Why?

It seems, however, that this liability to sin and to fall is not to continue forever. The destiny of the redeemed, as well as of all holy angels, will be forever fixed at or before the day of judgment. Of this we have given the most clear and satisfactory evidence in the following passages:

1. Matthew xxv, 46: "And these (the wicked) shall go away into everlasting punishment; *but the righteous into everlasting life.*"

2. Luke xx, 35, 36: "But they who shall be accounted worthy to obtain that world and the resurrection from the dead, neither marry nor are given in marriage; *neither can they die any more: for they are equal to the angels;* and are the children of God, being the children of the resurrection."

3. 1 Corinthians xv, 53, 54: "For this corruptible must put on incorruption, and this mortal must put on immortality. *So when this corruption shall have put on incorruption, and this mortal shall have put on immortality, then shall be brought to pass the saying that is written, Death is swallowed up in victory.*"

4. Revelation xxii, 11: "He that is unjust, (after the judgment,) let him be unjust still: and he that is filthy, let him be filthy still: *and he that is righteous, let him be righteous still: and he that is holy, let him be holy still.*"

Whence, then, we naturally inquire, comes this great change that is to take place in the moral status and liability of men and angels? Will they be deprived of their freedom, and governed henceforth as mere machines? Will the problem of governing the moral universe on moral principles be then abandoned, and the whole spiritual universe be henceforth propelled, like the Sun, Moon, and stars, by forces *ab extra?* This is not at all probable. Such an allegation is inconsistent with all enlightened reason, as well as with the plain and unequivocal teachings of the Word of God.

We find a far more satisfactory solution of this

problem in the richly developed provisions and resources of the Scheme of Redemption. From all that is said in the Scriptures on this subject, it seems pretty evident that through the incarnation, death, burial, resurrection, atonement, coronation, and gloriously triumphant reign of the Lord Jesus, there will be given, at least to the redeemed of our own race, such a demonstration of the awful nature of sin, the beauty and the necessity of holiness, and also of the unyielding and inflexible nature of Divine justice, as to render it *morally impossible* for them ever to sin again. And hence Jesus says, "They can die no more." And hence, moreover, the decree of the Almighty that the holy at and after the judgment shall be holy still.

God's eternal purpose respecting this Scheme.

But if such is to be the conservative influence of the Scheme of Redemption on our own race, is it not at least quite probable that it would have a similar influence on other minds capable of understanding and comprehending, to any considerable extent, the infinite love, and justice, and grace of God which are revealed in it, and by it, and through it? And if so, is it not also probable that God would use this moral power for the purpose of preventing any further outbreaks and demonstrations of sin in any and all other parts of his dominions? And is not this, in fact, the very lesson that Paul by the Spirit designs to teach us in the following sublime and beautiful passage? "To me," he says, "by far the least of all saints, was this grace given to preach among the Gentiles the unsearchable riches of Christ, and to enlighten all as to what is the stewardship of the mystery which has been hidden from all time in God who created all things: *that there might now be made known to the princedoms and the authorities in the heavenly realms, through the Church, the manifold wisdom of God, according to a purpose of all time which he brought about in Christ Jesus our Lord.*" Eph. iii, 8–11.

Conclusion.

I am well aware that such themes are too high for us, and that we are all too prone to theorize and speculate on such matters beyond what is, perhaps, either warrantable or profitable. But, nevertheless, I am constrained to conclude, from all the premises submitted, that the conservative influence of Christ's incarnation, death, atonement, and mediatorial reign extends far beyond the narrow limits of this Earth, and that it may, in fact, be a powerful means, in the Divine administration, of preserving forever, in a state of holiness and happiness, not only the redeemed of our own race, but also, and in like manner, untold millions of other happy spirits that now occupy other parts and provinces of Jehovah's empire.

PART V.

THE HOLY SPIRIT.

Scope of Part Fifth.

THE Divine nature of the Holy Spirit, as well as its distinct personality, has, I think, been sufficiently proved and illustrated under the subject of Christology; and I will, therefore, now confine my remarks simply to its agencies,

I. In revealing to mankind the Scheme of Redemption, and demonstrating its Divine origin.

II. In turning sinners from darkness to light, and from the power and dominion of Satan unto God.

III. In comforting, sanctifying, and saving the saints

CHAPTER I.

REVELATIONS AND DEMONSTRATIONS OF THE HOLY SPIRIT.

The Scheme of Redemption revealed by the Holy Spirit.

THERE was a time previous to which the whole Scheme of Redemption was concealed in the depths of the Divine mind. No creature had ever discovered it, nor was it possible that any creature, however exalted, ever could discover it. For, as Paul said to his Corinthian brethren, "What man knoweth the things of a man save the spirit of a man which is in him? Even so the things (or purposes) of God knoweth no man but the Spirit of God." 1 Cor. ii, 11. And hence it belonged to the Spirit, and to the Spirit alone, to reveal to mankind this scheme of God's philanthropy, as well as to demonstrate its Divine origin, "for the Spirit searcheth all things, even the deep things of God." 1 Cor. ii, 10.

Use made of second causes.

In doing so, however, it availed itself of existing means and instrumentalities, as far as possible. Indeed, this may be laid down as a universal law of the Divine administration. So far as we know or have the means of judging, God has never put forth any unnecessary power in any of the works of creation, providence, or redemption. His first miracle was, of course, wholly independent of second causes. By it nature was brought into being, and second causes were thus produced. But henceforth the laws and forces of nature were made in all cases to subserve the Divine purposes, as far as practicable. And hence we find that, in most cases, when the exercise of miraculous power became necessary the miraculous and natural forces used were supplementary to each other, and made to coöperate in effecting the end proposed. The recorded exceptions to this law are but few. They occurred only when it was necessary, for some wise and benevolent reason, to change, suspend, or modify in some way the laws and forces of nature.*

Definition of a Miracle.

* As, for instance, in the separation of the waters of the Red Sea, etc. And hence I would define a miracle as *an extraordinary manifestation of Divine power, operating either independently of the laws and forces of nature, as in the original creation, or in opposition to them, as in the separation of the waters of the Red Sea, or in connection and harmony with them, as in the Noachic deluge.* This, of course, implies in all cases the exercise of a power that is superior to the laws and forces of

This, then, is the law by which the Spirit of life operated in revealing to mankind the Scheme of Redemption. All written as well as most oral communications were made through human instrumentality. Human learning and human talents were employed in all cases, so far as they could be made available, in working out a *perfect* result, and no further. And hence it follows that not only every book, but also every word and sentence of the Original Scriptures, is the product of two factors, the human and the Divine. In some cases a preponderance seems to have been given to the former, and in some cases to the latter, depending on the nature and character of the truth that was to be expressed. But in no instance was any portion of the sixty-six canonical books of the Old and New Testaments recorded without the joint agency and coöperation of both these factors. As evidence of this see, for instance, the second chapter of First Corinthians.

Two factors in all of God's written Revelations to man.

To the Holy Spirit it belonged, also, to demonstrate the Divine origin of the Scheme of Redemption as it is now revealed to us in the Living Oracles. Nothing short of miracles was sufficient for this purpose. As is the proposition, so must also be the proof, in every department of literature, science, and philosophy. If the proposition is historical, the proof must also be historical; if the proposition is demonstrative, the proof must be demonstrative; and if the proposition is miraculous, then the proof must also be miraculous. And hence we have recorded, in immediate connection with the various developments of the Scheme

Divine Origin of these Revelations demonstrated.

nature. And hence it follows that no creature can work a *real* miracle. All such pretenses are but signs, and wonders, and miracles of falsehood. 2 Thessalonians ii, 9.

of Redemption, a series of miracles that put to silence, for the time being, even some of the most violent opposers of God's chosen and inspired embassadors. The Magicians of Egypt, for example, after having done all that they could to throw discredit on the Divine legation of Moses, were finally constrained to say of his miracles, "*This is the finger of God.*" Exodus viii, 19. Nebuchad nezzar had to concede that no other God could delive like the God of Shadrach, Meshech, and Abednego Daniel iii, 29. Darius the Mede, perceiving in the de liverance of Daniel the most clear and convincing evidence of the direct interposition and interference of Jehovah, made a decree that all nations should serve and obey him. Daniel vi, 26. And Nicodemus expressed but the common sentiment of all honest men who were cognizant of the miracles of Christ when he said to him, "Rabbi, we know that thou art a teacher come from God; for no man can do these miracles that thou doest except God be with him." John iii, 2.

Miracles no longer necessary.

These miraculous demonstrations of the Spirit were continued till the Scheme of Redemption was fully revealed, and the Canon of the Holy Scriptures was placed on a historical basis so firm and enduring that nothing can ever shake it. A rejection of the miracles and facts of the Bible would now be equivalent to a rejection of all history. Jesus Christ is to-day the Alpha and the Omega not only of the whole Christian System, but also of the world's civilization. Without him and his religion all the splendid monuments and improvements of the last eighteen hundred years are but as the baseless fabric of a vision. And hence we no longer need miracles to prove the

Divine origin of a scheme which is now sustained and illustrated by the history, philosophy, and literature of the whole civilized world.*

CHAPTER II.

AGENCY OF THE SPIRIT IN THE CONVERSION OF SINNERS.

Evidence of the Spirit's Agency in Conversion.

THAT the Holy Spirit has an agency in the conversion of sinners is evident from many such passages of Scripture as the following:

1. Genesis vi, 3: "And the Lord said, *My Spirit shall not always strive with man*, for that he also is flesh;" or rather, "by his erring he is become flesh;" *i. e.*, a sensual, corrupt, perishing creature.

2. Nehemiah ix, 30: "Yet many years didst thou forbear them, *and testifiedst against them by thy Spirit in the Prophets*. Yet they would not give ear. Therefore gavest thou them into the hand of the people of the land."

3. Jeremiah vii, 25, 26: "Since the day that your fathers came forth out of the land of Egypt unto this day, I have even sent unto you all my servants the Prophets, (speaking by the Spirit,) daily rising up early and sending them: yet they hearkened not unto me nor

Miracles of Knowledge.

* I refer here simply to miracles of power as previously defined. But if with many modern writers we include also under the head of miracles every manifestation and demonstration of God's *foreknowledge*, then, indeed, we have still occurring in the fulfillment of prophecy a series of miracles no less convincing to every honest and enlightened mind than were the manifestations of Divine power witnessed in the miracles of Christ and his Apostles.

inclined their ear; but hardened their neck. They did worse than their fathers."

4. Ezekiel xxxix, 29: "Neither will I hide my face any more from them, (the Children of Israel:) *for I have poured out my Spirit upon the house of Israel, saith the Lord God.*" The Prophet here refers to the future conversion of the Israelites, concerning which Paul speaks in the plainest terms in Romans xi, 11–31.

5. Joel ii, 28–32: "And it shall come to pass afterward *that I will pour out my Spirit upon all flesh;* and your sons and your daughters shall prophesy: your old men shall dream dreams, your young men shall see visions. *And also upon the servants and upon the handmaids, in those days will I pour out my Spirit.* And I will show wonders in the Heavens and in the Earth; blood, and fire, and pillars of smoke. The Sun shall be turned into darkness, the Moon into blood, before the great and terrible day of the Lord come. And it shall come to pass that whosoever shall call on the name of the Lord shall be delivered: for in Mount Zion and in Jerusalem shall be deliverance, as the Lord hath said, and in (or upon) the remnant whom the Lord shall call." In this passage the Prophet refers to the miraculous gifts of the Holy Spirit bestowed on the primitive Christians for the conversion of the world as well as for the edification of the saints.

6. Zechariah xii, 10: "*And I will pour out on the house of David, and upon the inhabitants of Jerusalem, the Spirit of grace and of supplications:* and they shall look upon me whom they have pierced; and they shall mourn for him (the Messiah) as one that mourns for an only son; and shall be in bitterness for him, as one that is in bitterness for his first-born." Zechariah refers here

to the same event previously alluded to by Ezekiel the future conversion of the Israelities. See, also, Joel iii, 17–21.

7. John iii, 5: "Jesus answered, Verily, verily, I say unto thee, *except a man be born of water and of the Spirit, he can not enter into the Kingdom of God.*"

8. John xvi, 7–11: "Nevertheless (said Christ to his Apostles) I tell you the truth: It is expedient for you that I go away. *For if I go not away, the Comforter will not come unto you; but if I depart, I will send him unto you. And when he is come, he will reprove* (ἐλέγχω, rather *convince*, or *convict*) *the world of sin, and of righteousness, and of judgment; of sin, because they believe not on me; of righteousness, because I go to my Father and ye see me no more; of judgment, because the Prince of this world* (Satan) *is judged.*"

9. Acts vii, 51: "Ye stiff-necked and uncircumcised in heart and ears, *ye do always resist the Holy Spirit;* as your fathers did, so do ye."

10. "And my speech and my preaching was not with enticing words of man's wisdom; *but in demonstration of the Spirit and of power.*"

11. Titus iii, 4–7: "But after that the kindness and love of God our Savior toward man appeared, not by works of righteousness which we have done, *but according to his mercy he saved us, by the washing of regeneration and the renewing of the Holy Spirit;* which he shed on us abundantly through Jesus Christ our Savior; that being justified by his grace, we should be made heirs according to the hope of eternal life."

The *fact*, then, that the Holy Spirit has an agency in turning men from darkness to light, and from the power of Satan to God, is quite obvious. But this is not enough to satisfy the inquisitive disposition of this inquiring and speculative age. We must go further, and inquire also *how* it is that the Spirit operates on the minds and hearts of the people. And this is, no doubt, all right and commendable, provided only that we do not carry our speculations too far and endeavor to become wise above what is written. But just here lies the danger. Some writers and speakers have, by their vain philosophies, most unwarrantably and presumptuously set undue limits to the *power* of the Holy Spirit, while others have gone to the opposite extreme, and ascribed to it an agency which absorbs and nullifies every thing else, ignores human agency and human responsibility, and which, moreover, serves to cherish and cultivate a spirit of the most wild and extravagant fanaticism. Extreme caution is therefore very necessary just here, lest while we are attempting to avoid Scylla, we should, like many an unfortunate adventurer, fall into the vortex of Charybdis.

Further inquiry about the Spirit's operation.

Tendency to extremes.

It may be well, therefore, to pause here for a moment, and to ascertain, as far as possible, in the first place, what is the proper and legitimate ground of inquiry now before us; what it does and what it does not comprehend. This may serve to eliminate some extraneous matters, and thereby to greatly simplify the real and only legitimate question that is now to be considered.

Limitation of the Question.

Be it observed, then,

I. *That this question has nothing to do with the agency of the Spirit in fitting those who die in their infancy for a place in the everlasting kingdom of our Lord and Savior Jesus Christ.* This is obvious for two reasons:

Nothing implied in it concerning Infants.

Two Reasons.

1. Because infants are not proper subjects of conversion. In its usual religious acceptation, conversion always implies a change of *conduct.* It is ceasing to do evil, and learning to do well. But infants are of course incapable of such a change.

2. The change that is necessary in order to the salvation of all who die in their infancy does not, therefore, come within the scope of those moral means and second causes which God has made necessary in order to the remission of our own personal sins. Salvation from the effects and consequences of Adam's first transgression, and salvation from the effects and consequences of our own personal transgressions, are not to be ranked in the same category. They belong to different chapters of the Divine administration, which should never be blended together. The former is unconditional, and will, therefore, be universal. The latter is conditional, and will, therefore, as we learn from the Scriptures, be enjoyed only by those who, in their own persons, observe and respect the conditions which God has himself prescribed. If in Adam we all died, it is just as certain that in and through Christ we will all be made alive. 1 Cor. xv, 22. "If by one man's disobedience the many were made sinners, equally sure is it that by the obedience of Christ the many will, to the same extent, be made righteous." Romans v, 19. And hence it follows that we need have no concern about our own deliverance or the deliverance of any one else from the dreadful effects and terrible consequences of Adam's first transgression. Christ has undertaken this work for us, and we may rest assured that he will finish it. If one miracle or ten thousand miracles should be necessary for its accomplishment, they will all be wrought in due season. There can be no failure on

his part. That power that can deliver the body from all physical corruption can also free the soul from all moral corruption. But *how* this will be done is not a matter that now concerns us.

II. It is well to remember, also, that *the question now before us is not a question of* POWER *but of* FACT. It is not, What power the Holy Spirit could exercise over the human mind in its conversion to God, but it is simply, What power it actually does exercise in the conversion of all sane, rational, and responsible persons. It does not become such a being as man, whose breath is in his nostrils, and who has not yet learned the nature, constitution, and capabilities of his own mind, to set limits to the power of either the Father, the Son, or the Holy Spirit. This the archangel himself would not presume to do.

A Question of *fact*, not of *power*.

III. Nor does it belong to our present subject to ascertain and to estimate fully and accurately even *all the power and influence which the Holy Spirit does actually put forth and exercise over the human mind in its conversion.* It *may* exert many influences of which we know nothing. Who but God himself is competent to say what power he does and what he does not exercise over the physical and spiritual universe? Manifestly all such inquiries reach far beyond the narrow limits of our comprehension. And hence it follows,

Not the full extent of the Spirit's influence.

IV. That the only legitimate question now before us is simply this: *What do the Scriptures teach us concerning the way and means in and through which the Holy Spirit operates on the minds and hearts of actual sinners, in order to their conversion?*

The only proper Question for consideration.

It seems to me, then, that all that we can learn from the Scriptures on this subject may be comprehended under the two following propositions:

Two Propositions.

I. *The Holy Spirit, as our great and benevolent Educator, often exercises a providential influence over the minds of men, preparatory to their conversion.* Of this we have many instances given in the Scriptures, as well as in our own experience.

First: the Spirit operates providentially.

Illustrations.

The miraculous and providential events that occurred on the ever-memorable day of Pentecost, served to prepare the minds of many then present for the address of Peter, which was to follow. And thus the Lord by his Spirit providentially opened the hearts of three thousand persons on that occasion, so as to induce them to give heed to the words of the Apostle. In like manner, he also opened the hearts of Cornelius and his household; of the Philippian jailer and his household; and of Lydia and her household. And just so it would seem, not indeed by working miracles, but by the workings of his providence, the Holy Spirit still strives with at least all who hear the Word of God, and who have not committed the unpardonable sin. How often, for instance, does sickness in a family or in a community open the hearts of careless sinners, and incline them to attend to the one thing needful!

But be it observed that there is really no renewing nor regenerating power in any such events, whether miraculous or providential, without the Word of the Gospel. They can benefit the sinner only by leading and inclining him to attend seriously to the teachings of the Holy Spirit. And hence the great importance of our second proposition, which is as follows:

Second: the Spirit operates through the Word.

II. *The Holy Spirit operates on the minds and hearts of men in order to their conversion through the Word of God.* As evidence of the truth of this proposition take the following passages:

Illustrations.

1. Psalm xix, 7: "*The law of the Lord is perfect, converting the soul:* the testimony of the Lord is sure, making wise the simple." From this passage we learn that the Word of the Lord converts the soul. But what is done by the Word may, of course, be said to be done by the Spirit, who is the Author of the Word.

2. Luke viii, 4–15: "And when much people were gathered together and were come out of every city, he (Jesus) spake by a parable, saying: A sower went out to sow his seed; and as he sowed, some fell by the way-side; and it was trodden down, and the fowls of the air devoured it. And some fell upon a rock; and as soon as it was sprung up, it withered away, because it lacked moisture. And some fell among thorns, and the thorns sprung up with it and choked it. And others fell on good ground, and sprang up and bore fruit a hundred-fold. And when he had said these things he cried, He that hath ears to hear let him hear. And the disciples asked him saying, What might this parable be? And he said, . . . the parable is this: *The seed is the Word of God.* Those by the wayside are they that hear; then cometh the Devil and taketh away the Word out of their hearts, lest they should believe and be saved. They on the rock are they who, when they hear, receive the Word with joy; and these have no root, who for awhile believe, and in time of temptation fall away. And that which fell among thorns are they who, when they have heard, go forth and are choked with the cares, and riches,

and pleasures of this life, and bring no fruit to perfection. But that on good ground are they *who, in an honest and good heart, having heard the Word, keep it, and bring forth fruit with patience.*" From this beautiful narrative it is evident that the Word of God is the seed sown in the heart, by means of which all the fruits of the Spirit are produced. The reader will observe that the persons who receive the Word are often, by metonymy, put for the Word itself, and that the scope of the parable is simply to show that the fruits of the Gospel depend on the state and condition of the hearts of those who hear it.

3. John vi, 44, 45: "No man (says Christ) can come to me except the Father who hath sent me draw him; and I will raise him up at the last day." And then he immediately adds, by way of explanation, "*It is written in the Prophets, And they shall all be taught of God,* (*i. e.*, of course, by his Spirit.) *Every man, therefore, that hath heard and hath learned of the Father* (through his Spirit) *cometh to me.*"

4. Romans i, 16: "For I am not ashamed (says Paul) of the Gospel of Christ: *for it is the power of God for salvation to every one that believeth; to the Jew first, and also to the Greek.*" The Gospel in this passage is equivalent to the whole Scheme of Redemption, as it is revealed to us in the Scriptures by the Holy Spirit. And hence it follows that the written Word is the power of the Spirit of God for the salvation of every believer. For it is by faith that God purifies the heart, (Acts xv, 9;) but faith comes by hearing the Word of God." Romans x, 17.

5. 1 Corinthians iv, 14, 15: "I write not these things to shame you, but as my beloved sons I warn you. For

though ye have ten thousand instructors in Christ, ye have not many fathers: *for in Christ Jesus I have begotten you through the Gospel.*" From this we learn that all the members of the Corinthian Church had been begotten by or through the Gospel. But the Spirit is the author of the Gospel. And hence this passage serves to explain how it is that every Christian is begotten or born of the Spirit. See John iii, 5.

6. James i, 18: "*Of his own will begat he us with the Word of truth,* that we should be a kind of first-fruits of his creatures." Here the Father is said to do what he does by his Spirit, for "it is the Spirit that quickeneth." John vi, 63.

7. 1 Peter i, 22, 23: "Seeing ye have purified your souls in obeying the truth through the Spirit, unto unfeigned love of the brethren, see that ye love one another with a pure heart fervently; *being born again, not of corruptible seed, but incorruptible, by the Word of God, which liveth and abideth forever.*" This is another beautiful commentary on John iii, 5; and also on 1 John iii, 9.

Conclusion.

From these, and many other similar passages of Scripture, we may, I think, justly conclude not only that the Holy Spirit operates on the minds of the unconverted through the Word of God, but also that it never converts any man without the Word. This was never done, so far as we know, even in the days of miracles; and certainly there is not in the whole Bible the shadow of evidence that the Holy Spirit now saves any actual transgressor in any other way than by purifying his heart and regulating his whole life through the influence of that faith which worketh by love, and which in all cases depends on the testimony which God has given us concerning his Son. Romans x, 17. And hence the Apostles were commanded to "*go into all the world and preach the Gospel to every creature.*" Mark xvi, 15. And hence, I may add, their great zeal in carrying out and fulfilling this commission. In all cases and under all circumstances they proceeded as if the whole world were lost without the Gospel; and as if the salvation of every man depended on their preaching, "*we thus judge,*" says Paul, "*that if one died for all, then were all dead: and that he died for all that they who live should not henceforth live unto themselves, but unto him who died for them and rose again.*" 2 Cor. v, 14, 15. O, that the spirit of these holy men would but animate the Church of the nineteenth century! How soon in that case would the wilderness and the solitary parts of the Earth be made glad, and the deserts of the pagan world rejoice and blossom as the rose!

CHAPTER III.

AGENCY OF THE SPIRIT IN COMFORTING AND SANCTIFYING THE SAINTS.

The Spirit does not enter the Heart before its purification.

It is a law of the universe that like loves its like. There can be no communion between light and darkness; no concord between Christ and Belial. And hence the Holy Spirit can not and will not take up its abode in the heart of any man until after that it has been purified by the blood of Christ. Till then it stands at the door and knocks. Rev. iii, 20. But it never presumes to enter until the body of sin has been destroyed, and the soul of the believer cleansed by the blood of atonement. This may be proved,

I. By referring to the laws of purification under the Old Covenant. The Priests had in all cases to be *washed* before they were *anointed.* Exodus xxix, 4, 7, 21. But the former was symbolical of inward cleansing, and the latter of the gift of the Holy Spirit. See Acts x, 38; Hebrews i, 9, etc.

Proof of this.

II. It is proved by the unequivocal testimony of Christ himself. Speaking of the Holy Spirit in John xiv, 17, he says positively that *the world can not receive it.* And hence the law of the Kingdom of Heaven as laid down by Peter on the day of Pentecost is this: *that the penitent believer shall first repent and be baptized, by the authority of Christ, into the name of the Father, and of the Son, and of the Holy Spirit, for the remission of his sins; and that he shall then and there receive the gift of the Holy Spirit."* Acts ii, 38.

Law of the Kingdom respecting the gift of the Holy Spirit.

By the gift of the Holy Spirit in this passage we are not to understand the miraculous powers of the Spirit bestowed on the Apostles and many other primitive Christians, but the Holy Spirit itself. This is evident from several considerations.

Evidence that this Gift of the Spirit is the Spirit itself.

I. From the fact that the word *gift* (δωρεά) is used in the singular number. Had Peter meant the miraculous powers of the Spirit it is most likely that he would have used the word *gifts* (χαρίσματα) in the plural number, as Paul does in 1 Cor. xii, 4, 9, 28, 30, and 31.

II. From the fact that this gift was limited to the baptized; but not so the miraculous gifts of the Spirit. These were bestowed sometimes even on wicked men; such as Balaam, Judas, Caiaphas, etc. And as we learn from Acts x, 44–46, Cornelius and other Gentiles, who were present and heard Peter's address, all received the Holy Spirit in its miraculous powers and manifestations, before they were baptized or inducted into the Kingdom.

III. From the fact that *this gift was promised to all who, like the three thousand Pentecostal converts, would comply with the prescribed terms and conditions of discipleship.* "For," says Peter, "the promise is to you and to your children, and to all that are afar off, even as many as the Lord our God shall call." Acts ii, 39. But the miraculous gifts or powers of the Spirit were bestowed on but a small portion of the primitive Christians.

IV. From the fact that the same important truth is also clearly taught in many other parallel passages. Take for illustration the following:

Evidence from parallel passages.

1. Ezekiel xxxvi, 25–27: "Then will I sprinkle clean water upon you, and ye shall be clean: from all your filthiness and from all your idols will I cleanse you. A new heart, also, will I give you, and new spirit will I put within you; and I will take away the stony heart out of your flesh, and I will give you a heart of flesh. *And I will put* MY SPIRIT *within you,* and cause you to walk in my statutes, and ye shall keep my judgments to do them." Jehovah, in this address to the Israelites, refers to their future conversion; and he promises that after their hearts shall have been cleansed and purified he will put his own Spirit within them.

2. John vii, 37–39: "On the last day, the great day of the feast, Jesus stood and cried, saying: If any one thirst let him come to me and drink. He that believes on me, as the Scripture has said, Out of his belly shall flow rivers of living water. *But this he spoke of the Spirit, which those who believe on him were about to receive; for the Holy Spirit had not yet been given, because Jesus had*

not yet been glorified." From this passage two things are evident:

(1.) That the gift of the Spirit, that is, the Spirit itself, is promised to every believer under the personal reign of the Messiah.

(2.) That this marvelous gift is one of the leading characteristics of Christ's administration. For in the sense in which the Holy Spirit is here promised it was never enjoyed by any one previous to his coronation and glorification. This passage, therefore, throws much light on the words of Peter in Acts ii, 38. See also John xiv, 17, 23.

3. Romans v, 5: "And hope makes not ashamed; *because the love of God is shed abroad in our hearts by the Holy Spirit which is given to us.*" The word "*us,*" in this connection, represents all Christians; and hence it follows that the Holy Spirit is given to all; and, moreover, that it is given to all for the purpose of shedding abroad the love of God in their hearts. This agency of the Holy Spirit is more fully and comprehensively stated by the same Apostle in his Epistle to the Galatians, when he says: "*The fruit of the Spirit is love, joy, peace, long-suffering, gentleness, goodness, fidelity, meekness, and temperance.*" And again, in 1 Cor. vi, 11, he says: "And such were some of you, (alluding to the licentious characters previously named,) but ye are (now) washed, but ye are sanctified, but ye are justified in the name of the Lord Jesus and by the Spirit of our God."

4. Romans viii, 9–11: "But ye are not in the flesh but in the Spirit, *if so be that the Spirit of God dwell in you. Now, if any man have not the Spirit of Christ he is none of his.* And if Christ be in you, the body is dead because of sin; but the spirit is life because of righteousness

But if the Spirit of Him that raised up Jesus from the dead dwell in you, He that raised up Christ from the dead shall also quicken your mortal bodies *by his Spirit that dwelleth in you.*" No evidence could be more direct and conclusive than that which is here given. According to Paul the indwelling of the Spirit is the distinguishing badge, the peculiar characteristic of the Christian. "If," says he, "the Spirit dwells in you, then indeed you are Christ's; but if it does not, the evidence is conclusive that you are not of the family and children of God. See also 1 Cor. iii, 16; vi, 19, etc.

5. 2 Corinthians i, 22: "Who also hath sealed us, *and given the earnest of the Spirit in our hearts.*" The word *earnest* (ἀῤῥαβών, עֵרָבוֹן) may denote any thing given in token that a bargain is ratified, and that the terms of the contract or covenant will all be fulfilled in due time Here it means simply the Spirit itself, which God has put into our hearts as a pledge that the eternal inheritance is ours. In the same sense it is also used in 2 Corinthians v, 5, and Ephesians i, 14.

6. Galatians iv, 6: "*And because ye are sons, God hath sent forth the Spirit of his Son into your hearts, crying, Abba, Father.*" Here we have stated not only the fact that God has given us his Spirit, but also that he has done so because we are his children. This passage is, therefore, in beautiful harmony with the saying of Christ, that the world can not receive the Holy Spirit.

7. Ephesians iv, 30: "*And grieve not the Holy Spirit of God, whereby ye are sealed unto the day of Redemption.*" In the thirteenth verse of the first chapter of this same Epistle we are told that this sealing of the Ephesians by the Holy Spirit took place, according to the aforesaid law of the Kingdom, after that they believed.

8. Ephesians v, 18: "And be not drunk with wine, wherein is excess; *but be filled with the Spirit.*" Here Paul draws a contrast between wine and the Spirit. The heathen were wont to be filled with the former; but the Apostle exhorts his Ephesian brethren to be filled with the latter, which implies, of course, that this was then possible, and, moreover, that it is still possible. By cherishing impure thoughts in our hearts we may grieve the Spirit, quench the Spirit, or even cause it to forsake us entirely. But if we hunger and thirst after righteousness, and strive to keep our hearts pure, then, indeed, we may, like Stephen, Barnabas, and other holy men of the primitive Church, be filled with the Spirit of holiness, and enjoy richly in our souls all its renewing and sanctifying energies.

Conclusion from preceding premises.

From these, then, and many other similar passages, it is abundantly evident not only that the Holy Spirit dwells in us, but also that it does so for the purpose of *comforting* us, (John xiv, 16,) *helping our infirmities*, (Romans viii, 26,) and *strengthening us with might in the inner man*, (Ephesians iii, 16,) that we may thus be made partakers of the Divine nature, having escaped the corruption that is in the world through lust.

The Spirit's *mode* of operating.

If it be asked *how* the Holy Spirit accomplishes all this in our hearts, we must, I think, again confess our ignorance, and humbly acknowledge our inability to answer the question. A being like man, who knows so little about the functions and operations of his own spirit, who can not tell how it is connected with his body, how it causes his blood to circulate in his body, nor how it even moves and animates a single member, should be very modest in his attempts to define and set limits to the powers and capabilities of the Spirit of God. It is evident, however,

Through the Truth.

I. *That it operates on the heart of the Christian, as it does on the heart of the sinner, through the Word of truth.* The good seed of the Kingdom is the Word of God, without which there can be no fruits of righteousness. And hence Christ's prayer to his Father (John xvii, 17, 19) that he would sanctify his Apostles through the truth; "thy Word," said he, "is truth." See, also, John xv, 3; Acts xv, 9; xx, 32; Eph. v, 26; 1 Thess. ii, 13; James i, 21; 1 Peter i, 22, 23, etc.

Through the providence of God.

II. *That it operates on the hearts of the saints providentially.* All nature is but a case of instruments in the hand of God, by means of which, through the agency of the Spirit, he not unfrequently accomplishes his benevolent designs in reference to the sanctification of the saints, as well as in reference to the conversion of sinners. In this way he often corrected and purified his ancient people (2 Saml. xii, 13–23; Psa. cxix, 67, 71; Mal. iii, 7–12); and in this way, he still works in us, and by us, and through us, both to will and to do of his own good pleasure (2 Cor. iv, 17; Heb. xii. 4–11; 1 Peter iv, 12–19).

Some additional influence of the Spirit, rendered probable for several reasons.

III. *It seems probable moreover that the Holy Spirit operates on the hearts of the saints directly, or at least by ways and means unknown to us, so as to strengthen our infirmities, and cause the word of truth to become more productive in fruits of holiness.* That the Spirit does so seems probable.

1. From the fact that it dwells in the heart of every Christian. That it does so is abundantly proved by the passages of Scripture already cited in this chapter. But if it operates on the heart of the Christian only

by means of the word of truth, and through the ordinary events of God's providence, then why does it sustain to him a relation different from that which it sustains to the unbeliever? Why is it *given* to us; and why does it *dwell* in us?

2. From sundry declarations of Christ and his apostles. Take, for instance, the passage previously cited from John vii, 38, 39. From this it appears

(1) That Christ is speaking here of what is peculiar to his own personal reign and administration. He manifestly refers in this passage to something which had hitherto been enjoyed by no one, and which could be enjoyed by none until after that he himself was glorified.

(2) This, it would seem, could not have reference to the mediate agency of the Spirit, through the written word and the ordinary workings of God's providence; for through these media the Spirit had always operated on the minds of both Jews and Patriarchs.

(3) And hence Christ most likely refers here to an influence of the Spirit, over and above that which it exercises through the word of truth and the ordinary workings of Divine providence; an influence, by means of which it helps our infirmities (Rom. viii, 26); strengthens us with might even into the inner man (Eph. ii, 16); and enables us to bring forth abundantly in our lives the fruits of "love, joy, peace, long suffering, gentleness, goodness, fidelity, meekness, and temperance" (Gal. v, 22, 23). See also John xv, 1, 2; Phil. ii, 12, 13, etc.

But the work of the Spirit is in no sense intended to set aside our own agency. God does not convert men into machines in order to save them. But he calls on every man to do what he can, and all that he can, with the assurance that he will do the rest. And who that has any just conceptions of his new relations, his privi leges, and his birthrights as a son of God and an heir of Heaven, would not be animated and encouraged to the greatest possible extent by such a call? Who that realizes that the Spirit of the living God dwells and works within him would not also labor with all diligence to work out his own salvation, and especially to keep his heart pure? It is said that Linnæus, the great Swedish naturalist, was so accustomed to contemplate God in and through his works that he finally saw him symbolized in every flower that he analyzed. And he had written over the door of his laboratory the following admonitory words:

Practical influence of this on the believer.

INNOCUI VIVITE: NUMEN ADEST.
Live harmless: the Deity is present.

But with how much more propriety can the Christian say, in the light of God's inspired Word, THE DEITY IS PRESENT!

Various agencies in the Scheme of Redemption.

But, finally, how wisely and how beautifully arranged is this glorious scheme of Redemption! How admirably are all the different agencies employed adapted to each other and to the accomplishment of the one great purpose of the whole system! The Father sent the Son to seek and to save the lost. The Son, having accomplished the object of his mission to this earth, reascended to the Heavens and commenced his mediatorial reign. The Holy Spirit was then sent on its mission of love and mercy, while holy angels were sent to minister to the heirs of salvation, and holy men were enlisted to the full extent of their capacity in the great and mighty conflict for the redemption of the world. The last of these agencies is, of course, that which now most concerns us; and to it we shall, therefore, devote the next general division of our subject.

BOOK THIRD.

SCHEME OF REDEMPTION DEVELOPED IN AND THROUGH THE CHURCH OF CHRIST.

THE redemption of fallen man is a work of immense magnitude, as well as of immense importance. It has enlisted all the wisdom and energies of the Father, and of the Son, and of the Holy Spirit; and it was designed, moreover, to enlist all the energies and capabilities of man, with all the manifold provisions and resources of the whole Earth, so far as this could be done without infringing on the freedom of the human will.

Extent of the means employed for man's salvation.

For this purpose, indeed, and for this purpose alone, the world exists as it now is. Had not the Scheme of Redemption been a certainty, a fixed reality in the mind and purposes of Jehovah, no doubt he would have put an end to the present state and order of things as soon as man sinned and fell. For in Matthew v, 13, the righteous are said to be the salt of the Earth. Compare Genesis xviii, 23–32. But without the Scheme of Redemption there would be none righteous; no, not even one. Romans iii, 9–20. And hence it would follow, on this hypothesis, that the world would have been as ripe for destruction when Adam first sinned as it was in the days of Noah, or as were the cities of Sodom and Gomorrah in the days

Evidence that the World exists as it is for this purpose.

of Lot. Take away the Remedial System through which alone any fallen son or daughter of Adam can be made righteous, and, so far as we can see, there would have been nothing left to preserve this sin-stained world for a single hour.

But even then God had resolved on the salvation of all who would be obedient to his just and righteous requirements, and he had resolved, moreover, that they themselves should have an important agency in this work, and that in order to this the world should be spared for a time, and that all its vast resources of vegetable, animal, and mineral wealth should be consecrated to the same great end and purpose.

Organization and coöperation necessary.

But it has been often said, and truly said, that in union there is strength. Men can accomplish but little without order and coöperation; and this is just as true in religion as it is in politics, education, internal improvements, or any thing else. And hence the paramount necessity of a religious organization through which all the truly pious might coöperate for the enlightenment, conversion, sanctification, and salvation of the world.

This a part of God's original plan, proved by the Types and Prophets.

Such an organization had long been contemplated. It was a part of the original plan devised by Jehovah, and was very strikingly and beautifully illustrated by many of the typical provisions of the Levitical Priesthood. The Prophets also often dwelt with great interest on this element of the Scheme of Redemption. Isaiah, for instance, at one time described it as a luminary rising on the benighted nations, (lx, 1–3;) and then again he speaks of it as a city into which all the tribes and families of the Earth were pouring their wealth and influence.

Lx, 4–22. Others spoke of it in like manner through various figures and emblems; but Daniel was, perhaps, the first who laid aside all symbolical imagery, and plainly announced the fact that at some time between the reign of Nebuchadnezzar and the fall of the Roman Empire the God of Heaven would set up a kingdom on Earth that should never be destroyed. Daniel ii, 44. A little more than six hundred years after this John the Baptizer appeared in the wilderness of Judea and repeatedly announced the fact that the Kingdom of Heaven was at hand, (Matt. iii, 2, etc.;) and the same proclamation was afterward made by both Jesus and his disciples throughout all Palestine. Matt. iv, 17, etc. And finally, on the day of Pentecost, A. D. 34, the fact itself was fully realized. For while the one hundred and twenty disciples spoken of in the first chapter of Acts were all assembled "in one place, suddenly there came a sound from Heaven as of a rushing mighty wind, and it filled all the house where they were sitting. And there appeared unto them cloven tongues like as of fire, and it (one tongue) sat on each of them. And they were all filled with the Holy Spirit, and began to speak with other tongues as the Spirit gave them utterance." Acts ii, 1–4.* To this miraculous event the Apostle Peter

Proclamation of John and Christ.

Beginning of the Kingdom.

* That this refers to the one hundred and twenty disciples, and not merely to the twelve Apostles, I am inclined to think for the following reasons:

Evidence that the Holy Spirit was poured out on the 120 Disciples.

I. Because this construction is most in harmony with the logical and grammatical relations of the passage. The word "*disciples*," in Acts i, 15, is, I think, the proper grammatical antecedent of "*they all*" in Acts ii, 1. For it was to the 120 disciples that Peter delivered his address, (Acts i, 16–22;) after which *they* (the 120) appointed two . . . ; and *they* (the 120) prayed . . . ; and *they* (the 120) gave forth their lots; and the lot fell on Matthias; and he was appealed on the same occasion as furnishing conclusive evidence that God had made Jesus both LORD and CHRIST; that is, the anointed Sovereign of the universe. And accordingly, *for the first time, believers were immediately required to be baptized by his authority into the name of the Father, and of the Son, and of the Holy Spirit.* By the authority of Jehovah, John the Immerser had baptized many of the Jews as Jews into repentance for the remission of their sins, but never before the day of Pentecost, A. D. 34, was any man baptized by the authority of Jesus Christ into the new and sacred relationship which is implied in the formula of Christian Baptism. And hence we find that from that day forward the Kingdom of Heaven, or the Church of Jesus

numbered with the eleven Apostles. And when the day of Pentecost was fully come, *they* (the 120) were all with one accord in one place, etc. By connecting these clauses together it seems pretty evident that the reference to the eleven Apostles in Acts i, 26, is but incidental, and that the 120 disciples constitute the proper *subject* of the whole narrative in Acts i, 23–ii, 4.

II. Because this seems to be implied in the introductory words of Peter's address. The eleven Apostles stood up with Peter as his coequals and coadjutors. And hence it is more natural to suppose that by the word "*these*" (οὗτοι) he intended to designate others than the Apostles. Had he referred simply to himself and his co-workers and fellow-laborers, in the apostolic office, he would, no doubt, have said "*we* (ἡμεῖς) are not drunken," etc., as he does in the thirty-second verse.

III. Because this best accords with the prophecy of Joel, to which Peter immediately referred for an explanation of the very strange and remarkable phenomena. "It shall come to pass in the last days, saith God, I will pour out of my Spirit upon all flesh: *and your sons and your daughters shall prophesy;* and your young men shall see visions, and your old men shall dream dreams; and on my servants and on my *hand-maidens* I will pour out in those days of my Spirit, and they shall prophesy." Acts ii, 17, 18. All this is most appropriate and just to the point, provided that the women mentioned in Acts i, 14, were included in the "*all*," Acts ii, 1.

IV. Because this explanation is corroborated by the pouring out of the Spirit on the household and friends of Cornelius. Acts x, 44: "While Peter was speaking these words, *the Holy Spirit fell on all them who heard the word.*" Compare Acts xi, 15.

Christ, is ever spoken of and recognized as a distinct and living reality. See, for instance, Acts ii, 47; v, 11; vii, 38; viii, 1, 3; xi, 15. In this last passage Peter clearly and unmistakably refers to the aforesaid day of Pentecost as the *beginning* of the Kingdom of Heaven and the commencement of Christ's mediatorial reign on Earth.

Names and Epithets given to the Kingdom.

This organization has received different names according to the stand-point from which it is viewed and the various relations under which it is contemplated. It is called *the Kingdom of Heaven* in Matt. iii, 2; iv, 17; xiii, 24, 31, 33, 38, 44, 45, 47, 52; xvi, 19, etc.; *the Kingdom of God,* Matt. vi, 33; Mark i, 14, 15; iv, 11, 26, 30; x, 14, 15, 23, 24, 25, etc.; *the Kingdom of God's dear Son,* Col. i, 13; *the Kingdom of Christ and of God,* Eph. v, 5; *the Kingdom of Jesus Christ,* Rev. i, 9; *the Church of God,* 1 Cor. xi, 22, 1 Tim. iii, 15; *the Church of Christ,* Matt. xvi, 18; *the Church,* Acts ii, 47; v, 11; 1 Cor. xv, 9; Eph. i, 22; iii, 10, 21; v, 23, 24, 25, 27, 29, 32; Col. i, 18, 24, etc. And again, when it is contemplated with reference to the several congregations of which it is composed, it is variously called *the Churches of God,* 1 Cor. xi, 16; 1 Thess ii, 14; 2 Thess. i, 4; *the Churches of Christ,* Romans xvi, 16; *the Churches of the Saints,* 1 Cor. xiv, 33; *the Churches of the Gentiles,* Romans xvi, 4; *the Churches of Judea, Asia, Macedonia, Galatia, etc.,* Gal. i, 22; 1 Cor xvi, 19; 2 Cor. viii, 1; Gal. i, 2; or simply *the Churches* Acts xv, 41; xvi, 5; 1 Cor. vii, 17; xiv, 34; 2 Cor. viii 18, 19, 23, 24, etc.

The propriety of these various designations will at once be perceived and acknowledged by the intelligent reader. The *implied* elements of the Kingdom of Christ and of the Church of Christ are of course identical.* But the name *Kingdom of Christ* is more *expressive.* It fixes our minds directly on Christ himself as the King and absolute Sovereign; whereas the name *Church of Christ* refers primarily to the whole body of believers, of which Christ is the Supreme Head.† See, for instance, Ephes.

Difference between the Kingdom of Christ and the Church of Christ.

* The elements of the Kingdom of Heaven are, 1. The King; 2. The Subjects; 3. The Constitution; 4. The Laws and Ordinances; 5. The Ministers; 6. The Territory. And the elements of the Church of Christ are, 1. The Head; 2. The Body; 3. The Constitution; 4. The Laws and Ordinances; 5. The Ministers; and, 6. The Territory. In the former Christ is the King; all persons begotten by the Spirit and born of water are the Subjects; the gracious purpose of God revealed in the New Covenant is the Constitution; the rules and institutions established by the Apostles are its Laws and Ordinances; the Ministers of the Gospel, both ordinary and extraordinary, are its Officers; and the whole Earth is its Territory. In the latter the same elements are all *implied* with but slight modifications.

Elements of the Kingdom of Christ and of the Church of Christ.

† The word *church* or *kyrke* is but a corruption of the Greek word *kuriakos*, (κυριακός,) and means primarily *whatever belongs or pertains to the Lord*, (κύριος.) It was at first most likely used merely as an adjective for the purpose of defining the noun *ekklesia*, (εκκλησία.) The latter was used among the ancient Greeks to denote an assembly of any kind whatever. Thus, for instance, Herodotus, Thucydides, and other Greek writers, frequently use it to designate the legislative assembly of the Athenians. In Acts xix, 32, 41, it is applied to the lawless and excited assembly of citizens called together and headed by Demetrius; and in the Septuagint it is several times used for the Hebrew word *kahhal*, (קָהָל,) to denote the whole assembly of the Jewish nation. See Acts vii, 38, and Hebrews ii, 12. It was, therefore, quite natural that instead of this somewhat indefinite term, the Greek Fathers should use the more definite name ἡ ἐκκλησία κυριακή, "*The Lord's assembly*," for the purpose of designating more clearly and distinctly the Church of Christ. But in time the noun was omitted; and the adjective and article only were used, just as ἡ κυριακή is used in Rev. i, 10, for *the Lord's Day;* and as τό κυριακόν is often used in Greek literature for *the Lord's house.* From the Greeks of Constantinople the Goths of the lower Danube got the word κυριακή, as the proper name of the Church of Christ, instead of ἐκκλησία; and from the Goths it was carried by the Anglo-Saxons into England and Scotland, where it is commonly written *church*, or *kyrke*, or *kirk*.

Origin and use of the word *Church* or *kyrke*.

i, 22, 23; ii, 16; iv, 4, 12, 16; v, 23, 24, 30; Col. i, 24; ii, 19; iii, 15. See also 1 Cor. xii, 12–27. It is in this sense that we propose to consider this Institution. For the sake of brevity and order we will speak,

I. Of its Officers.
II. Of its Laws and Ordinances.
III. Of its Members; and,
IV. Of its Organization, Coöperation, and Discipline.
V. Of its Fortunes and its Destiny.

PART I.

MINISTRY OF THE CHURCH.

Derivation and meaning of the word *minister*.

THE English word *minister* comes directly from the Latin *ministro*, which means *to wait on, to serve*, etc. Its Greek synonym is διάκονος, though it is used also sometimes for λειτουργός and ὑπηρέτης.* It is found thirty times in the Common English Version of the New Testament; in twenty of which it is used for διάκονος; five for λειτουργός, and five for ὑπηρέτης. It may, therefore, denote any one who waits on or serves another. This is evident from many such passages as the following:

Illustrations.

1. Matt. xx, 25–28: "But Jesus called them (the Apostles) to him, and said, Ye know that the princes of the Gentiles exercise dominion over them, and they that are great exercise authority upon them. But it shall not be so among you; but whosoever will be great among you, let him be your *minister*, (διάκονος;) and whosoever will be chief among you, let him be your servant, (δοῦλος:) even as the Son of Man came

Derivation and meaning of διάκονος, λειτουργός, and ὑπηρέτης.

* Διάκονος is from διάκω or διήκω, *to run, to hasten*; and hence it means properly *a runner, a messenger; a minister in actual service.* Λειτουργός, from λεῖτος, *public*, and ἔργον, *a work*, means simply *one who ministers for the good of the public.* Ὑπηρέτης, from ὑπο, *under*, and ερέσσω, *to row*, is a military term, and means properly *an under-rower*, or *a common sailor*, as distinguished from οἱ ναῦται, *shipmen*; and hence it came to signify an attendant or minister. Thus we find that John Mark was the ὑπηρέτης of Paul and Barnabas. Acts xiii, 5.

not *to be ministered unto*, (διακονέω,) but *to minister*, (διακονέω,) and to give his life a ransom for many."

2. Matt. xxii, 3: "Then said the King to the *servants*, (διάκονος,) Bind him (the man without a wedding garment) hand and foot, and take him away, and cast him into outer darkness: there shall be weeping and gnashing of teeth."

3. Matt. xxiii, 10, 11: "Neither be ye called masters, (καθηγητής,) for one is your Master, even Christ. But he that is greatest among you shall be your *servant*, (διάκονος.)"

4. Mark ix, 33–35: "And he came to Capernaum; and being in the house, he asked them, What was it that ye disputed about among yourselves by the way? But they held their peace; for by the way they had disputed among themselves who should be the greatest. And he sat down and called the twelve and said unto them, If any man desire to be first, the same shall be last of all and *servant* (διάκονος) of all."

In this generic sense the word διάκονος, or some one of its cognates, is applied to all church officers. And hence it is evident that they are not to be *lords* over God's heritage, but *servants* of the Church.*

The Ministry of the Church may be divided,

Division of the Christian ministry.

I. With respect to the period of their service, into Ordinary and Extraordinary.

II. With respect to their field of labor, into Local and Universal.

III. With respect to their rank, into Apostles, Prophets, Evangelists, Elders or Bishops, and Deacons. Eph.

* In England, where the Ministers of Parliament are *Lords* over both the Church and the State, it is perhaps not surprising that there should be some opposition to the use of the word *minister* among Dissenters and Reformers. But in its Scriptural sense this title certainly implies nothing that should be offensive to any one.

iv, 11; 1 Cor. xii, 28. Compare Phil. i, 1; 1 Timothy iii, 1–3. All this will be manifest as we proceed with the discussion.

CHAPTER I.

APOSTLES OF CHRIST.

Meaning of the word *apostle*.

THE word *apostle* (ἀπόστολος, from ἀποστέλλω, *to send forth*) means simply a missionary, or one who is sent out by the authority of another. Matthew xv, 24; Mark ix, 37; John iii, 17; Acts xiv, 14; 2 Cor. viii, 23; Gal. iv, 4; Phil. ii, 25; Heb. iii, 1, etc.

Three Orders of Apostles.

There are three orders of Apostles mentioned in the New Testament:

I. Apostles of God, such as Moses and Christ. Hebrews iii, 1.

II. Apostles of Christ, such as Peter, James, and John. Matthew x, 2–5, and Luke vi, 13–16.

III. Apostles of the Church, such as Paul and Barnabas. Acts xiv, 14, and 2 Cor. viii, 23.

Number and Names of Christ's Apostles.

For the present we will speak only of the second order, or the Apostles of Christ. Of these there were but thirteen, viz.: "Peter, and James, and John, and Andrew, Philip, and Thomas, Bartholomew, and Matthew, James, the son of Alpheus, and Simon Zelotes, and Judas, the brother of James," Matthias, who was elected in place of Judas Iscariot, and Paul, who was "as one born out of due time." Compare Matthew x, 2–4; Mark iii, 13–19; Luke vi, 12–16; Acts i, 12, 13, 26; and Acts ix, 1–22.

Some, indeed, infer from such passages as Matthew xix, 28, and Rev. xxi, 14, that there were, in reality, but twelve Apostles; and hence they suppose that Matthias was not an Apostle. But such an allegation is manifestly inconsistent with the plain and unequivocal statements made in Acts i, 23; ii, 14; vi, 2, etc. And it is, therefore, more probable that Paul, being an Apostle *extraordinary*, is not included in the aforesaid passages; or, otherwise, that the number twelve is used, in such cases, in a technical sense, as it frequently is when applied to the Tribes of Israel. These were, in reality, thirteen, though they are commonly called the twelve Tribes.

These thirteen Apostles were Christ's plenipotentiaries on Earth, and were invested with all the power and authority that were necessary in order to the full establishment and proper administration of the Kingdom of Heaven. See Matthew xviii, 18; xix, 28; Luke xxii, 28–30.

Power and authority of the Apostles.

To them, therefore, it belonged,

I. *To bear testimony in behalf of Christ.* "But ye shall receive power," said Christ to his Apostles, "after that the Holy Spirit is come upon you; and ye shall be WITNESSES unto me, both in Jerusalem, and in all Judea, and in Samaria, and unto the uttermost parts of the Earth." Acts i, 8. See, also, Luke xxiv, 48; John xv, 27; Acts xxvi, 16, etc.

Extraordinary Functions of the apostolic office.

II. *To reveal to mankind the essential truths and principles of the Scheme of Redemption.* "Howbeit, when he, the Spirit of truth, is come, he will guide you into all truth; for he shall not speak of himself; but whatsoever he shall hear, that shall he speak; and he will shew you things to come." John xvi, 13. See, also, Luke xxiv, 49; John xiv, 26.

III. *To enact all the necessary laws, and to establish all the required ordinances of the Kingdom.* "And Jesus came and spake unto them, (the Apostles,) saying, All authority is given unto me in Heaven and on Earth. Go ye, therefore, and make disciples of all the nations, baptizing them into the name of the Father, and of the Son, and of the Holy Spirit, teaching them to observe all things whatsoever I have commanded you; and lo, I am with you always, even to the end of the world." Matthew xxviii, 18–20. See, also, xviii, 18; xix, 28; Luke xxii, 29, 30, etc.

IV. *To demonstrate, by various miraculous signs and wonders, that Jesus had been exalted to be a Prince and a Savior, and that they themselves were his own chosen and appointed embassadors to proclaim his will to every creature.* "And behold I send the promise of my Father upon you; but tarry ye in the city of Jerusalem until ye be endued with power from on high." Luke xxii, 49. See, also, John xv, 26; Acts i, 8; iii, 1–26, etc.

V. *To confer on others the power to work miracles* Acts viii, 14–17; xix, 6; 2 Timothy i, 6.

Qualifications of the Apostles.

From this brief survey of the special duties and prerogatives of the Apostles it is obvious that they should all have the following qualifications:

I. *That they should have seen Jesus Christ, and been eye and ear witnesses of what they testified to the world concerning him.* See John xv, 27; Acts i, 21, 22; xxii, 14, 15; xxvi, 16; 1 Cor. ix, 1; xv, 8; 1 John i, 1.

II. *That they should have been chosen and appointed to their office by Christ himself.* Authority to choose an Apostle was never delegated to any man or body of men. Even Matthias was appointed by lot, the disposing of which is, in all cases, from the Lord. Proverbs xvi, 33. See, also, Luke vi, 13–16; Acts ix, 15; xxii, 14, etc.

III. *That they should have the gift of plenary inspiration.* This was necessary in order to enable them to understand aright the oracles and teachings of the Old Testament, to reveal fully and infallibly the remaining mysteries of the Scheme of Redemption, and to give to the Church such a code of laws and regulations as would, in all ages and under all circumstances, be to her a perfect rule of faith and practice. That this gift was abundantly bestowed is evident from the following passages: Matthew x, 16–20; John xiv, 15–18; xvi, 12–15; Acts i, 5, 8; ii, 1–4; 1 Cor. ii, 4–16; Gal. i, 11, 12.

IV. *That they should have the gift of tongues, and the power to work divers sorts of miracles.* This was one of their necessary credentials, and was largely bestowed on all the Apostles. Acts iii, 1–26; Hebrews ii, 4, etc.

The Apostles had no successors.

From these premises, then, it follows, of necessity, that the Apostles could have no successors in office. Neither the Pope of Rome nor the Archbishop of Canterbury can ever possess their qualifications, or discharge the special duties of their office. The fact is that in, and by, and through their writings they themselves still live and preside over the whole Church of God, according to the promise of Christ given to them in Matthew xix, 28, and in the same sense it is that Christ himself will be with them, even to the end of the world. Matthew xxviii, 20. And hence we conclude that the twenty-seven Canonical Books of the New Testament are the only proper successors of the Apostles of Christ now on Earth.

Other duties performed by the Apostles.

Besides the aforesaid special duties of their office, the Apostles discharged, also, as far as possible, all the various duties of the Prophets, the Evangelists, the Elders, and the Deacons.

They and the Prophets were, indeed, for a time the only Ministers of the Church. But when the number of disciples was increased, helps became necessary. The number of Prophets was then also increased, and besides, Evangelists, Pastors, and Teachers were then created, and for a time supernaturally qualified by the gifts of the Spirit "*for the perfecting of the saints, for the work of the Ministry,* (διακονία,) *for the edifying of the body of Christ,*" till the Canon should be completed, and the whole Church come to the full knowledge of the truth and to the measure of the stature of the fullness of Christ. See Ephesians iv, 11–13, and 1 Cor. xii, 28. All these matters, God willing, we will consider in order.

CHAPTER II.

PROPHETS.

Definition of a Prophet.

A PROPHET, (Gr., προφήτης, from πρό, *before,* and φημί, *to say;* Heb., נָבִיא, from נָבָא, *to boil up like a fountain,*) in both the Old and the New Testament, is one who, under the influence of the Holy Spirit, speaks the words and the thoughts of God, whether they relate to the past, to the present, or to the future. For proof and illustration see Deut. xviii, 18, 19; 1 Kings xii, 22–24; 1 Chron. xvii, 3, 4; Isaiah i, 1, 2; xxviii, 13, 14; Jeremiah x, 1, 2; Ezek. i, 3; iii, 4, 10, 11; Hosea i, 1; Joel i, 1; Amos iii, 1, 2; Obadiah i, 1; Jonah i, 1, 2; Micah i, 1; Zeph. i, 1; Haggai i, 1–4; Zech. i, 1–3; Malachi i, 1, 2; Acts ii, 17, 18; iii, 18, 21; xi, 27, 28; 1 Cor. xii, 10; xiv, 24–33; Eph. iii, 5; Hebrews i, 1; 2 Peter i, 19, 21.

And hence we find that the special business of the Prophets was,

Functions of the Prophetic Office.

I. *To predict future events.* This is evident from the following passages:

1. Acts xi, 27, 28: "And in those days came Prophets from Jerusalem to Antioch. And there stood up one of them, named Agabus, and signified by the Spirit that there should be great dearth throughout all the world; which came to pass in the days of Claudius Cæsar."

2. Acts xxi, 10, 11: "And as we tarried there (at Cæsarea) many days, there came down from Judea a certain Prophet, named Agabus. And when he was come to us, he took Paul's girdle, and bound his own hands and feet, and said, Thus saith the Holy Spirit, So shall the Jews at Jerusalem bind the man that owneth this girdle, and shall deliver him into the hands of the Gentiles." See, also, xx, 23.

II. *To reveal the counsels and purposes of God.*

1. Ephesians iii, 4, 5: "Which (mystery) in other ages was not made known to the sons of men, as it is now revealed to his holy Apostles and Prophets by the Spirit; that the Gentiles should be fellow-heirs, and of the same body, and partakers of his promise in Christ by the Gospel." Compare 1 Cor. ii, 7–16.

2. 1 Timothy iv, 14: "Neglect not the gift that is in thee, which was given thee by prophecy (διὰ προφητείας) with the laying on of the hands of the presbytery." Compare 1 Tim. i, 18, and 2 Tim. i, 6. This shows that it was God's purpose, made known most likely through some of the Prophets of Lystra or Iconium, that Timothy should be invested with this spiritual gift.

III. *To distinguish between the inspired Word of God and the uninspired teachings of men.*

1. 1 Cor. xiv, 37: "If any man think himself to be a Prophet, or a spiritual man, let him acknowledge that the things which I write unto you are the commandments of the Lord."

2. 1 John ii, 20, 27: "But ye have an unction from the Holy One, and ye know all things. . . . But the anointing which ye have received of Him abideth in you; and ye need not that any man teach you; but as the same anointing teacheth you of all things, and is truth, and is no lie, and even as it hath taught you, ye shall abide in him." Compare iv, 1.

IV. *To unfold the meaning of the Holy Scriptures, or the spoken Oracles of God.*

1. Exodus vii, 1: "And the Lord said unto Moses, See, I have made thee a God to Pharaoh; and Aaron thy brother shall be thy Prophet;" that is, thy interpreter.

2. 1 Cor. xiv, 1–4: "Follow after love and desire spiritual gifts, but more especially that ye may prophesy. For he that speaketh in an unknown tongue, speaketh not unto men but unto God: for no man understandeth him; howbeit in the Spirit he speaketh mysteries. But he that prophesieth speaketh to edification, and exhortation, and comfort. He that speaketh in an unknown tongue edifieth himself; but he that prophesieth edifieth the Church."

It is in this sense that Apollo was called the Prophet of Jupiter, and that the ancient poets were called the prophets of the Muses.

V. *To reveal the secrets of the human heart.* This is proved by the following passage: 1 Cor. xiv, 23–25: "If the whole Church were come together into some place, and all speak with tongues, and there come in those that are unlearned or unbelievers, will they not say tha ye are mad? But if all prophesy, and there come in one that believeth not, or one unlearned, he is convicted by all, he is judged (or searched into) by all. And thus are the secrets of his heart made manifest; and so falling down on his face, he will worship God, and report that God is in you of a truth." One of the leading characteristics of the Word of God is, that it searches the heart and reveals its secrets. This is beautifully illustrated by the following passage from Hebrews iv, 12: "For the Word of God is living and powerful, and sharper than any two-edged sword, piercing even to the dividing asunder of soul and spirit, and of the joints and marrow, and is a discerner of the thoughts and intents of the heart."

VI. *To exhort, comfort, confirm, and edify the Church.*

1. Acts xv, 32: "And Judas and Silas being Prophets also themselves, exhorted the brethren with many words and confirmed them."

2. 1 Cor. xiv, 31: "For ye may all prophesy one by one, that all may learn, and that all may be comforted."

The following observations will serve to illustrate still further the nature and design of the prophetic office in the Christian Church:

The Prophets chosen and qualified by Christ.

I. *The Prophets were not like the Evangelists, Elders, and Deacons, the creatures of the Church; but in all cases they were chosen and qualified by Christ himself, either directly or through the instrumentality of the Apostles.* From the narrative given in the second chapter of Acts it seems probable that one hundred and eight Prophets were qualified simultaneously with the twelve Apostles by the first baptism in the Holy Spirit; for they all began to speak with tongues as the Spirit gave them utterance. That Christ was the Baptizer in this case is evident from the thirty-third verse of the same chapter. Compare Matt. iii, 11, and Acts i, 5

Another instance in which the prophetic gift was bestowed directly by Christ himself is found in the history of the conversion of the first Gentile converts. Compare Acts x, 44–46, with xi, 15–17.

But that this miraculous gift was in some instances bestowed also through the instrumentality of the Apostles is evident from the following passages:

1. Acts viii, 14–18: "Now when the Apostles who were at Jerusalem heard that Samaria had received the word of God, they sent unto them Peter and John, who, when they were come down, prayed for them that they might receive the Holy Spirit; for as yet it had fallen upon none of them; only they were baptized in the name of the Lord Jesus. *Then laid they their hands on them and they received the Holy Spirit.* And when Simon *saw* that through the laying on of the Apostles' hands the Holy Spirit was given he offered them money," etc.

2. Acts xix, 6, 7: "And when Paul had laid his hands on them, the Holy Spirit came on them; *and they spake with tongues and prophesied.* And all the men were about twelve."

3. 2 Tim. i, 6: "Wherefore I put thee in remembrance, that thou stir up the gift of God which is in thee by the putting on of my hands."

Rank and dignity of the Prophets.

II. *In point of rank and dignity the Prophets were next to the Apostles.* This is evident from the following passages:

1. Ephesians iv: "And he gave some Apostles, and some Prophets, and some Evangelists, and some Pastors and Teachers, for the perfecting of the saints," etc.

2. 1 Corinthians xii, 28: "And God hath set some in the Church: first, Apostles; secondarily, Prophets; thirdly, Teachers; after that miracles; then gifts of healing; helps; governments; diversities of tongues."

III. *The Prophets were not selected from among persons of any particular age, rank, or even sex.* For God's promise through Joel to Israel was this: "I will," said he, "pour out of my Spirit upon all flesh; and your sons and your daughters shall prophesy; and your young men shall see visions, and your old men shall dream dreams; and on my servants and on my handmaidens I will pour out, in those days, of my Spirit, and they shall prophesy." Compare also Acts xxi, 9; 1 Cor. xi, 5; Exodus xv, 20; Judges iv, 4; 2 Kings xxii 14; Neh. vi, 14; Isaiah viii, 3; and Luke ii, 36.

Confined to no age nor sex.

IV. *The prophetic office, like the apostolic, was only temporary.* "Love never faileth," says Paul; "but whether there be prophecies, they shall fail; whether there be tongues, they shall cease; whether there be knowledge, (miraculous, of course,) it shall vanish away." 1 Cor. xiii, 8.

The Prophetic Office temporary.

From all these premises, then, I think it is quite evident that *the Prophets were an extraordinary class of Ministers chosen by Christ himself for the purpose of assisting the Apostles in the work of establishing the Church and preparing the saints for the work of the ministry; but were not intended to officiate either as Teachers or as Rulers in any fully organized and well-instructed congregation.* The sixty-six books of the Old and New Testaments are now our only Apostles and Prophets, and contain every thing that is really necessary in order to our edification and progress in the Divine life.

Conclusion.

CHAPTER III.

EVANGELISTS.

THE third class and order of ecclesiastical or church officers, given in Ephesians iv, 11, are called Evangelists. But who are they, what are they, and what are their duties and necessary qualifications?

Third class of church officers.

The word *evangelist* comes from the Greek verb *εὐαγγελίζω*, and this again from the noun *εὐαγγέλιον*. The latter means *good news;* and the former, *to proclaim good news*. And hence the word *evangelist*, according to its etymology, means simply *a proclaimer* of good news.

Meaning of the word according to its etymology.

But this gives us only its generic meaning. And in this sense Christ himself was an Evangelist, and so was every Apostle and Prophet; and so also is every faithful disciple. For it is certainly the duty as well as the privilege of every Christian to say to his neighbors, and friends, and fellow-citizens, "that Christ died for our sins, according to the Scriptures; and that he was buried, and that he rose again the third day, according to the Scriptures." 1 Cor. xv, 3, 4.

But in Ephesians iv, 11, the word *evangelist* is evidently used in a more definite and official sense:

Proof that it is used also in an official sense.

1. Because it is here used in connection and in contrast with other official names.

2. Because, on any other hypothesis, there would be

no propriety in making a distinction between Evangelists and any other class of Christians.

What, then, is its *official* meaning? In order to answer this question properly, and in the light of the Living Oracles, it is necessary that we first ascertain what was the work of the primitive Evangelists. What did these public functionaries do under the guidance, direction, and supervision of the Apostles?

The title is first given to Philip in Acts xxi, 8. He was one of the seven Deacons who were first chosen and appointed to attend to the secular wants of the Church at Jerusalem. But it seems that he afterward became an Evangelist, and proclaimed the Gospel with great success to the Samaritans, and was afterward instrumental in converting the Ethiopian eunuch, and evangelizing all the cities from Azotos to Cæsarea. Acts viii. From this very brief account, then, of the evangelical labors of Philip, we would naturally infer that his chief business was to convert the people; to turn them from darkness to light, and from the power and dominion of Satan to God.

Given first to Philip as an official title.

Scope of Philip's labors.

The next specific use of this term occurs in 2 Timothy iv, 5: "But watch thou in all things," says Paul to Timothy; "endure afflictions, *do the work of an Evangelist, fulfill your ministry.*"

Proof that Timothy was an Evangelist.

In this passage it is clearly implied that Timothy was an Evangelist,

I. Because it is evidently Paul's object, as we learn from the context, to express, in a few words, a summary of all the duties that pertained to his ministry. He had made quite a number of specifications in his first Epistle to Timothy, and had added several particulars in the second. He had, for instance, commanded him to preach the Word, to see that Elders and Deacons were duly chosen and appointed to their office, to labor earnestly for the edification of the Church, etc. But now, in the conclusion of his second letter, and while many things were weighing heavily on his mind, he aims to sum up in a few words, all that he would have Timothy observe and do. This he has done, most appropriately and effectually, by simply urging and exhorting him to do the whole work of an Evangelist, and to see that nothing pertaining to his ministry was neglected. The last clause is amplificative as in Hebrew parallelism.

II. Because it is very absurd to suppose that a man in one office would in terms so very general and comprehensive, be urged and required to perform the duties of another. On what reasonable ground can it be alleged that in a body where all is intended to be order and harmony, where every joint and every ligament is expected to perform its own proper functions, one member would be required to perform all the duties of another! The Elder, for example, to do the work of the Deacon, and either or both of these to do that of the Evangelist! "*Credat Judæus Apella; non ego.*"*

Extent and variety of his evangelical labors.

I will, therefore, regard it as a settled fact that Timothy was an Evangelist according to the ancient order, and proceed now to ascertain, as far as we can, what were his labors and his duties. We learn, then, from his history, as it is given by Luke and Paul,

I. That, about A. D. 51 or 52, he accompanied Paul on an evangelizing tour through Asia Minor, thence to

* The credulous Jew, Apella, may believe it; not I.

Philippi, and thence to Thessalonica, Berea, and Corinth. Acts xvi–xviii.

II. About A. D. 56 he and Erastus were sent by Paul on missionary business from Ephesus to Corinth. Acts xix, 22; 1 Cor. iv, 17; xvi, 10. A short time after this he met Paul in Macedonia, and united with him in sending Christian salutations to the Church of Corinth and the saints throughout all Achaia. 2 Cor. i, 1.

III. In the Spring of A. D. 58, he was with Paul at Corinth, and joined him in his salutations addressed to the brethren at Rome. Romans xvi, '21. Here he is called Paul's *workfellow*.

IV. From Corinth he accompanied Paul on his last recorded journey to Jerusalem, A. D. 58. Acts xx, 4.

V. We next find him with Paul while he was a prisoner at Rome, and still acting as his fellow-laborer in the Gospel. Phil. i, 1; ii, 19; Col. i, 1; Philem. i. These letters were all written in A. D. 61 or 62. Not long after this he is again honorably mentioned in Hebrews xiii, 23.

VI. Finally, he was left at Ephesus, about the same time that Titus was left in Crete, most likely A. D. 65, to set in order the things that were wanting in the Ephesian Church: that is, as we learn from the two epistles addressed to him, to see that none taught any thing contrary to sound doctrine; that all things were done in love, out of a pure heart, and of a good conscience, and of faith unfeigned; that supplications, prayers, intercessions, and thanksgivings were made for all men; that women behaved themselves in a manner becoming their sex and relations; that well-qualified Elders and Deacons were chosen and set apart to their proper spheres of labor; and that the

An Outline of what he was required to do in the Church of Ephesus.

disciples were admonished to beware of seducing spirits and doctrines of demons. He was commanded, also, to be "a pattern to the believers, in word, in behavior, in love, in spirit, in faith, and in piety;" to give attention to reading, to exhortation, and to teaching; not to neglect the spiritual gift which he had received through prophecy by the imposition of Paul's own hands, with the laying on of the hands of the Presbytery; to give himself wholly to the work, that his proficiency might be manifest to all; not to rebuke an old man severely, but to beseech him as a father, and the younger men as brothers, the elder women as mothers, and the younger women as sisters, with all purity; and to provide for the comfort and support of superannuated widows. His instructions required, also, that all faithful Elders or Bishops should be duly honored and rewarded; that an accusation against an Elder should not be received unless it was supported by the testimony of two or three witnesses; that those convicted of sin should be publicly rebuked before all, for the sake of a warning to others; that in the solemn work of ordination he (Timothy) should impose hands suddenly and rashly on no man; that he should have a proper regard for his own health and physical comforts; that the servants of both believing and unbelieving masters should be careful to fulfill all the duties and obligations of their several relations; that the members of the Church should all be warned against the errors and follies of those who, contrary to the doctrine which is according to godliness, place man's chief good in his mere external relations, honors, and possessions; that he (Timothy) himself should especially avoid all these evils; that he should follow after righteousness, godliness, fidelity, love, patience, and meekness; that he should fight the good fight of faith, and lay hold on eternal life; that he should admonish the rich not to trust in uncertain riches, but in the living God, and be rich in good works; and that, as a teacher of Christianity, he should avoid profane and vain babblings, and oppositions of science falsely so called. In his second epistle Paul further admonishes Timothy not to be ashamed of the testimony of the Lord, but to be a partaker of the afflictions of the Gospel; to hold fast the form of sound words in which he had been taught; to be strong in the grace which is in Christ Jesus; to provide for the spiritual wants, and especially for the future instruction of the Church and the world, by committing to other able and faithful men the same things in which he had himself been instructed; to endure hardness as a good soldier of Jesus Christ; to keep the disciples mindful of the facts, precepts, promises, and threatenings of the Gospel; to give very special heed to his ministry, that he might be a workman who would have no occasion to be ashamed, rightly dividing the Word of truth; to avoid youthful lusts, and to follow righteousness, faith, love, and peace with all them who call on the Lord out of a pure heart; not to engage in debate about foolish and untaught questions, but to be patient and gentle to all men, and to persevere in sound doctrine, notwithstanding the many errors that would be taught and the apostasies that were about to happen. And, finally, in view of his own approaching death, and of the solemn realities of the future judgment, the Apostle again repeated a very brief summary of all the duties that devolved on Timothy in the very responsible position in which he was placed: he exhorted and commanded him to preach the Word; to be instant and vigilant in all seasons, whether favorable or unfavorable; to bear evil treatment; to do the work of an

Evangelist; and to fully and faithfully perform all the duties of his ministry.

Labors of other Evangelists.

We might greatly extend this induction of facts by referring to the labors of Mark, Luke, Titus, Silas, Epaphras, Trophimus, and other Evangelists.* But from the data now furnished it is evident that the work of an Evangelist, as it is defined and illustrated in the New Testament, is threefold:

Summary of the Duties of an Evangelist.

I. To convert and baptize the people according to the teaching and example of the Apostles.

II. To collect the converts into such congregations as may be found most convenient for their own improvement and edification, and to watch over, edify, and instruct them until they are capable of sustaining themselves, when Elders and Deacons should be appointed, and the Evangelist relieved from his local charge.

III. To have a constant oversight, as far as practical, over all the Churches, and to give to those that are *weak* and *sickly* such aid as may be necessary for their support and for their restoration to a state of healthfulness and usefulness.†

* Philip and Timothy are the only Ministers who are personally called Evangelists in the New Testament. But it is evident from Ephesians iv, 11, that this title was applied to a *class* of ministers, and hence, no doubt, to all who, like Philip and Timothy, went every-where with the Apostles, and, under their instructions, preaching the word; such, for instance, as Apollos, Barnabas, Mark, Luke, Silas or Silvanas, Sopater, Crescens, Gaius, Secundus, Trophimus, Epaphras, Clement, Aristarchus, Tychicus, Fortunatus, Stephanas, Achaicus, Demas, Epaphroditus, etc.

Alleged objection to this arrangement.

† I am well aware that just at this point it will be urged by some as an objection that this interferes with the rights and prerogatives of the Elders. But such an objection always reminds me of the petty disputes which the Apostles themselves had in their infancy as to which of them should be the greatest. See Matt. xx, 20–28; Mark ix, 33–37; Luke ix, 46–48; xxii, 24–27. It is founded on the false assumption that there are to be lords of different ranks and

The next question which naturally arises respecting the Evangelical office has reference to the period of its duration. Has it ceasea to be, or will it continue while the Church continues in her present militant state? The former is the opinion of some. They allege that this is clearly taught in Ephes. iv, 11–16, where it is said that Christ gave some (that is, qualified some) to be Apostles, and some to be Prophets, and some to be Evangelists, and some to be Pastors and Teachers, for the purpose of adapting and fitting the saints for the work of the ministry, for the edifying of the body of Christ, until the whole Church should be brought to such a degree of perfection that she would be able to sustain herself and perform all the duties of her high and holy calling by the joint labors and coöperation of her several members. Then, it is alleged the evangelical office

Duration of the Evangelical Office.

First hypothesis.

orders over God's heritage. But nothing of this kind is known or recognized in the New Testament. The ruling principle of the Kingdom of Heaven is love. And from this it follows that the man who is greatest in authority and endowed with the greatest gifts, is also the greatest *servant*, (See the preceding references.) So long, then, as this principle prevails, (and any other state of the Church is abnormal,) so long there can be no conflict of rights, privileges, and prerogatives among the followers of Christ.

Reply to said objection.

What Evangelist, for instance, under the influence of this principle, would ever think of interfering with the regular instruction and discipline of a well-ordered and well-instructed congregation? And on the other hand, what Elder, influenced by the law of love, would not most willingly and anxiously avail himself of all the assistance that he could get from any and every Evangelist that would in any way serve to edify the body of Christ or any member of it? What Elders ever complained of the interference of such Evangelists as Alexander Campbell, John T. Johnson, Jacob Creath, William Morton, John Smith, John Rogers, etc.? And what would now be the condition of many congregations throughout the Mississippi Valley had not these eminent Evangelists exercised a timely and judicious watch-care over them? The fact is, that our own experience has fully demonstrated both the wisdom and the necessity of this apostolic rule and regulation ceased, and ceased forever, just as did the apostolic office.

But on this hypothesis the office of Pastors and Teachers ceased also at the same time. And hence it would follow that the Church is now left without any officers, unless, peradventure, the diaconate should be continued. But this would prove too much for all men of common sense and common experience. None but a mere visionary enthusiast, carried away by his own vain theories and speculations, can believe that the Church will ever accomplish her mission here on Earth without Pastors and Teachers. And hence we may here again apply the old adage and say that "what proves too much proves nothing."

Objection to this view.

Evidently, then, the Apostle designed to teach us a very different lesson in this passage. But what is it? What does he mean when he says that these gifts were to continue until all who compose the Church should come to the unity of the faith and of the knowledge of the Son of God, to a perfect man, even to the measure of the stature of the fullness of Christ?

To my mind it is evident that he refers here simply and exclusively to the continuance of supernatural or miraculous gifts. Two classes of ecclesiastical officers are clearly recognized in this chapter, as well as in many other portions of the New Testament. The first were necessary to establish the Church on a firm foundation, and to administer her affairs until the Scheme of Redemption should be fully revealed and the Canon of the Scriptures completed. The second are necessary to her perpetuity, power, and efficiency. To the former the miraculous gifts of the Holy Spirit were indispensable.

True hypothesis.

Two classes of ecclesiastical officers in the Primitive Church.

but to the latter the Oracles of God are a sufficient guide. As soon, therefore, as miraculous gifts ceased, those offices that depended essentially on them, such as the Apostolic and prophetic, ceased also.

But the evangelical office belonged to a different category. True, indeed, it was for a time necessary that Evangelists and all other teachers and preachers of the Gospel should be divinely inspired.* The New Testament was not then written, and the Apostles could not always be present to tell them what to say and what to do for the edification of the Church and the conversion of the world. And hence it is most likely that all the first-appointed Evangelists were miraculously qualified to reveal the truth, the whole truth, and nothing but the truth to the people. But that the office itself was designed to be perpetual, and did not, like the apostolic office, necessarily depend on miraculous gifts of any kind, is evident from several considerations:

Evidence that the Evangelical office was designed to be perpetual.

I. *The evangelical work is a perpetual work.* While time endures it will be the duty of the Church, through her own chosen and appointed representatives, to convert and baptize the people; to gather the converts together into separate and distinct organizations for their edification, improvement, and efficiency; and to have a watch-care over many weak and sickly congregations.

From the perpetuity of the Evangelical work.

II. *Evangelists from the beginning received their commission from the Churches, and not directly from Christ, as did the Apostles and Prophets.* This may be illustrated

* The Deacons seem to have been the only class of officers in the primitive Church who, *as such*, had not the gift of inspiration. In their case it was not necessary, as their business was not to teach, but simply to attend to the secular affairs and interests of the Church.

by the case of Timothy, one of the most prominent and efficient of all the primitive Evangelists. He was well reported of by the brethren of both Lystra and Iconium, and was ordained as an Evangelist by the laying on of the hands of the Presbytery. Acts xvi, 1–3; and 1 Timothy iv, 14. The imposition of Paul's hands (2 Timothy i, 6) was for the purpose of imparting to him those miraculous gifts which in that age were necessary in order to enable him to fulfill the commission which he had received from the Church of Lystra and Iconium. See also Acts xiii, 1–4.

From the source of their Commission.

Here, then, we have a clear distinction drawn between the apostolic and evangelical offices. The former was not only created, but it was also filled by Christ himself, for the purpose of establishing the Church and preparing her members for the work of the ministry. The latter was created for the purpose of enabling the Church to fulfill her mission in converting and saving the world. And hence it follows that every Evangelist is but a creature and servant of the Church. From her he receives his commission, and to her he is responsible. Every such office was evidently intended from the beginning to endure while time endures.

III. *It is, furthermore, very clearly intimated by Paul, in his second letter to Timothy, that the evangelical office is to be continued throughout all coming time.* "The things," said he, "which thou hast heard from me through many witnesses, the same commit thou to faithful men, who shall be able to teach others also." 2 Timothy ii, 2.

From the instructions of Paul to Timothy.

That this has reference to Evangelists, and not to Elders or Bishops, seems clear from two considerations:

1. The Apostle had but a short time previous to this

(in his first letter) given full instructions to Timothy respecting the appointment of Elders and Deacons; and it is not, therefore, probable that he would think it necessary to refer again to the same subject in his second letter.

2. From the whole scope of the passage it is evident that the Apostle refers to persons of the same official rank and order with Timothy himself. "Do you, my son," said he, "be strong yourself in the grace which is in Christ Jesus. And in order that the work may not fail when your warfare shall have ended, do you commit to other faithful men, who shall be able to teach others also, the same things which you have heard from me through many witnesses." *

Here, then, we have not only very clear and conclusive

Argument drawn from Ecclesiastical History.

* It might be urged, as a fourth argument in favor of the permanency of the Evangelical office, that it has actually been continued from the beginning to the present time; not always, indeed, under the same name. Even in the primitive Church Evangelists were sometimes called Apostles or Missionaries of the Church, (Acts xiii, 4, 14;) just as Elders are often called, also, Bishops or Overseers. But that *evangelist* was the name by which these servants of the Church were usually designated in primitive times seems evident from the testimony of several of the Christian fathers. Eusebius, for instance, the learned Bishop of Cesarea, who flourished A. D. 315-340, thus speaks of the Evangelists who lived and labored during the reign of Trajan, A. D. 98-117: "Leaving their own country," he says, "they performed the office of *Evangelists* to those who had not heard the faith; whilst with a noble ambition to proclaim Christ, they also delivered to them the Books of the Holy Gospels. After laying the foundation of the faith in foreign parts as the particular object of their mission, and after appointing others as *Shepherds* of the flocks, and committing to these the care of those who had been recently introduced they went again to other regions and nations, with the grace and coöperation of God. The Holy Spirit also wrought many wonders as yet through them; so that as soon as the Gospel was heard, men voluntarily in crowds, and eagerly, embraced the true faith with their whole minds." Eusebius' Eccl. Hist., Book III, Chapter xxxvii. The name *evangelist* was, at an early date, given to Matthew, Mark, Luke, and John, because they bore written testimony to the main facts of the Gospel.

evidence that the evangelical office is to be continued until the Church shall have accomplished her earthly mission, but we have also given the necessary qualifications of all who are to be appointed to this office. These are,

Qualifications of Evangelists.

I. *Ability to make known to others, in a clear, forcible, and becoming manner, the whole counsel of God.*

II. *Fidelity in the discharge of all their duties and obligations.*

These are both very remarkable generalizations, and comprehend severally a vast number of subordinate particulars. Let every candidate for the evangelical office consider them well.

In the evangelical work much is of course left to the wisdom and discretion of each individual. Many questions of ways and means can be properly decided only by considering all the circumstances of each particular case. But that all the Evangelists of any given district, state, or territory, as the case may be, should often meet and confer together, and adopt some plan of coöperation in harmony with the Word of God, is evident from several considerations:

Evidence that Evangelists should coöperate with each other.

I. *It follows, of necessity, from the extent and character of the work committed to them.* Their field of labor is the world. By them, as the representatives and servants of the Church, the Gospel is to be preached to every creature: to the rich and to the poor, to the bond and to the free, to the wise and to the unwise. Their office is no sinecure. Their warfare is offensive as well as defensive, and it must be carried on with energy until all the strongholds of sin and Satan are broken up, and the kingdoms of this world

From the extent and character of their work.

shall have become the kingdoms of our Lord and of his Christ. But to do this most successfully will, of course, require much counsel and earnest coöperation on the part of these soldiers of the Cross.

From the diversity of their talents.

II. *From the great diversity of their talents, learning experience, etc.* Much, very much, depends on every man's being in his own proper place. Some men are, by nature and education, qualified to command an army of one hundred thousand men, others can command but ten thousand, and others one, while others, again, are fitted for but a sort of guerrilla warfare. Each, however, may be useful in his own proper sphere. But much experience, wisdom, and coöperation are necessary, in order that each and every one may be allowed to work in that position for which he is, by nature and education, best qualified.

From the general rules and principles of the Kingdom.

III. *It is required by the general laws, rules, and regulations of the Kingdom.* Specific rules would, of course, be here wholly out of place. But the religion of Christ is, from its alpha to its omega, a social system. It teaches us that we are all members of the one body, and that we should all labor together for the same end. This is, of course, as true of the officers of the Church as it is of the other members See, for further proof and illustration, Romans xii, 3–8; 1 Cor. xii, 12–30; Ephesians iv, 16.

From primitive example.

IV. *It is clearly taught by the example of the Apostles and primitive Evangelists.* There was evidently an agreement among the apostles as to their respective fields of labor. See Gal. ii, 9. And, after their separation, each one seems to have called to his aid as many well-qualified Evangelists as possible, and to have assigned to each of them that part and portion of the work for which he was best qualified. What a noble band of young evangelical heroes followed Paul in all his labors and travels! And these, we find, were constantly coöperating, not only with him, but also with each other in every way that they could to promote the cause of Christ.

Would it not be well if the advocates of primitive Christianity would profit more by the example of these primitive soldiers of the Cross? If all our aged Evangelists would adopt Paul's plan, call young men to their aid, and assign to each of them his proper sphere of labor, what a host of able and faithful men might soon be gathered together and brought up to the help of the Lord against the mighty!

From the common practice of mankind.

V. *Such coöperation is authorized and required by the common consent and universal practice of mankind in all similar cases.* No body of men ever accomplished a great work such as Evangelists are expected and required to perform without much conference and coöperation. Even the Elders of a single congregation, consisting of a few hundred persons, find it necessary to meet together, appoint their chairman and secretary, agree on the best conceivable division of labor, and make their weekly or monthly reports. Why, then, should Evangelists be debarred from the same privilege in their earnest efforts to discharge with efficiency and fidelity the still more difficult and embarrassing duties of their office?*

The election, ordination, and responsibility of Evangelists will be best considered in connection with the

* It would be well if some good brethren, who think they see in all such meetings a tendency to Popery, would remember that this monster of iniquity grew out of an abuse of the Elder's office. The Pope is an overgrown Bishop not an Evangelist.

election, ordination, and responsibility of Bishops and Deacons. And I will, therefore, now proceed to the Elder's office.

CHAPTER IV.

ELDERS.

THE fourth class of ecclesiastical officers known in the New Testament are variously called Elders, Bishops, Overseers, Pastors or Shepherds, and Teachers.

Names given to the fourth class of Ecclesiastical Officers.

That these names are all used to designate the same class of officers will appear evident from a comparison and proper consideration of the following passages of Scripture:

I. Acts xx, 17, 28: "From Miletus he (Paul) sent to Ephesus, and called the ELDERS of the Church. And when they were come he said to them, . . . take heed to yourselves, and to all the flock over which the Holy Spirit has made you OVERSEERS, that you be SHEPHERDS to the Church of God which he has purchased with his own blood." Here the same persons who are called Elders in the seventeenth verse are called, also, Overseers in the twenty-eighth, and are, furthermore, exhorted to be Shepherds or Pastors to the flock.

Evidence that these all refer to the same class of Officers.

On this passage Dr. Bloomfield remarks as follows: "As these persons (the πρεσβύτεροι, Elders of the seventeenth verse) are, in verse twenty-eight, called ἐπίσκοποι, (Bishops or Overseers,) and especially from a comparison of other passages, (as 1 Tim. iii,

Remarks of Dr. Bloomfield.

1,) the best Commentators, ancient and modern, have, with reason, inferred that the terms *as yet* denoted the same thing. Ἐπίσκοπος might denote either an *overlooker* or a *care-taker*, and these senses would be very suitable to express the pastoral duties."

II. Titus i, 5–9: "I (Paul) left you (Titus) in Crete for this purpose, that you might set in order the things that are wanting, and ordain ELDERS in every city as I commanded you: if any one is blameless, the husband of one wife, if he has faithful children that are not accused of riotous living or disobedient. For a BISHOP must be blameless, as the steward of God; not self-willed, not passionate, not fond of wine, not quarrelsome, not one who makes money by base means; but hospitable, a lover of goodness, sober-minded, just, holy, temperate, holding fast the sure word as it is taught, that he may be able, *by sound teaching*, both to exhort and to convince the opposers." It is evidently Paul's intention, in this passage, to use the words *elder* and *bishop* interchangeably, and, furthermore, to indicate that every Elder or Bishop is an ordained Teacher of the Gospel; at least, he must be able, by sound teaching, both to exhort and to convince the gainsayers.

III. 1 Peter v, 1–4: "The ELDERS that are among you I exhort, who am a FELLOW-ELDER, (συμπρεσβύτερος,) and a witness of the sufferings of Christ and a sharer in the glory that is to be revealed, act as SHEPHERDS of the flock of God which is among you, *taking the oversight*, (ἐπισκοποῦντες,) not by compulsion, but willingly; not for the sake of sordid gain, but from readiness of mind: neither as being lords over God's possessions, but being examples (τύποι) to the flock. And when the CHIEF SHEPHERD shall appear, you will receive the crown of glory that fades not away." Here again the Elders are exhorted to be shepherds to the flock of God, and to take the Episcopacy or oversight of it willingly. And hence it is evident that, in the estimation of both Paul and Peter, the Elders and Bishops were officers of the same rank and order, and that they were severally to be both Teachers and Shepherds of the flock.*

Bishop Stillingfleet's account of the origin of Episcopacy.

* Some of my readers may be anxious to know how it came to pass that even in the generation next after the apostolic age Bishops and Elders were in many cases regarded and spoken of as two separate and distinct orders of Church officers. This question is well answered in the main by Bishop Stillingfleet, as follows: "After this, when the Apostles were taken out of the way, who kept the main power in their own hands of ruling the several Presbyteries, or delegated some to do it, (who had the main hand in planting Churches with the Apostles, and thence are called in Scripture sometimes fellow-laborers in the Lord, and sometimes Evangelists, and by Theodoret Apostles, but of a second order,) after, I say, these were deceased and the main power left in the Presbyteries, the several Presbyteries enjoying an equal power among themselves, especially being many in one city, thereby great occasion was given to many schisms, partly by the bandying of the Presbyters one against another, partly by the sidings of the people with some against the rest, partly by the too common use of the power of ordinations in Presbyteries, by which they were more able to increase their own party by ordaining those who would join with them, and by this means to perpetuate schisms in the Church—upon this when the wiser and graver sort considered the abuses following the promiscuous use of this power of ordination, and withal having in their minds the excellent frame of the government of the Church under the Apostles and their deputies, and for preventing of future schisms and divisions among themselves, they unanimously agreed to choose one out of their number who was best qualified for the management of so great a trust, and to devolve the exercise of the power of ordination and jurisdiction to him; yet so as that he act nothing of importance without the consent and concurrence of the Presbyters, who were still to be as the common council of the Bishop. This I take to be the true and just account of the original Episcopacy in the primitive Church according to Jerome." *Irenicum, p.* 281.

This is rather too much of a *per saltum* operation. Episcopacy did not at once spring into perfect manhood from all the different Presbyteries of Christendom, like Minerva from the brain of Jupiter. It was one of the gradual but rapid developments of that "mystery of iniquity" which was at work even in the time of Paul. 2 Thess. ii, 7. But its growth was much retarded until the Apostles were taken out of the way. Then many a good

But why, it may be asked, should the same class of officers be designated by so many different appellations?

This question will be best answered by a careful examination of the origin and historical usage of these several titles. Let us then consider them briefly in order:

Origin and meaning of *elder* as an official title.

I. Elder, (זָקֵן; Gr., *πρεσβύτερος*,) as an official title, is of Hebrew or rather of patriarchal origin. Literally, it means an old man, or one who is older than another. But wisdom is to be acquired only by age and experience. And hence we find that the sentiment has prevailed in all ages and in all countries that Rulers, both civil and ecclesiastical, should be men of age and experience. The Greeks had their *Γερουσία*, (*γέρων*, an old man,) and their *Πρεσβεία*, (*πρέσβυς*, or *πρεσβύτης*, an old man,) their Council and their Assembly composed of old men; the Romans had their Senatus as we have our Senate, (senex, an old man;) and the Israelites had their זְקֵנִים, or Courts and Councils, composed of men distinguished for their age, wisdom, and experience.

It does not follow, however, that every old man should be an elder in an official sense. Something more than mere age is necessary in our Rulers. They must have wisdom, and prudence, and moderation, without which age is really of no value. And hence it is, no doubt, that the age of eligibility to the office of Bishop

and influential Bishop, who, by the suffrages of his fellow-presbyters, was made President of the Presbytery, or *Primus inter pares*, often did much unintentionally by his example to establish an order of Bishops, who in a short time were very generally regarded as superior to the Elders. But be it observed that even according to Jerome and Bishop Stillingfleet, Episcopacy originated after the death of the Apostles. It was, therefore, born out of due time, and has, of course, no place in the Sacred Canon.

or Elder is no where defined in the New Testament. That man is old enough who has the wisdom that is profitable to direct in all things.

For the varied uses and applications of the word *elder* in an official sense, among the Hebrews, Egyptians, Moabites, Midianites, etc., see Genesis l, 7; Exodus iii, 16, 18; iv, 29; xii, 21; xvii, 5, 6; xviii, 12; xix, 7; xxiv, 1, 9, 14; Leviticus iv, 15; ix, 1; Numbers xi, 16, 24, 25, 30; xvi, 25; xxii, 4, 7; Deut. v, 23; xix, 12; xxi, 2, 3, 4, 6, 19, 20; xxii, 15, 16, 17, 18; xxv, 7, 8, 9; xxvii, 1; xxix, 10; xxxi, 9, 28; Joshua vii, 6; viii, 10, 33; ix, 11; xx, 4; xxiii, 2; xxiv, 1, 31; Judges viii, 14, 16; xi, 5, 7, 8, 9, 11; xi, 16, etc. From such passages it is manifest that the official sense of the word *elder* is derived from the primitive or patriarchal form of government, under which every father was both a ruler and a priest.

References.

II. Overseer (ἐπίσκοπος) is of Greek origin. It is used by the classical writers to denote,

Origin and meaning of the title Episcopos, or Overseer.

1. Any guardian or superintendent whatever.

2. A municipal officer, or one who was appointed to oversee and take care of the interests of some particular town or district.

3. A viceroy, or magistrate, sent to superintend the affairs of conquered provinces.

It occurs but five times in the New Testament: viz., in Acts xx, 28; Phil. i, 1; 1 Tim. iii, 2; Titus i, 7; and 1 Peter ii, 25. From all of which it is obvious that in its technical and official sense, as used in the New Testament, it denotes simply an officer who has been appointed to oversee and superintend the interests of some particular congregation.

III. The word *bishop* is but a corruption of the Greek ἐπίσκοπος. It was introduced into the English language through the medium of the Anglo-Saxon, and has, consequently, the same meaning as the word *overseer*.

Origin and meaning of the word bishop.

IV. The word *pastor* is of Latin origin. It comes from the verb *pasco, to feed*, and corresponds with the Hebrew participle noun רֹעֶה, and the Greek ποιμήν, and the Anglo-Saxon *sceap-herd*, or *shepherd*.

Origin and meaning of the word *pastor*.

The Hebrew word רֹעֶה occurs in the Old Testament 103 times, and is variously applied.

Its use in the Old Testament.

1. To keepers of sheep, as Abel, Genesis iv, 2; Abraham's and Lot's herdmen, Genesis xiii, 7, 8; the sons of Jacob, Genesis xlvi, 32, etc.

2. To God himself. Genesis xlviii, 15; Psalm xxiii, 1; lxxx, 1.

3. To Christ. Ezekiel xxxiv, 23; xxxvii, 24; Zech. xiii, 7.

4. To Moses as the leader and keeper of Israel Isaiah lxiii, 11.

5. To the Priests and Prophets of Israel. Jeremiah iii, 15; x, 21; xvii, 16; xxiii, 1, 2, 4; Ezek. xxxiv, 2, 5, 7, 8, 9, 10, etc.

6. To Cyrus as God's appointed guardian and shepherd of Israel. Isaiah xliv, 28.

7. To an intimate companion; one who eats and drinks with another. Prov. 13, 20; xxviii, 7; xxix, 3, etc.

The Greek word ποιμήν occurs in the New Testament 18 times, and is used to denote,

Its use in the New Testament.

1. Keepers of sheep. Matt. ix, 38; xxv 32; Luke ii, 8, 15, 18, 20, etc.

2. Christ himself. John x, 11, 14, 16; Hebrews xiii, 20; 1 Peter ii, 25.

3. The Elders of the Church. Eph. iv, 11.

The verb ποιμαίνω, to be a shepherd to a flock, occurs eleven times in the New Testament. It is applied to Christ, Matt. ii, 6; Rev. xix, 15; to the Apostle Peter, John xxi, 16; to the Elders of the Church of Ephesus, Acts xx, 28; to the Elders of the Churches of Pontus, Galatia, Cappadocia, Asia, and Bithynia, 1 Peter v, 2; to the finally victorious saints, Rev. ii, 27; and to Constantine as the ruler of the Roman empire, Rev. xii, 5.

Use of the Greek verb ποιμαίνω in the New Testament.

V. The name *teacher* (διδάσκαλος) is indicative of very high honor and authority. Christ himself is often called, by way of eminence, THE TEACHER, (ὁ διδάσκαλος;) and the same title is given to Nicodemus, John iii, 10. But in 1 Cor. xii, 28, and Eph. iv, 11, it is manifestly used to denote one of the leading functions of the Elder's office. Compare, also, 1 Tim. v, 17, and Titus i, 9.

Use and import of the word *teacher* in the New Testament.

The reader will now readily understand why it is that so many titles are used to designate the same class of officers in the Christian Church. They are called Elders on account of their superior age and implied wisdom and experience. They are called Bishops or Overseers, because it is their duty to watch over and superintend all that pertains to the edification and welfare of their respective congregations. They are called Pastors or Shepherds, because they are all required to have a shepherd's care over their several flocks: they are to watch for souls as those who must finally give an account to God. They are called Teachers, because it is a part of their duty to instruct all who are under their charge

Why so many terms are used to designate the same office.

From these premises, then, compared with sundry other portions of Scripture, it is obviously the duty of all Elders,

Duties of the Elders.

I. *To have a constant watch-care over their respective congregations.* "Be shepherds to the Church of God, which he has purchased with his own blood," is one of the most solemn and impressive charges ever delivered to mortal man; and those who would meet it must do it in the spirit of their Master. If need be, they must, like him, lay down their lives for the sheep. They must not only see that all the public services of their congregations are duly and regularly attended to, but, like Paul, they must also go from house to house, pray with the sick, comfort those that mourn, strengthen the weak, instruct the ignorant, and see that all are living in the regular and habitual use and enjoyment of the various means which God has appointed and wisely ordained for our growth in grace and our progress in the Divine life; and especially must they see to it that every member of the Church is actively and earnestly engaged in doing what he can to promote the welfare and to increase the influence of the whole body. There should be no drones in the Kingdom of God. There is work provided for all. And he is not always the best Bishop who does most of the work himself, but who is most successful in persuading and encouraging others to work most.

II. *They are the divinely appointed Teachers of all who are under their charge, not only in the congregation assembled for public worship, but also in the Sunday School, in the family, and in the social circle.* And hence it is that every Elder must be "apt to teach." He must be able to hold forth the faithful word as he has been taught, so that by sound teaching he may both exhort and convict the gainsayers. True, indeed, it may not be necessary that he should at all times exercise his gifts as a teacher When there is a plurality of Elders, as there should be in every congregation, only a portion of them may have to labor regularly and constantly in word and doctrine. 1 Timothy v, 17. But whenever it becomes necessary, he must be prepared to feed the flock with the sincere milk of the word, that they may grow thereby.

III. *To the Elders are also committed the discipline of their respective congregations.* "Let the Elders that rule well be counted worthy of double honor." 1 Tim. v, 17. "Remember them who have the rule over you, who have spoken unto you the word of God." Heb. xiii, 7. "Obey them who have the rule over you, and submit yourselves; for they watch for your souls as those who must give an account." Hebrews xiii, 17. And again, Paul says to Timothy, "If a man know not how to rule his own house, how shall he take care of the Church of God?" 1 Tim. iii, 5. See also 1 Thess. v, 12. A Bishop, then, must be a ruler. Not indeed a lord over God's heritage; but as a wise, prudent, and benevolent parent admonishes, reproves, rebukes, corrects, and chastens his own beloved children, so, in the spirit of Christ, must the Elders of every congregation admonish, reprove, and rebuke, without respect of persons, all transgressors under their charge. And if all means of reformation should fail, they must, with the concurrence of the congregation, "withdraw from every brother that walketh disorderly." 2 Thess. iii, 6. The Elders, then, of every congregation are its divinely appointed Shepherds, Teachers, and Rulers.*

* In this division of the Elder's office I do not aim so much at logical accuracy in the use of terms as I do at a clear and explicit statement of the duties involved; and especially at giving prominence to that *watch-care* which

In the discharge of these several duties much liberty is, of necessity, given to the Elders. Many questions will arise in the course of their administration which can be settled only by a wise, prudent, and judicious application of general principles. And hence the necessity that they should all be men of rare and superior qualifications. These are very clearly stated by Paul in his letters to Timothy and Titus. See 1 Timothy iii, 1–7, and Titus i, 5–9. We will notice very briefly those that are given in the Epistle to Timothy.

Qualifications of the Elders.

I. "*A Bishop must be blameless*" (ἀνεπίληπτος:) a man who gives his adversary no hold on him; against whom no evil charge can be sustained.

II. "*The husband of one wife*" (μιᾶς γυναικὸς ἀνηρ.) These words, considered abstractly, would seem to imply that either celibacy or polygamy disqualifies a man for the office of a Bishop. But there are some reasons which seem to imply that the latter only is intended. And,

1. Celibacy is not, in itself, an evil. In no part of the Bible is it so regarded, and at least two of the most eminent members of the primitive Church were unmarried men. Hence it is not probable that Paul would condemn in all others what he considered right in his own case. It is unreasonable to suppose that the chief of all the Apostles would lay down as a necessary qualification for inferior officers what is proved, by his own example, to be

all will admit is a most important part of the shepherd's office, but which is, nevertheless, often practically neglected by many of our Elders. The shepherd's office, in its widest ecclesiastical and metaphorical sense, comprehends *all* the duties of an Elder, Acts xx, 28; and in Eph. iv, 11, it includes every thing but teaching. In this latter sense the word *ruler* is also frequently used in the New Testament. And hence it may ordinarily be best to include all the duties of the Elder's office under the two heads of *teaching* and *ruling* This is clearly Paul's conception of the matter as expressed in Eph. iv, 11 and 1 Timothy v, 17.

unnecessary for the superior, and which would, in fact, have rendered both himself and Barnabas ineligible to the Eldership or the Diaconate of any Christian congregation.

2. But polygamy is an evil. It is a violation of the implied will and purpose of God in man's creation. "In the beginning He made them *a* male and *a* female." Its tendency is also full of evil. It destroys or greatly weakens conjugal affection. It excites envy and jealousy where love and harmony should always reign. And hence its history is a melancholy illustration of the weakness and the follies of fallen human nature.

It is, therefore, probable that monogamy is here opposed only to polygamy, and that to free the Church, as far as possible, from this then prevalent evil was the benevolent object of the Apostle. On this subject Thomas Scott makes the following judicious remarks: "Christ and his Apostles," says he, "expressly condemned polygamy, as well as divorces, except for adultery. Yet there was no direct command for a man who had previously taken more wives than one to put the others away when he embraced the Gospel; such a requisition might, in some instances, have produced very bad consequences in domestic life, and increased the opposition of the civil powers to the preaching of Christianity. But the rule that no man, however qualified in other respects, should be admitted into the pastoral office who had more than one wife, or who had put away one and taken another, tended to show the unlawfulness of polygamy and divorces on frivolous pretenses, and their inconsistency with the Christian dispensation, and concurred, with other things, to bring them into total disuse in the Christian Church, yet without violence and confusion."

III. "*Vigilant*" (νηφάλιος.) The Bishop must not go to sleep as a drunkard. He must be watchful with regard both to himself and the congregation.

IV. "*Sober*" (σώφρων.) He should be a man of a sound and well-balanced mind, possessing a large amount of good common-sense. This qualification will often be brought into requisition.

V. "*Of good behavior*" (κόσμιος.) He should be a man of good manners, chaste, courteous, and polite in his whole demeanor. A man of slovenly, rough, and boorish manners should never be made an Overseer of the Church of God.

VI. "*Given to hospitality*" (φιλόξενος.) He should be a lover of strangers; a man of the same spirit as the good Samaritan, always ready to pour into the wounds of bleeding and suffering humanity the oil and the wine of the Gospel, and especially to receive into his house and entertain any and every stranger that is in want.

VII. "*Apt to teach*" (διδακτικός.) He should have an accurate and comprehensive knowledge of the whole Scheme of Redemption, and be able to communicate it to others. This is a necessary qualification of *every* Elder, Bishop, or Overseer. And hence an order of merely "Ruling Elders" is not an order of the Apostolic Church. Every Elder is officially a Teacher as well as a Ruler, and consequently he should always be well qualified for the full and faithful discharge of all the duties of this twofold office.

VIII. "*Not given to wine*" (μὴ πάροινος.) A Bishop should not indulge in the habit of drinking wine, or any other kind of intoxicating liquors. He should keep himself pure from the evil effects of this and every other species of intemperance.

IX. "*No striker*" (μὴ πλήκτης.) He must not be quarrelsome and pugnacious in a physical sense, but a peaceable man.

X. "*Not greedy of filthy lucre*" (μὴ αἰσχροκερδής.) He must not be a person who gains money by base and dishonorable means. This would exclude from the Eldership, for example, many who are now engaged in the traffic of ardent spirits.

XI. "*Patient*" (ἐπιεικής.) He should be distinguished for his general mildness and amiability of character; "in meekness instructing those who oppose themselves, if God peradventure will give them repentance to the acknowledging of the truth."

XII. "*Not a brawler*" (ἄμαχος.) He should not be disposed to fight, in a metaphysical sense. He should not be captious, not given to strife and debate, not too tenacious of his own rights; but quiet and peaceable, and, in the spirit of the great Apostle, while contending earnestly for the faith once delivered to the saints, he should, as far as possible, accommodate himself to the prejudices of all, that he may gain the more.

XIII. "*Not covetous*" (ἀφιλάργυρος.) He should not be avaricious, not a lover of money; for "the love of money is a root of all evil."

XIV. "*One that ruleth well his own house, having his children in subjection with all gravity.*" It is important, just here, to distinguish between that which is, in itself, a qualification, and that which is a mere proof of its existence. If the view which we have taken of the second qualification is correct, it does not follow that, in order to become a Bishop, a man must, of necessity, have a family This test, as we have said, would have excluded Paul himself from the Eldership of a congregation in which, for three years, he had discharged with fidelity all the duties of an Overseer. But this much certainly does follow, that, if a man who is a candidate for the office of a Bishop has a family, it should be well governed; if he has children, then, indeed, they should be brought up in the nurture and admonition of the Lord. The Bishops were chosen from among the old men, and, of course, they generally had families. And their qualifications for the instruction, care, and government of a congregation would be most apparent from the manner in which they had educated their own families. It was a maxim with Confucius, the great Chinese philosopher, that "He who knows not how to govern and reform his own family can not rightly govern and reform a people." And a greater than Confucius has said, "If a man know not how to rule his own house, how shall he take care of the Church of God?"

XV. "*Not a novice*" (μὴ νεόφυτος.) He must not be a neophite—a new convert—"lest, being lifted up with pride, he fall into the same kind of condemnation as that into which the Devil fell."

XVI. "*Moreover, he must have a good report of them that are without*"—of them who are not Christians—"lest he fall into reproach and the snare of the Devil."

Such, then, are, in brief, the essential qualifications of every Christian Bishop, Elder, or Overseer. Those who do not possess them should beware that they touch not the ark of God.

The required number of Elders in every congregation.

The next point to be considered is the number of Bishops that should be appointed in each congregation. This will, of course, depend very much on the number of its members and the amount of labor to be performed.* In a congregation composed of but few members but few Elders are necessary. But in all cases it seems from the teachings of the New Testament that *there should be at least a plurality of Elders in every Church.* This is clear from such passages as the following:

Evidence of this.

1. Acts xi, 29, 30: "Then the disciples, every man according to his ability, determined to send relief unto the brethren who dwelt in Judea. Which also they did, and sent it to the ELDERS by the hands of Barnabas and Saul."

2. Acts xiv, 23: "And when they had ordained them ELDERS in every Church, and had prayed with fasting, they commended them to the Lord, on whom they believed."

3. Acts xv, 4: "And when they (Paul and Barnabas) were come to Jerusalem, they were received by the Church and the Apostles and ELDERS; and they declared all that God had done with them." See, also, verses 22 and 23.

4. Acts xx, 17: "And from Miletus he (Paul) sent to Ephesus and called the ELDERS of the Church."

5. Philippians i, 1: "Paul and Timothy, the servants of Jesus Christ, to all the saints in Christ Jesus, who are at Philippi, with the BISHOPS and Deacons."

* In some of the primitive and post-apostolic Churches the number of members and officers was very great. In the Church of Rome, for instance, in A. D. 252, there were one Bishop, forty-six Presbyters, seven Deacons, (after the original model of the Jerusalem Church,) seven sub-Deacons, forty-two Acolyths, or attendants, and fifty-two Exorcists, Readers, and Janitors. But there were in the Church at the same time more than fifteen hundred widows and other needy and afflicted persons, besides an immense number of other members, some of whom were in opulent and others in only moderate circumstances. *Euseb. Eccl. Hist.*, VI, 43.

6. 1 Timothy iv, 14: "Neglect not the gift which is in thee, which was given thee according to prophecy, with the laying on of the hands of the PRESBYTERY, (τοῦ πρεσβυτερίου,) an assembly of aged men or Elders. Luke xxii, 66, and Acts xxii, 5.

7. 1 Timothy v, 17: "Let the ELDERS that rule well be counted worthy of double honor, especially those who labor in word and teaching."

8. Titus i, 5: "For this cause left I thee in Crete, that thou shouldest set in order the things that are wanting, and ordain ELDERS in every city, as I commanded thee."

9. James v, 14: "Is any sick among you, let him call for the ELDERS of the Church; and let them pray over him, anointing him with oil in the name of the Lord."

10. 1 Peter v: "The ELDERS who are among you I exhort who am also an Elder, and a witness of the sufferings of Christ, and also a partaker of the glory which shall be revealed."

Alleged exception to this general rule.

The only apparent exception to this rule is found in Revelation, first, second, and third chapters, where each of the seven Churches of proconsular Asia is represented as having but one *angel* to preside over it. This title is by many supposed to denote the presiding Bishop of each Church. And hence it is that these chapters are often cited to prove that the Episcopal form of Church government was prevalent in the Churches even in the apostolic age.

But in reference to this matter it is enough to say,

Reply to this allegation.

I. *That we should be very cautious not to give to any word or passage in the Bible a meaning which is manifestly in conflict with the plain and obvious meaning of other passages.* The Bible is a unit, and every word in it must be interpreted in the light of every book, and chapter, and verse of both the Old and the New Testament.

II. *That it is especially important to observe this rule in interpreting those books which are confessedly symbolical.* The language of symbols is a sort of short-hand writing, and it must, therefore, be interpreted in the light of the more plain, simple, and didactic portions of the Scriptures. We have reason to suspect the correctness of any theory which has its *origin* in the Apocalypse.

III. *That in symbolical language it is very common to put one for many, an individual for a class, or a species for a genus.* In the prophecies of Daniel, for instance, the word *king* means sometimes a kingdom and sometimes a whole dynasty, or race of kings. And just so it is in this most symbolical of all books, the Apocalypse of the Apostle John. The four Living Creatures and the twenty-four Elders are evidently but the representatives of the Redeemed out of every kindred, and tongue, and people, and nation. Rev. v, 8–10. The star which fell from Heaven (ix, 1) denotes the Teachers of Christianity in Western Asia, most or all of whom had fallen before the Mahometans came as locusts out of the religious darkness that was then brooding over a large portion of the Eastern world. And the Angel of the fourteenth chapter, who had the everlasting Gospel to preach to all mankind, is manifestly but a symbolical representation of all those faithful missionaries of the Church who are even now going forth to fulfill this sublime and beautiful prophecy.

IV. *It is, therefore, most probable that the name angel is used in like manner in the first, second, and third chapters, to denote simply all the elders who were then presiding* *over each of the several Churches of Asia.** And hence, I think, we may safely conclude that it is a law of the Kingdom of Heaven that a plurality of Elders shall preside over every congregation which has attained to its majority, and which, of course, no longer needs the instruction and guardian care of an Evangelist.

Organization of the College of Elders.

These Elders are of course all *officially* equal. But this does not forbid their appointing a Chairman and Secretary of their own Board, and adopting such subordinate rules and regulations for their own benefit as may be necessary in order to the full and faithful discharge of all the trusts committed to them. All native-born American citizens are, *according to the Constitution*, free and equal. But it does not hence follow that they are all fit to be presidents, governors, judges, and legislators. Our representatives in Congress, having their proper credentials, all go to the Capitol on terms of legal equality. But it does not follow from this that they are all equally entitled to the Speaker's Chair. There are in every body of men natural and educational differences, which should ever be regarded in its organization; and to this general law the Presbytery of a congregation forms no exception. It is absurd to suppose that five, ten, or twenty men elected to the Eldership of a Church are all equally well prepared to discharge all the duties of their calling. The best Ruler is not

* Another mode of interpreting the word "*angel*" in these letters rests on the assumption that each of the seven Churches named had sent a messenger to John in Patmos, as Epaphroditus was sent to Paul in Rome, (Phil. iv, 18,) and that John was directed to send these epistles to the aforesaid Churches *by* their several *messengers*. This interpretation is favored by the etymology of the word ἄγγελος, which primarily means *a messenger;* but it does not well harmonize with the fact that throughout these seven epistles the angels are addressed as the responsible rulers and guardians of their several Churches.

always the best Teacher; and the best Teacher is not always the best Pastor. Every one has his proper gift from God. In the primitive Churches all Elders were Rulers, but only some of them labored constantly in word and doctrine; and hence it is obviously both the duty and the privilege of every college of Elders to form just such an organization of their own body, and to make such a division of their labor as will best enable them to meet all the wants of the congregation over which the Holy Spirit has made them Overseers.

Their field of labor extends no further than the limits of their own congregation. To preach the Gospel to the heathen is no part of the Elder's office; and to rule over other congregations would be usurpation. The Elder who leaves his own Church and goes to another enters it simply as a private member, just as the Governor of Kentucky would have no rights in Ohio beyond the rights of citizenship.

The Elders' field of labor.

That the Elder's office is to continue while the Church continues is evident,

Perpetuity of the Elder's office.

I. *From the fact that Elders will always be needed in the Churches.* Their work is a perpetuity, and hence so, also, is their office. Christ has not created a body without giving to it the necessary members.

II. *From the fact that no Church in primitive times was regarded as complete and capable of sustaining itself without Elders.* Paul and Barnabas ordained Elders in every Church that they established during their first missionary tour through Asia Minor, Acts xiv, 23; and Titus was left in Crete that he might ordain Elders in every city Titus i, 5.

III. *From the fact that the office has been continued*

without interruption, though often very greatly perverted from the beginning to the present time. To this fact al ecclesiastical historians bear witness.

CHAPTER V.

DEACONS.

THE word *deacon* is from the Greek διάκονος, a waiter, attendant, servant, or minister; and this is from the verb διακονέω, to wait upon, to serve, to minister; and this again is derived from διάκω or διήκω, to run, to hasten. The radical idea is, therefore, *active service.*

Derivation and primary meaning of the word *deacon.*

In this generic sense it is applied,

Illustrations.

1. To Christ himself. Romans xv, 8; and Gal. ii, 17.

2. To him who would be chief of the Apostles. Matt xx, 26; xxiii, 11; Mark ix, 35; x, 43, etc.

3. To any and all of the Apostles. 1 Cor. iii, 5; 2 Cor. iii, 6; vi, 4.

4. To Evangelists. Eph. vi, 21; Col. i, 7; iv, 7; 1 Thess. iii, 2; 1 Tim. iv, 6.

5. To any and every faithful servant of Christ. John xii, 26.

6. To civil magistrates. Romans xiii, 4.

7. To the emissaries of Satan. 2 Cor. xi, 15.

8. To waiters at festivals, etc. Matt. xxii, 13; John ii, 5, 9.

But besides these various applications of the word in its first intention, it is used, also, in a more limited and official sense to denote a particular class of Christian Ministers. This is obvious from the following passages:

Evidence that it is used, also, in an *official* sense.

1. Philippians i, 1: "Paul and Timothy, the servants of Jesus Christ, to all the saints in Christ Jesus who are at Philippi, with the BISHOPS and DEACONS." Here the Deacons are distinguished from the saints in general, and are ranked with the Bishops as an order of Ministers.

2. 1 Timothy iii, 8–13: "Likewise must the DEACONS be grave, not double-tongued, not given to much wine, not greedy of filthy lucre; holding the mystery of the faith in a pure conscience. And let these also first be proved; and then let them use *the office of a Deacon*, being found blameless. Even so must their wives be grave, not slanderers, sober, faithful in all things. Let the DEACONS be the husbands of one wife, ruling their children and their own houses well. For they who have used *the office of a Deacon* well purchase to themselves a good degree and great boldness in the faith which is in Christ Jesus."

In this passage Paul again associates the Deacons with the Bishops as a distinct order of ecclesiastical officers. Like the Elders they must first be proved; and then they are permitted to officiate (διακονείτωσαν) as Ministers of the Church. And those who perform the office of a Deacon (διακονήσαντες) well we are assured procure for themselves a good standing-place and much confidence in the faith. These passages, therefore, prove, beyond all reasonable doubt, that the Deacons of the primitive Church were a distinct order of Christian Ministers.

But what was their rank, and what duties were they required to discharge?

This question will be best answered by referring to the occasion of their first appointment. This is given in Acts vi, 1-7, as follows: "*And in those days, when the number of the disciples was multiplied, there arose a murmuring of the Hellenists against the Hebrews, because their widows were neglected in the daily ministration. Then the Twelve called the multitude of the disciples to them, and said, It is not reason that we should leave the word of God and serve tables. Wherefore, brethren, look ye out among you seven men of honest report, full of the Holy Spirit and wisdom, whom we may appoint over this business. But we will give ourselves continually to prayer and to the ministry of the word. And the saying pleased the whole multitude: and they chose Stephen, a man full of the Holy Spirit, and Philip and Prochorus, and Nicanor, and Timon, and Parmenas and Nicolas, a proselyte of Antioch; whom they set before the Apostles. And when they had prayed they laid their hands on them. And the word of the Lord increased; and the number of the disciples multiplied in Jerusalem greatly; and a great company of the priests became obedient to the faith.*"

Circumstances which led to the appointment of the first Deacons.

From this narrative, then, it appears,

I. That it was made the duty of these men to attend simply to the *secular* wants and interests of the congregation. It is true that the neglect of a particular class of widows was the immediate occasion of their appointment. But surely no one would thence infer that they were officially restricted to the particular case which suggested the necessity of their appointment; that in case of further neglect by the congregation it would be necessary to appoint others to feed the Hebrew widows, others to clothe the naked, others to

Duties of the Diaconate.

wait on the sick, and others, again, to administer to the wants of the superannuated. This would be to multiply offices and officers rather too fast for even the most visionary. The historian here records a fact, not as an isolated abstraction, but rather as an *exponent* of a great principle. The fact is a simple one, but the principle involved is very broad and comprehensive. It embraces all that pertains to the secular business of the Church. Those who feed the widows must have under their control the treasury of the congregation. And hence the proposition of the Apostles was to surrender this department of labor entirely to the seven, and give themselves exclusively "*to prayer and to the ministry of the Word.*"

To wait on the secular concerns of the Church was, therefore, the limit of their *official* duties. Their office comprehended nothing less, and it certainly embraced nothing more. It conferred no authority whatever, either to teach or to preach, in either the public or the private assembly. The Elders must all be *apt to teach*, and every Evangelist is required *to preach the Word.* But, in all that is said of the Deacons in the New Testament, there is not given a single intimation that either teaching or preaching is any part of their office.

They may, indeed, in a certain sense, preach the Word *unofficially.* This is, to a certain extent, the duty and privilege of every disciple. Rev. xxii, 17. And certainly there is no better time to administer to the wants of the soul than when we are feeding and clothing the body. Every Deacon should, therefore, "know his opportunity," and improve it. He should ever be ready to speak a word of comfort and consolation to the weary soul while he is laboring to supply the wants of its clay tabernacle. But, in doing so, it is well to remember that he acts simply as a Christian, and not as an officer of the Church.

Qualifications of Deacons.

II. From these premises we also learn that, in order to be eligible to this office, every candidate must possess the three following qualifications:

1. *He must be a man of honest report.* That is, he must have a good reputation, a well-attested character, both in the Church and out of it.

2. *He must be full of the Holy Spirit,* so that its fruits, love, joy, peace, long-suffering, gentleness, goodness, fidelity, meekness, and temperance, may characterize his entire demeanor.

3. *He must also be full of wisdom,* and distinguished, of course, for his prudence, and other practical virtues which are necessary to the proper discharge of his officia. duties. For, if a man can not manage his own tempora. affairs well, how can he take care of the house and treasury of the Lord?

All this is but a summary of what Paul says of the qualifications of Deacons in the third chapter of his first letter to Timothy.

Required number of Deacons in a Church.

It is not probable that the number seven is given here as an *essential* element of the Diaconate. The number of Deacons, like that of the Elders, should, no doubt, vary according to the various wants of each congregation. So we would judge from all the data furnished in the New Testament. But, nevertheless, many of the primitive Churches followed strictly, in this respect, the example of the Mother Church. And, to supply the deficiency in the Diaconate, they appointed Sub-Deacons, Acolyths, etc. In the Church of Rome, for example, about the middle of the third century, there were only seven Deacons, though the number of Elders was forty-six. Euseb. Eccl. Hist. vi, 43.

The Diaconate of the primitive Church was not confined to male members. Deaconesses were also appointed to attend to the wants of the sick and the needy, especially of their own sex. This is evident from Rom. xvi, 1, and 1 Timothy v, 9–15. This order was continued, in the Greek Church, till about the beginning of the thirteenth century, and it is to be regretted that it was ever discontinued in any Church. The poor and the needy will always be with us, and will require the attention of both Deacons and Deaconesses just as much as they did in the Churches of Jerusalem, Cenchrea, and Ephesus.

Deaconesses of the primitive Church.

CHAPTER VI.

APPOINTMENT OF OFFICERS.

THIS, in its widest and most comprehensive sense, implies three things:

Three things implied in the appointment of Officers.

I. The law in reference to their qualifications.

II. The law in reference to their election.

III. The law in reference to their ordination.

Of the first of these I have already spoken with sufficient fullness, and I will, therefore, now proceed to the brief consideration of the second and third.

SECTION I.—ELECTION OF OFFICERS.

I speak now only of the permanent Ministry of the Church, consisting of Evangelists, Elders, and Deacons

By whom should they be elected to their respective offices? Should they be chosen by the few, or by the many; by the Church herself, or by her officers?

General law with respect to the election of Officers.

That it is the law of Christ that THE CHURCH SHOULD ELECT ALL HER OWN OFFICERS is evident from several considerations.

Evidence drawn from her being constituted a self-governing and self-perpetuating body.

I. *Because the Church is now, under Christ, a self-governing and self-perpetuating body.* There was a time when she was incapable of this. In her infancy extraordinary helps were necessary, both to her growth and to her prosperity. But these helps were to be continued only during her minority, "till we should all come to the unity of the faith, and of the knowledge of the Son of God, to a perfect man, to the measure of the stature of the fullness of Christ; that we might no longer be children tossed and carried about with every wind of doctrine, through the artifice of men, and cunning craftiness whereby they lie in wait to deceive; but speaking the truth in love, we might grow up in all things into Him who is the Head, even Christ; from whom the whole body fitly joined together, and compacted by that which every joint supplieth, according to the effectual working in the measure of every part, maketh increase of the body, unto the edifying of itself in love." Ephesians iv, 13–16. This point having been reached soon after the Canon of the Holy Scriptures was completed, all miraculous helps were then taken away, and henceforth the Church was to govern, extend, and edify herself by her own inherent energy, and through the agency of such officers as she might herself choose and appoint.

II. *Because the Church herself, and not the Ministry*

of the Church, is the pillar and support of the truth 1 Timothy iii, 15. She is herself the stone cut out of the mountain without hands, which is to utterly destroy and consume the iron, and the clay, and the brass, and the silver, and the gold of all antichristian power and dominion. Daniel ii, 44. She is the Golden Candlestick in the hand of the Lord to dispense the light of the Gospel to the ends of the Earth. Rev. i, 20. She is the Temple and dwelling-place of Jehovah, where all the pure in heart may now find refuge. 1 Cor. iii, 9–17. She is the body of Christ; the fullness of Him who filleth all in all. Ephesians i, 23.

From her agency in supporting and propagating the Truth.

III. *Because the Church herself is the heritage* (κλῆρος, clergy) *of God, and all her Ministers are but her servants.* 1 Peter v, 2; 2 Cor. iv, 5, etc. And hence it is nothing more than becoming and right that she should choose those who are to minister to her wants and comfort.

From her relations to God and to the Ministry.

IV. *Because the members of the Church at Jerusalem were required to choose their own Deacons, notwithstanding the presence of the most august and impartial body of Christian Ministers ever found in any one congregation on Earth.* Acts vi, 1–7. Surely, if ever there was an occasion when the popular vote might, with propriety, be suspended, and the officers of a congregation be elected by the suffrages of a few, that was the time when the first Deacons were chosen in Jerusalem. There was evidently danger that party spirit would be excited unless the whole matter were disposed of with great prudence. And there were the Apostles, who knew all the members well, and their respective qualifications, and in whose judgment and impartiality

From the example of the Jerusalem Church.

the whole congregation had entire confidence. Surely to the eye of sense and finite reason, the shortest and best way to settle the whole matter would seem to be that the Apostles themselves should choose and appoint men to wait on the poor and the needy. But no; under the infallible guidance of the Holy Spirit, the Apostles thought very differently. They knew well that one of the great and important objects for which the Church was established on Earth was to elevate and educate her own members; to call out the energies and the resources of all; to make every one feel that he should be a *living* stone in the Temple of our God, and that he is, to some extent, responsible for the edification, growth, and influence of the whole body. And hence they, as the plenipotentiaries of Christ and the inspired lawgivers of the Kingdom of Heaven, said to the whole multitude of disciples: "Look ye out among you seven men of honest report, full of the Holy Spirit and wisdom, whom we may appoint over this business. . . . And the saying pleased the whole multitude; and they chose Stephen, a man full of faith and of the Holy Spirit, and Philip, and Prochorus, and Nicanor, and Timon, and Parmenas, and Nicolas, a proselyte of Antioch." Acts vi, 3, 5. This one example, then, when fairly and fully considered, should really be an end of the whole controversy touching the election of Church officers.

From the case of Timothy.

V. *Because Timothy was recommended to Paul as a man well qualified for the Evangelical work, by the brethren of Lystra and Iconium.* The testimony of Luke is as follows: "Then came he (Paul) to Derbe and Lystra. And behold a certain disciple was there named Timothy, the son of a certain woman who was a Jewess, and believed, but his father was a

Greek, who was well reported of by the brethren who were at Lystra and Iconium. Him would Paul have to go forth with him; and he took and circumcised him, because of the Jews who were in those quarters: for they all knew that his father was a Greek." Acts xvi, 1–3.

From this it seems that it was in compliance with Paul's wish that Timothy was at this time set apart to the Evangelical work. But in making this choice he was evidently influenced by the recommendation of the brethren of both Lystra and Iconium. And as these things were written for our instruction, we are, I think, warranted in the conclusion that every candidate for the Evangelical office should, as a condition of his ordination, be first recommended by at least a plurality of Churches.*

VI. *Because it was the custom of the primitive Churches to choose their own messengers and agents, even for temporary purposes.* This is proved by such passages as the following:

1. 1 Corinthians xvi, 3: "And when I (Paul) come, *whomsoever ye shall approve by your letters*, them will I send to bring your liberality to Jerusalem." From this we learn that even the Apostle Paul, with all his plenary

Reason of the difference between the election of Timothy and that of the seven Deacons.

* This case is somewhat different from that of the Deacons before mentioned. They were chosen by the members of but one Church; but it seems that the brethren of both Lystra and Iconium concurred in the choice of Timothy, or at least in recommending him as a person well qualified for the Evangelical work. The reason for making this difference is most likely owing to the fact that every Deacon is a servant of but one congregation. Beyond its limits he has no official authority. But all the Churches are, to some extent, interested in the labors of every Evangelist. And hence it is eminently becoming and proper that at least two or more of them should concur in his appointment.

power and inspiration, would not interfere with the right of the Corinthians to appoint their own messengers to convey their bounty to the suffering brethren in Judea.

2. 2 Corinthians viii, 18, 19: "And we have sent with him (Titus) the brother (unknown, probably Luke) whose praise is in the Gospel throughout all the Churches. And not only (is his praise in all the Churches, but it is he) *who was also chosen by the Churches* to travel with us with this grace, which is administered by us to the glory of the same Lord, and declaration of your ready mind."

3. 2 Corinthians viii, 22, 23: "And we have sent with them (Titus and the brother whose praise was in all the Churches) the brother (unknown) whom we have oftentimes proved diligent in many things, and now much more diligent through the great confidence which he has toward you. If any inquire concerning Titus, he is my partner and fellow-laborer for you: *or if our brethren be inquired of they are the messengers* (ἀπόστολοι) *of the Churches, and the glory of Christ.*" See, also, Acts xv, 22.

Election of Elders: how determined.

This evidence is, I think, abundantly sufficient to establish our main proposition. True, indeed, there is nothing in all this which relates directly and specifically to the election of Elders; and there is nothing of this kind in the New Testament. The reason is obvious: it is not necessary: the law of election is made sufficiently plain without it If the Churches are competent to elect their own Deacons, Evangelists, and special agents and messengers, surely they are also competent to elect their own Elders.

Conclusion.

And hence we conclude that *it is a law of the Kingdom of Heaven that the Churches should severally elect all their own officers.*

How they shall do this is no where stated clearly, distinctly, and definitely in the New Testament. Much is here left to be determined by the Churches themselves, or their chosen and acting representatives. There are, however, many general laws which should be as strictly regarded in all such cases as if they were a thousand-fold more specific and definite.* Such, for example, are the following:

Specific mode of election un determined.

General laws.

I. "*Whether, therefore, ye eat or drink, or whatsoever ye do, do all to the glory of God.*" 1 Cor. x, 31. This law positively excludes all selfishness, party spirit, and every thing else that is inconsistent with the glory of God and the unity, harmony, and prosperity of the Church.

II. "*Let all things be done decently and in order.*"

* Had the Divine Founder of Christianity attempted to govern his Church in all cases simply by specific rules and precepts, truly, indeed, the world itself would not have contained the books which would have been written. The "*lex scripta*," or written code of England, consists of thirty-five large quarto volumes, besides cart-loads of local and private acts of Parliament. And yet it very rarely happens that an existing law can be found which is in all respects applicable to a given case. Almost every new case of law and equity differs, in some respects, from every antecedent one. Every lawyer knows that it is only by analogy that court-decisions are generally applied to new cases of litigation. What, then, would have been the magnitude of the Divine code had God attempted to govern his people in all ages and under all circumstances by specific rules and regulations! Surely we can not too much admire that wisdom which for such a code has substituted a little volume of a few hundred pages, and which, notwithstanding its great brevity, has made it a perfect rule of faith and practice for every accountable being in every kindred, and tongue, and people, and nation while time endures! In doing so he has, in the first place, made the whole Bible, and especially the New Testament, *a book of motives*; secondly he has enacted some very *general laws and regulations*; thirdly, he has illustrated these laws and the general principles of his government by a great variety of *authoritative examples*; and finally, he has given to us such *specific laws and ordinances* as are necessary to make the Bible a perfect Rule of faith and practice.

Impracticability of governing the Church in all cases by *specific* laws.

1 Cor. xiv, 40. This law requires that all those rules which have been found necessary for conducting and governing popular elections should be duly regarded in the election of Church officers, and that the house of God should appear to all persons and under all circumstances as a house of order.

Much, indeed, must always be left to the force of circumstances. The same degree of formality, for instance, is not always required in small assemblies which would be necessary in larger ones. But in all cases the general rules and precepts of the New Testament require that something like the following order should be observed in the election of all Church officers:

Order of electing Church Officers.

I. *That the Church should, through her own chosen representatives, determine how many persons should be elected.* In every organized Church the Elders are, of course, the proper persons to determine all such questions after due consultation and conference with the members. But in unorganized Churches prudence would require that a committee of the more aged and thoughtful brethren should be appointed to prepare such matters for the action and approval of the congregation. No exhibitions of licentiousness nor of a wild and reckless democracy should ever be allowed to appear in the house of God.

II. *That said Representatives should also act in the case as a committee of nomination.* The views, wishes, and sentiments of all should, of course, be duly considered and regarded; and as many persons may be nominated as the members severally desire, provided that in the judgment of the committee they be not notoriously destitute of the required qualifications. But all nominations should be made through the Elders or other chosen representatives, and never at random in the popular assembly.

III. *Due notice as to the time of the election having been given, at a meeting called for the purpose, the suffrages of the congregation should be taken by ballot; each member voting for as many of the nominees as are to be elected.* In some cases it may not be expedient for all to vote. Very young persons and others not well acquainted with the character and qualifications of the nominees, would do well to waive their right of suffrage in so important a matter. But all the members of the Church should be allowed to vote who desire to do so.

IV. *The votes having been counted, the persons, to the number previously agreed on, having the greatest number of votes, should be declared the officers elect of the congregation; provided, however, that each has received a majority of all the votes cast.* No one should attempt to serve any Church in any capacity who has not been elected by the suffrages of at least a majority of his brethren; and, if possible, the vote should be made unanimous.

SECTION II.—ORDINATION OF OFFICERS.

General Proposition.

The persons duly elected should then be ordained or set apart to their respective offices by the whole congregation, with prayer and fasting, and through the imposition of the hands of their Elders, or other chosen representatives.

It is not enough that they be elected by the suffrages of the people. The common-sense of mankind requires that all candidates for important offices, whether civil or ecclesiastical, shall be installed with some solemn and impressive ceremonies. And hence the Apostles said to the disciples at Jerusalem, Do ye *choose* and we *will appoint.* This is all that is meant in the Scriptures by ordination. *It is simply a solemn setting apart of such persons to their respective offices as have been previously elected by the suffrages of the disciples, according to the standard of qualifications laid down by the Holy Spirit.*

Meaning of Ordination.

That this was always done by the imposition of hands, with prayer and fasting, seems clear from the following passages of Scripture:

Evidence that it was always done with prayer, fasting, and the imposition of hands.

1. Acts vi, 5, 6: "And the saying pleased the whole multitude. And they chose Stephen, a man full of faith and of the Holy Spirit, and Philip, and Prochorus, and Nicanor, and Timon, and Parmenas, and Nicolas, a proselyte of Antioch, whom they set before the Apostles; *and when they had prayed they laid their hands on them.*"

2. Acts xiii, 1–3: "Now there were in the Church which was at Antioch certain Prophets and Teachers: as Barnabas, and Simeon, who was called Niger, and Lucius of Cyrene, and Manaen, who had been brought up with Herod the tetrarch, and Saul. As they ministered to the Lord and fasted, the Holy Spirit said, Separate to me Barnabas and Saul, for the work whereunto I have called them. *And when they had fasted and prayed, and laid their hands on them, they sent them away.*"

3. Acts xiv, 23: "And when they had ordained them Elders in every Church, *and had prayed with fasting*, they commended them to the Lord, on whom they believed."

4. 1 Timothy iv, 14: "Neglect not the gift which is in thee, which was given thee according to prophecy, *with the laying on of the hands of the presbytery.*" Compare 2 Timothy i, 6.

In the first of these passages mention is made only of prayer and the imposition of hands; in the second, prayer, fasting, and the imposition of hands are all mentioned; in the third, only prayer and fasting; and in the fourth, only the laying on of hands. And hence some have too hastily inferred that in the primitive Church there was no uniform practice in the solemn rite of ordination.

False inference from these premises.

But this is a very loose and unsatisfactory way of interpreting the facts and phenomena of the Bible. To the ancients the celestial system was, in like manner, a labyrinth of confusion. The phenomena of the heavens seemed to be without order and without harmony. But the genius of Sir Isaac Newton has removed this false impression. That great interpreter of nature's laws has demonstrated that the God of nature is a God of order; that every sun, and moon, and planet, and comet, and asteroid, moves under the influence of one general principle, which binds in eternal harmony the whole material universe.

Illustration drawn from Astronomy.

It is so, also, in Revelation. To the superficial reader of the Bible there seems to be a want of uniformity in many other cases, as well as in ordination. In the Great Commission, for example, Christ said to his Apostles: "He that believeth and is baptized shall be saved." Some ten days after this, in reply to the anxious inquiry of the multitude, "Men and brethren, what shall we do?" the Apostle Peter said: "Repent and be baptized, every one of you, in the name of Jesus Christ, for the remission of sins, and ye shall receive the gift of the Holy Spirit." To the important question of the Philippian jailer, "Sirs, what must I do to be saved?" Paul replied, "Believe on the

Illustration drawn from the conditions of pardon.

Lord Jesus Christ and thou shalt be saved, and thy house." But in his letter to the Roman brethren the same Apostle says: "With the heart man believeth unto righteousness, and with the mouth confession is made unto salvation."

From such premises some have hastily concluded that the Bible is a chaotic mass of palpable contradictions. Others have inferred that the apparent want of harmony is owing to the unimportant character of some of the conditions specified. They allege, for instance, that it is evident from Paul's reply to the Philippian jailer, that confession and baptism may be dispensed with as unnecessary to salvation. But others again see none of these imaginary difficulties. They have made Christianity a study; they have surveyed the whole Christian System, from its center to its circumference, just as Newton surveyed the celestial system; and to them, therefore, all things pertaining to it seem to be in perfect order and harmony. They see in the circumstances under which these responses were given a sufficient reason for not expressing what was then well understood, or what was evidently implied and about to be practically illustrated; and hence they very rationally and properly conclude that none of these conditions can, in any case, be safely dispensed with. They infer that these are all divinely appointed means of salvation; that no one can, in fact, have a well-grounded assurance that his sins are all forgiven until he has believed with his heart, confessed with his mouth, repented of his sins, and been baptized into the name of the Father, and of the Son, and of the Holy Spirit.

The same rule of interpretation evidently applies to those passages which relate to ordination. Luke says that the Apostles prayed and laid their hands on the seven Deacons; but he does not say that they did not fast at the same time. One of these seven afterward became an Evangelist; and nothing is recorded concerning either his election or his ordination. But will any one hence infer that, like some precocious youths in modern times, he went out to do the work of an Evangelist on his own responsibility, without any of the formalities of a regular appointment? Paul says that his own hands and the hands of the Presbytery were laid on Timothy. He says nothing here about prayer and fasting. But will any one presume to say that in the ordination of Timothy these solemnities were omitted? Such an inference is just as illogical as the conclusion that repentance, confession, and baptism are not conditions of pardon in the Christian System, because, forsooth, Paul said to the Philippian jailer, "*believe* on the Lord Jesus Christ and thou shalt be saved, and thy house."

The Law of ordination in this respect analogous to the Law of pardon.

But enough has been said on this subject—enough to warrant the conclusion *that all the Deacons, Elders, and Evangelists of the primitive Church were ordained by the imposition of hands, with prayer and fasting, and, consequently, that no one can, even now, be legally and properly set apart as an officer or minister of the Christian Church without these solemnities.*

Conclusion.

I know it is alleged by some that, in the cases cited, hands were imposed for the purpose of imparting spiritual gifts, and not for the purpose of ordination. But such an allegation is wholly unwarranted by the facts as they stand recorded. For,

Whether hands were imposed in these cases for the purpose of imparting Spiritual Gifts.

1. In Acts vi. 3. 6, it is clearly implied that the

Apostles laid hands on the seven merely as a part of the ceremony of ordination, or for the purpose of setting them apart as the Deacons of the Church. Their instruction to the multitude was simply as follows: Do ye choose seven men *whom we may appoint over this business.* The disciples did so, and set them before the Apostles; *and when they had prayed they laid their hands on them.* Here there is not a word said about spiritual gifts, and nothing is to be found in the context which warrants the conclusion that any thing of the kind was then imparted.

Examination of Acts vi, 1-6.

II. The case of Paul and Barnabas, given in Acts xiii, 1-3, is even more conclusive against any and every such allegation. For,

Examination of Acts xiii, 1-3.

1. The command of the Holy Spirit to the Prophets and Teachers was not to qualify Paul and Barnabas for the work to which they had been called, but simply to set them apart to the work. Nothing is here said about imparting spiritual gifts.

2. It does not appear from the inspired record that these Prophets and Teachers had the power to impart such gifts. This was one of the peculiar and incommunicable functions of the Apostolic office. Even Philip the Evangelist, though able to work miracles himself, was not able to bestow this power on the Samaritans whom he had converted. And hence the necessity that Peter and John should go down from Jerusalem to Samaria for this purpose. They did so. And when they had prayed and laid their hands on some of the young converts they immediately began to work miracles, to the astonishment of Simon Magus and the whole multitude. Acts viii, 5-25.

3. But even if it could be proved, which it can not.

that these Prophets and Teachers had power to confer on others the gift of working miracles, it would, nevertheless, be sufficient for our present purpose to know that Paul at least stood in need of no such gifts. He was not dependent on these, or on any other set of men, for his qualifications to preach the Gospel. See Galatians i–ii.

III. The case of Timothy is equally clear and conclusive. From 1 Timothy iv, 14, compared with Acts xvi, 1–3, it is evident that the Elders of Lystra laid their hands on him for some purpose. But to impart miraculous gifts they had no power. And hence we are constrained to believe that it was simply for the purpose of ordaining Timothy as an Evangelist, and that the same order should be observed in the Church throughout all coming time. See Numbers viii, 9–11, etc.

Examination of 1 Tim. iv, 14.

But who, it will be asked, should impose hands on candidates for ordination? This is a very grave question, and it is one which should be very seriously considered.

The persons who should ordain.

In the ordination of the seven Deacons in the Jerusalem Church this was done by the twelve Apostles. But in what capacity did they then and there officiate? Did they act in this case with all their plenary authority as the Apostles of Christ? Or, as Evangelists, did they labor, like Timothy and Titus, to set in order the things which were wanting? Or, did they officiate merely as the Elders of the Church?

In what capacity the Apostles acted in ordaining the first Deacons.

In order to answer this question satisfactorily we should, I think, distinguish between the legislative part of this important transaction and the mere act of ordination. To legislate was an exclusive function of the apostolic office. The Apostles alone had a right to make laws and ordinances for the Kingdom of Heaven? To them as the plenipotentiaries of Christ, it certainly belonged exclusively to say what should be done in the pending crisis. But the work of ordination was transferable. It was transferred. Titus was left in Crete to set in order the things which were there wanting, and to ordain Elders in every city. And one of the purposes for which Timothy was left in Ephesus was, evidently, to ordain Evangelists, Elders, and Deacons. Besides, as we have seen, the Elders of the Church at Lystra took part in the ordination of Timothy. And hence I think it follows, beyond all reasonable doubt, that in the ordination of the first Deacons the Apostles did not act as Apostles, but merely as the representatives of the Church in Jerusalem. And when it is remembered that all existing orders of the Ministry, whether they be Evangelists, Elders, or Deacons, are but the servants of the Church, the conclusion seems to be inevitable *that it is the business of the Church to ordain, as well as to elect all her own officers.*

Conclusion with regard to the work of ordination.

In all fully organized Churches this should, of course, be done by their Elders as their duly chosen and appointed representatives, with the aid of such Evangelists as they may see fit to invite. But in every unorganized Church the officiating Evangelist should act, as did Timothy and Titus, as the representative of the congregation, in connection with such other persons as she may herself select for the purpose of coöperating with him. But in the New Testament there is no clear evidence that any *one* man was ever authorized to ordain another. Titus was required to ordain Elders in every city, *as Paul had commanded him:* and that. as we learn from all the examples

Who should officiate for organized and unorganized Churches.

recorded, was by the joint agency and coöperation of several persons.

As a general rule, ordained Ministers should be allowed and encouraged to remain in office so long as they continue to labor faithfully within the sphere of their appointment. But it is always implied that those who confer the gift of office have also power to take it away whenever, in their judgment, the glory of God requires it. The power to create implies, of course, the power to destroy.

Period of Ministerial service.

In view of all that has been said, then, on the subject of the Christian ministry, how very great are their responsibilities! How very solemn is the account which every servant of the Church will have to render to Christ at the judgment of the great day! Let me entreat you, then, my dear brethren, as many of you as may read this work, and especially my *young* brethren,

I. *To make the Word of God your constant and only guide.* Tradition may mislead us, and so also may all speculative philosophy; but "all Scripture is given by inspiration of God, and is profitable for teaching, for reproof, for correction, for instruction in righteousness, that the man of God may be perfect, thoroughly furnished for every good work."

II. *Be men of prayer.* Pray always. Pray without ceasing. It is not enough that you study the Bible to know your duty. You must also look to God constantly for help to enable you to perform it. "Ask," then, "and ye shall receive; seek, and ye shall find; knock, and it shall be opened to you."

III. *Be men of energy.* Give all possible diligence to make your ministry a success. We have abundant reason to rejoice and thank God that primitive Christianity is making constant and rapid progress in the world. But how much, alas! how very much still remains to be done before the world is converted and the Church herself brought up to the Divine standard of spiritual purity and practical godliness! Remember, then, dear brethren, that for much of all this you are personally responsible.

IV. *While you labor to do every thing for the glory of God, study at the same time to cultivate a spirit of kindness and benevolence toward all men.* Remember that "the end of the commandment is love out of a pure heart, and out of a good conscience, and out of faith unfeigned." Cultivate, then, in this respect, the spirit of your Divine Master. "Bless those who curse you; do good to those who hate you; and pray for those who insult you and persecute you," and soon you will sit down with Christ on his throne, even as he has overcome and sat down with the Father on his throne.

"Ye servants of the Lord,
  Each in his office wait;
With joy obey his heavenly word,
  And watch before his gate.

Let all your lamps be bright,
  And trim the golden flame;
Gird up your loins, as in his sight,
  For awful is his name.

Watch! 't is the Lord's command;
  And while we speak he 's near;
Mark the first signal of his hand,
  And ready all appear.

O, happy servant he
  In such a posture found!
He shall his Lord with rapture see,
  And be with honor crowned."

PART II.

CHRISTIAN ORDINANCES.

Origin and meaning of the word *ordinance*.

THE word *ordinance* is from the Latin *ordino*, to set in order, to arrange, to regulate. It is used in the Common English Version of the Old Testament for the Hebrew חֹק and חֻקָּה, a statute; מִצְוָה, a command; מִשְׁמֶרֶת, a charge, or office, intrusted to any one; and מִשְׁפָּט, judgment; and in the New Testament it is used for the Greek words διαταγή, an arrangement or disposition; δικαίωμα, a just or righteous deed, a decree or precept; δόγμα, a decree or edict; κτίσις, a creature or creation; and παράδοσις, delivery, tradition, traditional law, etc. It is evident, therefore, that the word *ordinance* may denote any law, right, decree, institution, or constitution given by Divine authority. And hence I do not present this to the reader as a strictly logical division of our subject. But under this general head I wish to consider, merely for the sake of convenience, a few of the most prominent ordinances of the Christian System, such as the Preaching of the Word, Prayer, Praise, Fasting, Christian Baptism, the Lord's Day, and the Lord's Supper.

The subject to be considered only in part.

CHAPTER I.

THE PREACHING OF THE WORD.

Announcement of God's purpose to save men by preaching.

THERE was a time when the Jews were trusting in the Law and the Greeks were seeking after wisdom as a means of justification, sanctification, and beatification. But after that, in the wisdom of God, the world by wisdom knew not God, it pleased God, by what the Greek philosophers were wont to call the foolishness of preaching, to save those who through it were led to believe in the Lord Jesus. 1 Cor. i, 21. And hence the commission of Christ to his Apostles, "Go ye into all the world and preach the Gospel to every creature; he that believeth and is baptized shall be saved, and he that believeth not shall be damned." Mark xvi, 15, 16. And hence, after they were endowed with power from on high, they went every-where preaching the Word, so that in about thirty years after the ascension of Christ, Paul could truthfully say to the Colossians, (i, 23,) that the Gospel had been preached to every creature under heaven.

Evidence that this arrangement was designed to be permanent.

That this arrangement was permanent and designed to be continued as an ordinance of God through all coming time, is evident from many considerations, such as the following:

I. *From the nature and necessities of the case.* The whole Bible is a demonstration of the fact that it is God's will and purpose to save all who will call him in sincerity and truth. But, as Paul says, (Rom.

x, 14, 15,) "How shall they call on Him in whom they have not believed? and how shall they believe in Him of whom they have not heard? and how shall they hear without a preacher? and how shall they preach except they be sent? As it is written, How beautiful are the feet of them that preach the Gospel of peace, and bring glad tidings of good things!" To say, therefore, that the Gospel is no longer to be preached to the world is virtually to say that God has abandoned his purpose to save mankind.

II. *From the fact that the Church has been constituted the pillar and support of the truth.* 1 Tim. iii, 15. In this respect she is compared to a Sun rising on the benighted nations, (Isa. lx, 1–3;) and then again to a golden candlestick. Zech. iv, 2; Rev. i, 20. And hence, as we have seen, the necessity of an order of ecclesiastical officers, who, as the servants and representatives of the Church, may go into all the world and preach the Gospel to every creature.

III. *This important truth is also frequently taught and variously set forth and illustrated in the prophetic writings.* Take, for instance, the following passages:

1. Romans xi, 15: "For if the casting away of them (the Jews) be the reconciling of the world, what shall the reception of them (into the Kingdom of God) be, but life from the dead?" Here Paul compares the effect of Israel's conversion on the Gentile world to a resurrection from a state of death in trespasses and in sins to a life of holiness. But such an effect can and will be produced only through the preaching of the Gospel by these faithfu missionaries of the Cross. See Daniel xii, 3, and Ezekie xlvii, 1–12.

2. Revelation xiv, 6, 7: "And I saw another ange

flying in the midst of Heaven, having the everlasting Gospel to preach to them that dwell on the Earth, even to every nation, and kindred, and tongue, and people, saying with a loud voice, Fear God and give glory to him, for the hour of his judgment is come; and worship Him who made Heaven and Earth, and the sea, and the fountains of water."

The word *angel* in this passage is used to denote not one of the celestial host, such as Michael or Gabriel, but simply the messengers of the Church. "For the gifts and calling of God are without repentance;" and if having committed to us the word of reconciliation, he would not allow an angel to preach the Gospel to Cornelius and his household, we may feel perfectly sure that he will never allow any but his redeemed and ransomed saints to preach it to mankind hereafter. To the Church of God it belongs, by Divine appointment, to convert the nations by preaching to them the everlasting Gospel in its primitive purity and simplicity, through the agency and instrumentality of her own evangelical missionaries. This, thank God, she is now doing; and soon, therefore, we may expect to hear the announcement of the second messenger, that Babylon the Great is fallen, and that the kingdoms of this world are become the kingdoms of our Lord and of his Christ.

In what the preaching of the Word consists.

But in what does the preaching of the Word consist? This is a very grave question; and it is one which should be very carefully considered by every Christian, and especially by every Christian Preacher. It may be well, therefore, to answer it briefly, both negatively and positively. And,

I. *It does not consist in preaching one's self.* The Preacher should, if possible, never appear in his own discourse. This treasure has been put into "earthen vessels, that the excellency of the power might be of God, and not of us." 2 Cor. iv, 7.

II. *It does not consist in the defense and advocacy of any party views and measures.* This is a weakness to which all men are, perhaps, more or less prone; and it is, therefore, a weakness against which the Christian Preacher especially should be on his guard. It is often much easier to glory in a party than in the Cross of Christ. But remember that the end of the Commandment is not the love of Calvinism nor of Arminianism, but that it is love out of a pure heart, and of a good conscience, and of faith unfeigned. 1 Tim. i, 5.

III. *It does not consist in the defense and demonstration of any system of science, literature, or philosophy.* It is very well to understand the book of nature, and to be well read in the whole encyclopædia of the sciences, literature, and the arts; but, at the same time, it is well to remember that there is nothing in all these that can either justify, or sanctify, or redeem a soul. A man might preach eloquently on natural science, and metaphysics, and politics all his life, and lie down in sorrow at last, to suffer as keenly from the piercings of the undying worm, and from the flames of the unquenchable fire, as the most ignorant and stupid of his admiring auditors. But,

IV. *It does consist simply in preaching Jesus Christ and him crucified.* This was the scope of Paul's entire ministry. "We preach Christ crucified," said he, "to the Jews indeed a stumbling-block, and to the Greeks foolishness; but to them who are called, both Jews and Greeks, Christ the power of God and the wisdom of God." 1 Cor. i, 23, 24. And hence he could say to the Corinthians, "I determined not to know any thing among you, save Jesus

Christ and him crucified." 1 Cor. ii, 2. And, again, to the Galatians: "God forbid that I should glory, save in the Cross of our Lord Jesus Christ, through which the world has been crucified unto me, and I unto the world." Gal. vi, 14. It is faith in Christ, and not in any system of religious philosophy, or of the philosophy of religion, that saves the soul.

This, then, suggests to us the twofold object of all correct evangelical preaching:

Twofold object of preaching.

I. To convince the world that Jesus Christ is the Son of God, through whom alone any sinner can find peace and pardon.

II. To persuade men to receive, honor, love, serve, and obey him. "Blessed are they that do his commandments, that they may have a right to the tree of life, and may enter in through the gates into the city. Rev. xxii, 14. See these two points illustrated in Acts, *passim.*

With regard to the proper style and manner of preaching I would simply refer the reader to the example of Christ and his Apostles. Their discourses are still our best models of Sacred Rhetoric and Pulpit Oratory.

Best models of Sacred Rhetoric.

The following lines from Cowper are well conceived and happily expressed. They may be instructive to some of my young readers. He says:

Extract from Cowper.

"Would I describe a preacher, such as Paul
Were he on Earth would hear, approve, and own,
Paul should himself direct me. I would trace
His master-strokes, and draw from his design.
I would express him simple, grave, sincere;
In doctrine uncorrupt; in language plain,
And plain in manner; decent, solemn, chaste,
And natural in gesture: much impressed
Himself, as conscious of his awful charge,
And anxious mainly that the flock he feeds

> May feel it too; affectionate in look,
> And tender in address, as well becomes
> A messenger of grace to guilty men.
> He that negotiates between God and man,
> As God's embassador, the grand concerns
> Of judgment and of mercy, should beware
> Of lightness in his speech. 'T is pitiful
> To court a grin, when you should woo a soul;
> To break a jest when pity would inspire
> Pathetic exhortation." *The Task, Book II*

CHAPTER II.

PRAYER.

Derivation and meaning of the word *prayer*.

Prayer, from the Latin *prex*, means simply, according to its etymology, *a petition, a request*, or *an entreaty*. But in its Scriptural usage, as well as in common parlance, it includes not only petitions, but also confessions and thanksgivings.

Prayer is natural to man.

It proceeds from the natural instincts and impulses of every feeling and grateful heart. Every man who has a proper sense of his dependence on God will supplicate his favor; every one who has a proper appreciation of the benefits received will express to him his gratitude; and every one who has a realizing sense of his own delinquencies will seek relief for his broken and contrite spirit by confessing to him his many faults and aberrations.

Privilege of Prayer guaranteed to all of God's children.

It is, therefore, a most benevolent and gracious provision of the Scheme of Redemption that God permits, invites, and encourages his children to pray; to pray always, to pray every-where, and to pray for all things that are necessary to their present and eternal well-being. That this is now our privilege is evident from many such passages of Scripture as the following:

1. Matthew vii, 7–11: "Ask, and it shall be given you, seek, and ye shall find; knock, and it shall be opened to you: for every one that asketh receiveth, and he that seeketh findeth, and to him that knocketh it shall be opened. Or what man is there of you who, if his son ask bread, will give him a stone? or if he ask a fish, will he give him a serpent? If ye then, being evil, know how to give good gifts unto your children, how much more will your Father who is in Heaven give good things to them who ask him?" See, also, Luke xi, 5–13.

2. Matthew xviii, 19: "Again I say to you, that if two of you shall agree on earth as touching any thing that they shall ask, it shall be done for them by my Father who is in Heaven."

3. Matthew xxi, 22: "And all things whatsoever ye shall ask in prayer, believing, ye shall receive."

4. Luke xviii, 1–8: "And he spoke a parable unto them to this end, that men ought always to pray, and not to faint; saying, There was in a city a judge who feared not God, neither regarded man; and there was a widow in that city; and she came to him, saying, Avenge me of my adversary. And he would not for a while: but afterward he said within himself, Though I fear not God, nor regard man, yet because this widow troubleth me, I will avenge her, lest by her continual coming she weary me. And the Lord said, Hear what the unjust judge saith; and will not God avenge his own elect, who cry day and night to him, though he bear long with them? I tell you that he will avenge them speedily."

5. John xiv, 13, 14: "And whatsoever ye shall ask in my name, that will I do, that the Father mav be glorified

in the Son. If ye shall ask any thing in my name, I will do it."

6. John xv, 7: "If ye abide in me, and my words abide in you, ye shall ask what ye will, and it shall be done for you."

7. John xvi, 24: "Hitherto ye have asked nothing in my name: ask and ye shall receive, that your joy may be full."

8. Philippians iv, 6: "Be anxious about nothing; but in every thing, by prayer and supplication with thanksgiving, let your request be made known to God."

9. Colossians iv, 2: "Continue in prayer, and watch in the same with thanksgiving."

10. 1 Thessalonians v, 17: "Pray without ceasing." See, also, Romans xii, 12; Ephesians vi, 18, etc.

11. James v, 16–18: "Confess your faults one to another, and pray one for another, that ye may be healed. The effectual fervent prayer of a righteous man availeth much. Elijah was a man subject to like passions as we are, and he prayed earnestly that it might not rain; and it rained not on the earth for the space of three years and six months. And he prayed again, and the heavens gave rain, and the earth brought forth her fruit." See, also, 1 Timothy ii, 1–4.

12. 1 John i, 9: "If we confess our sins, he is faithful and just to forgive us our sins, and to cleanse us from all unrighteousness."

13. 1 John v, 14, 15: "And this is the confidence which we have in him, that, if we ask any thing according to his will, he heareth us: and if we know that he hears us, whatsoever we ask, we know that we have the petitions which we desire of him," etc.

From these and many other like passages it is obvious

not only that it is our duty and our privilege to pray to God at all times, in all places, and under all circumstances, but also that prayer is a means of procuring for ourselves and for others many great and precious benefits. Such, for example, are the following:

Benefits resulting from prayer.

I. *It serves to cultivate and educate our own spiritual nature.* If it is a law of the human constitution that all our faculties are developed and strengthened by exercise, then, indeed, what can be more serviceable in the way of self-culture than the devotions of the closet? There is no other place beneath the heavens which is so favorable for the proper exercise of all our moral powers and susceptibilities. Even in the religious assembly the attention is often arrested and the heart is made to wander by some improper display of the lusts of the flesh, the lusts of the eye, and the pride of life. But from the closet all such evil influences are excluded. Here there is no motive to deceive, or to make a vain display of our persons, our dress, and our good works. But there the mind turns in upon itself. There the conscience is awakened; there we see ourselves in the light of Heaven. And there, under the deep and solemn conviction that we are on holy ground, and that the eye of God is upon us, we are almost compelled to be humble, to repent of our sins, to forgive our enemies, to sympathize with the afflicted, to adore our Creator, love our Redeemer, and exercise all the powers of our souls in harmony with the will of God. There is, therefore, a deep significance in the words of our Savior when he says, "But when thou prayest enter into thy closet, and when thou hast shut the door pray to thy Father who is in secret; and thy Father who seeth in secret will reward thee openly." Matthew vi, 6

As a means of spiritual culture.

II. *It enables us to form a habit of close and intimate union, communion, and fellowship with God.* The law of habit is well understood. All men live and act more or less under its influence. The man who frequents the theater, the ball-room, the drinking or the gambling saloon soon feels that he is, by an invisible and almost irresistible influence, drawn to these haunts of idleness, vice, and dissipation. He may see poverty, disgrace, misery, and wretchedness before him, and he may feel keenly the awful forebodings and warnings of a guilty and awakened conscience; but, nevertheless, the force of habit overcomes all his fears and feeble resolutions. Under its still-increasing power he visits and revisits these charnel-houses of iniquity "till a dart strikes through his liver," and, by his own folly, he seals forever the doom of his eternal infamy.

As a means of communion and fellowship with God.

But the man who begins his course of life on the ascending scale, who forms habits of industry, frugality, temperance, patience, godliness, brotherly kindness, and philanthropy, will soon find that there is but little difficulty in ascending still higher and higher on the way that leads to the everlasting Zion. These habits become to him helps and encouragements in the way of virtue, and he now hungers and thirsts after righteousness, as the weary hart pants after the brooks of water.

The habit of prayer, and especially of secret prayer, is altogether in harmony with this general law of human character. In no other religious exercise are we brought so near to God; in no other can he be so familiar with the Creator of our bodies and the Father and Preserver of our spirits. And as it is a law of our nature that we form attachments to and for those with whom we associate, and even become assimilated to them in t elements of our character, it follows that no other acts of devotion are so favorable for the cultivation of godliness. And hence we find that those most devoted to the closet have always been the most pious and the happiest of men.

Its influence on the Passions.

III. *It serves to preserve us from many evils.* Our worst enemies are our own lusts and passions. But these may all be very much weakened and even subdued through the influence of prayer. How can a man, for instance, cherish pride in his heart while he is honestly communing with his Maker? How can he cultivate a spirit of revenge while he is imploring the forgiveness of Him who has said, "Vengeance is mine; I will repay, saith the Lord?" How can he indulge in anger, wrath, malice, or any of the other works of the flesh while he is seeking for the aid of that blessed Spirit whose fruits are always "love, joy, peace, long-suffering, gentleness, goodness, fidelity, meekness, and temperance?" Prayer, properly offered, must always have a soothing influence on the affections. Its tendency is to allay the passions, promote the virtues, and harmonize all the powers and faculties of the soul.

Its influence on God and his administration.

IV. *It secures to us and for us much positive good by fulfilling a condition on which God has promised that he will bestow his blessings.* It is a great mistake to suppose, as some have done, that the influence of prayer is wholly subjective, or at any rate that it never extends beyond the narrow limits of our own earthly associations. Nay, verily, it reaches God himself. It moves the arm that moves and governs the universe. This consoling truth is clearly taught in many such passages as the following:

Evidence of this.

1. Numbers xi, 1, 2: "And when the people com-

plained it displeased the Lord: and the Lord heard it, and his anger was kindled; and the fire of the Lord burned among them, and consumed them that were in the uttermost parts of the camp. And the people cried unto Moses; *and when Moses prayed unto the Lord, the fire was quenched.*"

2. Deuteronomy ix, 13–20: "Furthermore the Lord spake unto me, saying, I have seen this people, and behold it is a stiff-necked people: let me alone that I may destroy them, and blot out their name from under heaven: and I will make of thee a nation greater and mightier than they. So I turned and came down from the mount, and the mount burned with fire: and the two tables of the covenant were in my two hands. And I looked, and behold ye had sinned against the Lord your God, and had made a molten calf: ye had turned aside quickly out of the way which the Lord had commanded you. And I took the two tables and cast them out of my hands, and broke them before your eyes. And I fell down before the Lord, as at the first, forty days and forty nights: I did neither eat bread nor drink water, because of all your sins which ye sinned, in doing wickedly in the sight of the Lord, to provoke him to anger. For I was afraid of the anger and hot displeasure, wherewith the Lord was wroth against you to destroy you. *But the Lord hearkened to me at that time also. And the Lord was very angry with Aaron to have destroyed him: and I prayed for Aaron also at the same time.*"

3. 1 Samuel xii, 16–18: "Now therefore stand and see this great thing which the Lord will do before your eyes. Is it not wheat harvest to-day?* I will call unto

* Rain is almost wholly unknown in Palestine during wheat harvest, which occupies the latter part of May and the first of June. The storm

the Lord, and he will send thunder and rain, that ye may perceive and see that your wickedness is great which ye have done in the sight of the Lord in asking you a king. *So Samuel called unto the Lord; and the Lord sent thunder and rain that day:* and all the people greatly feared the Lord and Samuel."

4. 2 Kings xx, 1-6: "In those days was Hezekiah sick unto death. And the prophet Isaiah, the son of Amoz, came to him and said unto him, Thus saith the Lord, Set thy house in order, for thou shalt die and not live. Then he turned his face to the wall, and prayed unto the Lord, saying, I beseech thee, O Lord, remember now how I have walked before thee in truth and with a perfect heart, and have done that which is good in thy sight. And Hezekiah wept sore. And it came to pass, before Isaiah had gone out into the middle court, that the word of the Lord came to him, saying, Turn again and tell Hezekiah, the captain of my people, Thus saith the Lord, the God of David thy father, *I have heard thy prayer, I have seen thy tears. Behold I will heal thee; on the third day thou shalt go up into the house of the Lord. And I will add unto thy days fifteen years.*"

See, also, Genesis xix, 17-21; Numbers xiv, 11-20; Job xlii, 7, 8; Psalm xviii, 6-15; Daniel ii, 18, 19; Jonah iii, 1-10; Luke xi, 5-13; xviii, 1-8; Acts iv, 31; xii, 1-17; Rom. xv, 30-32; Eph. vi, 19; James v, 16-18, etc.

Folly of objecting to this important truth.

Let no one, then, ridicule the idea that the prayers and entreaties of poor, fallen, sinful worms of the dust should have an influence on the Divine administration. This is only to expose his own ignorance of the moral government of God.

that followed was, therefore, a sure and striking proof that in this case Samuel spoke by Divine authority.

If a father finds that it is consistent with his dignity, with the regulations of his government, and with the best interests of his children to bestow his favors in answer to their petitions, why may not the Almighty Father of the universe act on the same principle? Surely this is not, as some have alleged, a proper subject of ridicule. If we can not fully comprehend this matter let us humbly confess our ignorance and seek for more enlarged and correct views of the Divine government. To many persons it would appear just as absurd that the pen in my hand should have an influence on the most remote of the fixed stars as that the prayers of a poor, penniless, and despised follower of Jesus Christ should excite the sympathies of Heaven and affect the purposes and acts of the King of kings and the Lord of lords. But, nevertheless, these two problems have both been clearly and satisfactorily solved. Newton obtained an answer to the one and the Holy Spirit has demonstrated the other. And hence, of course, the question is forever settled with all those who regard the Bible as the Word of God and of paramount authority.

Influence of social prayer.

V. *It is a powerful and divinely appointed means of convicting, converting, sanctifying, and saving others.* This is especially true of the family. The relation of a parent to a child is one of the nearest, dearest, and most interesting on Earth; and hence it involves an influence which is peculiar to itself. The example of the parent is to the child, during the most tender and impressible period of its existence, the standard of all that is right, and noble, and magnanimous. Its greatest concern, therefore, is to imitate him. What he says and does, it attempts to say and do also. If he swears, it swears; if he prays, it prays; but if he neglects the throne of grace, it neglects the throne of the universe, and Him who rules upon it.

Responsibility of Parents in this matter.

For the proper exercise of this influence over the child the parent is of course responsible. Wherever much is given much will also be required. This is a law of the universe, from which none are exempt.

What an awful account, then, will some parents have to render with respect to this part of their stewardship, when every man shall appear before the great white throne, to be judged according to the deeds done in his own body, whether they be good or whether they be evil! To be able on that day to stand at the right hand of the Great Judge and say, Behold, here am I, Lord, and here also are the children which thou gavest me, would, methinks, be joy enough to fill the heart of any ransomed man!

But who could bear to stand on the left hand of the Judge, and there to hear the accusations and criminations of his own offspring? To hear, for instance, a doomed son or daughter say, Father, *you* have brought me to this end! You never taught me to read and to study that Book by which I am now to be judged! You never directed me to the Lamb of God who once died to take away the sins of the world! You never taught me to pray to Him who once said: "Ask, and ye shall receive; seek, and ye shall find; knock, and it shall be opened to you." You never led me to the sanctuary, to the house of prayer and praise! You taught me to swear, to profane the name of God; to seek pleasure at the theater, the ball-room, and the card-table! But you never taught me, either by precept or by your example, to seek for happiness at the Fountain of life! You never taught me to seek forgiveness at the throne of grace! And now the harvest is past, the Summer is ended; and we are compelled to stand together on the ill-boding side of the throne of judgment!

Courteous reader, where will you stand on that day? And if you are a parent, where will your children and your servants stand? This is the proper time to answer and settle these solemn questions. If you have no delight in the worship of God here, do not flatter yourself that you will delight in it hereafter. If you do not teach your children to pray in the world that now is, they may never be permitted to pray in that which is to come.

Conditions of acceptable prayer.

The great importance and benefits of prayer, properly offered, must, then, I think, be obvious to all. But it is well to remember, just here, that prayer is not, of necessity, a blessing in itself. It is but an ordinance ordained by God as a means of securing and enjoying his blessings. And hence, in order that it may be made available, it must be offered in the way and on the conditions which God has himself prescribed. These are,

Faith

I. *That it be offered in faith.* For, says Paul by the Spirit, "Whatever is not of faith is sin." Rom. xiv, 23. And again he says: "Without faith it is impossible to please God; for he that cometh to God must believe that he is, and that he is the rewarder of them who diligently seek him." Heb. xi, 6. And hence it follows that the prayer of unbelief is but mockery, and that it can not be otherwise than offensive to God.

Repentance.

II. *That it be offered in the spirit of obedience; or with an honest purpose and intention to do the will of God; to cease to do evil, and to learn to do well.* "If I regard iniquity in my heart," says David, the Lord will not hear me." Psa. lxvi, 18. And Solomon adds: "He that turneth away his ear from hearing the law, even his prayer shall be an abomination." Prov. xxviii, 9.

Humility.

III. *That it be offered in the spirit of profound reverence and humility.* This indeed is implied in the two previous conditions; but in this licentious age it is well to be often reminded that "God resisteth the proud, but giveth grace to the humble." James iv, 6.

Attitude of prayer.

Even the proper attitude of prayer is not to be neglected. The sitting posture is exceedingly unbecoming and reprehensible. It ordinarily indicates a want of reverence and respect that would not be tolerated in the court of any earthly king, prince, or potentate. A mere hint, then, to those who are "at *ease* in Zion" will, I hope, be sufficient on this subject.

The attitude of standing is certainly much more respectful, as well as more favorable for the exercise and cultivation of the powers and susceptibilities of the soul. It has, moreover, been tolerated, if indeed it has not been sanctioned by Jehovah himself. Thus we read, for instance, that Abraham *stood* before the Lord while he made intercession for the cities of the plain. Gen. xviii, 22. In his intercessory prayer Solomon first kneeled, and then rose and blessed the people with continued prayers and supplications. 1 Kings viii, 54–61. The Jews, too, after their return from Babylon, when they had discovered the Book of the Law, "assembled with fastings, and with sackcloth and earth upon them. And the seed of Israel separated themselves from all strangers, and *stood* and confessed their sins and the iniquities of their fathers." Neh. ix, 1, 2. See also Mark xi, 25.

But the most natural and becoming attitude for the humble, confessing penitent, before a throne of grace, is unquestionably the *kneeling* posture. And hence it is that which is most frequently mentioned in both the Old and the New Testament. Indeed, so far as we know, this was the exclusive practice of the primitive Christian Church; and consequently it is still the most becoming in all those who take the Bible, the whole Bible, and nothing but the Bible as the rule of their faith and practice. The following references will suffice for illustration: 1 Kings viii, 54; 2 Chron. vi, 13; Psa. xcv, 6; Daniel vi, 10; Matt. xvii, 14; Mark i, 40; x, 17; Luke xxii, 41; Acts vii, 60; ix, 40; xx, 36; xxi, 5; Romans xi, 4; Eph. iii, 14; Phil. ii, 10, etc.

IV. *That it be offered in the spirit of forgiveness.* This, too, is implied in the first condition. But, nevertheless, many who now profess to believe the Gospel seem to forget the words of our Savior, that, "If ye forgive not men their trespasses, neither will your Father forgive your trespasses." Matt. vi, 15. See also Matt. xviii, 21–35.

A forgiving spirit.

V. *That it be offered through Christ as the great and only Mediator of the New Covenant.* This is one of the peculiar privileges of Christians. No patriarch or Jew ever prayed thus. Nor did Christ ever teach even his disciples to ask any thing in his name until he was about to leave them. John xvi, 24. But since the time of his coronation; since all authority in Heaven and on Earth was committed to him, it is the decree of Jehovah that all petitions shall be presented in the name of Jesus; and that all men shall honor the Son, even as they also honor the Father. And hence, says Paul in his letter to the Colossians iii, 17: "Whatsoever ye do, in word or deed, do all in the name of the Lord Jesus, giving thanks to God and the Father by him."

Christ the Mediator.

Then, dear reader, "seeing that we have a great High Priest who has passed through the Heavens, Jesus the Son of God, let us hold fast our confession. For we have not a High Priest who can not sympathize with our infirmities; but he was tempted in all things like ourselves, yet without sin. Let us come, therefore, with boldness to the throne of grace, that we may receive mercy, and find grace to help in every time of need." Hebrews iv, 14–16.*

CHAPTER III.

PRAISE.

Praise under the Old and the New Covenant.

From the earliest ages, praise has been commonly associated with prayer as a part of the worship of Jehovah. The Israelites were often admonished to praise the Lord, (Psalm cxlvii–cl,) and from the attention that was given to this matter by David and other kings of Israel, it is evident that it occupied a very important place in the services of the Old Covenant. See 1 Chronicles xxv; 2 Chronicles xxix, 30; Ezra iii, 10, 11, etc. Under the New Covenant all Christians are, in like manner, required to teach and to admonish one another in Psalms, and Hymns, and Spiritual Songs, singing and making melody in their hearts to the Lord. Ephesians v, 19, and Colossians iii, 16.

But what does the Apostle here mean by Psalms, and Hymns, and Spiritual Songs? The word *psalm* is from

* For a fuller discussion of this whole subject the reader is referred to "A Brief Treatise on Prayer," by the Author, published by H. S. Bosworth, of Cincinnati, Ohio.

Meaning of the words *psalms*, *hymns*, and *spiritual songs* in Eph. v, 19, and Col. iii, 16.

the Greek noun ψαλμός, and this again from the verb ψάλλω, to touch, to feel, to play on a stringed instrument with the fingers, and, finally, to make music or melody in the heart, as in Ephesians v, 19. The meaning of the noun corresponds with that of the verb, and denotes a touching, a playing on a stringed instrument, a song accompanying music on a stringed instrument, any song or ode. And hence it is evident that the word *psalm* may or may not refer to instrumental music. Its proper meaning, in any and every case, must be determined by the context. And, according to this fundamental law of interpretation, it is pretty evident that in Ephesians and Colossians the term ψαλμός has no reference whatever to instrumental music; for, in both cases, it is the strings or chords of the *heart*, and not of an instrument, that are to be touched.

The ancient Israelites, however, usually connected instrumental with their vocal music. And hence, in the Septuagint version of the Old Testament, the word ψαλμοι, *psalms*, is prefixed as the general title of the one hundred and fifty lyric odes used in their social worship. But the Hebrew title is תְּהִלִּים, which means *hymns* or *praises*, though the word מִזְמוֹר, *a psalm*, is prefixed to fifty-eight of these sacred odes, while but one (the 145th) has the distinctive title, תְּהִלָּה.

The word *hymn* is from ὕμνος, a song of praise, which comes from the primitive verb ὑδέω, to tell of, to celebrate. By the Greeks the word ὕμνος was used to denote the festive songs which they were wont to sing in honor of their gods and heroes.

The word ἀοιδή, contr. ᾠδή, which is used by the Apostle in Ephesians v, 19, and Colossians iii, 16, for *song*, is from ἀείδω, or ᾄδω, to sing. It is commonly used in the Septuagint for the Hebrew שִׁיר, and is the generic term for *ode* or *song*. The restricting and qualifying epithet πνευματικός, *spiritual*, may denote either that these songs were dictated to the spiritual men by the Holy Spirit, as were the songs of Elizabeth, Mary, and Zechariah, (Luke i, 42, 46, 67,) or simply that they were composed on spiritual and religious subjects.

On the whole, then, it is most probable that by *psalms* and *hymns* the Apostle meant the inspired odes of the Old Testament, and that by *spiritual songs* he meant all those pious and devout poetical effusions which resulted from the spiritual gifts bestowed on the primitive Christians. But of this we can not be entirely certain, for it seems that in 1 Cor. xiv, 26, one of the last class is called a psalm, (ψαλμός,) and Josephus uses both ὕμνοι and ᾠδαί in reference to the Psalms of David. Antiq. vii, 12, 3. These terms may, therefore, refer to some technical or conventional distinctions which were current in the apostolic age, but of which we can now know nothing.

Kind of matter appropriate to all Christian psalmody.

Be this as it may, one thing is evident from our premises: that the subject-matter of all Christian psalmody should be *spiritual*. God gave to the Jews a Book of Psalms, inspired both as to their matter and their form. He did so,

Why God gave the Jews a book of inspired odes.

I. *Because it was then a necessity*. In that age of comparative darkness, before the Scheme of Redemption was fully revealed, no uninspired man was qualified to write or compose any thing pertaining to a system of worship which had for its object not only the moral and religious education of the Israelites, but also the development of God's great and gracious purposes concerning our race. And hence it was that prophets were inspired, as in the first age of the Christian Church, to utter and compose spiritual songs for the people.

II. *Because, the Jews being of one language, it was as easy to express, for their benefit, appropriate sentiments of praise and thanksgiving in poetry as in prose.*

But for the Christian Church God has left no special form or collection of Psalms, Hymns, and Spiritual Songs on record.

Why he has not given a similar collection of inspired songs to Christians.

I. *Because this was not necessary.* Since the whole Scheme of Redemption has been revealed and the Canon completed, we have in the Greek and Hebrew Scriptures all things pertaining to life and to godliness. And by slightly varying the phraseology of the facts, promises, sentiments, admonitions, etc., of the Holy Scriptures, so as merely to adapt them to our own immediate wants and circumstances, we can now, without much difficulty, compose a book of sacred odes adapted to the condition of any and every kindred, and tongue, and people, and nation beneath the whole heavens, just as we can now make a prose translation of the Scriptures into all the languages and dialects of Earth.

II. *Because, in order to have done so successfully, it would have been necessary to give said form of psalmody in all the various languages and dialects of Earth.* No uninspired man can, with absolute precision and perspicuity, translate the poetry of one language into that of another The translation, at best, will be but an approximation to the original. Such has always been the result of every attempt to give to the world an English poetic version of the Psalms of David. Even the comparatively literal version of Rouse is only an approximation to the original Hebrew. The proof of this may be found in the very first verse of his translation. The meaning of the original stands about thus:

"O! the blessedness of the man who has
Not walked in the counsel of the impious,
Nor stood in the way of sinners,
Nor sat in the seat of scorners!"

This is rendered by Rouse as follows:

"That man hath perfect blessedness
Who walketh not astray
In counsel of ungodly men,
Nor stands in sinner's way,
Nor sitteth in the scorner's chair," etc.

The same sentiment is more elegantly but not quite so literally rendered into English by Dr. Watts as follows:

"Bless'd is the man who shuns the place
Where sinners love to meet,
Who fears to tread their wicked ways,
And hates the scoffer's seat."

The difference between these two versions is manifestly a difference in degree rather than in kind. Neither of them expresses the meaning of the Original, much less its *poetry*, with absolute accuracy. Nor do I think it at all necessary that they should do so. So long as the sentiment of the Scriptures is retained, the poetry and the music of our psalmody and hymnology may be so varied as to suit all the tastes, wants, and circumstances of mankind. But every thing which is false in sentiment, or which is in any way inconsistent with the dignity and purity of the Holy Scriptures, should be excluded from every collection of Psalms, and Hymns, and Spiritual Songs.

This will be still more obvious if we take into consideration some of the main objects for which this part of our social worship was instituted. These are,

Design and object of singing in social worship.

I. *To honor God as our Creator, Preserver, and Redeemer.* But it is evident that he should never be approached through falsehood, nor in any way that savors of lightness and frivolity.

II. *To cultivate and improve our own hearts.* The habit of *expressing* our sentiments has a very powerful influence on the development of our intellectual, moral, and religious faculties. And hence there should be no singing done by *proxy.* Good order, of course, requires that in every Christian congregation some one person, assisted and sustained by a sufficient number of others, should be appointed to lead in this part of our worship. But the whole congregation should always follow and express aloud their feelings of joy, or gratitude, or penitence, etc., as the case may be. "Let *the people* praise thee, O God," says the inspired Psalmist, "let ALL THE PEOPLE praise thee." Psalm lxvii, 3. Even in our social worship, though it is not, of course, consistent with good order that all should pray aloud at the same time, they should all, nevertheless, unite in saying the hearty AMEN (τὸ ἀμήν) at the close of each prayer. 1 Cor. xiv, 16.

III. *To convict sinners and persuade them to repent.* The well-known reflex influence of sympathy in popular assemblies is very great. And hence it is that the Gospel may sometimes be proclaimed even more successfully by singing than by preaching. But if our psalmody is erroneous in sentiment, instead of exciting in those present a zeal which is according to knowledge, and which is elevating, refining, and purifying in its influence, it may, of course, only serve to produce in them a wild, debasing, and extravagant enthusiasm.

In reply to the question whether instrumental music should now be used in Christian Churches as it was anciently among the Jews, I am constrained to give a negative answer chiefly for the following reasons:

Instrumental music in Churches.

I. *Such a practice is wholly unwarranted by any thing that is either said or taught in the New Testament.* The inspired Psalmist said to his Jewish brethren,

> "Praise him (Jehovah) with the sound of the trumpet;
> Praise him with the psaltery and harp;
> Praise him with the timbrel and dance;
> Praise him with stringed instruments and organs;
> Praise him on the loud cymbals;
> Praise him on the high-sounding cymbals." *Psalm cl*, 3-5.

But Paul says to all Christians, "Teach and admonish one another in Psalms, and Hymns, and Spiritual Songs, singing and making melody (ψάλλοντες, *psalming*) in your hearts to the Lord." Eph. v, 19. The antithesis here is certainly very marked, and seems to be intentional and significant.

II. *It is at least doubtful whether such a practice is in harmony with the tenor and spirit of the Christian Institution.* The Old Covenant was a covenant of rites and ceremonies, but the New Covenant deals mainly with realities. The shadow was given by Moses, but the substance came by and through Jesus Christ. And hence it would seem to be improper to connect with our worship any thing of a mere formal or ceremonial nature, save only such rites and ordinances as God has himself prescribed and commanded.

III. *The tendency of instrumental music is, I think, to divert the minds of many from the sentiment of the song to the mere sound of the organ, and in this way it often serves to promote formalism in Churches.* If all who attend religious meetings were as humble and as pious as they should be this might not be the case. All the organs and melodeons in Christendom could not seriously interfere with the devotions of some men. But I fear that many are not yet sufficiently advanced in the Divine life to use the organ with safety in our Churches; and perhaps when they arrive at the required stage of moral culture and spiritual development, they will not need an instrument to support and promote their devotions.

IV. *I am not aware that instrumental music has ever served to promote unity, peace, harmony, and love in any congregation of Christians; but I am aware that in some of them it has had a contrary effect.* If, therefore, we may judge the tree by its fruits, it would seem necessary to exclude all organs, melodeons, etc., from at least some Churches.

V. *It is often at variance with the law of love.* Grant, if you please, for the sake of illustration, that the use of the organ is not wrong in itself, still if it serves to offend a weak brother, it would certainly be very uncharitable in other members of the same Church to introduce it. To any and all who insist on their *right* to do so, I would respectfully recommend the profound study of the fourteenth chapter of Paul's letter to the Romans.

Conclusion.

For these and some other like reasons I am constrained to think that instrumental music should not be used in Churches. Whatever tends to division, strife, and formality should be excluded from the assemblies of the saints. Let all things be done in love, and let the world still have reason to exclaim with reference to our devotions, "*Behold, how good and how pleasant it is for brethren to dwell together in unity!*"

CHAPTER IV.

FASTING.

Fasting a natural and constitutional necessity.

It is a gracious law and provision of the human constitution that its nervous and vital energies may, in a great measure, be concentrated and directed to the accomplishment of one given object; its other functions being, in the mean time, either wholly or partially suspended. Thus, for instance, if while a man feels hungry and is about to take the required sustenance, he receives a message that his wife, or child, or some other very dear friend, is dead, he has no longer a desire for food; his vital energies are now mainly directed from his stomach to his brain, and to him the richest viands would now be altogether loathsome. He now chooses to go to the house of fasting rather than to the house of feasting, in order that he may give full scope and free exercise to the swellings and impulses of his soul.

When, where, and for what purpose observed.

And hence it is that on great and solemn occasions fasting has ordinarily, in all ages and in all nations, been connected with prayer as a means of spiritual strength and religious discipline. This fact is well illustrated by the following ordinance in reference to the most solemn of all the days of the Hebrew calendar: "On the tenth day of the seventh month there shall be a day of atonement. It shall be a holy convocation unto

Only fast prescribed by the Law.

you, and ye shall *afflict your souls*,* and offer an offering made by fire unto the Lord. And ye shall do no work on that same day; for it is a day of atonement, to make an atonement for you before the Lord your God. For whatsoever soul it be that *shall not be afflicted* in that same day, he shall be cut off from among his people. And whatsoever soul it be that doeth any work in that same day, the same soul will I destroy from among his people. Ye shall do no manner of work: it shall be a statute forever throughout your generations in all your dwellings. It shall be unto you a sabbath of rest, and *ye shall afflict your souls:* on the ninth day of the month at even, from even unto even, shall ye celebrate your Sabbath." Lev. xxiii, 26–32. See also Lev. xvi, 29–33; and Acts xxvii, 9.

Jewish voluntary fasts.

This was the only fast prescribed by the Law. But besides this the Jews observed, also, many voluntary fasts: some of which were occasional and extraordinary, and some were annual or weekly. See Zech. vii, 1-7; viii, 19; Matt. ix, 14; Luke xviii, 12, etc. The number of regular annual fasts now kept by the Jews amount to twenty-eight.

Evidence that Fasting is a Christian duty.

Under the dispensation of the New Covenant no regular fasts are prescribed by Divine authority. But that fasting is, nevertheless, an ordinance of God, and that as such it should be frequently observed by all Christians, is evident from the following passages:

* The word most commonly used in Hebrew for fasting is צוֹם: Gr., νηστεία, Lat., jejunium. It is not found in the Pentateuch; but it occurs frequently in the historical and prophetic books. The only term used in the Law of Moses to denote a religious fast is the very significant phrase עִנָּה נֶפֶשׁ: Gr., ταπεινοῦν ψυχήν; Lat., *affligere animam*, to afflict the soul. See Lev. xvi, 29, 31 xxiii, 27, 32; Numb. xxix, 7; xxx, 14; Isa. lviii, 3, 5, 10. In Psa. xxxv, 13. both terms are combined. Here David says: עִנֵּיתִי בַצּוֹם נַפְשִׁי. "I afflicted my soul with fasting."

1. Matthew ix, 14, 15: "Then came to him the disciples of John saying, Why do we and the Pharisees fast often, but thy disciples fast not? And Jesus said to them, Can the children of the bride-chamber mourn as long as the bridegroom is with them? *But the days will come when the bridegroom shall be taken away from them, and then shall they fast.*" From this passage it is evident that it was Christ's will and purpose that his people should fast often after his departure, and during his mediatorial reign.

2. Matthew xvii, 21: "Howbeit this kind (of demons) goeth not out *but by prayer and fasting.*" Here Christ connects fasting with prayer as a means and source of spiritual strength.

3. Acts xiii, 3: "*And when they had fasted and prayed, and laid their hands on them, they sent them away.*" Here we have apostolic example in favor of fasting, which, by all fair rules of interpretation, must be regarded as equivalent to an apostolic precept.

4. Acts xiv, 23: "And when they had ordained them Elders in every Church, *and had prayed with fasting*, they commended them to the Lord on whom they believed." Here fasting and prayer are again connected with ordination by apostolic authority.

5. 1 Corinthians vii, 5: "Defraud ye not one the other (husband and wife;) except it be with consent for a time, *that ye may give yourselves to fasting and prayer;* and come together again that Satan tempt you not for your incontinency." In this passage Paul not only sanctions but strongly commends both prayer and fasting as a means of moral culture and progress in holiness. Surely, then, we need no further evidence that fasting is a means ordained by God for the purpose of preparing the soul, on

all solemn occasions, for all manner of religious exercise and spiritual enjoyment.

With regard to all such questions as, On what particular occasions should we, like David, afflict our souls with fasting? how long should we fast? when should we abstain wholly from the use of food, and when will a partial abstinence be sufficient?—touching all such matters there are no specific rules laid down in the New Testament, for the obvious reason that none are necessary. The man who really loves God, and who desires to serve him with all his heart, and soul, and mind, and strength, need not be told that it is his *duty* to abstain from food on this, that, or the other special occasion. It is enough for him to know that it is his *privilege* to do so; that God has honored him by allowing him to decide for himself how often and to what extent he should chasten his body for the good of his soul. "Thy people," said Jehovah to his Son, "shall be FREEWILL OFFERINGS in the day of thy power, in ornaments of holiness; from the womb of the morning shall be to thee the dew of thy youth." Psalm cx, 3. This passage beautifully represents the *cheerful service*, the attractive piety, and the perpetual reproduction, in untold numbers, of the offspring and subjects of the Messiah during his mediatorial reign.

Details left chiefly to our choice and discretion.

Finally, as all religious ostentation is peculiarly odious and offensive to God, it would be well for all who fast, and especially for those who fast for their own personal benefit, to remember the following very impressive caution and admonition of our blessed Savior: "When ye fast be not as the hypocrites, of a sad countenance; for they disfigure their faces, that they may appear unto men to fast. Verily I say to you, they have their reward. But thou, when thou fastest, anoint thy head, and wash thy face; that thou appear not unto men to fast, but unto thy Father who is in secret; and thy Father who seeth in secret will reward thee openly." Matt. vi, 16–18.

CHAPTER V.

BAPTISM.

THIS subject will be most conveniently considered under the three following heads:

Division of the subject

I. The action expressed by the word *baptism.* What is it?

II. The design of Baptism. For what ends and purposes was it instituted?

III. The proper subjects of Baptism.

SECTION I.—ACTION OF BAPTISM.

Different views entertained of *baptisma* and *baptizo*.

The meaning of the word *baptisma* (βάπτισμα) rendered *baptism* in the New Testament has long been a subject of controversy. Some maintain that it is a generic term, and that it may denote either *a sprinkling, a pouring,* or *an immersion.* Others concede that it originally meant *an immersion;* but they insist that, as used by Christ and his Apostles it means only *a sprinkling* or *a pouring.* While others again maintain, that although it is used in the New Testament to denote a Christian ordinance, and has therefore in the Living Oracles a religious significance and application unknown to the ancient Greeks, it is nevertheless used here as in all other writings, in but the one definite and specific sense of *a dipping* or *an immer-*

sion. The same diversity of views is also entertained of its cognate verb *baptizo* (βαπτίζω).

In favor of the last of these views there is certainly a very strong presumption growing out of the fact that Baptism is a *Positive* ordinance. (See *Great Commission*, pp. 88–97, by the Author.) If Baptism is an exception to the general law, that *every Positive ordinance should be set forth in the plainest and most specific terms possible*, then certainly this should be very plainly indicated to us in some way. But quite the reverse of this is true. The historical use of both *baptizo* and *baptisma* shows beyond all doubt, that they were severally used in both classic and Hellenistic Greek to denote but one definite and specific action. This, the reader will perceive very clearly from the following illustrations.

Presumption in favor of the *specific* use of these terms.

I.—Examples from Classic Authors.

1. Pindar, the prince of lyric poets, was born in 522 B. C., and died about 440 B. C. In his Pythic odes (ii, 79, 80), comparing himself to a cork on a fishing net, which floats on the surface of the water, while the hook sinks beneath, he says,—"For as when the rest of the tackling is toiling deep in the sea, I, as a cork above the net, am *unimmersed* (ἀβάπτιστός) in the brine."

2. Aristotle, who flourished about 350 B. C. and who is justly celebrated throughout the world for his great accuracy in the use of terms, says in his work "Concerning Wonderful Reports," Vol. vi, p. 136,—"They say that the Phœnicians who inhabit the so-called Gadira, sailing four days outside of the Pillars of Hercules, with an east wind, come to certain desert places full of rushes and sea-weed;

which, when it is ebb-tide, *are not immersed* (μη βαπτίζεσθαι), but when it is flood-tide are overflowed."

3. Polybius flourished about 150 B. C. In his History, Book iii, ch. 72, 4, speaking of the passage of the Roman army across the swollen Trebia, he says, "They passed through with difficulty, the foot-soldiers *being immersed* (βαπτιζόμενοι) as far as to their breasts."

4. Lucian, the celebrated humorist and satirist, was born at Samosata about A. D. 130 or 135. In his "True History," Book ii, ch. 4, while humorously describing men with cork feet as walking on the sea, he says,—"We wondered therefore when we saw them not *immersed*, (βαπτιζομενους), but standing above the waves, and traveling on without fear."

5. Porphyry, a Platonic philosopher of Tyre, and violent opposer of Christianity, was born about A. D. 232. In his work "Concerning the Styx," while speaking of the "Lake of Probation," in India, and the custom of making criminals pass through it in order to test their guilt or innocence, he says,—"When the accused comes to it, if he is guiltless, he goes through it without fear, having the water as far as his knees; but if he is guilty, after proceeding a little way, he *is immersed* (βαπτίζεται) to the head."

In all these examples, which might be greatly multiplied, it is quite manifest that nothing but the word *immerse* or some one of its equivalents, will satisfy the requirements of the context. To substitute for it either *sprinkle* or *pour*, in any of these examples, would make sheer nonsense. And hence we conclude that from Pindar to Porphyry, the classical meaning of the word *baptizo* was simply *to dip* or *to immerse*.

II.—Examples from the Greek Versions.

1. The Septuagint version of the Old Testament was made in Egypt, under the patronage of Ptolemy Philadelphus, about 280 B. C. In it, the word *baptizo* (βαπτίζω) occurs but four times: twice in the canonical books and twice in the Apocrypha, as follows:—

(1) 2 Kings v, 14: "And Naaman went down and *immersed himself* (ἐβαπτίσατο) seven times in the Jordan."

(2) Isaiah xxi, 14: "My heart wanders, and iniquity *overwhelms* (βαπτίζει) me."

(3) Judith xii, 7: "Thus she abode in the camp three days; and went out in the night into the valley of Bethulia, and *bathed herself* (ἐβαπτίζατο) in a fountain of water by the camp."

(4) Wisdom of Sirach xxxiv, 30 (Eng. Version, Ecclesiasticus xxxiv, 25): "He that *immerses himself* (βαπτιζομενος) after touching a dead body, if he touch it again what is he profited by his bath?"

In the first of these examples, the word *baptizo* is manifestly used in its literal physical sense. There can be no doubt that Naaman "*dipped*" or *immersed* himself seven times in the Jordan. In the other examples the word is used figuratively; but nevertheless it retains in every case the ground idea of an *immersion.*

2. About A. D. 150 Aquila, a learned Jew of Pontus, translated the Old Testament into Greek. In Job ix, 31, he says, "Even then thou *wilt plunge* (βαπτίσεις) me in corruption:" for which we have in the English Bible, "Thou shalt plunge me in the ditch." Here the idea of an *immersion* is quite obvious.

3. Another version of the Old Testament into Greek was made by Symmachus of Samaria, about A. D. 200

In Psa. lxix, 3 (2), the author represents the Psalmist as saying, "I *am plunged* (ἐβαπτίσθην) into bottomless depths." Here again we have unmistakably the idea of an *immersion.* Neither pouring nor sprinkling would express the conception of the author.

III.—Examples from the New Testament.

The verb *baptizo* (βαπτίζω) occurs in the New Testament eighty times, and the noun *baptisma* (βάπτισμα) twenty-two times. Of these, the following examples will suffice for illustration.

1. Matthew iii, 5, 6: "Then went out to him Jerusalem, and all Judea, and all the region round about the Jordan, and *were immersed* (ἐβαπτίζοντο) by him (John) in the Jordan, confessing their sins."

2. Mark i, 9: "Jesus came from Nazareth of Galilee and *was immersed* (ἐβαπτίσθη) by John in the Jordan."

3. John iii, 23: "And John was *immersing* (βαπτίζων) in Ænon near to Salim, because there was much water there."

4. 1 Cor. x, 1, 2: "Moreover, brethren, I would not that ye should be ignorant, that all our fathers were under the cloud; and all passed through the sea; and *were immersed* (ἐβαπτίσαντο) into Moses, in the cloud and in the sea."

5. Col. ii, 12: "Buried with him *in the immersion* (ἐν τῷ βαπτίσματι), wherein also ye are risen with him."

In all these examples, the radical idea of an *immersion* is made quite obvious by the terms and conditions of the context. In the first and second, this is so very plain that no other words could express the idea more clearly. In the third, the reason assigned for choosing Ænon as a place to baptize, is wholly without significance on any other hypothesis than that John was an *immerser*. The word *Ænon* means *a fountain*, or more literally *a great fountain*. It comes from the intensive form of the Hebrew word *ahyin* (עַיִן) which means an *eye* or a *fountain*. In the fourth, the historical circumstances all go to show that the Israelites were *immersed* into Moses, in the cloud and in the sea. And from the fifth, it seems quite obvious, that in every legal baptism, there must of necessity be a symbolical representation of a burial and a resurrection. This is witnessed in every case of *immersion;* but never in a *sprinkling* or a *pouring*.

IV.—Examples from Josephus.

Flavius Josephus was born in Jerusalem A. D. 37, and died in Rome about A. D. 100. He was a Pharisee of the sacerdotal order, and was well instructed in both Greek and Hebrew literature. After the destruction of Jerusalem A. D. 70, he accompanied Titus to Rome, where he spent the rest of his days in literary pursuits. His "History of the Jewish War" and his work on "Jewish Antiquities" were both written in Hebrew, and afterward translated by himself into Greek. The former was published about A. D. 75, and the latter about A. D. 90. He is certainly one of the most learned of all the Hellenistic Greek writers; and as he was contemporary with the Apostles, his writings are of the highest value and authority in settling the question as to the New Testament meaning of the word *baptizo*. The following examples are sufficient to illustrate his use of this term.

1. Antiquities, Book ix, ch. 10, 2: Speaking of the case of Jonah, Josephus says, "Now at the first they durst not do so (cast Jonah into the sea), esteeming it a wicked thing to cast a man who was a stranger, and who

had committed his life to them into such manifest perdition. But at last when their misfortunes overbore them, and the ship was just going *to be submerged* (βαπτίζεσθαι), and when they were animated to do it by the prophet himself, and by the fear concerning their own safety, they cast him into the sea."

2. Antiquities, Book xv, ch. 3, 3: Describing the murder of the young High Priest, Aristobulus, who at the command of his brother-in-law, Herod the Great, was drowned in a swimming-bath, our author says, "Constantly pressing down and *immersing* (βαπτίζοντες) him, as if in sport, while swimming, they did not desist, till he was entirely suffocated."

3. Jewish War, Book ii, ch. 20, 1: Having described the retreat of Cestius, the Roman general, from the walls of Jerusalem, Josephus says, "After this calamity had befallen Cestius, many of the most eminent of the Jews swum away from the city, as from a ship when it is *going to be submerged* (βαπτιζομένης)."

4. War, Book iii, ch. 10, 9: Speaking of the unequal contest between the Jews and the Romans on the sea of Galilee, he says, "And when they (the Jews) ventured to come near the Romans, they became sufferers themselves, before they could do any harm to the others, and *were submerged* (ἐβαπτίζοντο), they and their ships together. . . . . And those of the *submerged* (βαπτισθέντων) who raised their heads above the water, were either killed by darts, or caught up by the vessels."

Other examples might be given; but these are quite sufficient to warrant the conclusion, that in the writings of Josephus, the word *baptizo* always means to *immerse*, *submerge*, *plunge*, or *dip*. To this there is no exception found in any of his works.

V.—Examples from the Greek Fathers.

As the testimony of Josephus is of the highest authority in settling the current Hellenistic meaning of the word *baptizo* in the first century of the Christian era, so also is the testimony of the Christian Fathers, of paramount value in determining what was the practice of the primitive Church in administering the ordinance of Baptism. This, it gives me pleasure to say, is full and unequivocal. The following examples from a few of the Greek Fathers, will suffice for illustration.

1. Cyril, Bishop of Jerusalem, was born at or near Jerusalem, about A. D. 315, and was made Bishop in 350. In his "Instruction on Baptism" he says, "For as Jesus assuming the sins of the world, died, that having slain sin he might raise thee to righteousness; so also thou going down into the water, and in a manner *buried* (ταφεὶς) in the water, as he in the rock, art raised again walking in newness of life." What a beautiful and impressive commentary is all this on Rom. vi, 4 and also on Col. ii, 12.

2. Basil the Great, Archbishop of Cæsarea, and one of the most learned of the Greek Fathers, was born at Cæsarea in Palestine, A. D. 328, and died Jan. 1st, 379. In his work on the Holy Spirit he says, "Imitating the burial of Christ *by the immersion* (διὰ τοῦ βαπτίσματος). For the bodies of those *immersed* (βαπτιζομένων) are, as it were, buried in the water." And again he says in the same passage, "The water presents the image of death, receiving the body as in a tomb."

3. Chrysostom, Archbishop of Constantinople, a man eminent for both his learning and his piety, was born at Antioch about A. D. 347, and died in exile A. D. 407. In his "Commentary on First Corinthians," Discourse xl,

he says, "For, *to be immersed* (βαπτίζεσθαι) and to sink down, then to emerge, is a symbol of the descent into Hades, and of the ascent from thence. Therefore Paul calls *the immersion* (το βάπτισμα) the tomb; saying, "We were buried therefore with him *by the immersion* (διὰ τοῦ βαπτισματος) into death."

Such extracts from both Greek and Latin writers might be multiplied indefinitely. But more than I have already cited would be quite unnecessary. These, in connection with the examples taken from the Greek Classics, Greek Versions, the New Testament, and Josephus prove beyond all reasonable doubt, that the proper meaning of *baptizo* is *to immerse;* and that *baptisma* means simply *an immersion.* And hence we conclude that *Christian Baptism consists in immersing a proper subject by the authority of Christ into the name of the Father, and of the Son, and of the Holy Spirit.*

Conclusion from all the premises submitted.

That this, and this only, was the primitive practice, has ever been maintained by the Greek and Baptist churches: and that it was for several centuries the common, if indeed not the exclusive practice of the primitive Christians, is conceded by the most learned and pious of the Pædobaptists. The testimony of the following eminent scholars and impartial witnesses will suffice for illustration.

Concessions of Baptists and Pædobaptists.

1. Luther "On the Sacrament of Baptism" says, "The name *baptism* is Greek; in Latin, it can be rendered *immersion*, when we immerse any thing in water, that it may be all covered with water. And although that custom has now grown out of use with most persons (nor do they wholly submerge children, but only pour on a little water), yet they ought to be entirely immersed and immediately

drawn out; for this, the etymology of the name seems to demand."

2. Calvin in his "Institutes of the Christian Religion," Book iv, ch. 15, speaking of Baptism, says, "The word *baptize* itself signifies *immerse;* and it is certain that the rite of immersing was observed by the primitive Church."

3. Dr. John Laurence Von Mosheim, speaking of the rite of Baptism as practiced in the first century of the Christian era, says, "In this century, baptism was administered in convenient places, without the public assemblies, and *by immersing the candidate wholly in water.* (*Eccl. Hist.*, Vol. i, p. 87, *Murdock's Ed.*) And of the same rite in the second century, he says, "Twice a year, at Easter and Whitsuntide, baptism was publicly administered by the Bishop or by the Presbyters, acting by his command and authority. *The candidates for it were immersed wholly in water.*" (*Eccl. Hist.*, Vol. i, p. 137).

4. Brenner, a learned Roman Catholic writer, in his "Historical Exhibition of the Administration of Baptism from Christ to our own times," says on page 306, "*For thirteen hundred years, was baptism generally and regularly an immersion of the whole person under the water;* and only in extraordinary cases, a sprinkling or pouring with water. The latter was moreover disputed as a mode of baptism, nay even forbidden."

5. Conybeare and Houson in their work on the "Life and Epistles of Saint Paul," page 384, "People's Edition," bear testimony as follows: "It is needless to add that baptism was (unless in exceptional cases) administered by immersion, the convert being plunged beneath the surface of the water to represent his death to the life of sin, and then raised from this momentary burial to represent his resurrection to the life of righteousness. It must be a

subject of regret, that the discontinuance of this original form of baptism (though perhaps necessary in our northern climates), has rendered obscure to popular apprehension some very important passages of Scripture." And again, speaking of Rom. vi, 4, they say, "This passage can not be understood, unless it is borne in mind that the primitive baptism was by immersion."

6. To the same effect is the testimony of Dr. Philip Schaff. In his "History of the Christian Church," Vol. i, p. 123, he says, "That the usual form of the act was *immersion* is plain from the original meaning of the Greek βαπτίζειν and βαπτισμός; from the analogy of John's baptism in the Jordan; from the Apostles' comparison of the sacred rite with the miraculous passage of the Red Sea, with the escape of the Ark from the flood, with a cleansing and refreshing bath, and with a burial and resurrection; and finally from the custom of the ancient Church which prevails in the East to this day."

Why sprinkling and pouring have become so prevalent.

Why then, it may be asked, has the practice of sprinkling and pouring become so prevalent? This may be readily inferred from what is immediately added by the same learned and pious author. On the same page of his history, he says, "Unquestionably, immersion expresses the idea of baptism more completely than sprinkling; but it is a pedantic Jewish literalism, to limit the operation of the Holy Spirit, by the quantity or quality of the water. Water is absolutely necessary to baptism, as an appropriate symbol of the purifying and regenerating energy of the Holy Ghost; but whether it be in large quantity or small, cold or warm, fresh or salt, from river, cistern, or spring, is relatively immaterial." So reasoned Cain when he brought of the fruits of the ground instead of a bleeding lamb, as an offering to God (Gen. iv, 3); and so reasoned King Saul, when in violation of the command of God, he spared of the flocks of the Amalekites for the purpose of offering sacrifice (1 Saml. xv, 15). But he was very promptly informed by Samuel, that, "To obey is better than sacrifice; and to hearken, than the fat of rams."

The reasoning of Pædobaptists on the action of Baptism, is rationalistic

It is not then with us a question of either Jewish or Gentile pedantry; but of obedience or disobedience to a positive command of God, whether we shall have a little water sprinkled or poured on our faces, or be "immersed into the name of the Father, and of the Son, and of the Holy Spirit." Let the earnest inquiry of every penitent believer be simply this: "*Lord, what wilt THOU have me to do,*" and very soon all controversy about the action of Baptism will cease in the Churches: for then, all who tremble at the word of the Lord, will be promptly *buried* with Christ in baptism, and rise with him "to walk in newness of life."

The real Question at issue.

SECTION II.—Design of Baptism.

Seldom, if ever, is the *full design* and import of a Divine ordinance formally stated in the Holy Scriptures. In this respect God often acts like the skillful physician. He has an object to be accomplished: some disease, if you please, to be eradicated from the human soul. He provides and administers the remedy, and leaves us to infer his design from the effects produced, and the general statements and incidental remarks made concerning it. This, I think, is true of Baptism; as it is also true of the Passover, the feast of Pentecost, the feast of Tabernacles,

Designs of God's Ordinances not always fully and formally stated.

the Sabbatical Year, the Year of Jubilee, and many other ordinances of the Old Covenant.

Remission of sins the general, but not the specific or *characteristic* design of Baptism.

True, indeed, it is often stated in the New Testament that Baptism is *for* (εἰς) *the remission of sins.* But this is just as true of faith, repentance, and confession, as it is of Baptism. They are all for, or, rather, ***in order to*** the remission of sins. Compare Mark xvi, 16; Acts ii, 38; iii, 19; xvi, 31; Rom. i, 16; x, 10, etc. They are all links in the chain of God's appointed means, which serve to bring the sinner under the influence of that blood which alone can procure his pardon and render him just before God. And hence, to say that Baptism is for the remission of sins is to give but its general design, which it has in common with faith, repentance, and confession. But besides this, it was, I think, evidently intended,

Its *characteristic* designs.

I. *To remind us of the burial and resurrection of Christ* This seems evident for the following reasons:

Commemorative.

1. It is certainly in harmony with the ***effect*** produced on the mind of every intelligent person who sees the ordinance properly administered. As he beholds the candidate for Baptism buried in the water and again raised out of it, he is involuntarily led to think of the burial and resurrection of Christ.

2. It is in harmony with God's gracious plan and purpose to commemorate the great and leading events of his administration by means of suitable rites and ordinances. The completion of the Adamic creation, for instance, was commemorated by the Sabbath; the sparing of the first-born of the Children of Israel when the first-born of the Egyptians were slain, by the Passover; the giving of the Law from Mount Sinai, by the feast of Pentecost; the sojourn of the Israelites in the desert.

by the feast of Tabernacles, etc. And hence it would seem to be peculiarly appropriate that the three great and leading facts of the Gospel, viz., the death, the burial, and the resurrection of Christ, (1 Cor. xv, 1–4,) should also be commemorated. The first has been commemorated by the Lord's Supper, and certainly nothing could more appropriately commemorate the second and third than Christian Baptism. True, indeed, in one sense and in one aspect the Lord's Day very forcibly reminds us of the resurrection and triumphs of our blessed Lord and Redeemer. But an event so very important as this is deserves to be commemorated and illustrated in every conceivable way. It was not enough to sacrifice the one goat as a sin-offering on the Day of Atonement to cover the sins of the people; a scape-goat was also found to be necessary in order to bear them away into a state of complete and everlasting separation. And just so it is with respect to the resurrection of Christ. The *time when* is *historically* represented and commemorated by the Lord's Day; but the *act* or the thing itself is *symbolically* represented and commemorated by the ordinance of Christian Baptism.

3. The Apostle seems to intimate this pretty clearly by connecting Baptism with the burial and resurrection of Christ. See Rom. vi, 4, and Col. ii, 12.

Symbolical of a change in our relations.

II. *To indicate to us in the most impressive way possible the great change which then and there takes place in our own relations; that is, our transfer from the kingdom of darkness into the Kingdom or Church of Christ.* Col. i, 13. And hence we are all baptized by the authority of the Lord Jesus Christ *into* (εἰς) the name of the Father, and of the Son, and of the Holy Spirit. Matt. xxviii, 19. Without the regenerating influence of the Holy Spirit producing in our hearts faith, hope, love, and repentance, Baptism is but an abortion, and can, of course, be of no benefit to any one. There must of necessity be a *renewing* influence of the Holy Spirit before there can be a normal birth of water. But the man who *has been begotten* by the Spirit of God is, according to the Divine arrangement, introduced by his Baptism into the Kingdom of Christ, (John iii, 5,) made partaker of the Holy Spirit, (Acts ii, 38,) and constituted an heir of the eternal inheritance. Rom. viii, 12–17.

Symbolical of a change in our state.

III. *To indicate to us, in like manner, our change of state; or, more particularly, our death to sin and our resurrection to a life of holiness.* This point is presented with great force by the Apostle Paul in the first part of the sixth chapter of his letter to the Romans. In the closing paragraph of the fifth chapter he speaks of the great and superabounding fullness of the grace of God in the Scheme of Redemption. "Moreover," says he, "the law entered that the offense might abound. But where sin abounded, grace did much more abound: that as sin has reigned unto death, even so might grace reign through righteousness, unto eternal life, by Jesus Christ our Lord."

But just at this point of his argument Paul perceived that the Jew would, in all probability, urge an objection. To the blind Pharisee or Sadducee this would seem to be entirely too much grace, and he would therefore, no doubt, attempt to turn Paul's whole argument into ridicule, or to reduce it to a practical absurdity, by endeavoring to show that its tendency would be to induce men to sin more and more. "What shall we say, then?" would be his reply. "Shall we continue in sin that grace may abound?" Certainly not, says Paul. The supposition implies a manifest absurdity; for "how," says he, "can we who have died to sin live any longer therein?" That is, how can we who have been separated from sin continue to live in it? But, Paul, will you please to inform us *when*, and *where*, and *how* we were separated from our sins? Why, says he, "do you not know that as many of us as were baptized into Christ *were baptized into his death?*"

A little reflection on the meaning and force of the preposition *into* (εἰς) will enable us to perceive and comprehend the force of the Apostle's argument. It is a particle of *transition*, and always implies a change of relations and a change of state, and hence, also, a change of influences. Thus, for instance, when a man, in order to avoid the violence of a storm, enters into a house, he is shielded and protected by the house; when he recklessly plunges into debt he suffers from the annoyances and inconveniences of debt; and when he falls into a paroxysm of anger, love, or any other passion he can not but feel and experience all its various influences, whether they be for good or for evil.

And just so the man who is, by the Divine arrangement, baptized *into* the death of Christ is made to realize and to enjoy all the blessings and benefits of his death. And hence we see why it is and how it is that Baptism is for the remission of sins. It procures for us pardon, not by virtue of any intrinsic efficacy in itself, abstractly considered, but simply by bringing us, through the Divine arrangement, into contact with that blood which cleanses from all sin. And "therefore we are buried with him (Christ) by Baptism into death, that like as Christ was raised from the dead by the glory of the

Father, even so we also should walk in newness of life." Compare, also, Acts ii, 38; Ephesians v, 26; Titus iii, 5; Hebrews x, 22, etc.

Symbolical of he final resurrection.

IV. *It is probable that baptism was intended also to typify or foreshadow our own death, burial, and resurrection.*

1. Because this is its natural and necessary tendency. Whenever and wherever we see a baptism properly administered, we are led to think not only of the death, burial, and resurrection of Christ, but also of our own.

2. Because, in 1 Cor. xv, 29, Paul draws from it an argument in proof of the final resurrection. "Else," says he, "what shall they do who are baptized for the dead, if the dead rise not at all? Why are they then baptized for the dead?" As much as to say, What is the meaning of baptism if there is no resurrection of the dead? On that hypothesis, why are you baptized for or on account of the dead? Of what avail or advantage will it ever be to you or to any one else thus to symbolize a falsehood?

SECTION III.—SUBJECTS OF BAPTISM.

Law of Christ with respect to the Subjects of Baptism.

THE law of Christian Baptism, with regard to its subjects, is thus clearly and definitely laid down by Christ himself, in the Great Commission: "Go YE," said he to his Apostles, "INTO ALL THE WORLD, AND PREACH THE GOSPEL TO EVERY CREATURE. HE THAT BELIEVETH AND IS BAPTIZED SHALL BE SAVED; BUT HE THAT BELIEVETH NOT SHALL BE DAMNED." Mark xvi, 15, 16.

Proof that this Commission does not include infants.

This Commission evidently embraces such persons, and such only, as are capable of hearing, believing, and obeying the Gospel. For if infants and idiots are included in it, then, indeed, they must all be damned with other unbelievers. But such an allegation is manifestly absurd. And, therefore, the hypothesis that the Apostolic Commission includes infants and idiots must be false.

This view of the matter is further sustained by all that is recorded in the New Testament touching the labors of the Apostles in carrying out the scope and object of this Commission. There is not, in all their history, a single intimation that they ever baptized either an infant or an idiot. The uniform testimony of the inspired record is simply this: that the people first heard the Word, and then believed, and then were baptized. See Acts ii, 41; iv, 4; vi, 7; viii, 12; x, 44-48; xvi, 30-34; xviii, 8, etc.

Evidence drawn from the labors of the Apostles.

And hence many even of the ablest pedobaptist writers now concede that infant baptism was not practiced by the Apostles and primitive Evangelists. The very learned Dr. Augustus Neander, for instance, says: "Baptism was administered at first only to adults, as men were accustomed to conceive baptism and faith as strictly connected. *We have all reason for not deriving infant baptism from apostolic institution*, and the recognition of it which followed somewhat later as an apostolic tradition serves to confirm this hypothesis." *Hist. of the Christ. Religion and Church*, Vol. I, p. 311.

Concession of many pedobaptist writers.

Whence, then, originated the practice of infant baptism? We will allow the very candid and erudite Neander to answer this question. He says: "Irenæus is the first Church teacher in whom we find any allusion to infant baptism, and in his mode of expressing himself on the subject he

Origin of infant baptism.

Views of Irenæus.

leads us, at the same time, to recognize its connection with the essence of the Christian consciousness; *he testifies of the profound Christian idea out of which infant baptism arose, and which procured for it, at length, universal recognition.* Irenæus is wishing to show that Christ did not interrupt the progressive development of that human nature which was to be sanctified by him, but sanctified it in accordance with its natural course of development, and in all its several stages. 'He came (says Irenæus) to redeem all by himself, all who through him are regenerated to God, infants, little children, boys, young men and old. Hence he passed through every age, and for the infants he became an infant, sanctifying the infants; among the little children he became a little child, sanctifying those who belong to this age, and at the same time presenting to them an example of piety, of well-doing, and of obedience; among the young men he became a young man, that he might set them an example, and sanctify them to the Lord.'

Explained and further developed by Neander.

"Infant baptism, then, (continues Neander,) appears here as the medium through which the principle of sanctification, imparted by Christ to human nature from its earliest development, became appropriated to children. *It is the idea of infant baptism that Christ, through the Divine life which he imparted to and revealed in human nature, sanctified that nature from the germ of its earliest development.* The child born in a Christian family was, when all things were as they should be, to have this advantage above others, that he did not first come to Christianity out of heathenism or the sinful nature-life, but, from the first dawnings of consciousness, unfolded his powers under the imperceptible preventing influences of a sanctifying, ennobling religion;

that with the earliest germination of the natural self-conscious life another divine principle of life, transforming the nature, should be brought nigh to him ere yet the ungodly principle should come into full activity, and the latter should find here its powerful counterpoise. In such a life the new birth was not to constitute a new crisis, beginning at some definable moment, but it was to begin imperceptibly, and so proceed throughout the whole life. Hence baptism, the visible sign of regeneration, was to be given to the child at the very outset; the child was to be consecrated to the Redeemer from the beginning of its life. *From this idea, founded on what is inmost in Christianity, becoming prominent in the feelings of Christians, resulted the practice of infant baptism.*"

Opposition of Tertullian.

But immediately after Irenæus, in the last years of the second century, "Tertullian appears as the zealous opponent of infant baptism, a proof that the practice had not yet come to be regarded as an apostolical institution, for otherwise he would hardly have ventured to express himself so strongly against it. . . It seems, in fact, according to the principles laid down by him, that he could not conceive of any efficacy whatever residing in baptism without the conscious participation and individual faith of the person baptized, nor could he see any danger accruing to the age of innocence from delaying it, although this view of the matter was not logically consistent with his own system.

Ground on which infant baptism was finally deemed *essential.*

"But when now, on the one hand, the doctrine of the corruption and guilt cleaving to human nature, in consequence of the first transgression, was reduced to a more precise and systematic form, and on the other, from the want of duly distinguishing between what is outward and what is inward in baptism, (the baptism by water and the baptism by the Spirit,) the error became more firmly established *that without external baptism no one could be delivered from that inherent guilt, could be saved from the everlasting punishment that threatened him, or raised to eternal life; and when the notion of a magical influence, a charm connected with the sacraments, continually gained ground, the theory was finally evolved of the unconditional necessity of infant baptism.* About the middle of the third century this theory was already generally admitted in the North African Church. The only question that remained was, Whether the child ought to be baptized immediately after its birth, or not till eight days after, as in the case of the rite of circumcision." *Hist. of the Christ. Religion and Church,* Vol. I, pp. 311–313.

Fallacy of this theory.

It seems, therefore, that infant baptism had its origin in a false and mistaken view of the design of the primitive apostolic Institution. For though it is certainly true that, by means of the first transgression of Adam, the whole human race have, without any agency on their part, been made sinful, it is equally true that, through the sin-offering and mediation of Christ, and without any agency on their part, they will, *to the same extent,* be made righteous: "*Wherefore, as by one offense, sentence came on all men to condemnation, so also, by one act of righteousness, the gift has come on all men to justification of life. For as by the disobedience of the one man the many have been made sinners, so also, by the obedience of the one, the many shall be made righteous.*" Rom. v, 18, 19.

To remove the influence of the sin of the first Adam from our suffering world is, therefore, the peculiar and exclusive work of the second Adam. It is a matter in which we can have no agency whatever. This is evident,

Evidence that the removal of this inherited depravity is a matter in which we have no agency, and for which we are not responsible.

I. *From the passage of Scripture just cited.* No language could more clearly and forcibly express the fact that we all inherit a sinful nature from the first Adam; but neither could any one, by any form of words, express more clearly than the Apostle has done the additional fact that our whole race, infants as well as adults, and heathens as well as Christians, will be finally and forever freed from all this inherited sinfulness, through the obedience and agency of the second Adam.

II. *From the fact that baptism has no influence whatever in removing this inherited sinfulness.* The baptized child is just as corrupt and as prone to sin as the unbaptized child. It is a thorn in the flesh of every human being, from which he can never be delivered, while his soul remains in its clay tabernacle.

III. *From the fact that there is not in the whole Bible a single intimation that any man was ever required to be baptized or to do any thing else, in order that he might be saved, or delivered from this inherited sinfulness.* Men are often called on and exhorted to repent of their own personal transgressions, but never on account of what they have involuntarily inherited from Adam.

IV. *From the fact that in the final judgment every man will be judged according to the deeds done in his own body, whether they be good or whether they be evil.* See Matt. xxv, 31–46; John v, 28, 29; Rom. xiv, 12; 2 Cor. v, 10; Rev. xx, 12, 13.

It is, therefore, quite probable that if the fifth chapter of Romans had been rightly understood by the Christian

Fathers the practice of infant baptism would never have had a place in the history of the Church.*

Ground of the second argument in favor of infant baptism.

As the controversy about infant baptism progressed other reasons were alleged and pleaded as a ground for continuing the practice. The most plausible of these is the argument drawn from analogy, or from the alleged identity of the two Churches under the Old and New Covenants. It is of course conceded that infants were embraced in the terms of the Old Covenant; and hence it is inferred by many that they are also, of necessity, proper subjects of the New Covenant.

Refutation of this argument.

But this again is manifestly in opposition to the teachings of the Holy Spirit in such passages as Jeremiah xxxi, 31–34; and Hebrews viii, 6–13. In each of these there is a contrast drawn between the two Covenants; and the points of difference are clearly and definitely stated. One of these has reference to the intellectual and moral attainments of the subjects of these two Covenants. Most of the subjects of the Old Covenant were introduced into it by a birth of flesh. And hence it was necessary that they should afterward be taught by their fellow-citizens even to know the Lord. But not so with the subjects of the New Covenant. "THESE," said Jehovah, "SHALL ALL KNOW ME, FROM THE LEAST OF THEM TO THE GREATEST."

I am aware that this declaration is by many referred to the whole population of the world at a given period.

Tendency of the human mind to run to extremes.

* We have in the history of this controversy about inherited depravity a melancholy illustration of the proneness of human nature to run from one extreme to another; and also of the evil fruits and bitter consequences of such extremes. The Pelagian party can very easily demonstrate the errors of the Augustinian, and the Augustinian can just as easily point out the errors of the Pelagian. But how few, alas! of those who are wedded to such vain theories and speculations can ever discover the *golden mean* of inspiration!

But in this sense it never was true, and never can be true while time endures. To the subjects of the New Covenant, and to them alone, it is manifestly applicable, according to all the terms and conditions of the context. And hence there can be no infants in the New Covenant, so far as it relates to the Church militant; but, nevertheless, all who die in their infancy will, through the rich merits of our Savior's blood, obtain an abundant entrance into God's everlasting Kingdom. And then will be fulfilled, in its highest sense, the saying, that, "*Out of the mouth of babes and sucklings thou hast perfected praise.*"

Conclusion.

CHAPTER VI.

THE LORD'S DAY.

We have in the New Testament abundant evidence that in and through the death of Christ were abolished all the typical and ceremonial institutions and ordinances of the Patriarchal and Jewish ages. See, for instance, Rom. vii, 1–6; 2 Cor. iii, 7–11; Gal. iii, 19–25; iv, 21–31; Col. ii, 14; Heb. viii, 6–13; xii, 26, 27, etc. And hence Paul says to the Colossians, "*Let no man therefore judge you in meat or in drink, or in respect to a feast, or the new moon, or Sabbaths: which things are a shadow of things to come; but the substance is in Christ.*" Col. ii, 16, 17. And again he says, in his letter to the Romans. "*One man thinks that one day is better than another, another thinks that every day is alike. Let each be fully assured in his own mind.* He that regards the day, to

Abrogation of all Patriarchal and Jewish types and ceremonies with the death of Christ the Lord he regards it; and he that does not regard the day, to the Lord he does not regard it. He that eats, eats to the Lord; for he gives God thanks; and he that eats not, to the Lord he eats not, and gives God thanks." Rom. xiv, 5, 6.

Erroneous conclusions drawn from these premises.

From these premises some persons have too hastily inferred that all distinctions between days are now abolished; that under the New Covenant no one is required to sanctify any portion of his time to the Lord, and that all seasons are, in fact, now equally holy.

But in this case we have an illustration of the very common fallacy of drawing a universal conclusion from particular premises. There is not in the passage cited the slightest evidence that the Apostle has reference to any thing more than the rites, and ceremonies, and voluntary customs of the Jews and Gentiles. And to extend his remarks any further is to commit what logicians call the fallacy of *illicit process*.

Evidence that mankind still need a day of sacred rest.

But that one day in seven should be sanctified wholly to the Lord may be fairly and legitimately inferred *from the common physical, intellectual, moral, social, and religious wants of mankind.* "The Sabbath," says Christ, "was made for *man*." Mark ii, 27. Of course, then, he needed it. And if he needed it in Eden, and during the Patriarchal and Jewish ages, does he not need it still? Does not the proper cultivation of his whole moral and religious nature require the sanctifying influence of a stated day of sacred rest as much now as it ever did?

This question is answered in the affirmative by the light and facts of all history. *Indeed, we may challenge the world to produce an instance of a Church or community distinguished for their virtue and piety who have lived in the habitual neglect of a Sabbath—of one day in seven consecrated to the service and worship of God.* I profess to have given some attention to this matter, and I think I am prepared to say that history furnishes no such example. Strange, then, it would be, indeed, if in an Institution like Christianity, gracious and benevolent in all its provisions, and designed especially for the moral and spiritual improvement of mankind, there were no Sabbath—no portion of time sanctified to the Lord! The omission of such an element would serve to mar the character of the whole Institution.

Evidence that the First Day of the week should be sanctified to the Lord.

We infer, therefore, *a priori*, that the Gospel has a Sabbath as well as the Law. But on what day does it occur? Evidently on the first day of the week, for the following reasons:

I. *On this day Christ rose from the dead, and thus brought life and immortality to light.*

From the resurrection of Christ.

Surely this of itself is enough to constrain every man who has a spark of the love of God in his soul to consecrate the day wholly to the Lord. For four thousand years previous to this event Death had been victorious. Seventy-three generations of the human race were then confined in the charnel-house of this relentless monster. The long-expected Deliverer appeared at length in the Land of Promise. He healed the sick, cleansed the lepers, cast out demons, and for a short time rescued even Lazarus and a few others from their chains and dungeons. But Death became alarmed, and all the hosts of Satan were summoned to the conflict. Finally, after a protracted struggle, the Prince of Life, the only hope of a fallen world, immersed in sufferings, bathed in blood, and pierced with agonies before unknown, bowed his head and expired on the Cross! Hope died, and all the expectations of the righteous perished!

But on the morning of the first day, what a contrast!

> "A silent prisoner in the tomb
> Our great Redeemer lay,
> Till the revolving skies had brought
> The third, the appointed day.
> Hell and the grave unite their force
> To hold our Lord in vain;
> The sleeping Conqueror arose
> And burst their mighty chains."

Need I say that on this event are suspended all our hopes of happiness for time and for eternity? "If Christ is not risen, then is our preaching vain and your faith is also vain." "But now is Christ risen from the dead and become the first-fruits of them that slept. For as in Adam all die, even so in Christ shall all be made alive." Redemption has been purchased, the grave has been opened, and life and immortality have been brought to light by the great Captain of our salvation. And hence the most feeble soldier of the Cross can now sing the victor's song, "O death, where is thy sting? O grave, where is thy victory?"

Regarding, then, the First Day of the week merely as commemorative, and having no other object than simply to celebrate the triumphs of the Prince of Life, and our victories through him, does any one calling himself a *Christian* still ask for authority to sanctify it and to consecrate it wholly to the Lord? Tell it not in Mecca, lest the worshipers of the false Prophet rejoice. Publish it not to the world, lest those who celebrate the birthday of a Paine, a Hume, and a Voltaire triumph. Tell it not to the American patriot, whose heart with each and every rising sun of the Fourth of July is carried back to the scenes of "seventy-six," lest he reproach you with falsehood.

From the example of Christ.

II. *On this day it seems that Christ was wont to meet with his disciples, between the time of his resurrection and ascension.* At least we have evidence of his meeting with them on two successive First Days, under circumstances which seem to indicate that he intended, by his example, to honor and sanctify the day. "Then the same day at evening, *being the first day* of the week, when the doors were shut where the disciples were assembled for fear of the Jews, came Jesus and stood in the midst, and said unto them, Peace be unto you. . . . And after *eight days* again, his disciples were within and Thomas with them. Then came Jesus, the doors being shut, and stood in the midst, and said, Peace be unto you," etc. John xx, 19–29. The attentive reader of this passage will at least pause and inquire, Why were the disciples assembled together *on the first day of the week?* Why did Jesus, *on that day*, appear in their midst and bless them? Why were the same things repeated on the eighth day following, or *the first day of the next week?* To these questions enlightened reason gives but one answer: as God gave the world an example by resting on the seventh day, so Christ has here left us *an example* by meeting with his disciples and blessing them on the day of his resurrection.

From the descent and gift of the Holy Spirit.

III. *On this day the Spirit came, and the Apostles were miraculously qualified for the work of their mission.* We learn from Acts ii, 1–4, that the descent of the Holy Spirit was on the day of Pentecost, and from Leviticus xxiii, 9–21, that Pentecost always came on the first day of the week.

From the beginning of Christ's reign and the commencement of the Church.

IV. *On this day the Christian Church began, and believers were for the first time baptized by the authority of Jesus Christ, into the name of the Father, and of the Son, and of the Holy Spirit.* See Acts xi, 15. This event is second in importance only to the resurrection of Christ and the gift of the Holy Spirit. Surely, then, a positive command to sanctify such a day as this would be wholly superfluous.

From the custom of the primitive Church.

V. *On this day the primitive Christians were wont to meet together for the purpose of attending to the Lord's Supper and engaging in other acts of social worship.* This is evident,

1. From Luke's testimony concerning the Church of Troas. Acts xx, 6, 7: "And we sailed away from Philippi after the days of Unleavened Bread, and came unto them (Sopater, Aristarchus, etc.) to Troas in five days, where we abode seven days. And on the First Day of the week, when the disciples came together to break bread, Paul preached to them, ready to depart on the morrow, and continued his speech till midnight." This was not an extraordinary or called meeting. Had such a meeting been in harmony with Paul's object in meeting with the Church of Troas, he would certainly not have remained there six days without calling the disciples together: for he *hasted*, if it were possible for him to be at Jerusalem the day of Pentecost. It is, therefore, evident from the whole narrative that the brethren of Troas came together, according to their usual custom, on the First Day of the week, to celebrate both the death and the resurrection of Christ.

From Paul's directions given to the Churches of Galatia and Corinth. 1 Cor. xvi, 1, 2: "Now concerning the collection which is for the saints, as I ordered the

Churches of Galatia, so also do you. *On the first day of every week* (κατὰ μίαν σαββάτων) let each of you lay somewhat by itself, according as he may have prospered, putting it into the Treasury; that there may be no collections when I come." It is evident, from all the facts and circumstances of this case, that the first day of the week was designated as the proper time for making these collections simply because that on this day the disciples of the aforesaid Churches were wont to meet together for public and social worship.

3. From the testimony of the Christian Fathers and other ecclesiastical writers. In a letter written about A. D. 72, by Barnabas, the companion of Paul, it is said, "The *eighth day* is the beginning of another world; and herefore with joy we celebrate the *eighth day*, on which Jesus rose from the dead." About eighty years later, A. D. 150, Justin Martyr, in his Apology to the emperor Antoninus Pius, says, "On the Lord's Day *all Christians* in the city or country meet together, because that is the day of our Lord's resurrection; and then we read the Apostles and Prophets. This being done, the President makes an oration to the assembly to exhort them to imitate and to practice the things which they have heard, and then we all join in prayer, and after that we celebrate the Lord's Supper; then they who are able and willing give what they think proper, and what is collected is laid up in the hands of the President, who distributes it to the orphans, and widows, and other necessitous Christians as their wants require." See *Mosheim's Eccl. Hist.*, Vol. I, p. 135, note 10. Still thirty years later, about A. D. 180, Irenæus says, "On the Lord's Day *every one of us Christians* keeps the Sabbath." And still later Eusebius, the father of ecclesiastical history, testifies as follows: "From

the beginning the Christians assembled on the first day of the week, called by them *the Lord's Day*, to read the Scriptures, to preach, and to celebrate the Lord's Supper."

To these statements might be added the testimony of Pliny, Ignatius, Clement of Alexandria, Tertullian, Origen, Athanasius, and Jerome, as well as that of Dr. Mosheim and other ecclesiastical historians. But this is not necessary. The facts already given concerning the Churches of Troas, Galatia, and Corinth are, of themselves, sufficient for our present purpose. They prove, beyond all reasonable doubt, that the first day of the week was, from the beginning, sanctified to the Lord by the Apostles and all other primitive Christians.

From the proper name given to the day by Divine authority.

VI. *The proper and specific name given to this day by the Holy Spirit shows, beyond all reasonable doubt, that it is the duty of every Christian to consecrate it wholly to the service of the Lord.* See Rev. i, 10. If, then, the first day of the week is the *Lord's* Day, it is not, of course, *our* day, and much less is it the *Devil's* day. A thousand precepts like the fourth commandment could not more clearly and specifically express God's *reserved right* to this portion of time than the name by which he has here seen fit to designate it. What belongs to *A* does not belong to *B*. And what belongs to God does not belong to man, any further than God, as the great Proprietor of all things, has delegated to him the right to use it. This right he has bestowed very liberally. The cattle on a thousand hills, all the fowls of the mountains, the fishes of the sea, and the entire vegetable and mineral kingdoms he has given to man in fee simple. Six days, also, out of every seven have been granted to mankind for secular pursuits, so far as may not be inconsistent with the glory of God and their own chief good. But one day in seven has been as certainly sanctified to the Lord as the *Lord's Supper* has been sanctified. If, then, some of the Corinthians were punished for appropriating some of this sacred feast to their own sensual gratification, is that man any less guilty before God who appropriates any portion of the Lord's Day to his own selfish or secular purposes?

From the ancient Prophets.

VII. *Some of the prophetic utterances of the Old Testament prove, also, very clearly that it was always God's purpose that a day of sanctified rest should be consecrated to his glory and to the good of his people, under the New Covenant as well as under the Old.* For the present I will cite but one example as an illustration. In Ezekiel xlvi, 1, the Prophet says: "Thus saith the Lord God: the gate of the inner court that looketh toward the East shall be shut during the six working days; but on the *Sabbath* it shall be opened." What is the meaning of this? What does this *Sabbath* signify? It is very evident that this prophecy relates to the future. There has not yet been a shaking in the valley of dry bones; the twelve tribes of Israel have not yet been restored to their own land; the stick of Judah and the stick of Ephraim have not yet become one; God has not yet led his unnumbered hosts against the mountains of Israel; the great battle of Armageddon has not yet been fought in the valley of Hamon Gog; the spirit of grace and of supplications has not yet been poured out on the house of David and on the inhabitants of Jerusalem; they have not yet looked upon Him whom they pierced; the symbolical Temple has not yet been reared, nor have the holy waters yet issued from its threshold for the sanctification and salvation of the world.

The last nine chapters of Ezekiel are not, therefore, a literal description of the rites and ceremonies of the Old Institution. The old partition wall has been demolished, and will never again be erected by Divine authority. The Gospel has placed the whole world, both Jews and Gentiles, on a common platform. "In Christ Jesus, neither circumcision avails any thing, nor uncircumcision."

"Now smoking sweets and bleeding lambs,
And kids and bullocks slain—
Incense and spice of costly names
Would all be burned in vain."

But the name of the type is often *metaphorically* transferred to the antitype. This is very common, especially in the writings of the Prophets. And hence it is evident that the last nine chapters of Ezekiel are but a symbolical representation of the organization, works, services, and missionary labors of the Israelites converted to Christianity, when the vail shall have been taken away from their hearts and they shall have seen the end of that Old Institution which was abolished in Christ more than eighteen hundred years ago. And hence the Temple is not a building of stone and cedar, of gold and silver; it is the Temple of the Living God, of which the tabernacle of Moses and the temple of Solomon were but mere shadows. Hence the waters which issued from under its threshold are not the overflowings of Siloam, Bethesda, or any other natural or artificial fountain, either within or without the walls of Jerusalem: they are the *living* waters of Calvary; they are the stream which flowed from the side of our Redeemer; they are the same in kind which issued from the Holy City eighteen hundred years ago for the healing of the nations, and which will again burst forth with all their healing efficacy when the scattered tribes of Israel shall have been converted and builded into a holy Temple in the Lord, on the foundation of the Apostle and Prophets, JESUS CHRIST himself being the chief corner-stone. And hence it follows that the *Sabbath* here spoken of is not the seventh day of the week; it is not the Patriarchal and Jewish Sabbath, for that will never be again restored by Divine authority; but it is the *Lord's Day*, the birthday of the new creation.* There remains, therefore, a rest, an earthly Sabbath for the converted Jew, and of course also for the converted Gentile, "where there is neither Greek nor Jew, Barbarian, Scythian, bond nor free; but Christ is all, and in all."

Summary of the evidence.

Our obligation, then, to sanctify the Lord's Day is enforced by the analogy of the primitive Sabbath; by the laws and wants of our own physical, intellectual, and moral nature; by the highest moral, social, and religious interests of society; by our natural desire to commemorate the great and leading events of history; by the resurrection and triumphs of the great Hero of man's redemption; by the example of Christ, of

Sanctification, also, of the seventh day by Jewish converts.

* It is true that previous to the destruction of Jerusalem the Jewish Christians observed both the first and the seventh days of the week. Schaff's Hist. of the Christ. Church, Vol. I, p. 129; and Mosheim's Eccl. Hist., Vol. I, p. 85. And hence, says Dr. Mosheim, on the same page, note (3,) "Some learned men labor to persuade us that in *all* the *early* churches *both* days, or the *first* and *last* days of the week, were held sacred. But the Churches of Bithynia, mentioned by Pliny, devoted but *one stated day* to their public worship; and beyond all controversy, that was what we call the *Lord's Day*, or the *first day* of the week." To this day, therefore, as the only day of the week that was ever set apart and sanctified to the Lord by *apostolic authority*, the Prophet Ezekiel here evidently refers. It is here, and also in Isaiah lxvi, 23, *metaphorically* called a *Sabbath*; just as Christ is called a *shepherd*, a *door*, a *lion*, a *lamb*, etc.; but its *proper name*, as given in the New Testament, is the *Lord's Day*.

Proper and metaphorical names of the first day.

his Apostles, and of all the primitive Churches; by God's reserved right to a portion of our time; and also by the consideration that when the Jews shall have been converted to Christ, and organized into one body, according to the pattern of Moses and the precepts of the Apostles, they will still have a Sabbath—a holy day for holy purposes.

Conclusions.

From these premises, then, we infer that every thing is sinful on the Lord's Day which in any way interferes with its own hallowed associations; with the proper discipline of our own hearts, and with the proper education of our own families; and, consequently, that much of the traveling, visiting, reading, conversation, and other exercises of this day, are an abomination in the sight of God, and utterly inconsistent with our Christian profession.

And, finally, it is evident from what is now before us, that the proper sanctification of the Lord's Day by all Christians would very greatly serve to promote their own enjoyment and to enlarge the sphere of their usefulness: that it would, moreover, be a powerful check on many of the social and national evils that now curse the world; and that it would, also, be one of the most efficient means of bringing about that most glorious era in the world's history, when "The wolf shall lie down with the lamb, and the leopard shall lie down with the kid; and the calf, and the young lion, and the fatling together; and a little child shall lead them. And the cow and the bear shall feed; their young ones shall lie down together; and the lion shall eat straw like the ox; and the sucking child shall play on the hole of the asp, and the weaned child shall put his hand on the cockatrice's den. They shall not hurt nor destroy in all my holy mountain says Jehovah; FOR THE EARTH SHALL BE FULL OF THE KNOWLEDGE OF THE LORD AS THE WATERS COVER THE SEA."

CHAPTER VII.

THE LORD'S SUPPER.

Material media necessary to our conception and appreciation of the *abstract* and the *spiritual*.

How very difficult it is for us, living as we do in houses of clay, whose foundation is in the dust, to rise to a just conception and appreciation of that which is purely spiritual! We now see, and hear, and taste, and feel, and smell through material organs. But we have not, strictly speaking, even one spiritual sense. That is, we have no sense by means of which our spirits can immediately and directly hold communion with other spirits.

This may be wholly owing to our present organization. Holy angels may feel no such restraints. They may need no material media as means of intercourse and enjoyment. And this, too, may be our condition when we shall see as we are seen, and when we shall know even as also we are known.

Illustrations.

But in our present state the picture must be presented to the eye, and the sound must be addressed to the ear. The mathematician must use his diagrams, the historian his charts, and the chemist his varied apparatus in order to illustrate properly and efficiently even the abstract and recondite principles of science.

And hence it is that God has from the beginning taught man by signs and symbols. Even in Eden the

Sabbath was instituted to remind man that this world is not eternal, that it is not the result of chance, and that it is not the work of any subordinate and inferior Demiurge, but that "in six days the Lord made heaven and earth, the sea, and all that in them is, and rested the seventh day."

On the same principle, and for a similar purpose, the institution of sacrifice was established immediately after the fall of man. And for the space of four thousand years the blood of innocent victims proclaimed to the world in the most impressive manner the holiness of God, the justice of God, the claims of his government on man, and the mysterious doctrine of expiation and reconciliation through the death and sin-offering of the great Antitype.

In the mean time Moses was directed to construct a system of symbolic worship. He made the Tabernacle and all its furniture, the Table of the shew-bread, the Candlestick, the Altar of incense, the Vail, the Ark of the covenant, and the Cherubim of glory for the purpose of instructing the Israelites, and through them the whole world in the sublime mysteries of redemption. Other inspired teachers of the Old Testament followed his example. Isaiah, Jeremiah, Ezekiel, Daniel, and the twelve Minor Prophets all taught the people through signs and symbols.

God's mode of instruction somewhat modified under the reign of Christ.

The beginning of the reign of Heaven was a new era in God's method of instruction. Great progress had been made under the Law in the development of truth. A religious vocabulary had been formed. And hence, when the great mystery was fully revealed, as it was for the first time on the day of Pentecost, A D. 34, the law of the New Institution was written, not on tables of stone, but on the fleshly tables of the heart. 2 Cor. iii, 3 The people were then much better prepared to understand the true nature and object of the Messiah's reign, and to comprehend more clearly and more fully the verbal teachings of the Holy Spirit.

But even then the symbolic method of instruction was not wholly abandoned. Our great Redeemer and Educator did not forget that we are still in the flesh, that we have bodies as well as spirits, and that while the world stands the former must ever be the medium of access to the latter. And hence, on "*the same night on which he was betrayed, he took bread; and when he had given thanks he brake it and said,* (to his disciples,) *Take, eat; this is my body which is broken for you: this do in remembrance of me. After the same manner also he took the cup, when he had supped, saying, This cup is the New Testament in my blood: this do ye, as oft as ye drink it, in remembrance of me. For as often as ye eat this bread and drink this cup, ye do show the Lord's death till he come.*" 1 Cor. xi, 23–26.

The primary object and design of the Lord's Supper.

In these words of our blessed and adorable Redeemer, he very clearly and impressively sets forth the object and design of this Institution. He teaches us very plainly that its primary object is commemorative, that it is designed to keep ever fresh in our memories the first great fact of the Gospel "*that Jesus Christ died for our sins according to the Scriptures.*" 1 Cor. xv, 3.

But to say that it is merely commemorative is not enough. It implies more than the mere recollection of a fact. *It is intended also to be the medium of furnishing and imparting spiritual*

Its secondary object and design.

nourishment to the hungry and thirsty soul. We are required *to eat* the bread and *to drink* the wine. But why is this, and for what purpose? Not because they are converted into the body, blood, soul and divinity of the Son of God. Nay, verily. They are still the meat that perishes. But there is here presented a beautiful analogy between the wants of the body and the wants of the soul. To supply the wants of the former it is not enough to remember that in our Father's house there is bread enough and to spare. It is not enough that we even look upon the rich provisions which have been bountifully supplied. We must also partake of them, we must masticate and digest them, we must eat and appropriate them to the nourishment and support of our frail bodies, or very soon our physical existence will terminate.

Illustration drawn from our physical wants.

And just so it is with our souls. They need their regular supplies of food as well as our bodies. And this food must be spiritually eaten, spiritually digested, and spiritually appropriated, or otherwise our souls will soon languish, and like our bodies perish forever.

This fact is very beautifully illustrated in the discourse of our Savior to the Jews recorded in the sixth chapter of the testimony of John. "*Verily, verily,*" said he, "*ye seek me, not because ye saw the miracles, but because ye did eat of the loaves and were filled. Labor not for the meat which perishes, but for that meat which endureth unto everlasting life, which the Son of Man will give unto you: for him hath God the Father sealed.* . . . I AM THE BREAD OF LIFE. *Your fathers did eat manna in the wilderness and are dead. This is the bread which cometh down from heaven: if any man eat of this bread he shall live forever;*

Illustration from the teachings of Christ.

and the bread which I will give is my flesh, which I will give for the life of the world.

"The Jews then strove among themselves, saying, How can this man give us his flesh to eat? Then Jesus said unto them, *Verily, verily, I say to you, except ye eat the flesh of the Son of Man and drink his blood, ye have no life in you. Whoso eateth my flesh and drinketh my blood hath eternal life, and I will raise him up at the last day. For my flesh is meat indeed, and my blood is drink indeed. He that eateth my flesh and drinketh my blood, dwelleth in me, and I in him. As the living Father hath sent me, and I live by the Father, so he that eateth me, even he shall live by me. This is that bread which came down from heaven: not as your fathers did eat manna and are dead; he that eateth of this bread shall live forever.*"

It is true that this very profound and impressive discourse has no direct reference to the Lord's Supper. The lesson which Christ here teaches us was suggested by the occasion. He had on the day previous fed four thousand persons on five barley loaves and two small fishes. And when the multitude followed him to Capernaum, eagerly seeking after the meat which perishes, he reminded them that other food was necessary, that neither the manna which God had rained down from heaven upon their fathers in the desert nor the food which he had miraculously supplied on the day previous, near the village of Bethsaida, could give to any one eternal life, and that if they would live forever they must all eat his flesh and drink his blood.

What is then required of all who partake of the Lord's Supper.

This may, no doubt, be done in various ways. Every ordinance of God is a medium of nourishment to the hungry soul. But no other institution is so well and so directly adapted to this end as the Lord's Supper. And hence it is that in it and through it we are commanded to eat of our Lord's broken body and to drink of his shed blood. For "the same night in which he was betrayed, he took bread: and when he had given thanks, he brake it, and said, Take, eat." Eat what? The bread merely? Nay, verily, for he immediately adds, "*This is my body.*"

We must then eat simultaneously of the commemorative loaf and of the bread of life; and while we literally drink of the symbolic cup, we must also at the same time drink spiritually of that blood which alone can supply the wants of the thirsty soul. Unless we do this the bread which we eat can in no sense be to us the body of the Son of God, nor can the wine which we drink be in any sense the blood of the New Covenant, which was shed for the remission of the sins of many.

Our proneness to formalism.

But to do this properly requires much preparation and discipline of both head and heart. How prone, alas! we all are to trust in forms and shadows, in the mere rites and ceremonies of religion, as if they were the end and object of all that God has ever revealed to man!

Illustrations from the history of the Israelites.

This was the common and ever-besetting sin of the ancient Israelites. It was manifest among them even in the days of Moses. It was seen at the altar, at the laver, and at the table. But it became worse and worse, more and more prevalent among all classes of the people, till finally the services of the Sanctuary were transformed into a system of cold, lifeless, and spiritless formality, and God expressed his abhorrence of even their most solemn acts of pretended devotion. "To what purpose," said he, "is the multitude of your sacrifices unto me? I am full of the burnt-offerings of rams, and the fat of fed beasts; and I delight not in the blood of bullocks, or of lambs, or of he-goats. When ye come to appear before me, who hath required this at your hand, to tread my courts? Bring no more vain oblations: incense is an abomination to me; the new-moons and Sabbaths, the calling of assemblies, I can not endure; it is iniquity, even the solemn meeting. Your new-moons and your appointed feasts my soul hateth; they are a trouble to me; I am weary to bear them." Isa. i, 11–14.

Similar admonitions and reproofs were often given and repeated by all the Prophets. But it seems that nothing could stay or stop the onward tide of formalism among the Jews. Even while listening to the earnest and heart-searching appeals of Him who spoke as never man spoke, they were much more attentive to the mint, and the anise, and the cumin than they were to the weightier matters of the Law, such as judgment, mercy, and fidelity.

Illustrations drawn from the history of the Christian Church.

Under the administration of Christ and the mission of the Holy Spirit, a great reformation might in this respect be reasonably anticipated. Christianity is a spiritual system. It has comparatively but little to do with the flesh. But it abounds in whatever serves to enlighten, purify, and sanctify the soul. It may, indeed, in one respect, be regarded as a sublime development of the oracle that "*God is spirit; and they who worship him, must worship him in spirit and in truth.*" John iv, 24. This was certainly a fundamental theme with all the New Testament writers. Paul never seems to forget it, nor to grow weary in warning the Churches against the sin of formalism. "He is not a Jew," says he, "who is one outwardly;

neither is that circumcision which is outward in the flesh. But he is a Jew who is one inwardly; and circumcision is that of the heart, in the spirit and not in the letter: whose praise is not of men, but of God." Rom. ii, 28, 29. And again he adds, "We are the circumcision who worship God in spirit, and rejoice in Christ Jesus, and have no confidence in the flesh." Phil. iii, 3.

But all the solemn instructions, warnings, and admonitions could not and did not save even the primitive Church from the sin of formalism. The Jew had long been educated in this vice, and so also had the Gentile. They had formed *habits* of formality and carnality; and habits once thoroughly formed become a second nature. They are commonly as enduring as life itself; they are as tenacious as the vital current. And hence says Jehovah by the mouth of Jeremiah, "*When the Ethiopian can change his skin, and the leopard his spots, then may ye also do good who are accustomed to do evil.*" Jer. xiii, 23.

True, indeed, the transforming power of the Gospel is almost omnipotent. In myriads of myriads of cases it has changed the vulture to the dove, the lion to the lamb. And hence, for a time, the primitive converts to Christianity seemed to forget every thing else, and to enjoy the truths and rich blessings of the Gospel in all their native fullness and simplicity. But soon the old leaven began to work. Both Jewish and Gentile formalism was revived in the Churches; and the plain and simple ordinances of the Gospel were perverted from their original design, just as had formerly been the ordinances and institutions of Moses.

This perversion of the Christian ordinances was first seen in the abuse of the Lord's Supper. The true spiritual import of Baptism and the Lord's Day seems to have been maintained in the primitive Churches for some time after the death of the Apostles. But in less than a quarter of a century after the death and coronation of the Messiah, Paul was constrained to say to the Corinthian brethren: "*When ye come together into one place, this is not to eat the Lord's Supper; for in eating every one taketh before another his own Supper; and one is hungry and another is drunken!*" 1 Cor. xi, 20, 21.

It is, indeed, evidently implied here that one of the objects for which the Corinthians professed to come together was to eat the Lord's Supper. But, nevertheless, they had so far perverted the original design of the institution that their manner of eating it was virtually not to eat it at all. They had converted it into a sort of idolatrous festival. After the example of the heathen at their appointed festivities, each one seems to have contributed to the common stock of provisions whatever he could afford, or whatever he thought necessary. But in eating the rich members of the congregation eagerly and greedily seized on that portion of the bread and wine which they themselves had provided. They ate and drank to satiety; while others were left destitute and put to shame on account of their poverty!

This was formalism in one of its rudest and most barbarous manifestations. It was monstrous to the eye of enlightened reason, and shocking to every sanctified susceptibility of the human heart. But it was not more so than was the practice of many nominal Christian Churches during the dark ages. And even in the middle of the nineteenth century the very same sensual spirit is often manifested in the more polite, but no less vain and empty ceremonies of many who profess to take the Bible as the rule of their faith and practice. *How many still profess to celebrate the Lord's death who never taste of any thing more than the mere symbols; who never eat the flesh nor drink the blood of the Son of God;* and to whom it might be said with just as much propriety as it was ever said to the Corinthian brethren, "*When ye come together into one place, this is not to eat the Lord's Supper?*"

I need not here enter into particulars. I need not go to Rome nor to Oxford for illustrations. A general reference to the past, and a special appeal to the personal experience of every child of God, is enough to convince all who are really such that formalism is one of the besetting sins of our entire race; that it grows out of the preternatural state of the human heart; and that every man, while in the flesh, is more or less liable to be overcome by its seductive influence.

The divinely prescribed antidote and preventive of formalism in the Lord's Supper.

What, then, is the remedy for this evil of universal tendency? If in the Gospel God has given to us all things pertaining to life and godliness, what provision has he made against the prevalence of formalism in the communion of the saints?

The answer to this question is given very clearly and specifically in Paul's admonition to the Corinthian converts. "LET A MAN," says he, "EXAMINE HIMSELF; AND SO LET HIM EAT OF THAT BREAD AND DRINK OF THAT CUP."

The means, then, ordained by God to prevent the growth and prevalence of formalism in the celebration of the Lord's Supper, is the practice of *self-examination.* "Let a man examine himself; and so let him eat of that bread and drink of that cup." If this were properly attended to by all who profess to be the followers of the

Lord Jesus, and no others are of course expected to sit down at his table, what an interesting occasion every Communion season would be! The Lord's Supper would then be to every communicant,

> "A feast of delicacies; a feast of old wines:
> Of delicacies exquisitely rich; of old wines perfectly refined."
>
> *Isaiah* xxiii, 6.

But how few, alas! how very few, have ever learned the art and mystery of self-examination! To see ourselves just as God sees us; to explore the deepest, darkest, and vilest recesses of our own hearts, with an honest purpose, through Divine grace, to forsake every false and wicked way; to cut off every right hand and to pluck out every right eye that causes us to offend; and to remove every obstacle, however near and however dear it may be, which intervenes between us and our blessed Redeemer, so that we may at once, with an humble boldness, approach him in the Institution designed to commemorate his own death, and partake of that flesh which is meat indeed, and of that blood which is drink indeed—this it is to be feared is an attainment which is but seldom made in the Christian profession. To succeed in this it is necessary,

Means and mode of self-examination.

I. *That the examination shall be conducted faithfully and honestly in the light of God's word.* In no other way can we comprehend how far we come short of the true standard of Christian excellence. If the carpenter must have his rule, and the surveyor his chain and compass, how much more necessary is it that the Christian should have that Word which is quick and powerful, and sharper than any two-edged sword, piercing even to the dividing asunder of the soul and spirit, and of the joints and marrow: and which is a discerner of the thoughts and intents of the heart," if he would examine himself as he will be examined, when the secrets of all hearts shall be revealed, and every man shall be judged according to the deeds done in his own body, whether they be good or whether they be evil. Job seemed to think that he was very righteous while he was conversing with his three friends. He attempted to justify himself from and against all their accusations. But when God spoke to him he was silent. When the heart-searching words of the Almighty penetrated the depths of his soul he abhorred himself, and repented in dust and in ashes. Job. xlii, 1–6. Peter, too, was very bold in his own defense, even in the palace of the High Priest. But when the Lord looked on him, and he remembered the words of Jesus, he went out and wept bitterly. Luke xxii, 61, 62. And just so it would now be with myriads who carelessly approach the Lord's Table and eat and drink their own condemnation, not discerning the Lord's body, if they would only lay aside the false *standards* of their own creation, and honestly try themselves by those words by which they shall be judged at the last day. But it is still true that many perish through lack of knowledge.

II. *It is also essential that self-examination should be conducted with prayer: prayer that God would himself search our hearts, and that he would help us to search them honestly, faithfully, and thoroughly; that he would purify them, and that he would enable us to forsake every false and wicked way.* "Search me, O God, and know my heart; try me, and know my thoughts; and see if there be any wicked way in me, and lead me in the way everlasting," was the prayer of the sweet Psalmist of Israel. Psalm cxxxix, 23, 24. And this, too, should also be the earnest prayer of every Christian before he presumes to approach the Table of the Lord for the purpose of partaking of the memorials of his broken body and his shed blood.

III. *Fasting, too, and even becoming apparel, is another very important aid in the work of self-examination.* While the body is covered with jewels it is very difficult to clothe the soul with humility; and while our appetite is more than satisfied with the luxuries and pleasures of this life, it is almost impossible for the spirit to hunger and thirst after righteousness. Under such circumstances we are greatly prone to imagine that we are rich and increased with goods, and that we have need of nothing, not knowing that at the same time we may be wretched, and miserable, and poor, and blind, and naked. O yes, there is a state of body, as well as a state of mind, that fits the soul for the work of self-examination, that helps to prepare the heart for the communion of the saints, and that serves to make the Lord's Supper, to every communicant, a foretaste of the marriage supper of the Lamb.

IV. *Another indispensable means of self-examination, in order to a profitable participation of the Lord's Supper, is the proper sanctification of the Lord's Day.* The work of self-examination is, indeed, a matter of constant obligation. It should never be wholly omitted, not even for a single day. But while the mind is busily occupied, as it usually is during the other six days of the week, with the ordinary cares and secular avocations of life, it is very difficult to examine the heart, to try the reins, and to weigh the motives with that extreme care and accuracy which the case requires. And hence God has most wisely and benevolently connected the commemoration of our Savior's death with the commemoration of his resurrection.* He has so arranged the ordinances commemorative of these two events that due attention to the one serves also to qualify and prepare us for the other. While with joy and wonder we behold the opening sepulcher, we are naturally led to the Cross. We are reminded that our blessed and adorable Redeemer hung upon it, that he was wounded for our transgressions, and that he was bruised for our iniquities. We are instructed in the awful nature and malignity of sin, and the necessity of holiness. And thus we are led almost unconsciously to the work of self-examination, and to that

*That the primitive Christians were wont to celebrate the Lord's Supper on every first day of the week is evident,

Evidence that the primitive Christians celebrated the Lord's Supper on every first day of the week.

I. *From what is recorded in Acts xx, 7, concerning the Church of Troas.* All the facts and circumstances of the case go to prove that this meeting of the disciples at Troas was a *stated* meeting, and for a *stated* purpose.

II. *From what is recorded of the Church of Corinth.* From 1 Cor. xi, 20, it is evident that when the disciples of Corinth came together at all their *stated* meetings one of the professed objects for which they met was to eat the Lord's Supper. And from 1 Cor. xvi, 2, we learn that they were in the habit of meeting on every Lord's Day. Thus the passage is correctly rendered by Dr. Macknight: "On the first day of every week (κατὰ μίαν σαββάτων) let each of you lay somewhat by itself, according as he may have prospered, putting it into the treasury, that when I come there may then be no collections."

III. *From the testimony of the Christian Fathers and other ecclesiastical writers.* Dr. Neander says: "As we have already remarked, the celebration of the Lord's Supper was still held to constitute an essential part of Divine worship on every Sunday, as appears from Justin Martyr, (A. D. 150,) and the whole Church partook of the communion after they had joined in *the Amen* of the preceding prayer. The Deacons carried the bread and wine to every one present in order. It was held to be necessary that all the Christians in the place should, by participating in this communion, maintain their union with the Lord and with his Church; and hence the Deacons carried a portion of the consecrated bread and wine to strangers, to the sick, to prisoners, and to all who were prevented from being present at the assembly." *Hist. of the Christ. Religion and Church,* Vol. I, p. 332.

During the first two centuries the practice of weekly communion was universal, and it was continued in the Greek Church till the seventh century. Such as neglected it three weeks in succession were excommunicated.

preparation of heart which makes the Lord's Supper a feast to the soul.

But how can that young sister expect to find any enjoyment at the Lord's Table who has spent the morning of the Lord's Day in the vanities of the toilet! How can that young brother expect to see in Jesus the "One altogether lovely and the chief among ten thousand," who has just laid aside the fashionable novel or the political newspaper to hasten to the Lord's Table! If men and women will first desecrate the Lord's Day, no wonder if they also profane the Lord's Supper. If they find no pleasure in going with Mary to the tomb of Joseph, it is no marvel that the Cross should appear to them as a root out of dry ground. The disciple who will rob God of his own hallowed time in the morning is not to be trusted with the rich viands of his Table in the evening.

Adaptation of the Lord's Supper to the wants of man.

But to the humble and faithful disciple who has properly examined himself, and who, through the emblematic bread and wine, really discerns and partakes of the Lord's broken body and shed blood, how exceedingly rich, and suggestive, and sanctifying in its tendencies is this most gracious ordinance! With what intense interest his soul lingers on the brow of Calvary! But he does not stop there. As he looks upon the Cross, the nails, the spear, the blood, the convulsions of nature, and the Divine majesty, meekness, loveliness, and benevolence of our adorable Redeemer he is almost compelled to think of the uncreated glories of the Divine Logos, and of his infinite condescension in taking upon himself, not the nature of angels, but the nature of the seed of Abraham, in order "that through his death he might destroy him who has the power of death, and deliver them who, through fear of death, were all th lifetime subject to bondage." And, led on by these associations, he is almost unconsciously carried forward to contemplate the future. He thinks of the second advent of Christ, of the resurrection of the saints, of the day of judgment, and of the honors and glories of God's everlasting Kingdom. And, while each new suggestion furnishes fresh aliment for his hungry soul, it at the same time serves to sanctify and purify his heart. What mind thus exercised can ever foster feelings of pride, vanity, envy, lust, or revenge! Who that really believes and feels all this can ever refuse to forgive from the heart every brother his trespasses?

God forbid, then, that we should ever glory save in the Cross of our Lord Jesus Christ; and may Heaven grant that through it the world may ever be crucified unto us and we unto the world!

PART III.

MEMBERS OF THE CHURCH.

A STRICTLY logical and chronological development of all the elements of the Church would require us to consider,

Logical outline of the development and history of the Church.

I. The Officers extraordinary by whom the Church was founded.

II. Their *preaching*, or the way in which they made disciples and the conditions on which they received them into the Church.

III. Their *teaching*, or the conditions on which the initiated were retained in the Church and finally received into God's Everlasting Kingdom.

IV. The ordinary and permanent Ministry of the Church.

V. The various relations and coöperative functions of the several Churches.

VI. The sufferings, triumphs, and destiny of the Church.

But for the sake of brevity and convenience I have thought it best to consider all the various classes of Officers, Ordinary and Extraordinary, under one general head, and the principal Ordinances of the Church under another. And hence the next thing in order, according to this arrangement, is to consider what is said of the members of the Church. In speaking of these we will notice,

Advantages of the plan adopted.

Items to be considered under the head or division of Church Members.

I. The terms and conditions on which persons are to be received into the Church.

II. The duties of Christians, or the conditions of continued membership and of final admission into God's everlasting Kingdom.

III. The Creed of the Church, or the Authoritative Standard by which the conduct and standing of her members are to be tested.

IV. The perfect adaptation of this Standard to the wants, capacities, and circumstances of all.

CHAPTER I.

CONDITIONS OF MEMBERSHIP; OR, THE TERMS ON WHICH PERSONS ARE TO BE ADMITTED INTO THE CHURCH.

These may be all understood from the following and other parallel passages.

Passages of Scripture indicating the terms and conditions of Church membership.

1. Matth. xviii, 3: "Except ye *be converted* (στραφῆτε, 2 pers. plu., aor. 2, sub. pass.) and *become as little children*, ye shall not enter into the kingdom of heaven."

2. Matth. xxviii, 19: "Go ye therefore and *make disciples* (μαθητεύσατε) of all the nations, *baptizing them into the name of the Father, and of the Son, and of the Holy Spirit.*"

3. Mark xvi, 16: "He that *believeth* and *is baptized* shall be saved; but he that believeth not shall be damned."

4. Luke xiv, 26, 27: "If any man come to me, and *hate not his father, and mother, and wife, and children, and*

brethren, and sisters, yea, and his own life also, he can not be my disciple. And whosoever doth not ***bear his cross, and come after me***, can not be my disciple."

5. John iii, 3, 5: "Jesus answered and said unto him, Verily, verily, I say unto thee, ***Except a man be born again***, he can not see the kingdom of God . . . . Jesus answered, Verily, verily, I say unto thee, ***Except a man be born of water and of the Spirit***, he can not enter into the kingdom of God."

6. Acts ii, 38: "Then Peter said unto them, ***Repent*** and ***be baptized*** every one of you, in the name of Jesus Christ, for the remission of sins, and ye shall receive the gift of the Holy Spirit."

7. Acts iii, 19: "***Repent*** ye therefore, and ***turn*** (ἐπιστρέψατε, 2 pers. plu., aor. 1, imper. act.), that your sins may be blotted out, so that times of refreshing may come from the presence of the Lord."

8. Acts viii, 12: "But when they ***believed*** Philip, preaching the things concerning the kingdom of God and the name of Jesus Christ, they ***were baptized*** both men and women."

9. Acts xvi, 30, 31: "And he brought them out and said, Sirs, what must I do to be saved? And they said, *Believe on the Lord Jesus Christ*, and thou shalt be saved, and thy house."

10. Acts xviii, 8: "And many of the Corinthians ***hearing, believed, and were baptized***."

11. Acts xxii, 16: "And now why tarriest thou? Arise and ***be baptized***, and wash away thy sins, ***calling on his name***."

12. Rom. i, 16: "For I am not ashamed of the Gospel of Christ; for it is the power of God unto Salvation to every one that ***believeth***."

13. Rom. vi, 4: "Therefore we *are buried with him by baptism into death;*" that like as Christ was raised up from the dead by the glory of the Father, even so we also should walk in newness of life."

14. Rom. x, 10: "For with the heart, man *believeth* unto righteousness; and with the mouth, *confession is made unto salvation.*"

15. Rom. x, 13: "For whosoever *calleth on the name of the Lord*, shall be saved."

16. 1 Cor. xiii, 1–3: "Though I speak with the tongues of men and angels, and have not *love* (ἀγάπη), I am become as sounding brass or a tinkling cymbal. And though I have the gift of prophecy, and understand all mysteries and all knowledge; and though I have all faith, so that I could remove mountains, and have not *love*, I am nothing. And though I bestow all my goods to feed the poor, and though I give my body to be burned, and have not *love*, it profiteth me nothing."

17. Gal. iii, 27: "For as many of you as *have been baptized into Christ have put on Christ.*"

18. Eph. ii, 4–6: "But God who is rich in mercy, for his great love wherewith he loved us, even when we were dead in sins, *hath quickened* us together with Christ (συνεζωοποίησε τῷ χριστῷ),—by grace ye are saved,—and hath raised us up together, and made us sit together in heavenly places in Christ Jesus."

19. 1 Tim. vi, 12: "Fight the good fight of faith, lay hold on eternal life, to which thou wast called, and thou *didst confess the good confession* (ὡμολόγησας τὴν καλήν ὁμολογίαν) before many witnesses."

20. Titus iii, 5: "Not by works of righteousness which we have done, but according to his mercy he saved us *by*

the washing (διὰ λουτροῦ, *through the bath*) of regeneration and *renewing* of the Holy Spirit."

21. Heb. iv, 14: "Seeing then that we have a great High Priest, who has gone through the heavens (διεληλυθότα τοὺς οὐρανούς), Jesus the Son of God, let us hold fast *the confession* (τῆς ὁμολογίας)."

22. 1 Peter i, 23: "*Being born again*, not of corruptible seed, but of incorruptible, *by the word of God which liveth and abideth forever*."

From these and many other like passages, it is quite obvious that the law of initiation into the Church of Christ requires (1) That all who would become members of this Divine Institution must first be renewed or begotten by the Holy Spirit, through the word of truth (John iii, 5; 1 Peter i, 23: See also 1 Cor. iv, 15 and Jas. i, 18); (2) That they must believe on or into (εἰς) the name of the Lord Jesus Christ, as the way, the truth, the resurrection, and the life (Mark xvi, 16; Acts viii, 12; xvi, 31; xviii, 8); (3) That they must love Christ more than they love even their own lives and their most dear and cherished earthly relations (Luke xiv, 26, 27; 1 Cor. xiii, 1–3); (4) That they must repent of their sins (Acts ii, 38; iii, 19); (5) That they must turn from Satan to God, and become humble, meek, and docile as little children (Matth. xviii, 3; Acts iii, 19); (6) That they must call on the name of the Lord in humble and earnest prayer and supplication (Acts xxii, 16; Rom. x. 13); (7) That they must confess Christ as the Son of God and Savior of sinners (Rom. x, 10; 1 Tim. vi, 12; Heb. iv, 14); and (8) That they must be baptized by the authority of Christ into the name of the Father, and of the Son, and of the Holy Spirit; receiving at the same time, according to God's appointment, the forgiveness of

Conditions of Church membership.

all their past sins, and the gift of the Holy Spirit (Mark xvi, 16; Acts ii, 38; xxii, 16; Titus iii, 5).

It is not my aim in giving these several specifications to arrange them in their strictly logical or philosophical order; but merely to present them to the reader in such a way as will best serve to accomplish the practical purposes that I have in view. This will appear more obvious as we proceed with the discussion.

I.—Renewing of the Holy Spirit.

Difference between the Renewal of the Holy Spirit and Regeneration

This, in the modern theological nomenclature, commonly means the same thing as the word *regeneration*; but not so in the Holy Scriptures. In these inspired Oracles, the word *regeneration* (παλιγγενεσία, from παλιν *again* and γένεσις *generation*) is used in a much wider sense than *the renewal of the Holy Spirit*; and denotes properly the whole process of quickening, converting, and initiating persons into the kingdom of Christ. Thus in his conversation with Nicodemus, Christ makes regeneration or the new birth equivalent to both being begotten by the Spirit and being born of water. (Compare John iii, 3 with John iii, 5). And Paul says, "If any man be in Christ he is *a new creature*" (2 Cor. v, 17); but it is in the initiating ordinance of baptism that we put on Christ (Matth. xxviii, 19; Gal iii, 27). And so also the same Apostle calls baptism "*the bath* of regeneration" (Titus iii, 5), showing very plainly that baptism is included in the process of regeneration. But it is no part of the renewing or quickening process. The sinner is dead in trespasses and sins (Eph. ii, 1); and it is the work of the Holy Spirit to beget a new life in the soul. This it does by implanting in it, through human instrumentality, the good seed of the kingdom (Luke viii,

11), the word of God which is itself living and powerful (Psa. xix, 7; John vi, 63; Heb. iv, 12, 13). And hence Paul speaking as the agent of the Spirit says to the Corinthians, "Though ye have many instructors in Christ, yet have ye not many fathers; for in Christ Jesus, I *have begotten* (ἐγέννησα, aor. 1, indc. act. of γεννάω *to beget, to bring forth*) you *through the gospel*" (1 Cor. iv, 15). Hence also James says, "Of his (God's) own will *begat* (απεκύησεν, aor. 1, indc. act. of ἀποκυέω *to bring forth, to beget*) he us *with the word of truth*, that we should be a kind of first fruits of his creatures" (Jas. i, 18). And to the same effect is the testimony of Peter. In his first letter "to the strangers scattered throughout Pontus, Galatia, Cappadocia, Asia, and Bithynia," he says, "See that ye love one another with a pure heart fervently; *being born again* (αναγεγεννημένοι, part. per. pass. of αγεννάω), not of corruptible seed, but of incorruptible, by the word of God, which liveth and abideth forever" (1 Peter 1, 23). After the child of God has been thus begotten again by the Holy Spirit, by means of the word of truth, he is through a birth of water introduced into a new state of being; and henceforth he walks with Christ "in newness of life" (John iii, 5; Rom. vi, 4; Col. ii, 11–13). The renewal of the Holy Spirit is therefore an essential part of the process of regeneration; but it is not the whole of it. To complete the process, the child of God must be born of water, as well as be begotten by the Spirit. See John iii, 5 and Titus iii, 5.

How, or by what means, the Spirit renews the soul of man.

II.—Faith in Christ.

This is very intimately connected with the renewal of the Holy Spirit, as above described. Indeed it is the means by and through which the Spirit begets a new life in the soul. And, hence, in a strictly philosophical discussion, it might be best to speak of faith first; and afterward of the renewal of the Spirit: for certain it is that all spiritual life comes to us by faith, just as faith itself comes "by hearing, and hearing by the word of God" (Rom. x, 17). In this respect, God deals with us as free, rational, and accountable creatures. He first communicates to us, by his Spirit, the word of his grace, sustained by such evidence as is necessary to prove that it is a message from himself. The sinner hears the word, and weighs the accompanying evidence of its Divine origin and authenticity. He sees that the testimony is full and complete; and he becomes satisfied that the Gospel is a message from God to guilty men. Its moral power now penetrates his heart. He is convicted "of sin, and of righteousness, and of judgment;" and under the influence of this conviction, he begins to manifest the new life thus begotten in his soul, by crying out for mercy, and earnestly inquiring what he must do to be saved. No longer is he disposed to counsel with flesh and blood; but believing now in Jesus with all his heart, he repents of his sins, makes the good confession of his faith, puts on Christ in baptism, and rises with him "to walk in newness of life." He is now "a new creature." Old things are passed away, and all things are become new (2 Cor. v, 17.)

Origin of Faith, and its relations to the renewal of the Holy Spirit.

Proof of this, from the several cases of conversion recorded in the Acts of the Apostles.

So we are taught and so we learn from all that is recorded in the Holy Scriptures on the subject of conversion. When, for instance, Peter rose up with the eleven on the day of Pentecost, to open the Kingdom of heaven to such of his Hebrew brethren as would accept of salvation through Christ, after having briefly repelled the insinuation of certain scoffers, he proceeded to show

1. *That the miraculous events which then and there so much astonished the people, were but a fulfillment of the prophecy of Joel touching the reign of the Messiah.* "And it shall come to pass in the last days," said God by this ancient prophet, "I will pour out of my Spirit upon all flesh; and your sons and your daughters shall prophesy, and your young men shall see visions, and your old men shall dream dreams; and on my servants, and on my handmaidens I will pour out in those days of my Spirit, and they shall prophesy. And I will show wonders in heaven above, and signs in the earth beneath: blood, and fire, and vapor of smoke: the sun shall be turned into darkness, and the moon into blood, before that great and notable day of the Lord come. And it shall come to pass, that whosoever shall call on the name of the Lord shall be saved" (Acts ii, 17–21).

Analysis and applicaton of Peter's Pentecostal address.

The application which Peter made of this prophecy is so obviously correct, that no one could gainsay or deny it. There were the one hundred and twenty men and women actually prophesying, and announcing to the multitude in their own several dialects, "the wonderful works of God." This was therefore a very happy and most appropriate introduction; and served greatly of course to open the hearts of the people to attend to the words of the Apostles. And hence having fairly gained the attention of the multitudes, Peter next proceeded

2. *To announce to them the facts of the Gospel; and especially to submit to them the evidence of Christ's resurrection.* This he proves

(1) By referring to the sixteenth Psalm; in which

David says, "I foresaw the Lord always in my presence; for he is at my right hand that I should not be moved. Therefore my heart rejoiced, and my tongue was glad: moreover also my flesh shall rest in hope; because thou wilt not leave my soul in Hades (לִשְׁאוֹל, *εἰς ᾅδου, to Hades*), neither wilt thou suffer thy Holy One to see corruption. Thou hast made known to me the ways of life; thou wilt make me full of joy with thy countenance."

Now, says Peter in commenting on these words, David can not here refer to himself; for he is dead; his flesh has seen corruption, as you all very well know. "But being a prophet, and knowing that God had sworn to him with an oath, that of the fruit of his loins according to the flesh, he would raise up Christ to sit on his throne,—he seeing this before, spake of the resurrection of *Christ*, that *his* soul was not left to Hades, nor did *his* flesh see corruption" (Acts ii, 22–31). Here again then, the application of prophecy is clear and unmistakable.

(2) He proves it by the direct testimony of the Apostles themselves; for the confirmation of which they were ready if necessary to lay down their own lives (Verse 32).

(3) He proves it by the miracle itself. There were the miraculous demonstrations before them; plain, clear, and manifest to all. These manifestations of Divine power proved not only that the Apostles were the chosen embassadors of God, and as such spoke as they were moved by the Holy Spirit; but they served moreover to prove through the testimony of the Apostles, that Jesus was himself the author and worker of the miracle. "*He*," exclaimed the bold and heroic Peter, "*he* having been exalted to the right hand of God, and having received of the Father the promise of the Holy Spirit,—*he* hath shed forth this which ye now see and hear" (Verse 33).

(4) And finally, he proves still further Christ's exaltation, and, by implication, also his resurrection, from Psalm cx, 1. "For David," he says, "has not ascended into the heavens; but he himself says, Jehovah said to my Lord, Sit thou on my right hand till I make thy enemies thy footstool" (Verses 34, 35).

3. *From these premises Peter very forcibly concludes that Jesus had even then begun his mediatorial reign.* "Therefore," he says, "let all the house of Israel know assuredly, that God has made that same Jesus whom ye crucified, both Lord and Christ" (Verse 36).

Effect of Peter's address on the minds and hearts of the people.

This conclusion was wholly irresistible. There was no fair way of avoiding it. The people were pierced to their hearts by the sword of the Spirit; and under the conviction of their own sinfulness, the righteousness of Christ, and the just claims of the Divine government on them, they cried out to Peter and to the rest of the Apostles, "*Men and brethren, what shall we do?*"

Evidence that the people were begotten by the Spirit, through the belief of the truth.

In these words of earnest inquiry, we have given unmistakable evidence of faith in Christ, and also of the renewal of the Holy Spirit, as effected in the hearts of the people through the preaching of Peter. For before the delivery of his sermon, all that were then present, save only the one hundred and twenty disciples, were without faith in Christ, and also without that spiritual life which unites the soul of the believer to God in holiness and love. But now what a change. Many who had previously cried out with the multitude, "Crucify him, crucify him," are now convinced that he is the promised Messiah; "the Chief among ten thousand, and the One altogether lovely." Their hearts are no longer filled with enmity to him, but are now deeply agitated with sundry other emotions, indicative of the new life which is springing up in their souls through the belief of the truth. And hence when they were commanded to repent and be baptized, in the name of Jesus, for the remission of their sins, and in order that they might receive the gift of the Holy Spirit, they at once submitted to the Divine injunction; and on the same day three thousand persons, begotten by the Spirit and born of water, were added to the infant Church. And just so it was in every other case of conversion recorded in the Acts of the Apostles. The people always heard the word, believed it, obeyed it, and then went on their way rejoicing.

Nature of faith, and its proper functions in the scheme and economy of redemption.

From these premises then it is an easy matter to perceive what is the nature of faith, and what also are its proper functions. The word of God, sustained by its accompanying evidences, is first addressed to the understanding, where after due examination it is received as the truth. But this truth is "living and powerful." It contains within itself moral elements adapted to the entire moral nature of man. And hence we find, that unless interrupted by extraneous influences, it at once permeates the heart, and fills it with sundry living and powerful emotions. Through the heart, it affects the will; and through the will, it helps to control the life of all who honestly receive and retain it. In the course of this process, we have then clearly and distinctly marked (1) A change of views and sentiments; (2) A change of heart; (3) A change of will; and (4) A change of life. These are all *implied* in the faith of the Gospel, though they are not all *expressed* by the word *faith* (πίστις) as it occurs in the New Testament. The third change is commonly expressed by the word *repentance;* and the fourth, by the word *conversion* and its cognates. And hence we find that the word *faith* is usually and properly applied to the first and second of the aforesaid changes. But even these are indicated by it only in part. From each of them some things must be eliminated which do not properly belong to that state of mind and heart which, in the Holy Scriptures, is commonly designated by the word *faith.* It seems however, when used to denote a condition of salvation, to embrace in all cases (1) A strong *conviction* of the truth of the Gospel, as "the power of God for salvation to every one that believeth;" and (2) A firm and abiding *trust* in Christ, as the way, the truth, the resurrection, and the life. To believe in a fact, is simply to be fully persuaded that it did actually occur; but to believe in Christ is, not only to believe that he exists, but also to trust in him as our wisdom, justification, sanctification, and redemption. For it is not only with the intellect but also with the heart that "man believeth unto righteousness" (Rom. x, 10).

III.—Love of Christ.

Origin and importance of our faith in Christ.

This is a very important element of the Christian system. Without it indeed even faith itself is valueless. For "Though I have all faith," says Paul, "so that I could remove mountains, and have not love, I am nothing." And again he says, "Now abideth faith, hope, and love, these three; but the greatest of these is love" (1 Cor. xiii, 2, 13). It is however one of the legitimate fruits of faith, and springs up in the heart of every true believer, as soon as he has just conceptions of Christ in his various personal and official relations, as the greatest and best of all God's gifts to man, and the very highest manifestations of his love. "We love him," says John, "because he first loved us" (1 John iv, 19). This is therefore one of the very first and clearest manifestations of that spiritual life which unites the soul of every true believer to God through Christ. Indeed "the end of the commandment is love, out of a pure heart, and of a good conscience, and of faith unfeigned" (1 Tim. i, 5). And hence we learn from the highest authority, that no one can be a disciple of Christ, who does not love him supremely (Luke xiv, 26, 27).

IV.—Repentance.

The word *repentance* (μετάνοια) means according to its etymology, *a change of mind.* It implies therefore that the sinner has obtained new views of Christ, of sin, and of holiness. He is made to realize that it was for him that Jesus wept, and bled, and died. And this conviction begets in his heart a godly sorrow for his sins. As he now looks on Him who was pierced for his transgressions and bruised for his iniquities, he is himself greatly grieved in spirit on account of his manifold sins and transgressions; and he resolves that with the help of God he will henceforth cease to do evil and learn to do well. This resolution is no sooner formed than a change begins to be effected in his life. His simple inquiry now is, "Lord, what wilt thou have me to do?" And having obtained an answer to this question, he "no longer confers with flesh and blood; but with a loyal, loving, praying, and obedient heart, he at once takes the yoke of Christ upon him, and submits in all things to his will and government.

How the truth of God affects the sinner who receives it.

Here, then, as before stated, we have given four distinct and radical changes. The first of these is an intellectual change, caused by the force of the truth and the testimony submitted; the second is a change of heart, brought about by the antecedent change of the understanding; the third is a change of the will, affected by the change of the heart; and the fourth is a change of conduct, resulting from the change of the will. Which then of these four elementary changes constitutes true and genuine repentance? They are all essential links in the same chain of causation; and it may therefore be conceded, that they are all *implied* in the word repentance. But the question is not, What is *implied* in it, but what is *expressed* by it, as it is used in the inspired writings?

Four changes wrought in the sinner by means of the truth.

Which of these constitutes the *essential* element of repentance?

That it denotes a change subsequent to that which is effected in the intellect by means of testimony, and also to that which takes place in the heart, is manifest from such passages as the following. "Now I rejoice," says Paul, "not that ye were made sorry, but that ye sorrowed *to repentance* (εἰς μετάνοιαν); for ye were made sorry after a godly manner, that ye might receive damage by us in nothing. For godly sorrow *worketh repentance* (μετάνοιαν) to salvation, not to be repented of; but the sorrow of the world worketh death. For behold this self-same thing that ye sorrowed after a godly sort, what carefulness it wrought in you, yea, what clearing of yourselves, yea, what indignation, yea, what fear, yea, what vehement desire, yea, what zeal, yea, what revenge! In all things, ye have approved yourselves to be clear in this matter" (2 Cor. vii, 9–11). From this it seems that Paul, by a prudent and judicious presentation of the truth, had wrought a logical change in the minds of

Proof, that repentance *follows* a change of the Intellect and also of the Heart.

these Corinthians; and this change of judgment had produced in turn a corresponding change in their feelings. Their hearts were now filled with godly sorrow by means of Paul's first Epistle to them. But neither of these changes constitutes repentance. It is something which follows after all this in the chain of moral causation; for, says Paul, "*Ye sorrowed to repentance;*" and again he says, "*godly sorrow worketh repentance.*" Godly sorrow, then, is essential to repentance, as an adequate cause is always essential to every effect. But repentance follows godly sorrow, as godly sorrow itself follows also a certain class of our moral judgments.

Does repentance, then, consist in a change of the will, or in a change of conduct, or in both?

Proof that repentance *precedes* conversion and reformation.

Peter answers this question in Acts iii, 19, when he says to the multitude, "Repent then and *turn* (ἐπιστρέψατε) in order that your sins may be wiped out; and that there may come times of refreshing from the presence of the Lord." Here the word *turn* manifestly expresses all that is properly included in the required change of conduct. And as repentance is antecedent to this, it follows as a logical necessity that *repentance consists properly and essentially in a change of the will*, effected by means of godly sorrow in the heart. That his word is often used in a more comprehensive sense, so as to include godly sorrow, and also conversion and reformation of life, is, I think, manifest from sundry passages of Scripture. The latter is indeed clearly implied in the passage already cited from 2 Cor. vii, 9–11. See also Matth. iii, 3; iv, 17; xi, 20, 21; xii, 41; Luke xiii, 3, 5; xv, 7, 10; xvi, 30; Acts

Repentance consists *essentially* in a change of the will.

Repentance in its widest and most comprehensive sense.

xvii, 30; Heb. vi, 1; Rev. ii, 5, 16, 21, 22; iii, 3, 19; ix, 20, 21, etc. But the essential element of repentance in all cases is a change of the will. Genuine repentance consists always in a full and unreserved submission of the will of the sinner to the will of God. This change is effected by means of godly sorrow in the heart, and always leads to reformation of life.

Relation of Repentance to Faith.

It is manifest therefore that repentance is the result of faith, as faith itself is the result of testimony. No testimony, no faith; no faith, no repentance; no repentance, no conversion; no conversion, no reformation; and no reformation, no salvation. The truth understood, begets in the understanding of the sinner, a conviction that Jesus Christ is the Son of God and Savior of sinners. This conviction under favorable circumstances, penetrates the heart, and fills it with godly sorrow; and this sorrow leads to repentance. But while it is quite manifest that there can be no repentance without godly sorrow, and that there can be no godly sorrow without some faith in the testimony of God concerning Christ, it is at the same time equally obvious, that the faith of the sinner is in turn greatly increased and strengthened by his repentance. This arises of necessity out of the very terms and conditions of offered pardon. The promise of salvation is to those who believe, repent, and reform. But faith, as we have seen, implies both belief in the testimony of God, and trust in God himself through Christ. But how can the *impenitent* sinner trust fully and confidently in God? Manifestly, this is impossible. He may indeed, under a firm persuasion that Jesus has by the grace of God tasted death for every man, cherish some degree of hope, and exercise some measure of trust in God, even before he fully repents of his sins, and resolves to reform his life. But it is not until after that his will is wholly subjected to the will of God, that he can fully trust in God, and rely on him with confidence for every needed blessing. And hence it is that faith and repentance have always a mutual and reflex influence on each other. Faith leads to repentance, while repentance again serves very greatly to increase our faith; and especially that element of it which we call *trust in God,* through our Lord Jesus Christ. From these premises, then, the necessity of repentance in order to salvation is very obvious.

How Faith and Repentance serve to mutually increase and strengthen one another.

V.—Conversion.

Conversion means simply and properly a *turning* (ἐπιστροφή): but in a religious sense, it means the turning of a sinner mentally, morally, and physically, from the service of Satan to the service of God. True indeed it has reference primarily to the turning of the soul; but this involves also of necessity a turning of the body; for as is the soul of a man religiously, so also are all the outward manifestations of his life. If his will is to serve "the world, the flesh and the Devil," then indeed his whole life will be given up to "the lusts of the flesh, the lusts of the eye, and the pride of life." His face will be hellward; and every step he takes will be toward the bottomless pit, prepared for the Devil and his angels. But let his will be changed, and then also his life will change with it. As his mind turns, so also his body turns. His face is now heavenward; and every step of his life now brings him nearer and nearer to the celestial city "whose builder and maker is God." And hence it is that conversion always implies a

In what Conversion consists.

turning of the body, as well as of the soul and spirit to God. The man who turns mentally from darkness to light and from the power of Satan to God, at the same time ceases to do evil, and learns to do well. His only inquiry now is, "Lord what wilt thou have me to do?" and henceforth his whole life is devoted to the service of God. Otherwise we are constrained to believe that he is really not a converted man. "Hereby we know," says John, "that we know him, if we keep his commandments. He that saith, I know him, and keepeth not his commandments, is a liar, and the truth is not in him. But whoso keepeth his word, in him verily is the love of God perfected: hereby know we that we know him. He that saith he abideth in him, ought himself also so to walk even as he walked" (1 John ii, 3–6).

Evidence of genuine Conversion.

It is easy therefore to perceive the importance and necessity of conversion. Christ came, not to save men in their sins, but to save them from their sins. And hence the cry of Mercy to all is, "Turn you, turn you; for why will you die?

Necessity of Conversion.

VI.—Prayer.

Prayer is the natural outpouring of every believing, grateful, and penitent heart; and hence it is always one of the very first indications that the soul has been truly converted to God. I do not say that this alone is in all cases sufficient evidence of conversion. Sometimes men are prompted to pray from motives of mere selfishness. They are convinced that God is, and that he bestows his blessings in response to the prayers of his people. And feeling, as they do, their own weakness and utter insufficiency, they often, in times of severe trial and affliction, instinctively and self-

Prayer an evidence of Conversion.

ishly pour out their prayers and supplications to him for mercy. But no prayer is acceptable to God which does not flow from a heart that is truly converted to him. "He that turneth away his ear from hearing the law," says Solomon, "even his prayer shall be an abomination" (Prov. xxviii, 9). But when the heart is really converted to God, it as naturally seeks after him, as it seeks for the common comforts and blessings of life. "*Behold he prayeth*," is the testimony of Jesus himself in proof of the conversion of Saul of Tarsus (Acts ix, 11). And what was true of Saul, is also true of every one who like him feels deeply his own spiritual poverty and wretchedness, and his great need of salvation, through the infinite merits of our Savior's blood. Prayer is therefore as really a condition of pardon and church fellowship, as is faith, or repentance, or confession, or baptism. Were it otherwise, Joel and Paul would never have said by the Spirit, "*Whosoever shall call on the name of the Lord shall be saved*" (Joel ii, 32; Rom. x, 13).

Prayer, a condition of pardon.

But by this I do not mean, that when a man believes, repents, and is converted, he has nothing more to do than simply to pray that God would pardon his sin and bestow on him the gift of the Holy Spirit. Certainly not. He must pray; and if he is a truly and thoroughly converted man he will pray; and he will pray for the pardon of his sins as well as for every other needed blessing. But he will do more than this. God hears and answers the prayers of the *obedient*. And hence Ananias said to Saul, "Why tarriest thou? Arise, and be baptized, and wash away thy sins, calling on the name of the Lord." This is still Heaven's order of pardon. It is not faith alone, nor repentance alone, nor conversion alone, nor prayer alone,

Prayer, to be acceptable, must be followed by obedience.

nor confession alone, nor baptism alone, but all of these combined in God's own appointed order, that secures for us the forgiveness of our sins through the rich merits of our Savior's blood. And hence it follows that every believing penitent should, like Saul of Tarsus, be instructed to arise and wash away his sins, "CALLING ON THE NAME OF THE LORD."

VII.—CONFESSION.

It is said of Christ, that before Pontius Pilate he witnessed "the good confession; (τὴν καλὴν ὁμολογίαν); and of Timothy that he confessed "the good confession" (τὴν καλὴν ὁμολογίαν) before many witnesses (1 Tim. vi, 13). And after the same formula of speech, all Christians are exhorted to hold fast "the confession" (Heb. iv, 14; x, 23, etc). From such expressions, then, it is very manifest that, in the Apostolic Church, a particular truth, most likely expressed in a given formula of words, was publicly confessed by all candidates for church membership, and which on account of its very important practical bearings in the scheme and economy of redemption was commonly known and designated as "THE GOOD CONFESSION." This seems to be implied in the use of the definite article in all cases where this confession is spoken of.

Evidence, that all the members of the Apostolic Church made a public confession of their faith.

But what was this "good confession," to which so much prominence is given in the New Testament?

The answer to this question is, I think, found in Matth. xvi, 16. "When Jesus came into the coasts of Cæsarea Philippi, he asked his disciples, saying, Who do men say that I the Son of man am? And they said, Some say that thou art John the Baptist; some, Elias; and others Jere-

In what this good confession consists. Proof.

mias, or one of the prophets. He said unto them, But who say ye that I am? And Simon Peter answered and said, THOU ART THE CHRIST, THE SON OF THE LIVING GOD. And Jesus answered and said unto him, Blessed art thou Simon Bar-jona; for flesh and blood hath not revealed it unto thee, but my Father who is in Heaven. And I say unto thee, that thou art Peter (πέτρος), and upon this ROCK (πέτρα) I will build my Church; and the gates of Hades shall not prevail against it" (Matth. xvi, 13–18). From this it seems pretty evident that it was the purpose of Jesus to build his Church on the fundamental truth that *he is himself the promised Messiah, the Son of the living God*, by requiring all who would become members of his Church to confess this truth as did Peter. And if so, then it follows that the confession of Peter is really "the good confession" of the Church, the same that was made by Timothy before many witnesses. And this view of the matter is further supported by the fact that Christ himself made this confession before Caiaphas (Matth. xxvi, 63, 64), and no doubt also before Pilate (1 Tim. vi, 13). True indeed this is nowhere recorded by Matthew, Mark, Luke or John; but neither is the important saying of Christ, found in Acts xx, 35, recorded by any of these four witnesses. And as John tells us that he had purposely omitted in his narrative, many of the sayings and doings of Christ, we have no right to call in question the accuracy of Paul's statement as given in his first Epistle to Timothy.

The central and fundamental truth of the whole Bible.

If any further evidence is needed on this point, it may be found in the fact that the truth confessed by Peter is in fact the great central and fundamental truth of the whole Bible; for "the testimony of Jesus is the spirit of prophecy" (Rev.

xix, 10). "To him gave all the prophets witness, that through his name, whosoever believeth in him, shall receive the remission of sins" (Acts x, 43). The confession of Peter is therefore one of the most wonderful generalizations in the whole Bible. To believe it understandingly, is in fact, to believe all that is recorded in both the Old and the New Testament. And hence it is eminently proper that this fundamental truth of the Christian religion should receive the prominence that is given to it by Christ and his Apostles; and that while it is believed with the heart, it should also be confessed with the mouth that "Jesus is the Christ, the Son of the living God" (Rom. x, 10).

Creed of the Church.

It is manifest moreover that this fundamental truth may with propriety be regarded as the Creed of the Church; and many do so actually consider it. But as the word *creed* is now commonly used to denote not only what we believe as essential to our salvation, but also what we receive as *our authoritative standard of faith and practice*, it may be best to call the whole Bible, Old Testament and New, our Creed. For "all Scripture is given by inspiration of God, and is profitable for doctrine, for reproof, for correction, for instruction in righteousness, that the man of God may be perfect, thoroughly furnished for every good work" (2 Tim. iii, 16).

VIII.—Baptism.

Qualifications for Baptism.

The man who has been begotten by the Holy Spirit, through faith in Christ; who has repented of his sins; has been converted to God; and who with an humble, loving, prayerful and obedient heart has made "the good confession," is now ready in submission to the authority of Christ, to be baptized "into the name of the Father, and of the Son, and of the Holy Spirit" (Matth. xxviii, 19). This is the next step in the economy of grace; and in this, he, according to the Divine appointment, receives through the blood of Christ the remission of all his past sins (Mark xvi, 16; Acts ii, 38; xxii, 16); is formally introduced into the kingdom of God (John iii, 5); and receives the gift of the Holy Spirit (Acts ii, 38; Gal. iv, 6), as an earnest of the eternal inheritance, "until the redemption of the purchased possession" (Eph. i, 13, 14). Having died to sin practically, it is fitting that he should be buried with Christ in baptism, and rise with him "to walk in newness of life" (Rom. vi, 4; Col. ii, 12; iii, 1). Henceforth Sin has no longer dominion over him; but as the servant of Righteousness he now brings forth fruit unto holiness, and rejoices in hope of the glory of God.

Benefits received in and through Baptism.

From our present stand-point and the premises submitted in this chapter, we are now prepared to explain to advantage certain alleged difficulties, which are by some regarded as inconsistencies in the Christian economy. We see, for instance,

Alleged inconsistencies in the conditions of offered pardon and church membership.

1. Why it is, and how it is that the offered conditions of pardon and church membership seem to differ so much under different circumstances. Jesus said to his Apostles, "He that believeth and is baptized shall be saved" (Mark xvi, 16); but Peter said to the inquiring multitude on the day of Pentecost, "Repent and be baptized every one of you in the name of Jesus Christ, for the remission of sins, and ye shall receive the gift of the Holy Spirit" (Acts ii, 38); and Paul and Silas said to the Philippian jailer, "Believe on the Lord Jesus Christ, and thou

shalt be saved, and thy house" (Acts xvi, 31); while Ananias, as we have seen, simply said to Saul, "Arise, and be baptized, and wash away thy sins, calling on the name of the Lord" (Acts xxii, 16). These instructions may at first seem to involve some inconsistencies. But they are all plain to him who understands properly the conditions of pardon, and who at the same time takes into due consideration the various circumstances of the persons and parties addressed. For as we have already seen, the faith of the Gospel, from its very nature, always implies of necessity the obedience of the Gospel. It is not, as we have shown, a mere logical assent of the understanding to the truth of the proposition that "Jesus is the Christ the Son of the living God;" but it is a living, active, fruit-bearing principle, which, while it has its root in the understanding, at the same time pervades the heart; and through the heart it influences the will; and through the will it controls the life. And hence it is often given as a summary of all that is required of the sinner in order to salvation. Thus, for instance, to the jailer who knew nothing of Christ, nothing could be more appropriate than the address of Paul, "Believe on the Lord Jesus Christ, and thou shalt be saved, and thy house;" but to the inquiring Pentecostal believers, the response of Peter, "Repent and be baptized," was better adapted, than would have been such a reply as Paul made to the jailer. And in the case of the believing, praying, and penitent Saul of Tarsus, nothing more was necessary than simply to say to him, as did Ananias, "Arise, and be baptized, and wash away thy sins, calling on the name of the Lord." And hence it must be evident to every reflecting mind, that the laws of the Kingdom of heaven are like the laws

Explanation of these apparent discrepancies.

of nature, uniform. Whatever was required of any one person as a condition of pardon and church membership, is still required of all.

2. We see how it is that we are said to believe *into* (εἰς) Christ (John i, 12; iii, 15, 16, etc.), and also to be baptized *into* (εἰς) Christ (Matth. xxviii, 19; Gal. iii, 27, etc). Here again there is really no discrepancy. For it is not by faith alone, nor by repentance alone, nor by prayer alone, nor by confession alone, nor by baptism alone, nor even by love alone, but by virtue of all these combined, that we put on Christ, and so become members of his body.

How it is that we both believe *into* Christ, and are baptized *into* Christ.

We say, for the sake of illustration, that the Mississippi river floats steamboats. But where? At its source? No; but after that it has united with sundry other streams. And just so it is with respect to our faith. It too is a stream, a living stream which runs through the whole Christian life, and gives character to every thought, and word, and action. Faith then in connection with repentance, love, prayer, confession, and baptism, puts us into Christ, and gives us a right to all the privileges of the sons of God.

3. We see why it is, that so many things are *for* or *in order to* the remission of sins. In Matth. xxvi, 28, for instance, it is said that the blood of Christ was shed for (εἰς) the remission of sins; in John iii, 16; Acts x, 43; xvi, 31, and many other parallel passages, it is very clearly implied that faith is for the remission of sins; and in Acts ii, 38, repentance and baptism are both specifically required for (εἰς) the remission of sins. So also it might be very easily shown that conversion, love, prayer, and confession are all for the remission of sins. But to the

Various requirements *in order to* the remission of sins.

careful and diligent student of the economy of redemption, it is scarcely necessary to say that the preposition *for* in these several cases is used in very different senses, and is expressive of very different relations. It has of course in all such instances the same general signification; but it is used specifically in different senses, according to the nature and character of the antecedent or consequent. The shedding of Christ's blood, for instance, was necessary not only to purge our consciences from dead works, and to so qualify us in various ways for the service of the living God (Heb. ix, 14); but it was furthermore also necessary to so meet and satisfy the claims of the Divine government on man, as to make it possible for God to be just in justifying every one that believes in Jesus (Rom. iii, 25, 26). But not so with regard to faith. There is really nothing meritorious in it; nothing to make an atonement for the sin of any one. It is however absolutely necessary in order to so prepare the sinner's heart, as to make it morally possible for God to pardon his transgressions, even by virtue of the blood of Christ. And hence it has in all ages and under all circumstances been required as a condition of forgiveness in case of personal transgressions (Rom. xiv, 23; Heb. xi, 6). And the same is also true of repentance. The will of the sinner must yield to the claims of the Divine government, or, by a moral necessity, he must be banished "with an everlasting destruction from the presence of the Lord and from the glory of his power" (2 Thess. i. 9). But baptism is a positive ordinance. It has no foundation in nature; but it depends for its existence and its place in the economy of redemption, solely on the will and appointment of the Divine Lawgiver. Thousands

Various senses in which the preposition *for* is used in such cases.

during the Patriarchal and Jewish ages were saved without it; and if any are now really in like circumstances, we may indulge the hope that they too will be saved, as were Abraham, and Isaac, and Jacob. But like the forbidden tree in the garden of Eden, baptism is given under the Christian dispensation as a test of our loyalty to God. And hence it follows, that the man, who, with the New Testament in his hand, willfully neglects this Divine ordinance, shows by this very omission of duty, that his heart is not right in the sight of God; and he has therefore need that some one teach him the way of the Lord more perfectly.

God's work and man's work in the economy of redemption.

4. We see how it is, and in what respect it is, that both God and man have an agency in the work of regeneration. To God, and to him alone it belonged to *provide* salvation for our lost and perishing world. In this part of the work man could do nothing; absolutely nothing. But "God so loved the world that he gave his only-begotten Son, that whosoever believeth in him should not perish, but have everlasting life" (John iii, 16). Nor was this all: but knowing as he did our ignorant, fallen, and helpless condition, he sent also his Spirit to beget in us a new life through the word of truth, and so to help our infirmities, as to give us a victory "over death and him that has the power of death." And hence we may all say with Paul, "By grace ye are saved through faith; and that not of yourselves, it is the gift of God" (Eph. ii, 8). But nevertheless it has pleased God to make our *enjoyment* of the great salvation depend in a great measure on our own voluntary agency. "Not every one," says Christ, "that saith unto me, Lord, Lord, shall enter into the kingdom of heaven, but he that doeth the will of my

Father who is in heaven" (Matth. vii, 21). And hence it is, that in the whole economy of redemption, man's own natural powers are always called into requisition so far as they can be made available. His ear, for instance, is made the medium through which the word of truth is communicated to his understanding; his understanding is made the medium of access to his heart; his heart is used to influence his will; and his will is made the regulator of his life. Thus it is that God encourages and requires us to work out our own salvation with fear and trembling, while he himself works in us "both to will and to do of his good pleasure" (Phil. ii, 12, 13).

Wisdom and benevolence of God's arrangement in giving to man an agency in the work of redemption.

The wisdom and benevolence of this arrangement will, on a little reflection, appear obvious to all. For in this way God permits and enables men (1) To demonstrate their loyalty to himself and to his government; (2) To educate themselves for higher spheres of enjoyment both here and hereafter; and (3) To imitate Christ, as good stewards of the manifold grace of God, by doing good to all men as they have opportunity. And hence we find that the most pious and godly men have always been the most active and zealous in every good work

Evidence that the Gospel is of Divine origin.

5. Finally, we see in this whole arrangement of the economy of redemption multiplied evidence of its Divine origin. What earthly legislator, governor, king, or potentate would ever think of offering pardon to his rebel subjects on such conditions as the foregoing? To open all jails, prisons, and penitentiaries, and say to the depraved inmates, You may all go free, and enjoy the highest honors, privileges, and emoluments of the commonwealth, on condition that you confess your faults, bow to the author-

ity of the government, and live in harmony with its requirements,—such a course, as every one knows, would very soon result in the overthrow and ruin of any earthly monarchy. But God's thoughts are not as our thoughts, nor are his ways as our ways. But as the heavens are higher than the earth, so are his ways above our ways, and his thoughts above our thoughts (Isa. lv, 8, 9). And hence he has offered to all men pardon, justification, sanctification, and redemption, on terms which, though without a parallel in the history of all human governments, are nevertheless alike honorable to God himself and to man who was made in his image and after his likeness. And now we realize that in the economy of grace, "Mercy and Truth have met together; Righteousness and Peace have kissed each other" (Psa. lxxxv, 10).

CHAPTER II.

DUTIES OF CHRISTIANS; OR, THE TERMS AND CONDITIONS OF CONTINUED MEMBERSHIP, AND OF FINAL ADMISSION INTO GOD'S EVERLASTING KINGDOM.

In the Commission given by Christ to his Apostles, Matt. xxviii, 18–20, they were required,

Three items embraced in the Great Commission.

I. To make disciples of all the nations.

II. To baptize them into the name of the Father, and of the Son, and of the Holy Spirit.

III. To teach them to observe all things which Christ had commanded them, and which the Holy Spirit would bring to their remembrance.

To ascertain definitely and precisely what all these things are would require a critical analysis and examination of all that is taught in the New Testament, from the beginning of Acts to the end of Revelation. But for such a work I have neither the time nor the space at present. All that I aim to give in this chapter, is a very brief outline or summary of Christian duty. Such a summary is contained in 2 Peter i, 5–11. The Epistle is addressed to Christians;* to those who, through faith, repentance, confession, and baptism, had been received

Detailed account of the things commanded.

Summary of Christian duty.

* In the New Testament the members of the Christian Church are variously designated as follows:

Names given in the New Testament to the followers of Christ.

I. They are called *Disciples* (μαθηταί, *learners*, from μανθάνω, *to learn*,) Acts vi, 1, etc., because they professed to follow Christ as their Teacher. In like manner the pupils of the ancient Philosophers and Rhetoricians were called their disciples.

II. They are called *Christians*, (χριστιανοί, from Χριστός, *Christ*,) Acts xi, 26; xxvi, 28; 1 Peter iv, 16, because they professed to be the followers of Christ. It has long been a question whether this name was at first given to the Disciples by the heathen, or whether they voluntarily assumed it themselves, or whether it was given to them by Divine authority. Be this as it may, one thing is very certain, viz., that this name was, in a short time, received and indorsed as appropriate by the Apostles themselves, (1 Peter iv, 16, and James ii, 7;) and very soon after the death of the Apostles it became the common distinguishing appellative of all the followers of Christ. This is evident from the writings of Tacitus, Lucian, Justin Martyr, Tertullian, Archelaus, Eusebius, Chrysostom, etc. The apostate Emperor Julian, wishing to deprive them of a name in which they so much gloried, ordered that they should be called, not *Christians*, but *Galileans*. *Greg. Nazianzen. Orat.* iv, 86, p. 114.

III. They are called *Believers*, (πιστεύοντες and πιστοί,) Acts v, 14, and 1 Tim. iv, 12, because of their belief in Christ.

IV. They are called *saints*, (ἅγιοι, *pure*,) Acts ix, 13, 32, 41, etc., with reference to their consecration to God and the purity of their aims and objects.

V. They are called *Brethren*, (ἀδελφοί, *brothers*,) Acts ix, 30; x, 22, etc., with reference to their relations to each other.

VI. They are called the *Chosen* or the *Elect*, (ἐκλεκτοί, from ἐκλέγω, *to select*,) Rom. viii, 33; Col. iii, 12, etc., because they are chosen according to the foreknowledge of God the Father, through sanctification of the Spirit, in order to obedience and the sprinkling of the blood of Jesus Christ. 1 Peter i, 2.

VII. They are called *the People of God*, (λαὸς τοῦ Θεοῦ,) Hebrews iv, 9; 1

into the Church of Christ. To all such the Apostle says: "*Giving* ALL DILIGENCE, *add to your faith heroism; and to heroism, knowledge; and to knowledge, temperance; and to temperance, patience; and to patience, godliness; and to godliness, brotherly kindness; and to brotherly kindness, love.* For if these things be in you and abound, they make you that you shall be neither barren nor unfruitful in the knowledge of our Lord Jesus Christ. But he that lacketh these things is blind, and can not see afar off, and hath forgotten that he was purged from his old sins Wherefore the rather, brethren, give diligence to make your calling and election sure. *For if ye do these things, ye shall never fall; for so an entrance shall be ministered to you abundantly into the Everlasting Kingdom of our Lord and Savior Jesus Christ.*"

It would be very difficult to give a more plain and simple directory to any one, and for any purpose, than that which is here given by the Apostle to all Christians, respecting the way of holiness. A few words of expla-

Peter ii, 10; and *the Children of God,* (τέκνα Θεοῦ,) 1 John iii, 1, 2, etc., because of their covenant relation to him.

VIII. They are reproachfully called by the Jews *Nazarenes,* (Ναζωραῖοι, Acts xxiv, 5.

The primitive Christians had an intense feeling of opposition to all human and party names; and for a long time they held to the name *Christian* as a symbol of unity, and as a safeguard against all schisms. Gregory Nazianzen says, about A. D. 350: "I honor Peter; but I am not a Petrian: I honor Paul; but I am not a Paulite; because I am of God. *He* is my Father." Epiphanius says: "The general Church is called by but one name. *Sects* only are called after their founders: as the Donatists, Manichæans, etc. So also testifies Chrysostom, Basil, Augustine, etc.

Primitive opposition to party names.

The name *Catholic* (καθολικός, κάθολος, κατὰ, and ὅλος, *on the whole, general*) originated from an intense feeling of opposition to all sects and parties. For a time it was used merely as an *epithet,* but afterward it became the distinctive *name* of the Church. The common style of confessors in the third century was this: "Christian is my name, and *Catholic* is my surname."

The name *Catholic.*

nation and illustration are all that is here necessary for our present purpose. Notice, then,

I. The preface to this directory: "GIVING ALL DILIGENCE, add," etc. This implies a great deal; but nothing more than is really necessary,

Comprehensive character of the Preface to this Directory.

1. *In order to the full and faithful discharge of our duties to God.* We are not our own. We have been bought with a price. Our bodies, our spirits, our time, our influence, and our all, belong to God. He has, therefore, the right to require all this of us; and it would certainly be very ungrateful and wholly inexcusable on our part to withhold it.

Threefold necessity of all this.

2. *It is necessary in order to the preservation and increase of our own spiritual life, health, and happiness.* There can be no growth nor progress in the Divine life without activity. And hence it is that God has most wisely and benevolently permitted us to coöperate with him in the great work of saving ourselves and redeeming a world. It is, indeed, a striking evidence of the Divine origin and adaptation of the Scheme of Redemption that it does not leave dormant and unemployed a single faculty of our nature. It calls into active exercise for the sake of our own happiness and improvement all the powers and susceptibilities of our bodies, our souls, and our spirits. And hence we are exhorted and encouraged to work out our own salvation with fear and trembling, while God himself works in us both to will and to do his own good pleasure. Phil. ii, 12, 13.

3. *It is essential to our own usefulness and the fulfillment of our various obligations to society.* Christ has, by the grace of God, tasted death for every man. He has, by his atoning sacrifice, rendered it possible for God to

be just in justifying every true believer. But he has committed to us the word of reconciliation. To us it now belongs to preach the Gospel to every creature, and to do good to all men as we have opportunity. Gal. vi, 10. And to do this as it ought to be done will certainly require *all diligence* on our part.

Specifications of the Christian's Directory.

II. Notice, secondly, the several specifications of this Divine directory, and which are to be sought after and cultivated with all diligence. These are,

1. *Heroism*, (ἀρετή, from Ἄρης, *Mars, the god of war.*) This term is not equivalent to virtue in general, but it seems to include all the heroic virtues, such as courage, fortitude, manliness, bravery, and intrepidity. Every Christian must be a soldier of the Cross. As he rises from the liquid grave he enters the army of the faithful and engages in the mightiest conflict that is known in the annals of earth and time—a conflict that will never end till the last enemy, Death, shall be destroyed. Hence he has need of courage and bravery to meet danger, of fortitude and manliness to endure the trials of the conflict, and of intrepidity and vigilance so as to be always ready not only to meet the assaults of the enemy, but also to carry forward the standard of the Cross and put to flight the armies of the aliens.

2. *Knowledge*, (γνῶσις;) that is, the knowledge of his calling. It is very pleasant in some respects to have a knowledge of every thing. But much of this would be of but little value to any one as a means of saving himself and the world around him. "This is eternal life," said our Savior, "to know thee, the only true God, and Jesus Christ whom thou hast sent." John xvii, 3. It is to the study of the Bible, therefore, and such other

sciences merely as will serve to illustrate its sacred pages that the Christian is required to give all diligence.

3. *Temperance*, (ἐγκράτεια; from ἐν, *in*, and κρατος, *strength.*) This term is equivalent to *self-government.* It implies that the Christian should have the mastery of all his powers, passions, and appetites. For "he that is slow to anger is better than the mighty; and he that ruleth his spirit, than he that taketh a city." Prov. xvi, 32.

4. *Patience*, (ὑπομονή, *a remaining behind.*) This means simply *patient endurance.* Trials are now necessary for the purpose of developing and cultivating all our virtues. Rom. v, 3, 4; 2 Cor. iv, 17; Heb. xii, 5–13, etc. But it is only to those who are properly exercised thereby that they bring forth the peaceable fruits of righteousness. And hence we should labor to let patience have her perfect work, that we may be perfect and entire, wanting nothing. James i, 3.

5. *Godliness*, (εὐσέβεια; εὐ, *well*, and σέβω, *to honor, worship.*) Under this term is embraced simply that ardent *piety* which keeps the heart ever glowing with spontaneous feelings of love, reverence, and gratitude to God, and which serves, therefore, to make us like him.

6. *Brotherly-kindness* (φιλαδελφία; from φιλία, *love*, and ἀδελφός, *a brother.*) The Church of Christ is a family, and all its members are related to each other as brethren. And hence they should ever cherish for each other feelings of the most tender love and affection, so that the world may ever have reason to exclaim, "Behold how good and how pleasant it is for brethren to dwell together in unity." Psalm cxxxiii, 1.

7. *Love*, (ἀγάπη;) that is, love for all men. The Christian can never consistently be a *partisan* of any kind. He feels that he is a citizen of the world. and

that it is his duty and his pleasure to do good to ***all men*** as he has opportunity. And hence, like the good Samaritan, he is ever ready to pour the oil and the wine of the Gospel into the wounded and bleeding hearts even of those who despitefully use and persecute him, just as God "causes the sun to rise on the evil and on the good, and sends rain on the just and the unjust."

III. Consider the means by which all this is to be accomplished. These must be such and such only as God has himself provided and ordained for this purpose. It is not by a mere act of the will that we can increase our heroism, knowledge, power and capacity of self-government, patience, godliness, brotherly-kindness, and love to and for all men. Nay, verily. To do this we must give all diligence to the study of God's Word; we must pray always; we must sanctify the Lord's Day, and never neglect the weekly celebration of the Lord's Supper; we must not forget the assemblies of the Saints, as the manner of some is, but exhort one another daily, lest any of us be hardened through the deceitfulness of sin; and, in a word, we must, like Christ, be diligent in every good work.

Means of reaching and accomplishing all these ends.

IV. Consider the end and result of following with all diligence the aforesaid directory. This is given in unmistakable terms by the Apostle himself. "*If ye do these things*," says he, "*ye shall never fall: for so an entrance shall be ministered to you abundantly into the Everlasting Kingdom of our Lord and Savior Jesus Christ.*" This is enough. Any thing more is wholly inconceivable. An eternity of perfect bliss! Who can now realize it? Who can properly paraphrase such a thought?

"O, sweet employ, to sing and trace
Th' amazing hights and depths of grace;

And spend, from sin and sorrow free,
A blissful, vast eternity!

O, what a sweet, exalted song,
When every tribe and every tongue,
Redeemed by blood, with Christ appear,
And join in one full chorus there!

My soul anticipates the day;
Would stretch her wings and soar away
To aid the song, the palm to bear,
And praise my great Redeemer there."

CHAPTER III.

CREED OF THE CHURCH.

THE word *faith*, like the word *religion*, is not unfrequently used in three different senses, or, at least, with three different shades of meaning, in the Bible.

Threefold sense and application of the word *faith*.

I. *It is sometimes used by metonymy in an objective sense, to denote that system of doctrine which is revealed to us in the Holy Scriptures.* Such is evidently its meaning in the following passages:

1. Acts vi, 7: "And the word of God increased; and the number of the disciples multiplied in Jerusalem greatly; and a great company of the priests became obedient to *the faith*."

Instances of its being used in an *objective* sense.

2. Acts xiii, 8: "But Elymas the sorcerer withstood them, (Paul and Barnabas,) seeking to turn away the Deputy from *the faith*."

3. Gal. i, 23: "But they (the Churches in Judea) had only heard, That he (Paul) who persecuted us in times past, now preached *the faith* which he once destroyed."

4. Gal. iii, 23: "But before *faith* came, we were kept under the Law, shut up unto *the faith* which should afterward be revealed."

5. 1 Timothy v, 8: "But if any provide not for his own, and especially for those of his own house, he has denied *the faith*, and is worse than an infidel."

6. 1 Timothy vi, 10: "For the love of money is a root of all evil; which while some coveted after, they have erred from *the faith*, and pierced themselves through with many sorrows."

7. Jude 3: "Beloved, when I gave all diligence to write unto you of the common salvation, it was needful for me to write unto you and exhort you that ye should contend earnestly for *the faith* which was once delivered to the saints."

Examples of its use in a *subjective* sense.

II. *Most frequently it is used subjectively, in its literal and proper sense, for that state of the understanding and the heart which causes a man to trust in Christ, and to obey all his commandments* The following examples will suffice for illustration:

1. Matthew viii, 10: "When Jesus heard it, (the remark of the centurion,) he marveled, and said to them that followed him, Verily I say unto you, I have not found so great *faith*, no, not in Israel."

2. Matthew ix, 22: "But Jesus turned about; and when he saw her, he said, Daughter, be of good comfort; thy *faith* hath made thee whole."

3. Matthew xv, 28: "Then Jesus answered and said unto her, O woman, great is thy *faith:* be it unto thee even as thou wilt."

4. Acts vi, 8: "And Stephen, full of *faith* and power, did great wonders and miracles among the people."

5. Romans x, 17: "So then *faith* cometh by hearing, and hearing by the word of God."

6. Heb. xi, 1: "Now *faith* is the confidence of things hoped for, and the evidence of things not seen," etc.

III. *It is also used sometimes by metonymy for the obedience of faith.* Take, for instance, the following passages:

Examples of its use in *practical* sense.

1. Matthew xxiii, 23: "Woe unto you, scribes and Pharisees, hypocrites! for ye pay tithe of mint, and anise, and cumin; and have omitted the weightier matters of the Law, judgment, mercy, and *faith*, (fidelity.)"

2. Romans i, 8: "First, I thank my God through Jesus Christ, for you all, that your *faith* (fidelity) is spoken of throughout the whole world."

3. Romans iii, 3: "For what is some did not believe? Shall their unbelief make the *faith* (fidelity) of God without effect?"

4. Gal. v, 22: "But the fruit of the Spirit is love, joy, peace, long-suffering, gentleness, goodness, *faith*, (fidelity.)"

5. Titus ii, 10: "Not purloining, (speaking of servants,) but showing all good *fidelity*, (πίστις;) that they may adorn the doctrine of God our Savior in all things."

6. Heb. xiii, 7: "Remember them who have the rule over you, who have spoken unto you the word of God; whose *faith* (fidelity) follow, considering the end of their conversation."

Here, then, we have a sort of trinity in the word *faith:* not properly three separate, independent, and distinct things; but rather three phases and manifestations of one and the same thing. The first of these may, for the

Mutual relation of the *objective*, *subjective*, and *practical* elements of our faith.

sake of distinction, be called *objective* faith, or faith in the book; the second, *subjective* faith, or faith in the heart; and the third, *practical* faith, or faith in the life. The last is but the immediate and necessary effect of the second; and the second is, in like manner, the legitimate effect of the first: so that if we would have true and genuine faith in our lives, we must first have it in our hearts; and if we would have it in our hearts, we must first have it in our Creed. And hence it is that we are brought back to the Bible itself AS THE ONLY PROPER CREED OF THE CHURCH: *the only infallible and reliable standard of our faith and practice.* Our faith, subjectively considered, is always liable to be erroneous in many respects; and our practice is likely to be even more so. But the Bible is perfect, as its Divine Author is perfect. And hence it should be our constant aim and effort, day by day, to test our thoughts, our words, and our actions, by this Divine standard; and to bring them up as near to its requirements as possible, but never to go beyond it. All efforts to transcend this limit are attempts at reformation in the wrong direction: they are the bitter fruits of infidelity, come from what source they may.

The only proper Creed of the Church.

Its use as means of reformation.

Happy, then, thrice happy, would it be for the Church to-day if she had always contended earnestly for the Creed delivered to the Saints by the inspired Apostles. But the pride of the human heart is amazing. There is a constant inclination on the part of fallen man, weak, frail, and erring as he is, to make his own opinions the standard by which to judge of every thing else. And hence, at an early period, the subjective faith of the Church, or rather of her aspiring Bishops and Presbyters, was reduced to writing, and in a

Bad effects of substituting the *subjective* for the *objective*.

great measure substituted for the inspired Creed of the Apostles and Prophets. But the trouble did not stop here. Very soon different opinions were entertained respecting the meaning of the newly formed Creed; and hence the necessity of again correcting the objective by the subjective. A third Creed was formed, and a fourth, and a fifth; but every attempt at creed-making has only served to destroy the unity of the faith, to multiply sects and parties, and to lead away the minds and hearts of the people from the earnest and prayerful study of the Holy Scriptures, which alone are able to make us wise even unto salvation.

The only means of restoring the unity of the Church.

And hence it is evident that every attempt to unite the people of God on any human basis must ever prove utterly vain and abortive. The only possible way to accomplish this end is to throw aside all human Creeds, and take the Bible, the whole Bible, and nothing but the Bible, as our rule of faith and practice.

Alleged objection to the view presented.

But I am aware that, just here, some will be ready to urge an objection against the view presented. A man, for instance, they say, applies for membership in a certain Church. He says that he believes the Bible to be the word of God, and the only proper rule of faith and practice. But the Elders of the Church ascertain from him that he has totally misapprehended some of its teachings on certain very grave and important practical questions. He believes, for instance, that Jesus Christ is a mere man; that there is no Holy Spirit; that sprinkling is baptism; that when a person becomes a member of a Church he may do just as he pleases, being no longer under law, but under grace, etc. The Elders labor in vain in attempting to convince him that he is in error on all these matters; and finally they reject him as one who is wholly unfit for a place in the Church of God. Now, says the objector, do not these Elders reject this applicant simply on the ground that their *subjective faith* is different from his? And does not this prove, beyond all doubt, that *in practice* at least, every man's interpretation of the Bible is his Creed?

I answer, *no.* He is rejected not by the elders of the Church, but by the Apostles of Christ, who still sit on thrones, judging the twelve tribes of Israel.

Reply to this allegation.

But let me explain a little just here. It is a self-evident fact, that without assuming something, we can really prove nothing. This is universally conceded; and hence we have given in every department of literature and science certain axiomatic or self-evident truths, which are not to be proved themselves, but which are constantly used for the purpose of proving other more abstruse and complicated propositions with which they stand connected. Thus, for instance, we say in Geometry, that "Things which are equal to the same thing are equal to each other;" "If to equals, equals be added, the sums will be equal;" "The whole is equal to the sum of all its parts," etc. And, in like manner, we enter upon the study of Psychology, by assuming our own personal existence; our own personal identity; that every effect must have an adequate cause, etc. And just so it is in Biblical science. It, too, has its self-evident truths and propositions: among which we may, I think, safely rank the following:

Necessity of axioms in all reasoning.

Illustrations.

Self-evident propositions with regard to the Bible.

I. ***That when God spoke to man, he spoke for the***

purpose and with the design of being understood. The contradictory of this proposition is an absurdity.

II. *That every honest man, whose mind has not been biased by the influences of a false education, may, therefore, understand what God has said in the Holy Scriptures, so far as a knowledge of the truth is essential to his own happiness and the happiness of others.* The contradictory of this proposition would imply that God has failed in his purpose.

III. *That the fundamental facts and principles of the Christian faith are not, therefore, proper and legitimate subjects of debate.* True, indeed, some persons may object to them just as they object to almost every thing else. Even the evidences of sensation and consciousness are not sufficient to satisfy some minds. But the Bible was not made to suit such *abnormal* cases.

Elders act, therefore, like other men in similar cases.

When, therefore, we say that the Elders of a Church have a right to reject such persons as pervert, or deny the plainest propositions in the Word of God, we claim no more for them than we commonly concede to other men in all the various ranks, pursuits, and relations of life. It is true that they may sometimes err in applying the plainest rules and principles of our Creed. And so, also, may the mathematician err in applying the plainest and simplest axioms of Geometry; the merchant may err in applying his yard-stick; the surveyor may err in applying his chain and compass; and the farmer may err in the use of his half-bushel. But who would thence infer that the farmer measures his grain by his own conceptions of the capacity of a half-bushel? or that the surveyor measures his land by his conceptions of a chain and compass? or that the merchant measures his cloth by his conceptions of a yardstick! Why then, in reason's name, should any one charge the Elders of a Church with ignoring the Bible, and making their own conceptions of its plain and simple truths their practical rule and standard in the government and discipline of a Church?

Syllogistic presentation of the argument. But if any one can not perceive the force of this reasoning let him try the two following syllogisms:

I.

Whoever acts in harmony with the divinely authorized Creed will be saved.

Every man's own interpretation of the Bible is his divinely authorized Creed.

Therefore, every man who, like Saul of Tarsus before his conversion, **acts in harmony with his own interpretation of the Bible, will be saved.**

II.

Every man who acts in harmony with the divinely authorized Creed will be saved.

The Holy Bible is our only divinely authorized Creed.

Therefore, every man who acts in harmony with its precepts and requirements will be saved.

Now, gentle reader, which of these two syllogisms do you prefer? The first contains the logic of Sectarianism, and the second contains the logic of Christianity.

CHAPTER IV.

ADAPTATION OF THE BIBLE TO THE WANTS OF MAN.

It is now a well-established principle of all sound philosophy, that every effect must correspond with the nature and character of the cause which produces it. If the cause is perfect the effect will be perfect; but if the cause is in any way or in any measure inadequate, then the effect will also partake of the same marks of imperfection.

The proposition proved *a priori*.

For the proof of this proposition we may appeal to every effect in the universe, human and Divine. Man is imperfect; and so, therefore, are also all his works. I am well aware that there are many ultra views taken of the philosophy of human nature. The mind of man is a pendulum, always vibrating between extremes on this as well as on every other subject. Manicheism, etc., produced Pelagianism; and this again reacted in the school of Augustine. But without attempting to define the precise limits of human depravity, we may safely affirm that fallen man has never yet accomplished any thing which, when weighed in the Divine balance, has not been found wanting.

Illustrations drawn from the works of God and the works of man.

And hence man has always been experimenting, always aiming at perfection, but never reaching it. Sometimes advancing and sometimes retrograding, but never reaching the goal of the infinite. If the Scotch system of Metaphysics is better than the Grecian, it is because Reid, Stewart, Brown, and Hamilton were permitted to sit at the feet of the Great Teacher. If California has improved on the educational system of Virginia, it is because she has learned wisdom from the experiments of her sister Republics.

But God makes no experiments. His works are all perfect. When he had finished the drama of creation he looked upon the Earth and its tenantry and pronounced all "*very good.*" There was not a blemish, not a single imperfection in heaven, earth, or sea. The morning stars sang together, and all the sons of God shouted for joy when they beheld this new-born Earth rise out of chaos and roll on majestically in the very identical orbit which the great Engineer and Architect of the universe had marked out for it when he first set a compass on the face of the deep, when he weighed the mountains in scales and the hills in a balance.

The light was divinely adapted to the eye of man, the melody of nature to his ear, the atmosphere to the vital current and pulsations of his heart, and all the tenantry of Eden contributed to the enjoyment of Adam and his lovely bride, till stretching forth her hand she plucked, she ate

> "Of that forbidden tree whose mortal taste
> Brought death into the world, and all our woe."

Then it was that

> "Earth felt the wound; and Nature from her seat
> Sighing through all her works, gave signs of woe
> That all was lost."

I will not now attempt to refute the vain speculations which some have entertained respecting the origin of sin and the alleged imperfections of the Divine arrangement. It is sufficient for our present purpose to know that God is not the author of confusion, and that the most gifted son of Adam's race has never yet even imagined any thing that will compare with the universe which God has created. Even the abuse of their most exalted privileges by men and angels is but a shade in the picture, the permission of which was, no doubt, necessary to the perfection of the Divine plan.

> "Cease, then, nor order imperfection name;
> Our proper bliss depends on what we blame.
> All nature is but art unknown to thee;
> All chance, direction which thou canst not see,
> All discord harmony not understood,
> All partial evil universal good."

Now all this is just as true of the Bible as it is of nature. Let the Divine authenticity of the Scriptures be conceded, which for the present we will assume, and it follows with all the clearness and force of demonstration, *that they are perfectly adapted to the end and purpose for which they were given to man.* To suppose that it could be otherwise would be to ignore and set aside all the analogies of nature. It would imply that He who made the eye can not see; that He who made the ear can not hear; that He who formed the heart of man is ignorant of its powers and susceptibilities; that Omnipotence could not meet the wants of a fallen creature; or otherwise that He who so loved the world as to give his only begotten Son for its redemption could and would tantalize his own offspring by giving them stones for bread, and the bitterness of wormwood for the water of eternal life.

First general conclusion from these *a priori* premises.

But for what purpose was the Bible given to man? This is the great question. To man as he *is* it involves considerations of the very highest practical importance. I say particularly to man as he *is*, for there was a time when he had no

The only remaining question to be considered.

Bible, when he needed none, when no cloud intervened between him and his Creator, when God spoke to him face to face, as friend to friend, and when all was light, and life, and love in Eden's holy bowers.

Historical outline of the Scheme of Redemption from its conception to its complete development.

But sin destroyed that happy union. It separated man from the source and fountain of his being and blessedness. It severed the ties which bound humanity to Divinity. And had not God mercifully interposed in his behalf, man must have wandered as an outcast in the blackness of darkness forever and ever. The past and present state of the heathen world is, indeed, a partial though an awfully impressive illustration of what all men must have become without the Bible.

But God had graciously provided a remedy. Foreseeing the end from the beginning, and knowing that man would forfeit his birthright to all the joys of both the terrestrial and the celestial Paradise, he had made the Scheme of Redemption a part of his original plan. It was, no doubt, perfectly arranged in the Divine mind before his creative voice first broke the silence of eternity. Acts xv, 18; Rom. viii, 28–30; Eph. i, 4, etc.

Ages rolled on. Ten thousand suns lighted up the vast vault of creation, the planets revolved in their respective orbits, the morning stars sang together, and myriads of myriads of happy spirits reëchoed the praises of Jehovah from the center to the circumference of this vast and stupendous universe. But no ray of light from the Sun of Righteousness illuminated these heavens. In the unnumbered pages of Nature's immense volume there was not found one syllable on the Scheme of Redemption. No created eye had yet penetrated its depths; no human or angelic ear had yet been charmed with its

Divine harmonies. It remained a secret, a profound secret in the Divine mind till after the conception and development of sin—till Adam and his disconsolate wife were about to bid adieu to all the joys and pleasures of Eden. Then it was, in that dark and gloomy hour, when the poison of death was diffused throughout the entire constitution of that once happy pair, when despair filled their hearts, when they were about to look for the last time on the tree of life, on the groves, and flowers, and crystal streams of Eden, and when all the galleries of Heaven were filled with sympathetic spectators—then it was that Jehovah uttered that most mysterious and awfully sublime oracle, "*The Seed of the woman shall bruise the head of the Serpent.*"

This, I presume, was the most astonishing revelation that was ever made to Heaven, Earth, or Hell. It could, indeed, scarcely yet be called a revelation. It was rather an index of mercy pointing to some scheme of philanthropy in the Divine mind, which, however, no seraph yet understood, and which was for ages after called by way of eminence, "*The mystery.*"

Time passed on. A font of types was cast for the purpose of illustrating more perfectly this greatest of all wonders. Prophecy was also added for the same purpose. Moses, Isaiah, Jeremiah, Ezekiel, Daniel, and other prophets spoke in the most eloquent strains concerning a glorious system of things, which, however, they saw but obscurely in the far-distant future.

At length the Messiah himself appeared—God manifest in the flesh, the wonder of all wonders! He became a Prophet, and for three and a half years he instructed the people in things pertaining to the Kingdom of God. But finally the vail was rent, the new and living way was opened. and the great High Priest of the Christian Institution entered at once into the Holy of Holies, and there, in the presence of adoring millions, he demonstrated, through the offering of his own blood, how God can be just in justifying those who believe in Jesus. Rom. iii, 25, 26.

The mystery was then revealed to all the Cherubim, Seraphim, and redeemed in Heaven, and ten days after this it was also made known by the Apostles to the inhabitants of Jerusalem, through the inspiration of that Spirit which searches all things, yea, even the deep purposes and counsels of Jehovah. From Jerusalem the Apostles went to Samaria, thence to Antioch, and thence to the uttermost parts of the Earth. Every-where they proclaimed the mystery revealed, and the conditions on which all men might become citizens of Christ's Kingdom here, and obtain an abundant entrance into his Everlasting Kingdom hereafter.

What the Bible is, and what it is not.

The Bible, then, is a perfect revelation of a perfect system of Divine philanthropy, designed to promote the present happiness and to secure the eternal felicity of all who will believe it, receive it, and obey it. And hence says the beloved John, in the close of his narrative, "These things are written that ye may believe; and that believing ye may have life through his name." John xx, 31. And hence says Paul, in his letter to the Romans, "I am not ashamed of the Gospel of Christ; for it is the power of God for salvation to every one that believeth; to the Jew first, and also to the Greek: for in it," he says, "God's scheme of justification by faith *is revealed in order to faith.*" Romans i, 16, 17.

It is not necessary that I should pause to discuss here the true theory of inspiration. This is not required in order to a just and satisfactory conclusion. For whether we understand *how* God operates or not, of one thing we may always be assured, *that whatever he does is done perfectly*. And hence it follows, *a priori*, with all the certainty and force of demonstration, THAT THE HOLY SCRIPTURES ARE PERFECTLY ADAPTED TO THE PRESENT CONDITION, CAPACITY, WANTS, AND CIRCUMSTANCES OF MAN.

Result of the *a priori* argument.

I do not mean by this that the Bible contains a full and complete revelation of all the plans and purposes of Jehovah, nor that it contains such a revelation of even the whole system and economy of redemption, nor that it is all perfectly intelligible to any and every one who reads it. Such a book, however perfect in itself, would not be at all suited to the wants of man as he is. It is not merely the amount of knowledge contained in the Bible, nor the great simplicity of its language, which makes this wonderful Book what it is. *It is the perfect harmony of means and ends; it is the Divine adaptation of it a- a system to the entire wants of our nature*; *it is this which makes the Bible infinitely more perfect than any work which was ever composed by an uninspired man.*

In what the perfection of the Bible consists.

The Sun might have been so constituted as to impart ten times the present amount of heat and light to the solar system, but such an increase of these elements would certainly not have contributed to our enjoyment. The atmosphere might have been made to contain a much larger amount of the element which supports life and combustion, but this would very soon have exhausted the vital energies of the animal kingdom.

Illustrations.

There is a *relative* beauty, fitness, and adaptation in

every atom, sun, and system in the physical universe. And, in like manner, the elements of Divine harmony are just as perfectly adjusted and as gloriously displayed in all parts of the Holy Bible. The same Omniscient Being that created the oxygen, the hydrogen, the nitrogen, the carbon, and the other elements of our globe; that arranged and compounded them in reference to each other and to the wants and capacities of every species of organized beings, vegetable and animal, has also most benevolently framed the Holy Scriptures, and adapted them to the entire moral, social, and religious wants and circumstances of the whole human race.

Evidence drawn from the study and analysis of the Book itself.

This is not a mere theoretical or speculative inference. An analysis of the Book itself brings us to the same conclusion. Where, for instance, will you find another volume beneath the broad heavens which is so well adapted to the capacity of the old and the young, the wise and the unwise? The very child is often led, by the simplicity of the Bible narrative, to believe its Savior, to love him, and to rejoice through him on a bed of death as it would on a bed of roses, while at the same time the most gifted philosopher labors in vain in his efforts to comprehend the full import of its simple and unaffected utterances. He has, peradventure, exhausted the stores of human learning; he understands all that Leibnitz, La Place, Locke, and Newton ever wrote; he finds nothing in all the rich stores of human philosophy which is too profound for the genius and capacity of his mighty intellect: but he has read the Bible; he has re-read it; and a hundred times has he pondered, with equal profit, every word of its sacred pages; and yet he dies with the confession on his lips that he has never exhausted its rich treasures of wisdom and knowledge, and that, in fact, "the great ocean of truth still lies before him unexplored."

If any thing more is necessary in order to the full and complete demonstration of our main proposition, it may be found in the historical developments of Christianity. Even in the Patriarchal Age, those who followed the starlight of the Gospel were made holy and happy by it. "Enoch walked with God, and he was not; for God took him." Abraham was made and constituted the Father of the faithful, and in many respects honored above all the sages of antiquity, simply on account of his profound respect and reverence for the Word of the Lord. The wilderness of Arabia was a dark and gloomy solitude, but the Israelite who kept his eye on the Pillar of the Cloud by day, and the Pillar of Fire by night, was in no danger of falling into snares himself, nor of enticing others to forsake the narrow way which led to the Land of Promise. The Tabernacle, like the New Jerusalem, received no light from the Sun, the Moon, or the stars. A fourfold covering of fine linen, goats' hair, rams' skins, and badgers' skins excluded every ray of external light from the inner Courts of that symbolic edifice, but the Priests who walked in the light of the Shekinah and golden Candlestick had no need of the light of nature.

Evidence drawn from the historical developments of the Scheme of Redemption.

First, from the Patriarchal Age.

Secondly, from the Jewish Age.

But still more full and glorious was the light of the Sun of Righteousness. Looking down through the long vista of future ages, Isaiah beheld the wilderness and the solitary places rejoicing under the genial and transforming power of this most glorious luminary of the moral universe. Under his renewing influence the eyes of the blind were opened, the

Thirdly, from prophecies respecting the Christian Age.

ears of the deaf were unstopped, the lame man leaped as a hart, the tongue of the dumb began to sing, and the way of holiness became perfectly plain to the eye of the astonished Prophet.

This way seems to have especially attracted his attention; and therefore he very narrowly and carefully considered whatever he saw upon it. The passengers were all men and women of holy and spotless character. There was no lion there, nor any other kind of ravenous beast; and no unclean person polluted it. But there were the *pious* of every rank and order. There was the true philosopher; and there was the man of the weakest intellect—one

> "—— who never had a dozen thoughts
> In all his life, and never changed their course,
> But told them o'er, each in its customed place,
> From morn till night, from youth till hoary age.
> Little above the ox which grazed the field
> His reason rose: so weak his memory
> That the name his mother called him by he scarce
> Remembered; and his judgment so untaught,
> That what at evening played along the swamp
> Fantastic, clad in robe of fiery hue,
> He thought the Devil in disguise, and fled
> With quivering heart and winged footsteps home.
> The word philosophy he never heard,
> Nor science; never heard of liberty,
> Necessity, nor laws of gravitation:
> And never had an unbelieving doubt."

And yet that man was one of the Redeemed: he was one of the ransomed of the Lord, who were returning and coming to Zion with songs and everlasting joys on their heads; and who shall hereafter walk the golden streets of the New Jerusalem.

This glorious vision of the Prophet was even more than realized by the Primitive Church. In Jerusalem, for instance, through the simple instrumentality of the

Word of God and the demonstra..ons of the Holy Spirit, three thousand persons were on one day translated from darkness to light, and from under the power and dominion of Satan into the Kingdom of God's dear Son. No doubt was then entertained about the Apostles' meaning. The way of salvation was made so very plain that all understood it. *The people simply heard the Word; they believed it; they obeyed it; and on the same day or night, as the case might be, they were added to the congregation of the saved.* See Acts, *passim.*

Fourthly, from the history of the Primitive Church.

But they did not stop there. *They continued steadfast in the Apostles' teaching, and in the fellowship, and in the breaking of the loaf, and in the prayers. And great grace was upon them all.* Acts ii, 41-47.

Why, then, has not this happy state of things always continued in the Church? Why has not Christianity, ere this, triumphed over all opposition? Why have the kingdoms of this world not yet become the kingdoms of our Lord and of his Christ? Why has not every city on earth become a Jerusalem? And why has not every succeeding day of the reign of Heaven been a new Pentecost?

Why Christianity has not, ere this, universally triumphed.

It is not because the Gospel has changed. It is not because the Bible is now less adapted to the genius, wants, and circumstances of man than it was eighteen hundred years ago. But it is simply *because the followers of the Lord Jesus Christ have not always, like the primitive Christians, continued steadfast in the Apostles' teaching.* Like the ancient Jews, they have committed two great evils; they have, in a great measure, ignored the Bible, and they have substituted for it the vain and empty dreams and speculations of human philosophy.

These are certainly very strange and marvelous phenomena in the history of human nature. We might reasonably suppose that the children would have learned more wisdom from the experience of their fathers: that four thousand years of darkness, superstition, misery, and crime, would have taught mankind the folly of attempting to solve the great problems of human happiness and human destiny, without the aid of Divine Revelation; and that no one who had once beheld the full-orbed glories of the Sun of Righteousness would ever again be bewildered by the *ignis fatuus* of an empty, deceitful, and false philosophy.

Unreasonableness of this course of conduct.

"When the young eagle, with exulting eye,
Has learned to dare the splendor of the sky,
And leave the Alps beneath him in his course,
To bathe his wings in morn's empyreal source;
Will his free wing from that majestic hight
Descend to follow some wild meteor's light,
Which far below, with evanescent fire,
Shines to delude, and dazzles to expire?—
No! still through clouds he wings his upward way,
And proudly claims his heritage of day."

But it should be remembered that the eagle has never suffered from the evil and pernicious influences of a false education. It has never felt the enslaving power of prejudice. This is one of the evil demons that are found only in the human heart; and it is, moreover, the very last of the legion that relinquishes its dominion over the powers and susceptibilities of the soul.

How accounted for.

The Apostles were certainly as free from its influence as are most other men. Their occupations, habits of life, and idiosyncrasies of character, were all favorable to at least an ordinary degree of mental independence. But a term of three and a

Illustrations of the power of prejudice.

half years in the School of Him who taught as never man taught, was not sufficient to free their minds from the obnoxious biases of a false education. So great, indeed, was the power of prejudice over their whole intellectual and moral nature, that they did not and could not, for the time, understand some of the plainest and most important oracles that ever fell from the lips of their Divine Master. What, for instance, could be plainer than the language of the Commission: "Go ye, therefore, into all the world, and preach the Gospel to every creature?" But the demon of prejudice whispered in their ear: "This means every creature of the elect world." And when, on the day of Pentecost, Peter said to his inquiring auditors, "The promise is to you, and to your children, and to all that are afar off, even to as many as the Lord our God shall call," the broad and very comprehensive terms of this proclamation were at once restricted in his mind to the narrow limits of his own sectarian creed.*

The Apostles had yet no idea that the Gentiles were about to be made fellow-heirs with the Jews: the mystery was not even yet revealed to them in all its length, and breadth, and fullness. And hence it was necessary to convince Peter, by a special miracle, that God is no respecter of persons, but that in every nation, he that feareth him and worketh righteousness is accepted of him, before he would consent to proclaim the good news and glad tidings of life and salvation even to the family and friends of the devout Cornelius.

But while he was speaking, "the Holy Spirit fell on all them who heard the word. And they of the Circumcision who believed were astonished, as many as came

* It is evident, therefore, that even the fullest and highest degrees of inspiration bestowed on the Apostles did not make them *omniscient*

with Peter, because that on the Gentiles also was poured out the gift of the Holy Spirit: for they heard them speak with tongues and magnify God."

This was, of course, sufficient evidence to satisfy Peter and his six brethren who accompanied him. But the prejudice of the multitude was not yet removed. The report was, no doubt, soon circulated far and wide that Peter—yes, the bold, courageous, and heroic Peter—had transcended the limits not only of the Commission, but even of the Divine benevolence. And therefore, when he came up to Jerusalem, he was summoned to appear before his Jewish brethren to answer to the grave charge, "*Thou wentest in to men uncircumcised, and didst eat with them.*" But when they heard Peter's defense "they held their peace and glorified God, saying, Then hath God also to the Gentiles granted repentance unto life."

Mingling of Jewish Traditions and Gentile Philosophy with Christianity.

Henceforth the *extension* of the Commission was a settled question; but its *comprehension* was still a subject of earnest debate and bitter controversy. The Hebrew converts were exceedingly zealous for the traditions of their fathers, and many of their teachers still said to the people, "Unless ye be circumcised and keep the Law of Moses, ye can not be saved." From their infancy their minds had been thoroughly molded in their own Rabbinical traditions. They saw every thing through a false medium, and therefore they never did and never could enjoy the pure sunlight of Heaven's own effulgence. Like their fathers they still continued to make void the law of the Lord by mixing and commingling with it the doctrines, precepts, and commandments of men.

The influence of Gentile prejudice was equally pernicious. If the Jewish mind was fettered by the false theology of the Scribes and Pharisees, the Gentile mind was equally enslaved by the tenets of Plato, Aristotle, Zeno, Epicurus, Zoroaster, and other distinguished party leaders.

It is true, indeed, that for a short time the power of the Gospel seemed to neutralize and triumph over every thing else. Under its potent influence some of the worst forms of human nature were molded into the image and likeness of Him who became flesh and dwelt among us. Many of the Egyptian, Persian, Grecian, Roman, and other idolatrous tribes and families renounced their superstitions, destroyed their idols, and consecrated themselves in body, soul, and spirit to the service of the Lord.

Bad effects of this on the Church.

But the early impressions of a false education were not yet wholly eradicated. Nothing short of a special miracle could have done this. Evil habits became a second nature, and therefore it was an easy matter for the Tempter to revive old associations. Soon the old leaven began to work. The Bible was neglected. And from that hour the rites and ceremonies of Heathen Mythology have been more or less associated with the pure Gospel in nearly every society on Earth that claims to be the Church of Christ. Rome is full of them. And even Protestantism has not yet been wholly purified from the leprous contact of Pagan and Papal abominations.

Apology for the Leaders of the Protestant Reformation.

By this I do not intend to detract one iota from the honor that is due to the great and good Reformers of the sixteenth, seventeenth, eighteenth, and nineteenth centuries. They have turned many to righteousness, and will, therefore, shine as stars of the first magnitude in the firmament of God's Everlasting Kingdom.

But if the Apostles, inspired as they were, did not for some years understand the full import of their own mission, surely it is not wonderful that men, educated in the lore of mystic Babylon, should fail to comprehend at once the length and breadth, the depth and hight of the truth as it is revealed to us in the Living Oracles. If with an honest heart and a good conscience Peter could say to the people, "The promise is to you and to your children, and to all that are afar off," and nevertheless continue to treat the whole Gentile world as unclean, surely it is no marvel that Luther should disclaim against the errors of popery while he was himself celebrating mass; that Calvin should oppose the persecutions o. Rome and at the same time cause Michael Servetus to be put to death chiefly on account of his opposition to the doctrine of the Trinity; and that Chillingworth should proclaim that "the Bible, the whole Bible, and nothing but the Bible is the religion of Protestants," and yet consent to fetter the minds of the rising generation with the erroneous formulæ of an uninspired creed. Nay, verily, let us rather wonder that since these fathers fell asleep so few have risen to plead for the paramount claims of Divine Revelation.

Continued inexcusable neglect of the Bible.

It is true that during the present eventful century much has been done for the cause of the Bible and the restoration of primitive Christianity. But how much still remains to be done in order to restore the Holy Scriptures to their proper place as the only infallible and authoritative standard of Christian education, Christian faith, and Christian practice! How many parents in every community pay little or no regard to the religious education of their children! How many still continue to mold the minds of their infant offspring in the patent forms of Edinburgh, Westminster, or Philadelphia! How little Bible reading, not to speak of Bible *training*, is now required and practiced in the Church, in the School, or in the family! And even in our Theological Seminaries how often is the Bible laid aside and treated as a mere work of reference, while the minds of the students are thoroughly cast and molded in the Institutes of Calvin, the Divinity of Dwight, or the Theological System of some other uninspired man! And as a consequence of all this neglect, how seldom is the Bible made a theme of conversation in any of the public, or private, or social circles of modern Christendom!

No evidence of its want of power and adaptation that it does not produce effects where it is not.

Such, then, are, in brief, the reasons why the last eighteen centuries have not been one continued and uninterrupted season of refreshing from the presence of the Lord. It has not been owing to any fault or deficiency in Heaven's appointed means, but simply to the general and inexcusable neglect of them. The Bible can not produce or effect a change where it is not. It must be received into the understanding and cherished in the heart before it can reform the life. No one ascribes imperfection to the Sun because it does not give color to the flower that blooms in the dungeon. It is sufficient evidence of its perfection that it gives health and vitality to every thing that comes within the sphere of its influence. This is all that we claim for the light of Divine Revelation. And this much we have now proved *a priori* and *a posteriori*.

Still, however, it may be well to draw a few additional

facts from the records of history. Every successive period of the Christian Era furnishes some new proof that the Bible is divinely adapted to the wants and genius of human nature. Even during the world's midnight, when darkness covered the Earth, and gross darkness, the people, the few who followed the Star of Bethlehem, safely navigated the sea of life and found a calm and sure repose in the heaven of eternal rest.

Further historical evidence of its elevating and sanctifying power and tendencies.

As we pass from the eleventh to the sixteenth century the light gradually increases. And since the beginning of the German Reformation facts have so accumulated that the historical evidence of this period alone now amounts to a moral demonstration. Indeed, any correct geographical atlas or map of the present state of the world is sufficient to satisfy any one who honestly, and without prejudice, seeks for the truth on this subject. What is it, for instance, that has so far elevated Protestant England over Catholic Spain and priest-ridden Italy? Why are these United States so far superior to Mexico and the South American Republics in all that serves to adorn, refine, and purify human nature? The primary and chief cause of all this can be found only in their greater respect and reverence for the Holy Scriptures. You can not find it in the fertile soil of these countries; you can not find it in their balmy atmosphere; nor can you find it even in their civil and political institutions. But you can find it in the relative use that these people have made of that heaven-inspired Volume in which God has given to us all things which pertain to life and godliness.

Argument by approximation.

I know that this argument is only an approximation toward the point at which we aim.

But if the natural philosopher can justly infer that a ball rolled on a plane surface would forever move in a straight line, were it not opposed by some external forces—which forces, however, he can never wholly remove—then, indeed, may not the Christian philosopher conclude, with equal certainty, that if all things which now oppose the truth were taken out of the way, and the Bible were allowed to exert all its Divine influence on the human soul, it would, with the blessing of God and the renewing and sanctifying energies of the Holy Spirit, very soon reunite all the scattered fragments of the Christian world, and cause the moral deserts of the Earth to rejoice and blossom as the rose.

Argument drawn from the plastic nature of the infant mind and the power of truth.

Such, in fact, is the attractive power of the Living Oracles that all the obstacles of a false education and the inventions of modern priestcraft are not sufficient to keep apart the purest and most enlightened members of sectarian Churches. Ever and anon the unnatural and unscriptural bonds of these associations are burst asunder, and, like purest drops of heavenly dew, their kindred spirits mingle into one. This has often happened, especially during the last fifty years, and such events will become more and more frequent as we progress in Biblical knowledge and *Biblical education.* For if such is the plastic nature of the infant mind that it may, during the process of its development, be easily cast into the mold of Mahometanism, Brahmanism, Buddhism, Catholicism, or any of the numerous forms of Protestantism, it would be strange, indeed, if a system framed by the finger of God, and divinely adapted to all the wants, capacities, and circumstances of the human soul should fail to unite in the bonds of Christian love and affection all who have been properly educated in all its gracious provisions, and who honestly seek to know the truth as it has been revealed to us by the Holy Spirit.

The present great want of Christendom.

The great want, then, of Christendom, at this time, is a more general, thorough, and systematic course of BIBLE TRAINING. And by this I do not mean that we need merely more preaching, teaching, and exhortation. All these are, of course, necessary, but none of them will supply the want of *Bible training*. It is one thing to impart knowledge to the human mind, and quite another to so train, develop, and discipline that mind that it may be fully qualified to receive, appropriate, and enjoy the knowledge imparted. Many a youth ten years of age knows more now about the Scheme of Redemption than did Abraham, Moses, Isaiah, or even John the Baptist. But it would be very difficult to find a youth in the nineteenth century who has received a better *religious education* than that which was severally enjoyed by these ancient worthies.

The minds of the rising generation must, then, be developed and thoroughly molded in the Living Oracles. We would not, of course, exclude all other books and sources of information, but we would regard and treat them all as subordinate to the Bible. The Book of Life has too long been laid on the shelf as a mere work of reference. We would take it down from its neglected position; we would wipe away from it the accumulated dust of ages. We would substitute it for the licentious novel, and every other form of corrupt literature in the family circle; for all human systems and bodies of Divinity in the Theological Seminary; and in every School, Academy, College, and University we would make it a subject of as profound study and as rigid examination as the Logic of

Aristotle, the Geometry of Euclid, or the Fluxions of Newton.

Let this mode of instruction be generally adopted in every department of education; let the minds and hearts of the youth of both sexes be thoroughly molded in the Institutes of Heaven's own appointment; and soon, very soon, the voice of the apocalyptic angel will be heard proclaiming under the whole heavens, "*The kingdoms of this world are become the kingdoms of our Lord and of his Christs.*"

Anticipated results of such a course of Bible training.

PART IV.

CHURCH ORGANIZATION, COOPERATION, AND DISCIPLINE.

Fundamental principles of Church organization, coöperation, and discipline.

IT will, perhaps, be a saving of both time and space if we consider here, first of all, some of the fundamental principles of Church organization, coöperation, and discipline. Observe, then,

I. *That the Church of Christ is really but* ONE BODY. The proof of this will be found in the following passages:

Unity of the Church.

1. Romans xii, 4, 5: "For as we have many members in one body, and all the members have not the same office, so we, being many, are *one body* in Christ, and every one members one of another."

2. 1 Cor. x, 17: "For we, being many, are one bread and *one body;* for we are all partakers of the one bread."

3. 1 Cor. xii, 12, 13: "For as the body is one, and hath many members, and all the members of that one body, being many, are one body, so also is *Christ*; (that is, *the Church* as united in him. 1 Cor. vi, 15.) For by one Spirit are we all baptized into *one body*, whether we be Jews or Gentiles, whether we be bond or free; and have all been made to drink into one Spirit."

4. Eph. i, 22, 23: "And (God) hath put all things under his (Christ's) feet, and has given him to be the Head over all things to the Church, which is his *body*, the

fullness of Him that filleth all in all." See, also, Col. i, 24.

5. Eph. iv, 4: "There is *one body* and one Spirit, even as ye are called in one hope of your calling."

II. *This one body is composed of an indefinite number of members, all of whom are most intimately related to each other, and are required to labor and coöperate for each other's good, as well as for the increase and edification of the whole body.* See Rom. xii, 4–21; 1 Cor. xii, 7–27; Eph. iv, 16, etc.

Mutual relations and obligations of its members.

III. *But, nevertheless, for the sake of order, convenience, and efficiency, this one body may be divided into as many churches or congregations as may be thought necessary; each one of which, when fully organized, should have its own corps of Elders and Deacons.* And hence we read, in the New Testament, of the Church of Jerusalem, the Church of Antioch, the Church of Ephesus, the Church of Corinth, etc.

Local divisions of the one body; for what purpose.

IV. *Care should be taken, however, not to multiply congregations beyond what is really necessary.* We should never lose sight of the fact that, "in union there is strength; and in separation there is weakness." By carrying the process of division too far we may lose much more than we gain by the operation. And hence the unity of the Church, even in the matter of its organization, should be preserved and maintained as far as practicable. This is well illustrated by the history of the Church during the apostolic age. In the provinces of Galatia, Asia, Macedonia, Judea, etc., we read of a plurality of Churches; because, in such districts, the members could not, without great inconvenience, meet together in one place for public and social worship. 1 Cor. xvi, 1 19; 2 Cor. viii, 1; Gal. i, 22, etc. But in each of the large

Their numb limited.

cities, such as Jerusalem, Antioch, Ephesus, Corinth, etc., we read of but one congregation of Christians. Acts viii, 1; xiii, 1; xx, 17; 1 Cor. i, 2. It would seem, however, from sundry passages in the New Testament, that the members of at least some of these Churches were in the habit of meeting together in different parts of the same city for social worship; just as we now frequently meet for prayer and praise in such private houses as may best suit the convenience of members living in different localities. See Rom. xvi, 5; 1 Cor. xvi, 19; Col. iv, 15; and Philemon 2.

Every member of the one body, a member, also, of some one local congregation.

V. *Every member of the one body is, also, de facto, a member of some one congregation, to which he is personally responsible, and with which he is bound to coöperate in all that pertains to the glory of God, the edification of the Church, and the conversion of the world.* I have no objection to the common practice of giving to those recently baptized in a Church the hand of Christian affection, provided it be done, not for the purpose of receiving them into the Church as members, for which there is not the slightest authority in the word of God, but simply as a fraternal *recognition* of their existing membership. But I do protest against the opinion entertained by some, that a man may be baptized and yet be irresponsible to any Church or body of disciples; or that he may receive from the Church of which he is a member a letter of commendation, and then be irresponsible to any Church so long as he may see fit to retain said letter in his own possession. Good order requires that every Christian shall be responsible to the Church where he is baptized, and from the moment of his baptism. If for any valid reason he wishes to leave said Church, even on the self-same day of his adoption, let him receive from it a letter of commendation to the congregation nearest to the place of his destination. If he neglects or refuses to identify himself with it, let him be called to an account by the Church that recommended him, and to whom he is still responsible, so long as he retains their letter of commendation. It is high time that these wandering stars should be arrested in their erratic course, and that every Christian should be made to feel that he is responsible to his brethren for his regular attendance on the ordinances of God, and his general demeanor as a member of the body of Christ

VI. *In all purely local matters, such as pertain to their own order and discipline, the aforesaid congregations are independent of each other; and should ordinarily be allowed to manage their own affairs, according to the word of God, in whatever way they may think best.* This is evidently implied in the divinely authorized division of the one body into separate and distinct local congregations. The separation was made wholly for the sake of convenience; for the purpose of simplifying the machinery of the Church, and of more accurately defining the duties, obligations, and responsibilities of the several members in their several localities. And hence there is not given in the New Testament a single instance of one congregation's interfering in any way with the local interests of another. Every one was allowed and required to manage its own affairs according to the laws of Christ, without let or hinderance. See Acts and Paul's Epistles, *passim.*

Independency of the local congregations.

VII. *But in all matters of general interest, such as pertain to the increase, order, power, glory, and efficiency of the whole body, these several congregations may and should coöperate, whenever by*

Their right and duty to coöperate.

so doing they can better accomplish any of the great and benevolent objects for which the Church was established on Earth. Their right to do so is clearly implied,

1. In their relations to each other as members of the one body. Their separate organizations are purely for the sake of convenience and efficiency in relation to personal and local matters. But they are, nevertheless, still but members of the one body; and are, therefore, of course bound to coöperate with each other in all that pertains to its growth and prosperity. This follows with just as much certainty from our premises as that the different persons composing any one congregation are bound to coöperate with each other for its welfare.

2. It is implied in the example and practice of the apostolic Churches. The congregations of Galatia, Macedonia, and Achaia, for instance, coöperated with each other in giving relief to the poor saints in Judea. See Rom. xv, 26, 27; 1 Cor. xvi, 1–4; 2 Cor. viii, 1–5, 13, 14, 23; ix, 1–4, etc.

3. It is implied in the nature and extent of the work which is to be accomplished. This may all be summed up under the two following heads:

(1.) The conversion of the world, and

(2.) The edification or proper religious education of the converts.

Of these we will speak more particularly in the two following chapters.

CHAPTER I.

CONVERSION OF THE WORLD.

More than eighteen hundred years have passed away since the Gospel was first proclaimed to the world as "the power of God for the salvation of every one that believeth." But nevertheless its triumphs are yet very far from being complete. Of the twelve hundred millions of human being who now inhabit the Earth, more than eight hundred millions are still under the shadow of Death, without God and without hope in the world.

Triumphs of the Gospel as yet but partial.

Why is this? Is it because God is not willing that all men should be made happy by believing and obeying the Gospel? Surely not, for he "so loved the world that he gave his only begotten Son, that whosoever believeth in him should not perish, but have everlasting life." Is it, then, owing to any want of sympathy on the part of Christ or to any deficiency in the provisions of the Gospel? It can not be, for Christ is the same yesterday, to-day, and forever. His sympathy for our fallen, wretched race is just as great now as it was when, by the grace of God, he tasted death for every man, and the Gospel is in all respects the same to-day that it was when, eighteen hundred years ago, it triumphed over all the combined opposition of the Roman empire.

This not owing to a deficiency in any of the Divine elements.

But there is a human as well as a Divine side to this question. The Scheme of Redemption is itself all of

God, and in a very important sense, too, its success and final triumphs are all of God. 1 Cor. iii, 7, etc. But, nevertheless, to us has been committed the word of reconciliation, (2 Cor. v, 19;) the Church has been made the pillar and support of the truth, (1 Tim. iii, 15;) she is the candlestick or moral luminary by means of which the light of Divine truth is to be dispensed throughout the whole Earth. Isaiah lx, 1–3; Matt. v, 14; Rev. i, 20.

Part of the work assigned to man.

How this work is to be done is not fully stated in the Holy Scriptures. Many of the details of the enterprise are wisely and of necessity left to the discretion ot the Church herself. But,

Extent to which every man is responsible for the salvation of the world.

I. *It is made the duty of every man to do what he can, consistently with the word of God, for the conversion of the world.* "Let us not," says Paul, "grow weary in well-doing: for in due season we shall reap if we faint not. As we have, therefore, opportunity, *let us do good to all men,* but especially to them who are of the household of faith." Gal. vi, 9, 10. And again he says, "We thus judge that if one died for all, then were all dead; and that he died for all, that they who live should not henceforth live to themselves, but to him who died for them and rose again." 2 Cor. v, 14, 15. Every man, therefore, who has been redeemed by the blood of Christ, whatever may be his rank or calling, is solemnly bound to make the salvation of the world (including, of course, that of his own soul) the supreme object of his life and labors. This is, in fact, the only way in which he can live to and for Christ. No living man can serve him in any other way or in any other part of his dominions. The regulation and government of the Sun, Moon,

Evidence of this.

and stars fall not within the limits of our jurisdiction. The Earth is at present our only field of labor, and it presents but two ultimate objects in behalf of which it is possible for us to exert our energies. Every thought, every word, and every action of our lives, whatever may be its proximate results, must ultimately serve to establish and strengthen either the Kingdom of Christ or the Empire of Satan. It is a great delusion to suppose that *self* may constitute a third object, that we may live for ourselves without exercising an influence for good or for evil upon others. There is, of necessity, a reciprocal influence exercised between the one and the many. This is just as fixed as are the laws and forces of universal gravitation. You might as well attempt to place an atom of matter beyond the limits of solar attraction as to dissolve the ties that bind the individual to society. And hence it follows that the man who lives for self lives for Satan. The man who is not with Christ is against him, and he who gathers not into the Kingdom of God's dear Son is giving his influence to enlarge the dominions of the Evil One.

But the most direct evidence of this is to be found in the second and last great Commission given by Christ to his disciples, (Rev. xxii, 17:) "LET HIM THAT HEARETH SAY, COME." The first Commission was given directly to the Apostles and through them to the Church only by implication. Matt. xxviii, 18–20. But this second Commission is given expressly not only to the Church, but more particularly to every member of the Church. "Let him that heareth say, Come," is the gracious command of our blessed Lord to every one of his true and faithful disciples.

This does not, of course, imply that it is the duty of

every disciple to go, as did the Apostles, into all the world and preach the Gospel to every creature. For this he may not be qualified either by nature or by education. But these gracious and solemn words of Christ evidently do imply and require,

Import of the second and last Commission: "Let him that heareth say, Come."

1. *That every man who has the necessary qualifications should, as far as possible, devote his whole life to the ministry of the Gospel.* This is a call, a Divine call, to every disciple who has the necessary talents and acquirements to consecrate himself wholly and entirely to the proclamation of the Word. He is hereby authorized and required to say to all men, so far as he may have the opportunity to do so, Come to the Savior; come to the Lamb of God that taketh away the sin of the world; take his yoke upon you and learn of him, and you shall find rest to your souls.*

2. *It is evidently implied in these words of our Redeemer that every disciple of his, however destitute of intellectual and literary qualifications he may be, should communicate the good news and glad tidings of life and salvation to others, privately and socially.* He is hereby authorized and required to say, in all his social intercourse with his own family, and friends, and neighbors, and fellow-citizens, "Come to the Savior; come to Mount Zion, and to the city of the Living God, the heavenly Jerusalem; and to an innumerable company of angels; and to the general assembly and Church of the first-born whose names are enrolled in heaven; and to God the Judge of all; and to the spirits of just men made perfect;

*This passage, however, authorizes no one to go out as an Evangelist without the consent of his brethren. *They* must in all cases judge of his qualifications for the work.

and to Jesus the Mediator of the New Covenant; and to the blood of sprinkling which speaketh better things than Abel." Hebrews xii, 22, 24.

This was the primitive order of things, and this is the natural order. And hence they that were scattered abroad from Jerusalem on account of the first persecution went every-where preaching the Word. Acts viii, 4. There was no attempt made to compromise with the false etiquette of the world in this matter; no stopping to consider how men of wealth, and learning, and fashion would regard the simple story of the Cross. Not at all. Out of the abundance of their hearts they simply and joyfully communicated to others the good news of salvation through a once crucified, but now risen and glorified Savior. And just so it will ever be. So long as it is written, "Out of the abundance of the heart the mouth speaketh," (Matthew xii, 34,) so long will every *consistent* disciple of the Lord Jesus make the story of the Cross the main burden of his conversation in all his intercourse with his fellow-men. To all such it must ever be a source of unspeakable pleasure to be able to say to the dying and destitute every-where, "Come and take of the bread and water of life freely." Isaiah lv, 1, and Rev. xxii, 17.

3. *This is a commission to all the followers of the Lord Jesus Christ, to preach to the people not only in word, but also in deed; not only by precept, but also by example.* It is a commission to let our light so shine before others, that they, seeing our good works, may thereby be constrained to glorify our Father who is in heaven." And especially is it a commission to us all, and a most solemn requisition upon us all, *to contribute liberally of our means for the comfort and support of those who are able and willing to go forth into all the world and preach the Gospel to*

every creature. In this way we can all say indirectly to the benighted of all nations, "Come to the Lamb of God that taketh away the sin of the world."

Every congregation responsible for the proclamation of the Gospel.

II. *It is the duty of every congregation of disciples, so far as they have the ability and opportunity, to preach the Gospel to the unconverted in their midst, and also in other adjacent destitute communities.* This may be proved,

Proof.

1. From what has been said of the duties of the several members of the Church. For what is a congregation of disciples but an association of Christians united together for the purpose of doing jointly what they could not so well do by each one's acting in his own separate and individual capacity? Romans xii, 4–8, and 1 Cor. xii, 4–27, etc. And hence every congregation of Christians is really an evangelical society, divinely ordained and authorized to send out missionaries of the Cross whenever and wherever she may have the means and the opportunity to do so.

2. From the example and practice of the primitive Church. The Church of Jerusalem, for instance, sent out Barnabas as a missionary to Antioch, (Acts xi, 22,) and after that Church was firmly established and well supplied with Prophets and Teachers they were required to send out Paul and Barnabas on one of the most important and successful evangelical tours recorded in the New Testament. Acts xiii and xiv.

The Churches jointly responsible for the conversion of the world.

III. *It is the privilege, and, I may add, the duty, of all the Churches in any given district to coöperate with each other to the full extent of their ability, through their Elders, Evangelists, or other chosen representatives, in sending the Gospel to foreign lands, and in making disciples of all the nations*

This is a work which, of course, requires the *united* efforts of many Churches, and to the extent of this coöperation there is no limit whatever prescribed in the Word of God. Whether the association should consist of all the disciples within the limits of a village, or a city, or a county, or a state, or a nation, or a continent, or the world is a matter of mere expediency, which God has wisely and benevolently left to our own discretion. For be it remembered that after we shall have made all the divisions and subdivisions that may be thought necessary for the sake of convenience, there is, nevertheless, still, by Divine appointment, but the ONE BODY, (Ephesians iv, 4,) and that it has been made the pillar and support of the truth. 1 Timothy iii, 15.

Limited rights and privileges of such a coöperation of Churches.

In every such coöperation, however, great care should be taken to introduce no principle or line of policy which is inconsistent with the Scriptural rights and privileges of the several Churches. The delegates who compose it are but the *representatives* of their respective congregations, and they have, therefore, no right to legislate on matters of faith and piety, nor to make money in any way or in any sense a condition of membership, nor to adopt such a constitution or code of laws as will allow unconverted and wicked men to become members of the coöperation. But they have a right, as the representatives of the body of Christ, to transact all their legitimate business by the common rules of decorum and good order, and to use whatever means may be found necessary in order that the Gospel may be preached to every creature.

It is evidently, then, the duty of all Christians to labor and strive together in every way that they can consistently with the word of God for the conversion of the whole world. And if they had all done so from the beginning, how very different would now be the moral, social, and religious condition of our fallen and perishing race! How many of those in heathenish darkness might now be rejoicing in the full light of the glorious Gospel! And how many precious souls that are now in Hell, among the wailings and agonies of the damned—forever weeping, but not in Mercy's sight—O, how many of those lost ones might at this moment be tuning their golden harps among the redeemed in Heaven if the Church had but faithfully fulfilled her mission to the world!

Answer to query, *Why the Gospel has not universally triumphed.*

Here, then, we have the answer, and the only proper answer to the question, Why it is that the Gospel has not long since triumphed every-where. It is not, as before suggested, owing to any unwillingness on the part of God, or of Christ, or of the Holy Spirit; it is not owing to any deficiency in the Gospel scheme of salvation which God has so wisely and so perfectly adapted to the wants, capacities, and circumstances of all men; but it is simply owing to the fact that the Church has failed to do her duty. It is because so many of the professed followers of Christ have turned aside to vain jangling, and forgotten their mission of love and mercy to our perishing race, that the ways of Zion now mourn, and that the triumphs of the Gospel have been so very greatly retarded.

All that is wanting to success.

But let the Church be made pure; let her be forever separated from all her unholy alliances; let none but regenerated men and women be received into her communion and fellowship; let those be united as they should be in the bonds of love and peace; let them live worthy of their high and holy calling; let them make the Church, as far as practicable, the medium of all their active benevolence; let her be their alms society, their temperance society, their Bible society, and their missionary society; let her constitution be their only policy of insurance; let them regard her as their chief joy; let her courts be no longer deserted for the pleasures of the ball-room; let her social meetings be no longer forsaken for the honors of the lodge, or any other secular institution; let her increase and prosperity be the subject of their daily prayers; and soon will the iron, the clay, the brass, the silver, and the gold be broken in pieces together; soon will all vice be checked, oppressions cease, and error of every kind vanish as darkness before the rising Sun of the morning; soon will the world become one temple of praise; the nations will be united in the bonds of fraternal affection; glory will be ascribed to God in the highest; and on Earth peace and good-will abound to all men.*

* Queries for the Thoughtful.—I. Is it right for Christians to insure their lives and their property? Does such a course of conduct serve to cultivate in the hearts of those who indulge in it that sense of dependence on God, and that trust in his providence which the Scriptures so often commend, and which they always require? See, for instance, Matt. vi, 19–34.

II. Is it right for Christians to become members of such associations as the society of Masons, Odd-Fellows, etc.? Have they any time, money, or influence, for which they are not responsible to God, and which he does not require them to use in and through other channels of benevolence, for his own glory and the good of mankind? And, besides, is the obligation of secrecy enjoined by these societies entirely consistent with that spirit of candor, frankness, and mutual confidence, which is but the natural and legitimate effect of the Gospel on good and honest hearts; and which should, therefore, ever characterize all the members of the one body?

CHAPTER II.

EDIFICATION OF THE CHURCH.

Proof that the second great duty of the Church is to provide for the *edification* of her converts.

THAT it is the duty of the Church to provide for the edification (οἰκοδομή) of all her members is evident from the following passages:

1. Rom. xiv, 19: "Let us, therefore, follow after the things which make for peace, and things wherewith one may *edify* another."

2. Rom. xv, 2: "Let every one please his neighbor for his good to *edification*."

3. 1 Cor. x, 23: "All things are lawful for me, but all things are not expedient: all things are lawful for me, but all things *do not edify*."

4. 1 Cor. xiv, 3–5: "But he who prophesieth speaketh to men for *edification*, and exhortation, and consolation. He who speaketh in a foreign language *edifieth* himself; but he who prophesieth, *edifieth* the Church. I wish, indeed, that ye all spake in foreign languages, but rather that ye prophesied; for greater is he who prophesieth than he who speaketh in foreign languages, unless he interpret that the Church may receive *edification*."

5. 1 Cor. xiv, 12, 26: "Wherefore, ye also, since ye are earnestly desirous of spiritual gifts, seek them, that ye may abound for the *edification* of the Church. . . . . How is it, then, brethren? When ye come together every one of you hath a psalm, hath a doctrine, hath a foreign language, hath a revelation, hath an interpretation. *Let all things be done to edification*."

6. 2 Cor. xii, 19: "Again: think you that we excuse ourselves unto you? We speak before God in Christ, (that we do not;) but *we do all things*, dearly beloved, *for your edification*."

7. Eph. iv, 16: "From whom (Christ) the whole body fitly joined together and compacted by that which every joint supplieth, according to the effectual working in the measure of every part, maketh increase of the body unto the *edification of itself in love*." See, also, Acts ix, 31; 1 Cor. viii, 1; 2 Cor. x, 8; xiii, 10; Eph. iv, 12, 29; 1 Thess. v, 11, etc.

Derivation and meaning of the word *edify*.

The word *edify* (οἰκοδομέω, from οἶκος, a house, and δέμω, to build; Latin, *ædificio*, *ædes*, a house, and *facio*, to make,) means properly to build a house; then simply to build, to build up, to establish, to confirm. It is applied to the Church *metaphorically*, as the Temple, or habitation of God, through the Spirit; and in this very comprehensive sense it includes every thing which in any way serves to enlighten, educate, and improve the several members that compose the one body.

What the duty of Church edification comprehends and requires.

And hence it requires,

Instruction in the Holy Scriptures.

I. *That all the members of each and every congregation be regularly and systematically instructed in the Holy Scriptures.* Without this there can be no building up of the body of Christ. The Word of God is the food of the soul. Matt. iv, 4 It is that, says Paul, "which is able to *build you up*, and give you an inheritance among all them that are sanctified." Acts xx, 32. And hence it was that the primitive Christians "continued steadfast in the Apostles' *teaching*, and in the fellowship, and in the breaking of the loaf, and in the prayers." Acts ii, 42.

II . *That they be all required to study the Holy Scriptures for themselves.* Preaching and teaching are both necessary as a means of moral and religious edification. But they are not all that is necessary to this end. Unless the members of the Church can be induced to study the Scriptures for themselves, the most eloquent and appropriate instructions from others can accomplish but little. No one ever became an eminent mathematician, or linguist, or naturalist, or philosopher, by simply listening to a course of lectures. In order to excel in any of these departments of knowledge the hearer must become a ***student;*** he must himself be a co-worker with his instructors. And just so it is in religious matters. The man who would excel in his knowledge of the Scriptures, and have his soul cast into their mold of doctrine, must, like David, study them for himself by day, and meditate on them by night. And hence the necessity that every Christian family and Church shall be a school of Christ. We need the discipline of the nursery, and the Sunday school, and the Bible class, as well as the instructions of the pulpit.

The study of the Scriptures.

III. *That they diligently attend on all the ordinances of God's house.* These, like the ordinances of nature, are all divinely adapted to the capacity, wants, and circumstances of man as he is. They are the means by which, and the media through which, God pours into our hearts the rich streams of his grace, which ever flow from the unwasting fountains of his own benevolence. And hence we find that those who, like Zachariah and Elizabeth, "walk in all the commandments and ordinances of the Lord blameless," ***grow*** constantly in the favor, as well as in the knowledge of our Lord and Savior Jesus Christ.

Attention to God's Ordinances.

IV. *That they be all regularly and systematically engaged, according to their several capacities, in the work and service of the Church.* In no other way is it possible to educate properly their moral, social, and religious powers and susceptibilities. Every faculty of man's nature was made to be exercised, and hence the necessity that the life of every disciple should, like that of Christ, be one of constant activity. And just here lies the great secret of success in training and edifying a congregation; it consists simply in having every one of its members actively engaged in doing good in some way. It is a great mistake to suppose that the officers of a Church must do most of the work themselves. He is not the ablest and most successful general who does most of the fighting himself, but who so uses and manages his army as to bring out and successfully apply the strength, energy, and resources of all the men under his command. And just so it is in the army of the faithful. The Elders and Deacons of a congregation are but the generals and captains whose business it is to oversee, develop, direct, and apply to the best advantage the talents, learning, and other resources of its members. And hence their first duty is to see to it that all are earnestly and prayerfully engaged in some work of benevolence. Let every one do something. If a brother can not be a successful preacher or teacher he may, perhaps, make a good and efficient sexton. If a sister can not do the work of a Priscilla or a Phœbe, she may at least wash the saints' feet, or serve the Church in some way.

Activity of the members.

V. *That the wants of the poor, the sick, and the afflicted be well supplied.* No congregation of disciples can flourish while some of them,

Care for the poor.

like Dives, are faring sumptuously every day, and while others are, like Lazarus, lying at the gates and *begging* to be fed with the crumbs which fall from their tables. The rich must be made to feel that they are not their own, that they have been bought with a price, that their bodies, their souls, their spirits, their property, their time, their talents, and their all belong to God, and that it is, therefore, their business as good stewards of his manifold favors to dispense to the needy the rich bounties of his providence as they have opportunity. And on the other hand the poor must be made to realize that, if they are indeed the children of God, they are then heirs of all things, that their bread shall be given them, and their water shall be sure, and that those who seek the Lord and serve him faithfully shall not want any good thing. There is a *fellowship* (*κοινωνία*) in the Church of Christ which gives to all its members a right to whatever is really necessary to their comfort, and which, if properly understood, would render all secular policies of insurance wholly unnecessary.

Prompt payment of all debts.

VI. *That the Church herself, as well as her members, keep out of debt, and walk honestly toward them that are without.* "Owe no man any thing," says Paul, (Rom. xiii, 8,) "but to love one another." And this love must be out of a pure heart, and a good conscience, and faith unfeigned." 1 Tim. i, 5. Every other kind of indebtedness serves to paralyze our energies, disqualify us for the enjoyment of religion ourselves, and unfit us for exercising a proper influence on those around us. It is useless to recommend to others the religion of the Lord Jesus Christ while we are ourselves neglecting the principles of common justice. "*Let*," then, "your light so shine before men that they may see your good works and glorify your father who is in Heaven." Matt. v, 16.

VII. *That in order to meet promptly all the wants and liabilities of the Church, as well as for the purpose of cultivating in themselves habits of systematic benevolence, all her members be encouraged to contribute liberally of their substance to the treasury of the Lord on the First Day of every week, as they may have severally prospered.* That this was the practice of the primitive Church is, I think, evident from what follows: "Now concerning the collection which is for the saints, as I ordered the congregations of Galatia, so, also, do you. On the first day of every week let each of you lay by somewhat by itself, according as he may have prospered, putting it into the treasury: that when I am come there may then be no collections." 1 Cor. xvi, 1, 2.

Systematic contribution for benevolent purposes.

In this passage it is clearly implied and required,

1. That every member of the Church should give something for benevolent purposes.

2. That the amount contributed by each should be according to his ability, or in the ratio of his prosperity.

3. That this contribution, whatever it is, should be made weekly, on each and every successive Lord's Day.

The advantages of a scheme of systematic benevolence and ecclesiastical finance, founded on these elementary principles, are obviously very great. For,

Advantages resulting from a judicious scheme of systematic benevolence.

1. Such a practice would serve to create in every one an interest in the mission and welfare of the Church. "Where your treasure is," says Christ, "there will your heart be also." Matt. vi, 21 And hence it follows that, if we would induce men to

pray for the Church, to live for the Church, and, if need be, to die for the Church, we must first persuade them to contribute liberally of their means for her increase and support.

2. It would, also, serve to develop, mold, and perfect our Christian character, by the frequent and systematic exercise of all our moral and religious faculties. This is essential to the proper development and discipline of both head and heart. It is the means ordained by God for educating our whole spiritual nature, and making it subservient to the Divine will. And hence, if we would educate our benevolent affections properly, we must do so by contributing frequently for benevolent purposes. Giving annually, or quarterly, or even monthly, is not sufficient. It may, peradventure, be sufficient to relieve the wants of the poor and the destitute; but it can never secure to ourselves, as contributors, the full measure of God's benevolent purpose in making us the favored stewards of his bounty. It requires a long, severe, and systematic process of education in such matters, in order to enable us to *realize* the truth of the sentiment that "it is more blessed to give than to receive." Acts xx, 35.

3. These things, then, being so, it follows as another advantage of such a scheme, that more money can be raised in this way for benevolent purposes than by any system of annual, quarterly, or monthly contributions; and consequently, that by adopting it, the Church will always have at her command a greater amount of means for charitable and evangelical purposes. Whatever serves most to educate the heart and to engage the affections will, of course, have the greatest influence over the purse and fortunes of the individual.

VIII. *That all transgressors and delinquents be promptly waited on, and exhorted and encouraged to persevere in their begun Christian course.* "If a man be overtaken in a fault, ye who are spiritual restore such a one in the spirit of meekness; considering thyself, lest thou also be tempted." Gal. vi, 1. "Wherefore, lift up the hands which hang down and the feeble knees. Make straight paths for your feet, lest that which is lame be turned out of the way; but let it rather be healed." Heb. xii, 12, 13. "Brethren, if any of you do err from the truth and one convert him, let him know that he who converteth the sinner from the error of his way, shall save a soul from death, and hide a multitude of sins." James v, 19, 20. But any delay in this matter may be hazardous. It is generally an easy matter to check vice in its beginnings, but it is exceedingly difficult to do so after it has become a habit. And hence we are admonished to exhort one another daily while it is called *To-day*, lest any of us be hardened through the deceitfulness of sin." Heb. iii, 13.

Treatment of the weak and erring.

IX. *That the Church be kept in a pure and healthy condition.* That is, comparatively so. Absolute perfection is not to be expected in and of the Church militant. Some darnel will, of necessity, be found among the wheat till the time of the harvest. Matthew xiii, 24–30. But this is no reason why thorns, and briers, and thistles should be allowed to grow with it. Nothing can be more plainly taught in the Scriptures than that it is the duty of the Church to withdraw her fellowship from every member who persists in a disorderly course of conduct. Thus, for instance, Paul says to the Thessalonians, "Now we command you brethren, in the

Treatment of obstinate transgressors.

Right of the Church to excommunicate all such.

name of our Lord Jesus Christ, that you withdraw yourselves from every brother that walketh disorderly, and not according to the tradition which he received from us." 2 Thess. iii, 6. See, also, 1 Cor. v. And just so it was under the Law which was a shadow of good things to come. Every leprous and unclean person had to be removed from the camp in which God then dwelt symbolically as he now dwells in the Church by his Spirit. Numbers v, 1–4. It is not, then, a matter of choice or of privilege, but of imperative duty, that those who openly and obstinately transgress the laws of Christ shall be cut off from all the privileges of the Church and delivered to Satan for the destruction of the flesh, so that, if it be possible, their spirits may be saved in the day of the Lord Jesus.

Distinction between public and private offenses.

In dealing with such matters it is well to distinguish between public and private offenses; that is, between such as are committed against the Church herself, and those which are committed against some one of her members. The law in the latter case is laid down by Christ in Matthew xviii, 15–18, and requires,

The Law in relation to the latter.

1. That the offended party shall go to the offender, and tell him his fault between themselves alone. If they agree as to what is right and proper in the case, the matter is ended, and no further proceedings are necessary.

2. But if they do not agree, then the person offended is required to take with him one or two others who shall coöperate with him in trying to bring about a reconciliation. If they succeed, the whole matter is settled, the brother is gained, and peace restored.

3. But if the second effort should also fail to effect a

reconciliation, then the offended party is further required to lay the whole matter before the Church, and the brethren who coöperated with him in his last interview with the offender are now to serve as witnesses in the case. After this it is to be treated in all respects as a public offense.

Offenses committed against the Church are, of course, to be treated in like manner, with all allowable forbearance. The Elders, assisted by others distinguished for their wisdom, piety, and knowledge of the Holy Scriptures, are to do all in their power to bring the offender to repentance and reformation. If they succeed, all is well; the case may be simply reported to the Church, and the members allowed to express publicly, by rising or otherwise, their willingness to forgive the transgressor, and to retain and treat him as a brother.

Mode of treating public offenses.

But if the Elders do not succeed in bringing the offender to repentance, then their line of duty will generally be about as follows:

1. They should make out a clear and distinct *written* statement of the charge laid against him.

2. They should sustain the charge by clear and unmistakable evidence, or otherwise abandon the whole case.

3. If the charge is sustained, they should next decide the matter according to the law of Christ and the evidence submitted.

4. They should report the case to the congregation, stating clearly and distinctly the charge preferred, the facts proved, and the law of Christ in the case, in connection with their own verdict; and then they should require the whole congregation *to execute*, in a public and solemn manner, said verdict against the guilty person.

5. They should see to it that all the members act afterward in harmony with the expression given by the whole Church; that they really coöperate with each other in executing the sentence on the offender; that they abstain from holding any social intercourse with him; that might in any way serve to encourage him to persist in his sinful course.

6. They should still labor, however, as they best can, for his recovery and restoration. And if at any time they succeed in bringing him to repentance, they should immediately report his case to the Church, and again require the members to express publicly their willingness to forgive him and treat him as a brother in the Lord.

Authority for these proceedings.

For all this the following Scriptures furnish ample authority: Acts xx, 28; Romans xii, 8; 1 Thess. v, 12, 13; 1 Tim. iii, 5; v, 17; Heb. xiii, 7, 17, 24; 1 Peter v, 1–3; 1 Cor. v; and 2 Cor. ii, 6–11. From these and other like passages it is evident that in all such matters it is the business of the Elders *to teach* and *to rule*, and that it is the duty of the congregation *to execute* the sentence of the Elders on the guilty person according to the Law and evidence submitted. If this were done in all cases, the discipline of the Church would have an elevating and purifying influence that would soon be felt and acknowledged by all her members. But it is useless for a judge to pronounce sentence on a criminal if the sheriff and other officers of the government refuse to execute it.

Good effects of discipline properly administered.

Care for weak Churches.

X. *That all weak and sickly Churches, as well as individuals, be promptly and properly cared for.* True, indeed, as before said, the several Churches or congregations of which the one body is composed are largely independent of each other in all local matters. But, nevertheless, whenever any one of them is in danger of being corrupted or destroyed by false teaching, maladministration, or any thing else, it is the imperative duty of other Churches to interfere, in a prudent way, for its safety. This is plainly and positively required by the mutual relations that they all sustain to each other as members of the body of Christ. It will not do, as Paul very forcibly shows in his first letter to the Corinthians, for the hand to say to the foot, I have no need of thee; nor for the stomach to say to the other members, I will assert and maintain my independence by even taking poison whenever I please to do so. This is not in harmony with our mutual relations to each other as members of the one body. Every man is, in a certain sense and to a certain extent, independent of every other man. But, nevertheless, no true philanthropist would stand by and see his brother perish without interposing in his behalf, lest, peradventure, he might be charged with unduly interfering with his personal liberty! God did not so allow the world to perish in their folly.

Unity of faith and practice.

XI. *That unity of sentiment, faith, and practice be maintained, as far as possible, in all the Churches of the saints.* The great importance of this is well illustrated by the following passages:

Its importance illustrated.

1. Matthew xii, 25: "Every kingdom divided against itself is brought to desolation; and every city or house divided against itself can not stand."

2. John xvii, 20, 21: "Neither," says Christ, "pray I for these (my Apostles) alone; but for them also who shall believe on me through their word; that they all may be one· as thou Father art in me and I in thee, that thev

also may be one in us; that the world may believe that thou hast sent me."

3. 1 Cor. i, 10: "Now I beseech you, brethren," says Paul, "by the name of our Lord Jesus Christ, that ye all speak the same thing, and that there be no divisions among you; but that ye be perfectly joined together in the same mind and in the same judgment."

4. Ephesians iv, 1–6: "I, therefore, the prisoner of the Lord, beseech you that ye walk worthy of the vocation wherewith ye are called; with all lowliness and meekness, with long-suffering, forbearing one another in love; endeavoring to keep the unity of the Spirit in the bond of peace. There is one body and one Spirit, even as ye are called in one hope of your calling: one Lord, one faith, one baptism, one God and Father of all who is above all, and through all, and in you all."

And hence we find that *schismatics*, (Gr. *σχίσμα, a split*) that is, those who cause divisions in the Church of Christ, are every-where denounced in the Scriptures as carnal and unregenerate men. See, for instance, 1 Cor. iii, 1–4; Gal. v, 19–21; Jude 19, etc.

Meetings of consultation and conference.

XII. *That those who love and fear the Lord, and especially the officers of the Churches, should often meet and confer together on all the wants and interests of the Kingdom.* If it is essential to the growth of a single congregation that her Elders, Deacons, and other prudent and influential members shall often meet and confer with each other as to the best ways and means of supplying her wants, why may not this be, to some extent, equally true of all the Churches in a given district? It will not do to say that in all such deliberative assemblies there is danger of being misled by the unhallowed ambition of proud, vain, selfish, and angodly men. This may be true even of the presbytery of a single Church. The power to do good implies, of course, the power to do evil. And hence, if the principle of the objection is right and valid, we should all, like the foolish servant, bury our talents in the Earth, and simply do nothing, lest, perchance, we should be inclined to do evil.

But this, of course, proves too much for any and every one who longs for the increase and prosperity of Zion. Christianity is a power, and its influence must be aggressive. We dare not, if we would, avoid doing every thing that we can, individually, socially, and collectively, for the edification of the Church and the salvation of the world. The path of duty is here, as in every other case, the path of safety. Let every man be taught, as he should, to tremble at the Word of the Lord; let all Christians make it, in all cases, the man of their counsel; let them act in harmony with its precepts in their families, in their respective congregations, and in the assembly met for the purpose of considering the wants of the Churches in any given district, state, or territory, and then all will be well. Their own hearts will then be filled with love to God, and with an ardent sympathy for our race, while the world will look on and exclaim, "Behold how good and how pleasant it is for brethren to dwell together in unity."

PART V.

FORTUNES AND DESTINY OF THE CHURCH.

Trials and afflictions of the Church during the Dark Ages.

THE Church has passed through many days of adversity.* Foes without and enemies within have plotted her destruction; and at times the Gates of Hades seemed to have almost prevailed against her. The Dragon drove her into the wilderness: the Beast followed her with persecutions; and the False Prophet, animated with the malice and cunning of Satan, endeavored to blot out her very name and memory from the face of the Earth. The sun of her glory went down; and for more than one thousand years darkness, superstition, and idolatry, brooded over the face of this sin-cursed world.

Mysterious character of these events.

This is one of the most singular of all the moral phenomena in the government of the universe. That He who created all things, who supports all things, and who does what is pleasing in his sight in Heaven and among the inhabitants of the Earth, should permit the combined powers of darkness to gain even an apparent temporary advantage over the Church—an institution of his own appointment, and designed for the most benevolent of all purposes—is a problem too profound for all who have not been well instructed in the principles of the Divine government;

* For an account of her past trials and sufferings see the Ecclesiastical Histories of Neander, Mosheim, Gieseler, and Schaff.

and hence, this has been a standing objection with a class of skeptics for the last fifteen hundred years. They have never thoroughly studied the philosophy of the spiritual universe; they do not properly comprehend the laws and principles of the Divine administration; their minds have been molded in the grosser materials and false philosophies of the world. They have studied much more carefully the policy of Nebuchadnezzar, Alexander, Cæsar, and Tamerlane, than the wisdom of Him who has ever regarded with profound respect the *voluntary principle* of both men and angels.

Skeptical objection to this part of God's administration.

But it is not our design at present to philosophize. Facts are sufficient for our present purpose. To those who urge the past weakness, misfortunes, and inefficiency of the Church as an argument against Christianity, it is enough to say that they have made their discovery too late. All this was known to Christ, and made known by him to his disciples more than eighteen hundred years ago. See Matt. x, 16–39; xxiv, 9–13; Luke xii, 49–53; xxi, 12–18; John xv, 20; xvi, 2, etc. Paul also predicted that there would be a great apostasy from the truth, 2 Thess. ii. And John, in his Apocalyptic vision, saw the Church under the symbol of a forsaken and disconsolate woman, flying into the wilderness to escape from the persecutions of the great Red Dragon, animated and excited by that evil spirit which has ever worked in the hearts of the children of disobedience, Rev. xii. This, then, is no new discovery of infidels. It is one of the revelations of that Spirit which comprehends all things from the beginning.

Reply to this objection.

But there is a brighter view reflected on and from the same prophetic canvas. The same Spirit which so graphically described the misfortunes of the Church has also, in like manner, revealed to us her future glories. Of this all the Prophets and Apostles are witnesses. It is one of the favorite themes of the eloquent and evangelical Isaiah: see, for instance, the sixtieth chapter of his prophecies. And through his servant Jeremiah the Lord says to his Church: "I will restore health to thee, and I will heal thee of thy wounds, saith the Lord; because they called thee an outcast, saying, "This is Zion, which no man seeketh after." See Jer. xxx, 10–17.*

Revelations concerning the future prosperity of the Church.

The testimony of John, the beloved disciple, is also very clear and satisfactory on this point. No one who has carefully studied the Apocalypse can any longer entertain a doubt on this subject. The solemn and sublime scenes of this wonderful book bring us down three times to the glorious period of which we now speak. The seven vials and the seven trumpets respect chiefly the political events of the world; in which, however, the interests of the Church were very deeply involved. The last trumpet, like the two preceding, was a woe to the inhabitants of the Earth; but it was full of blessings to the citizens of Christ's Kingdom; for when the seventh angel sounded, "there were great voices in heaven, saying, The kingdoms of this world are become the kingdoms of our Lord and of his Christ; and he shall reign forever and ever. And the four and twenty Elders who sat before God on their thrones fell on their faces and worshiped God, saying, We give thee thanks, Lord God Almighty, who art, and wast, and art to come, because thou hast taken to thee thy great power and has reigned.

* In this passage there is a double reference, first to the type, and then to the antitype

And the nations were angry, and thy wrath is come, and the time of the dead that they should be judged, and that thou shouldest give reward to thy servants the Prophets, and to the saints, and them that fear thy name, small and great; and shouldest destroy them who destroy the Earth." Rev. xi, 15–18.

The second series of symbols is that of the symbolic monsters described in chapters twelfth, thirteenth, and fourteenth. It reveals to us still more clearly than the first series, the awful calamities of the saints of the Most High. But in the sequel we see the Lamb standing on Mount Zion, and with him a hundred and forty-four thousand, having God's name written in their foreheads, and singing a new song before the throne; while their persecutors are cast into the wine-press of the wrath of God.

The third series refers exclusively to God's judgments on the enemies of the Church. And hence, while the seven angels were preparing to pour out the bitter contents of the seven golden vials on the Earth, those who had gotten the victory over the Beast, and over his image, and over the number of his name, stood on a sea of glass, having the harps of God; and in anticipation of their glorious deliverance, they sang the song of Moses, the servant of God, and the song of the Lamb, saying, "Great and marvelous are thy works, Lord God Almighty; just and true are thy ways, thou King of saints. Who would not fear thee, O Lord, and glorify thy name, for thou only art holy; for all nations shall come and worship before thee; for thy judgments are made manifest." Rev. xv, 1–4.

But it is only by going somewhat into details that we can understand this matter aright. And as some knowledge of it is essential to our plan and purpose, we will bring our discussion of the scheme and economy of redemption to a close by considering, very briefly, in their probable chronological order, the main and leading events connected with the future developments and final triumphs of the Church. These, after much reflection on the whole subject, I am inclined to think will take place as follows:

Main events connected with the future progress and final triumphs of the Church.

I. *Fall of the Turkish or Ottoman empire.* This seems to be pretty clearly indicated,

1. By the series of events recorded in the eleventh and twelfth chapters of Daniel. That the Turkish Sultan is the present king of the North (Daniel xi, 40–45) we have already proved, I hope to the satisfaction of the reader, in "*Reason and Revelation,*" pp. 174–177 And that all has been fulfilled which is said of him previous to the forty-fourth verse of the eleventh chapter, has also been shown in the same work, and in the same connection. And hence we may anticipate that what is recorded in the two following verses will soon occur. "But tidings out of the East and out of the North shall trouble him. Therefore he shall go with great fury to destroy, and utterly to make away many. And he shall plant the tabernacles of his palace (or his palace-like tabernacles) between the seas, in the glorious holy mountain; yet he shall come to his end, and none shall help him."

Evidence from the Book of Daniel.

In this passage we have, I think, clearly given the last struggles and final overthrow of the Turkish empire. France and England may continue to sustain her for a short time, but all the powers of western Europe can not do so very long. She must and she will come to her end very soon, and none shall help her. When, how, and by what means this will take place is not so clearly revealed. But it is probable,

(1.) That Russia and some eastern power, most likely Persia, will be made the instruments of her overthrow. It has long been the fear of the Turks and the growing expectation of the Greeks that Russia will one day put an end to the Ottoman empire. These impressions have been strengthened by the events of more than two hundred and fifty years. Ever since the reign of Peter the Great Russia has been encroaching on the limits of Turkey, and all the world now knows that Constantinople would very soon be tributary to St. Petersburg were it not for the combined influence of England and France. But these western powers can not always serve as her guardians. The events of another year may change their policy in relation to her, and then tidings out of the North and East may very soon trouble her.

(2.) That the last great and decisive conflict, resulting in the complete overthrow of the Ottoman empire, will take place in the hill country of Judea, between the Dead Sea and the Mediterranean. "He shall plant his palace-like tabernacle between the seas, *in the glorious holy mountain*." In the forty-first verse of the same chapter the appellation "*glorious land*" is applied to the land of Canaan, and in other passages it is called "*the holy land*," "*the pleasant land*," "*the goodly heritage*," "*the glory of all lands*," etc., to distinguish it from the idolatrous territory of the Gentiles. It is, therefore, quite probable that this "glorious holy mountain" is the mount of Olives, Calvary, or some other sacred elevation near Jerusalem.

2. By the vision of the Apostle John, Rev. xvi, 12 "And the sixth angel poured out his vial on the great river Euphrates; and the water

Evidence from the Apocalypse

thereof was dried up that the way of the Kings of the East might be prepared." The most eminent commentators are, I think, generally agreed that the pouring out of the seven vials of the wrath of God on the Earth is symbolical of his righteous judgments on all the enemies of the Church, that the first five have already been poured out, and that the pouring out of the sixth has reference to the final ruin of the Ottoman empire, an event which can not, therefore, be very remote. Indeed, the signs of the eastern world would seem to indicate that we may reasonably anticipate the fulfillment of this prophecy at almost any time.

II. *A series of events involving great public embarrassments, most likely in relation to the division of the Ottoman dominions, and particularly in relation to the allotment of Palestine.* "And at that time shall Michael stand up, the great prince who standeth for the children of thy people; and there shall be a time of trouble, such as never was since there was a nation even to that same time; and at that time thy people shall be delivered, every one that shall be found written in the book." Daniel xii, 1.

Evidence from Prophecy.

It seems, then, from this, in connection with the previous section, that the fall of Turkey will be the first of a series of events that will cause very great trouble and excitement in the eastern world. And this, indeed, we might very readily anticipate, even without the aid and light of prophecy. The long-established policy of nearly all the great powers of the civilized world renders it highly probable that such will be the issue of events when the Ottoman empire shall fall to rise no more. If England and France would spend so much as they have recently done to

Evidence from the relations and established policy of European nations.

prevent the court of St. Petersburg from infringing on the borders of the Sultan, not on account of any sympathy that they have for the Turks or their respect for the rights of man, but simply for the purpose of preserving the balance of power among the nations of Europe by holding in check the ambition and avarice of Russia, what sacrifice would not they and other rival powers make to prevent Russia and Persia, or any other two kingdoms, from taking and appropriating to themselves the wealth of a fallen empire? If it is still a sound maxim that "Wherever the carcass is, there will the eagles be gathered together," what a tremendous conflict of nations may we reasonably anticipate in any attempt that may be made to divide and appropriate the spoils of Turkey! England, France, Germany, Austria, Prussia, Russia, Greece, Persia, Egypt, and the scattered Tribes of Israel will probably all be there to urge their respective claims, and to serve as umpires in the great controversy.

Guardianship of Michael.

But at that time Michael will again stand up in behalf of Israel. For many generations he was their prince and national guardian. Daniel x, 21. Under Jehovah, he seems to have been employed to lead them out of the land of Egypt and out of the house of bondage; to conduct them through the Red Sea and the dreary deserts of Arabia; to lead their armies to victories in Canaan, and to comfort them in their afflictions in Babylon; to move Darius to promote Daniel, and to stir up Cyrus to rebuild the temple; to accompany their emancipated hosts in their return from captivity; and for many years to preside over their interests in Palestine. Compare Exodus xxiii, 20–25; xxxii, 34; Numbers xx, 16; Joshua v. 13–15; Isaiah lxiii, 9; Daniel x, 21, and xii, 1. But the cup of their iniquity was at length filled to overflowing; the Spirit of God was grieved by their obstinacy and repeated acts of rebellion; Jerusalem was encompassed with armies; and soon after, if Josephus is worthy of credit, a voice—it may have been of this same guardian angel and his associates—was heard in the Temple saying, "LET US REMOVE HENCE." *Jewish War*, Book VI, chapter v. From that time Jerusalem has been trodden down by the Romans, the Persians, the Saracens, the Seljukians, the Mamelukes, and the Ottomans, and the Jews themselves have wandered as sheep without a shepherd. The predictions of Moses concerning this remarkable people have been most particularly fulfilled. They have been scattered among all people, from the one end of the Earth even to the other; they have found no ease nor rest, but have been oppressed and crushed always and every-where; they have been left few in number among the heathen; they have pined away in their iniquity in their enemies' land; and they have become an astonishment, a proverb, and a by-word among all nations.* Deut. xxviii.

Result of the controversy with regard to Palestine.

But the times of the Gentiles will soon be fulfilled. Luke xxi, 24. The Ottoman scepter is about to be broken. Michael will again stand up in behalf of Israel, "*and at that time shall be delivered every one that shall be found written in the book.*" Every Israelite on Earth who, like his fathers in the time of Ezra, can trace his genealogy to the stock of Abraham

* On this one chapter of fulfilled prophecy we might very safely rest the question touching the Divine authenticity of the whole Bible. No honest man can consistently read this chapter in the light of history and then refuse to believe that Moses wrote these words as he was moved by the Holy Spirit. But, if Moses was inspired, so also were all the other writers of the Old and New Testaments inspired. Of this there can be no reasonable doubt. The Bible is, like the Solar System, a unit. It must all stand or fall together.

will then be emancipated. And whatever disposition may be made of the other provinces of the fallen Sultan, Palestine will be again restored to the Tribes of Israel for an everlasting possession.

III. *Revival of the Israelites, and their return to Palestine.* "And many of them that sleep in the dust of the Earth shall awake; some to everlasting life, and some to shame and everlasting contempt." Daniel xii, 2.

Evidence from Daniel.

In all our attempts to interpret the Bible it is very important to discriminate between what is literal and what is figurative. The whole doctrine of transubstantiation is based on a misconception of a single term, and that, too, one of the smallest words in our vernacular: "This IS my body." The question to be determined is simply this Does the copula *is* express the relation of identity, or merely that of analogy between the subject and the predicate of this proposition? Is it used in a literal or in a metaphorical sense? The Roman Catholic maintains the former, and hence infers that the bread and wine in the Lord's Supper are transmuted into the body, blood, soul, and Divinity of our Lord and Savior Jesus Christ!

Importance of discriminating between what is literal and figurative.

Similar to this, I humbly conceive, is the error of those who refer the prophetic words at the head of this section to the final resurrection of the dead. Their interpretation is, in the main, too literal. It is, I think, inconsistent with the context for several reasons:

Query as to the meaning of this prediction.

1. In the final and literal resurrection the bodies of *all* will be raised. John v, 28, 29. But in the case to which the angel here refers only *many* of them that sleep in the dust shall awake.

2. There is, in several respects, a want of chronological harmony between the revival here described and the final resurrection.

(1.) The former must take place very soon, probably in about twenty-four years from this time. Thousands of the present generation may yet live to witness it. But the latter is an event that is yet far distant. At least a thousand years of peace and plenty shall intervene before all that are in their graves shall hear the voice of Jesus and come forth. All this will, I hope, appear more evident in the sequel.

(2.) After the revival here described the work of conversion will still go on. Some of these Israelites will, after their own resurrection, turn many to righteousness. Compare x, 14, and xii, 3. But after the literal resurrection of the dead there will be no more preaching, no more exhortation, no more calling on sinners to repent, no more conversion to God. See 1 Thess. iv, 15–17, and 2 Thess. i, 6–10, etc.

(3.) The partial and figurative resurrection of which the angel here speaks will take place at the end of three and a half years of prophetic time, when God shall have accomplished his purpose in scattering the power of the holy people. Daniel xii, 5–7. But the angel afterward defines two other periods of time which, if reckoned from the same chronological epoch as the first, which is most probable, will terminate, the one thirty and the other seventy-five years later.* Daniel xii, 11, 12.

The three periods spoken of in the twelfth chapter of Daniel.

* In the eleventh verse of this same chapter the taking away of the *Daily* in Jerusalem is given as the terminus from which it seems probable that all these periods are to be reckoned. This was first taken away in a typical sense, by the Romans, in A. D. 70, and in its true and proper antitypical sense by the Saracens, in A. D. 632; this, at least, was the year in which they

From these premises, then, we conclude that the words under consideration have no reference to the final resurrection, but simply *to the general revival of the oppressed Israelites in the lands of their dispersion, and to their restoration to Palestine through the agency and superior diplomacy of their guardian angel.*

Conclusion.

For the proof of this we rely chiefly on the following parallel passage from Ezekiel. The Prophet says: "The hand of the Lord was upon me, and carried me out in the Spirit of the Lord, and set me down in the midst of the valley which was full of bones. And he caused me to pass by them round about: and behold! there were very many in the open valley; and lo! they were very dry. And he said unto me, Son of man, can these bones live? And I answered, O Lord God, thou knowest. And he said unto me, Prophesy upon these bones, and say unto them, O ye dry bones, hear the word of the Lord. Thus saith the Lord God unto these bones: Behold! I will cause breath to enter into you, and ye shall live: and I will lay sinews upon you, and will bring up flesh upon you, and cover you with skin, and put breath in you, and ye shall live; and ye shall know that I am the Lord. So I prophesied as I was commanded; and as I prophesied there was a noise, and behold! a shaking, and the bones came together, bone to its bone. And when I beheld, lo! the sinews and the flesh came up upon them, and the skin

Corroborating evidence from Ezekiel.

commenced their conquests in Palestine. *Gibbon*, Vol. vi, pp. 402–407. If, then, to A. D. 632 we add, according to the year-day theory, 1260, 1290, and 1335 years we have given 1892, 1922, and 1967 as three important epochs in the future history of the Israelites. And hence it is probable that the first of these refers to the time of their return to Palestine, the second to their conversion to Christ, and the third to the conversion of the world through their agency.

covered them above; but there was no breath in them. Then said he unto me, Prophesy unto the wind; prophesy son of man, and say to the wind: Thus saith the Lord God: Come from the four winds, O breath, and breathe upon these slain, that they may live. So I prophesied as he commanded me, and the breath came into them; and they lived and stood up upon their feet; an exceeding great army." Ezekiel xxxvii, 1–10.

Had no explanation been given of this vision, how very few persons would have ever understood it! Most commentators would, no doubt, have regarded it as a symbolical representation of the final resurrection. But, fortunately for us, all uncertainty as to its true meaning and application has been removed; for, in explanation of it, the Lord himself immediately adds: "*These bones are the whole house of Israel.* Behold, they say, Our bones are dried and our hope is lost; we are cut off for our part. Therefore prophesy, and say unto them: *I will open your graves, and cause you to come up out of your graves, and bring you into the land of Israel.* And ye shall know that I am the Lord, when I have opened your graves, O my people, and brought you up out of your graves. And I will put my Spirit in you, and ye shall live; and I will place you in your own land. Then shall ye know that I, the Lord, have spoken it, and performed it, saith the Lord."

For further evidence on this point see Isaiah xi, 10–12; Jeremiah xxiii, 3–8; Ezekiel xxxvi, etc.

IV. *Purpose of many nations to dispossess the restored Israelites.* After describing symbolically the fall of Turkey, John says: "I saw three unclean spirits, like frogs, come out of the mouth of the Dragon, and out of the mouth of the

Testimony of John the Apostle.

Beast, and out of the mouth of the False Proph
they are the spirits of demons (δαιμόνων) working m
which go forth to the kings of the Earth and of the
world, to gather them to the battle of that grea
of God Almighty." Rev. xvi, 13, 14.

This very obscure and enigmatical language of J
becomes much more luminous when compared with
more full and explicit revelations of Ezekiel on the sam
subject. In the thirty-sixth and seventh chapters, the Prophet speaks chiefly of the return of the Israelites to Palestine, with an occasional reference to their conversion; and in the first seven verses of the thirty-eighth chapter he describes the various belligerent nations that will invade Palestine with the view of resubduing it. These are Gog, or the host of Magog, Meshech, and Tubal; with whom will be associated Persia, Ethiopia, Lybia, Gomer, the house of Togarmah, and many other tribes. Magog, Meshech, and Tubal, were sons of Japheth; and, according to the most reliable accounts, their descendants occupied the countries North of the Caspian and Black Seas; the same that now compose a large portion of the Russian empire. And when we connect with this fact the testimony of the Prophet, given in the fifteenth verse of this same chapter, that this despotic power will come from the North, that is, from the North of Palestine, we can scarcely entertain a doubt that Gog, the leader of this immense host, is the Russian army, or perhaps the Autocrat himself.

Testimony o Ezekiel with respect to the allied nations.

And this certainly corresponds well with the parallel passage cited from Rev. xvi, 13. The Dragon of the twelfth chapter evidently represents the pagan Roman empire. But that empire fell; and in its place rose the ten-horned Beast. The Dragon of the sixteenth chapter *al* with that of the twelfth; but it to denote a government very *simi-* mpire. And, be it observed, that nust exist now, or at least rise to on; for the contents of the sixth ured out. From all of which it hat the Dragon of the sixteenth ı empire. No other government on mbles the ancient Roman. In extent ırst for glory, and a desire for conquest, ussia may well be compared with that of

ıssia will not be alone in this invasion and ıt conquest. According to John, the same kind ean spirit will animate, also, the Beast and the Prophet. And Ezekiel says that Persia, Ethiopia, ıa, Gomer, the house of Togarmah, etc., will be asso- ted with Gog. Here, again, therefore, these two in- pired witnesses agree perfectly in their testimony; for it is generally conceded that Gomer settled in Asia Minor, and that from Togarmah and other sons of Gomer have sprung most of the interior and western tribes of Europe; and hence the bands of Togarmah may be regarded as identical with the Beast, which evidently represents the Catholic powers of the same locality. And it is of course known to all that the Persians, Ethiopians, and Lybians are followers of the False Prophet.* We, therefore, infer, with a good degree of certainty, that this immense host of invaders will consist chiefly of Russians, Catholics, and Mahometans.

From the eighth to the seventeenth verse of this

* This title is, by the common consent of all Christendom, given to Ma- homet and his followers.

chapter, (Ezekiel xxxvii,) the Prophet describe cumstances of this invasion. These enemies of Israel will come from the North, riding upon horses, in immense numbers; so that as a cloud the cover the land. And there they will be met by mercha from Sheba, Dedan, and Tarshish, who will flock to th camp with the hope of enriching themselves with th spoils of victory. But the Jews will take them captive, whose captives they were; and they shall rule over their oppressors. Isa. xiv, 2. And all this, it is said, shall be in the latter days, after that the Israelites shall have been gathered out of all nations into the land of Canaan. Then will Gog conceive a mischievous purpose, and say: "I will go to them that are at rest; that dwell safely, all of them dwelling without walls, and having neither bars nor gates, to take a spoil and to take a prey." This is the purpose of Gog; but the purpose of Jehovah is very different. "I will bring thee against my land," says the King of Israel, "that the heathen may know me, when I am sanctified in thee, O Gog, before their eyes."

V. *Utter overthrow of these hostile powers in the battle of Armageddon,* resulting in the general conversion of the Israelites.* "And they (the unclean spirits) gathered them (the kings of the Earth) together, into a place called in the Hebrew tongue Armageddon." Rev. xvi, 16.

Here again the words of John will be best understood by comparing them with the fuller and more explicit account which is given of the same great battle by Ezekiel. In the following paragraph,

Destruction of the invaders.

* Armageddon, or more properly Harmageddon, from הַר, *a mountain*, and מְגִדּוֹ, *Megiddo*, was the name of a hill near to which good king Josiah was slain in battle with Pharaoh Necho, 2 Chron. xxxv, 20–25. And hence the name is used metaphorically, like Marathon, Arbela, or Waterloo, for any decisive battle-field, or place of great mourning. See Zech. xii, 11.

8, to xxxix, 20, inclusive, the
efeat and massacre of these in-
ription is awfully animated and
God is kindled, and even all the
em to sympathize with their Cre-
ainst the invading foe: the Earth
ns fall, the pestilence rages; and
rain, hail, fire, and brimstone, are
e devoted multitudes. Every man's
d against his fellow; and of that immense
ered out of nearly all the principal nations of
e, Asia, and Africa, five-sixths fall down slain on
mountains of Israel.

Consequences of this victory.

The consequences of this victory are given in the remainder of the thirty-ninth chapter. Some of these have reference to the Jews, and some to their enemies. It is said, in particular, that "All the heathen shall see my judgment, which I have executed; and my hand which I have laid upon them;" "and the heathen shall know that the house of Israel went into captivity for their iniquity, because they have trespassed against me;" "so the house of Israel shall know that I am the Lord their God, from that day and forward. Then shall they know that I am the Lord their God who caused them to be led into captivity among the heathen; but I have gathered them into their own land, and have left none of them any more there; neither will I hide my face any more from them, *for I have poured out my Spirit upon the house of Israel, saith the Lord God.*"

From these premises it is evident,

Inferences drawn from the data of this section.

1. That this prophecy relates to the future. The heathen do not yet so recognize the hand of God in the government of the world, the

Jews are still in captivity on account of their sins, God's face is still concealed from them, and his Spirit has not yet been poured out upon them.

2. That the change here described in the relations, condition, and circumstances of the Jews seems to imply nothing short of their general conversion to Christianity. For thus saith the Lord, "*The house of Israel shall know me from that day and forward.*" They now know him as Jehovah, and have ever done so since they became a nation. But this language evidently implies that they will then know him as he is more fully and more perfectly revealed in the New Testament, under the threefold personality of the Father, the Son, and the Holy Spirit.

Testimony of Joel and Zechariah.

The reader will find strong corroborating evidence of all this in the third chapter of Joel and the twelfth of Zechariah, both of which refer to the same occasion described in the thirty-eighth and ninth chapters of Ezekiel. But we have stronger testimony than that of either Ezekiel, Joel, or Zechariah. The language of all these writers is highly symbolical, and we may, therefore, often fail to comprehend the precise import and bearing of their predictions. But in Romans xi, 11–32, Paul, in his usual plain, didactic style, places the fact of Israel's conversion beyond all legitimate controversy. He first argues the possibility and the probability of their conversion to Christ from several considerations, such as the great influence that it would have for good on the rest of mankind, the fact that a part of them which he here compares to the first-fruits had already been received into the Christian Church, etc., and then he plainly and positively announces the fact that all the Israelites will yet be saved. "For I would not, brethren, that ye should be ignorant of

Testimony of Paul.

this mystery, lest ye (Gentiles) should be wise in your own conceits, that blindness in part is happened to Israel until the fullness of the Gentiles be come in; AND SO ALL ISRAEL SHALL BE SAVED: as it is written there shall come out of Zion the Deliverer and shall turn away ungodliness from Jacob; for this is my covenant unto them when I shall take away their sins. As concerning the Gospel, they are enemies for your sake; but as touching the election, they are beloved for the fathers' sake: for the gifts and calling of God are without repentance. For as ye (Gentiles) in times past have not believed God, yet have now obtained mercy through their (Israel's) unbelief; even so have these also not now believed, that through your mercy they also may obtain mercy."

Conclusion respecting the conversion of Israel.

This, then, I think, is entirely conclusive. The word *Israel* in this connection evidently refers to the seed of Abraham according to the flesh, and the word *all* is used in the sense of the *greater part*, just as it is in many other parts of Scripture. And hence there can be no doubt that the time will come when the Jews, as a people, will be converted to Christ. The precise time of this important event is, of course, somewhat uncertain, but I am inclined to the opinion that this will all be fulfilled about A. D. 1922.

"Then, 'neath the fig-tree and the vine,
Shall Judah's daughters peaceful rest,
And gray-haired fathers safe recline
On sacred Calvary's hoary breast.

Those tuneful harps that hung so long
Upon the weeping willow's stem
Shall swell again old Zion's songs
Within thy walls, Jerusalem."

VI. *Destruction of Popery, Mahometanism, and other antichristian powers and combinations.* "And the seventh angel poured out his vial into the air; and there came a great voice out of the temple of Heaven from the throne, saying, IT IS DONE. And there were voices, and thunders, and lightning; and there was a great earthquake, such as has not been since men were upon the Earth, so mighty an earthquake and so great. And the great city was divided into three parts; and the cities of the nations fell; and great Babylon came into remembrance before God, to give unto her the cup of the wine of the fierceness of his wrath. And every island fled away, and the mountains were not found. And there fell upon men a great hail out of heaven, every stone about the weight of a talent: and men blasphemed God because of the plague of the hail; for the plague thereof was exceeding great." Rev. xvi, 17–21.

Effects following the pouring out of the seventh vial.

We have in these impressive words of the Apostle an awful presage of the speedy judgments of God on all the surviving enemies of his Church. She is now divinely authorized to bear the olive branch to all the nations. Those that regard her warnings, and that live in harmony with her laws and institutions, will still flourish as the palm tree; they will ever grow like the cedars of Lebanon. But woe to that nation that will not yield to the moral power and influence of the Church of the Living God. Its doom is sealed; its destiny is fixed. For says the Lord by Isaiah, in addressing his Church, "THE NATION AND KINGDOM THAT WILL NOT SERVE THEE SHALL PERISH: YEA, THOSE NATIONS SHALL BE UTTERLY WASTED." Isaiah lx, 12. The Gospel is to kindreds, and tongues, and sects, and nations, as it is to individuals, a savor of life unto life or of death unto death. It either kills or cures. It is the ax that is even now laid at the root of every tree in Christendom

God's Decree concerning all the enemies of the Church.

and every one which does not speedily bring forth good fruit must soon be cut down and cast into the fire.

Doom of mystic Babylon, the Beast, and the False Prophet.

Soon after the battle of Armageddon the seventh vial of the wrath of God will be poured out into the air, and then will follow a series of revolutions that will shake the political as well as the religious world, to its very center. During these convulsions "the Prince of the power of the air, the spirit that now worketh in the children of disobedience," will no doubt himself be greatly discomfited, and all his chief human organizations and fortifications will be totally destroyed. Babylon the Great, the mother of harlots, will sink *with violence*, to rise no more, (Rev. xviii, 21,) and the Beast and the False Prophet will both be cast *alive* into the lake of fire burning with brimstone. Rev. xix, 20.

It is all folly, then, to suppose that these antichristian powers can ever be reformed. No doubt there are still in them many individuals who are, or who may be, converted to Christ; and to all such the voice of warning has already gone forth: "Come out of her, my people, that ye be not partakers of her sins, and that ye receive not of her plagues." Rev. xviii, 4. This cry must yet be heard a little longer in these devoted kingdoms, and then will the end come.

Testimony of Daniel and Paul.

VII. *Conversion of the world by the Israelites.* "They that be wise shall shine as the brightness of the firmament; and they that turn many to righteousness, as the stars, forever and ever." Daniel xii, 3. The angel refers here exclusively to the Israelites; to those who are of the seed of Abraham according to the flesh. Daniel x, 14. And, again, Paul says concerning them: "If the fall of them be the riches of the world, and the diminishing of them the riches of the Gentiles, *how much more their fullness?* (That is, how much more will their general conversion be the riches of the world?) For I speak to you Gentiles, inasmuch as I am the Apostle of the Gentiles. I magnify my office, if by any means I may provoke to emulation them who are my flesh, and might save some of them. For if the casting away of them (as the people in covenant with God) be the reconciling of the world, what shall the receiving of them (into the Church of Christ) be, but A LIFE (or a resurrection of the whole Gentile world) FROM THE DEAD?" Rom. xi, 12–15.

Character of the life and resurrection spoken of by Paul in Romans xi, 15.

The Apostle here evidently speaks of a *spiritual* resurrection. The Jews will of course have no agency in raising the *bodies* of men from their graves. This is the exclusive work of Him who has said: "I am the resurrection." But that the Israelites, when converted to Christ, will have a powerful influence *in reviving the souls of men*, may be inferred from several considerations.

First element that will give efficiency to the preaching of the converted Israelites.

1. *Their conversion will most likely be a complete restoration of primitive Christianity.* The Gospel was corrupted at a very early period. Even in the days of the Apostles the spirit of schism and discord was at work in many of the Churches. One said I am of Paul; another, I am of Apollos; and another, I am of Cephas. Some attempted to combine with the doctrine of Christ the spiritual vagaries of a Plato; others labored to introduce the metaphysical abstractions of an Aristotle; while others again sought to make out a perfect system of religion and morality, by uniting the precepts of the Gospel with the licentious tenets of Epicurus, or with some other system of Jewish or Gentile philosophy. Many isms were the

natural and legitimate offspring of these vain attempts to improve what God had already made perfect; and it is a well-attested historical fact that, through the strife of debate, the abuse of human authority, and the vain pretensions of erring man, Christianity was almost wholly excluded from the popular theologies of the Middle Ages. And though Luther, Calvin, Arminius, Wesley, and a host of other great reformers, have done much to restore the pure Gospel, it is, nevertheless, true that all the Protestant parties are still too much devoted to the mere politics and metaphysics of Christianity. These abstractions are but poor nourishment for the hungry soul; they are miserable substitutes for the bread and the water of eternal life. And hence the comparative failure of nearly all modern missionary efforts to convert the world.

But it is not probable that the Jews will ever be converted to any mere abstract theory of Christianity, whether Papal or Protestant. They will never give up the traditions of their own Rabbis for any of the uninspired creeds of modern Christendom. It is Christ himself, the chief among the ten thousands, and the one altogether lovely, that will woo their hearts and bring their whole nature of body, soul, and spirit, under subjection to the will of God. It is the heart-felt consciousness that they have despised, crucified, and so long rejected the Lord of life and glory, that will work in them that godly sorrow described by Zechariah xii, 9–14; and that will induce them to cry out, like Saul of Tarsus, "Lord, what wilt thou have us to do?"

Like the primitive Christians, then, these new converts will go every-where preaching the Word. The spirit of the Apostles, which has for ages slumbered under the secularized and corrupted forms of Christianity, will be revived in these new heralds of the Cross. They will become the most zealous and devoted of all missionaries; and, with the influences of a pure Gospel in their heads and in their hearts, and stimulated by a thousand exciting reminiscences, who can estimate the changes and revolutions which these ransomed millions of our race may soon effect in the world? Even under the most unfavorable circumstances their influence must be immense. The Gospel has not lost a single element of its power. God, and Christ, and the Holy Spirit, and holy angels desire as much as ever the salvation of the world. And hence it would seem that the only thing which is now wanting to bind Satan and to fill the whole world with the glory of Jehovah, is just such a band of missionaries as the Jews are likely to become when the vail shall be taken away from their hearts.

Other elements of their success.

2. *But besides the great zeal of the Jews, and the restoration of the pure Gospel, there are some other matters connected with their present relations and the advanced state of the arts and sciences which, under God, will greatly serve to promote the object of their mission.* Nothing happens by chance in the moral changes and phases of society. He who made the universe still governs it; and to govern the whole, he must first take care of the parts: to regulate suns and systems he must first weigh and adjust their atoms; and in order to feed, clothe, and preserve man, he must number the hairs of his head, and regulate every pulsation of his heart. This he has always done. The history of the world is one continued illustration of his providential adaptation of means to the accomplishment of special ends. To save our race from utter ruin an ark was prepared. To preserve Jacob and his family, and to illustrate, at the same time, some of the most profound

Means always provided with reference to special ends.

principles of the scheme and economy of redemption, Joseph was born, loved, hated, sold into Egypt, imprisoned, and made governor over all the land. To restore the Israelites to Canaan, and to complete the shadow of which the Gospel is the substance, Moses was born, laid in an ark of bulrushes, adopted by Pharaoh's daughter, instructed in all the wisdom of the Egyptians, and then divinely commissioned and qualified to lead his brethren out of the house of bondage to the Land of Promise. And to prepare the world for the advent of the Messiah the folly of all human wisdom was exposed, the temple of Janus was closed, and an expectation was excited among all nations that some great reformer was about to appear,

> "Whose genial power would whelm Earth's iron race,
> And plant once more the golden in its place."

And hence it seems that God does nothing in vain; and that the feeblest instrumentalities for good are always provided with reference to some special end.

These things, then, being promised, we may now very properly ask, Why have the Jews been scattered among all the nations? Why, amidst the wreck of thrones and the fall of empires, have they always been preserved as a distinct people? Why do they now speak all the languages and dialects of this babbling Earth? What mean those important discoveries that distinguish the nineteenth from all preceding centuries? For what purpose has the telegraph been invented, the power of steam applied to machinery and the resources of Mathematics exhausted in the advancement of the physical sciences and the improvements of their kindred arts? Why is so much now said and done to promote the principles of civil and religious

Vast accumulation of means in the nineteenth century.

liberty among all nations? Why has education advanced so rapidly, and why have the Holy Scriptures been multiplied more than tenfold during the last fifty years?

Such an accumulation of means certainly seems to indicate that God is about to accomplish *some* great purpose. And what can this be but the conversion of the world? Men of secularized minds and limited conceptions may see nothing very remarkable in the fortunes of the Jews, and to such persons some slight improvements in commerce or in the science of agriculture may seem to be the grand ultimatum of all discovery. But the Bible reveals to us a very different philosophy. It teaches us that the kingdoms of this world are yet to become the kingdoms of our Lord and of his Anointed, that the increase and perfection of the Church is the end of all things earthly, and that every thing else pertaining to this world is a mere circumstance. And hence it is but reasonable to infer that the Israelites have been preserved for this very purpose, that they have been widely dispersed in order that they may acquire a knowledge of all the languages of the world, and that after their conversion they may return and announce to each nation, in its own vernacular, the glorious facts, precepts, and promises of the Gospel, and that to this same end may be referred the present wonderful progress in science and the astonishing improvements in all the arts of civilization.

End and object of all this.

This induction of facts might, of course, be very greatly extended. But I think enough has been said to illustrate the Apostle's meaning, and to show that he uses no undue exaggeration when he compares the effect of the influence which the converted Jews will exert over the unconverted portion of the Gentile world to a resurrection from the dead.

This subject may be further illustrated by Ezekiel's vision of the holy waters. Ezekiel xlvii, 1–12. Concerning which be it observed,

Scope of Ezekiel's Vision of the holy waters.

1. That they are evidently symbolical of the stream of Gospel light and influence which will go forth from the Church of the redeemed Israelites for the conversion of the world. No such river now flows from Mount Moriah. But when the symbolical Temple of converted Jews shall be erected on its summit, a stream of salvation will again flow from Jerusalem which will cause the wilderness and the solitary parts of the Earth to be made glad, and the very deserts to rejoice and blossom as the rose.

Proof that they are symbolical.

2. These waters greatly increase in depth and in breadth as they flow eastward. "And when the man who had the line in his hand went forth eastward, he measured a thousand cubits, and he brought me through the waters; and the waters were to the ankles. Again he measured a thousand cubits, and brought me through the waters; and the waters were to the knees. Again he measured a thousand, and brought me through the waters; and they were to the loins. Afterward he measured a thousand, and it was a river that I could not pass over; for the waters were risen, waters to swim in, a river that could not be passed over." xlvii, 3–5. The great and rapid increase of these waters very beautifully illustrates the speedy conversion of the whole Gentile world by these new missionaries of the Cross. The stream of their influence will be small at first, but it will become wider and wider, deeper and deeper, till it shall finally fill the whole world, and the knowledge of the Lord shall cover the earth as the waters cover the sea.

Their increase in volume.

3. The healing virtues of these waters are also very

remarkable. "And he said unto me, Son of man, hast thou seen this? Then he brought me and caused me to return to the brink of the river. Now when I had returned, behold at the bank of the river were very many trees on the one side and on the other. Then said he unto me, These waters issue out toward the East country, and go down into the desert, and go into the sea, (the Dead Sea;) which being brought into the sea, the waters shall be healed. And it shall come to pass, that every thing that liveth, which moveth, whithersoever the rivers shall come, shall live. And there shall be a very great multitude of fish, because these waters shall come thither: and they shall be healed; and every thing shall live whither the river cometh. And it shall come to pass, that the fishers shall stand upon it (the shore of the Dead Sea) from Engedi even unto Eneglaim; they shall be a place to spread forth nets; their fish shall be according to their kinds, as the fish of the great sea, (the Mediterranean,) exceeding many." Verses 6–10.

Their healing power.

This is a beautiful illustration of the sanctifying and soul-redeeming influences of the Gospel. The world is a sea—*a Dead Sea.* Mankind are all dead in trespasses and in sins. But a fountain has been opened in the house of David; a living stream has gone forth from the side of our Redeemer. It has purified the Sanctuary; it has cleansed the temple of God. But it can not be confined within the narrow limits of any one town, city, or continent. It is the remedy which God has provided to supply the wants of a fallen world, and hence he has made it as free as the air or the sunlight of heaven.

"Let the glad tidings reach the dead;
This river runs through death's dark shade;

Where'er it comes, this living spring
Gives life and health to every thing."

Evidence of some existing evil during the overflow of these waters.

4. "But the miry places thereof and the marshes thereof shall not be healed; they shall be given to salt." Verse 11. The meaning of these words is very obvious from the context. The influence of the Gospel will be felt and enjoyed under the whole heavens; it will cover the whole Earth as the waters cover the sea. But all parts of the Earth will not enjoy it equally. In some places the water will be so shallow and so mixed with clay that they will only produce mire. These localities will still, like the banks of the Dead Sea, remain unproductive. That is, some persons, and probably even some communities, will not receive the Gospel in the love of it. Like the ancient Pharisees and some modern professors of Christianity, they will still continue to make void the law of God by their traditions and their own inventions.

The particular forms of error to which the Prophet here refers we can not of course now determine with any degree of certainty. Some dregs of Popery may still continue to curse the world; or some new abominations, more in harmony with the then existing state of society, may spring up in those halcyon days of Gospel light and glory. But certain it is, that while the sanctifying and saving influence of the Gospel will be general, it will not be universal: while nations will beat their swords into plowshares and their spears into pruning-hooks, some persons will still continue to conceal, under the garment of the assassin, the revolver and the bowie-knife: while the wolf will dwell with the lamb, and the leopard with the kid, the growl of the hyena will still be heard in some dark corner of the Earth: and while the world will be a temple filled with sweet incense from a thousand altars, the moral miasma of this sin-polluted Earth will ever continue to rise from a few remaining bogs and quagmires. The saint and the sinner will, therefore, live together during even the Golden Age of Christianity. The tares and the wheat will grow together in the same field till the time of the world's great harvest.

5. And, finally, many perennial and fruitful trees will line the banks of this river of life. "And by the river, upon the banks thereof, on this side and on that side, shall grow all trees for meat, whose leaf shall not fade, neither shall the fruit thereof be consumed: it shall bring forth new fruit according to its months, because their waters issued out of the Sanctuary. And the fruit thereof shall be for meat, and the leaf thereof shall be for medicine." Verse 12.

Significance and import of the *trees* on the banks of the river.

The river is symbolical, and, therefore, so are the trees which grow on its banks. They represent the means through which God supplies his people with spiritual food and medicine adapted to the wants of their immortal souls. The figure is evidently drawn from the Tree of Life, which was watered by the river of Eden. That tree was, for a time, the panacea of Heaven; those who ate of it had no need of a physician. The Apostle John uses the same beautiful imagery in describing the New Jerusalem, and the abundant supplies of God's grace and goodness to his redeemed people in a future state. He saw a river flowing from the throne of God: on each side of it he saw the Tree of Life, which bears twelve kinds of fruit, and yields its fruit every month; and the leaves of the tree are for the healing of the nations.

Such, then, is a brief symbolical representation of the great and manifold blessings that will abound to all nations when the Jews shall be converted to Christ and become missionaries of the Cross. When they become preachers of righteousness the world will soon become a temple of God's praise; and these new heralds of the Cross, having turned many to righteousness, will themselves shine as the stars forever and ever.

No cessation of Gentile labor.

In the mean time the evangelical labors of the Gentiles will, of course, be continued. Thank God, there is no monopoly in the work of saving the world from sin. While there is a soul to be redeemed it will be the privilege, not to say the duty, of every Christian to labor for its salvation; but, owing to circumstances, it would seem from such passages of Scripture as we have examined, that to the converted Jews will belong largely the honor of binding Satan and filling the whole Earth with the knowledge and glory of Jehovah.

The Vision of John concerning it.

VIII. *Millennial reign of the saints.* Of this we have the most particular account given in Rev. xx. 1–6: "And I saw," says John, "an angel come down from heaven, having the key of the bottomless pit and a great chain in his hand; and he laid hold on the Dragon, that Old Serpent, which is the Devil and Satan, and bound him a thousand years; and cast him into the bottomless pit, and shut him up and set a seal on him, that he should deceive the nations no more till the thousand years should be fulfilled. After that he must be loosed for a little season. And I saw thrones; and they sat on them; and judgment was given to them. And I saw the souls of them that were beheaded for the witness of Jesus, and for the word of God; and who had not worshiped the Beast, neither his image, neither had received his mark on their foreheads, nor in their hands; and they lived and reigned with Christ a thousand years; but the rest of the dead lived not again till the thousand years were finished. This is the first resurrection. Blessed and holy is he that hath part in the first resurrection: on such the second death hath no power; but they shall be priests of God and of Christ, and shall reign with him a thousand years."

Absurdity of interpreting all this literally.

When we say that this language is symbolical we simply affirm that it is similar to other parts of the Apocalypse. Very few persons, we presume, would insist on a strictly literal interpretation of this passage. That an angel, in the ordinary sense of this term, will ever descend from heaven, and literally lay hold on the Dragon, that Old Serpent, which is the Devil and Satan; that he will bind him with a literal chain of gold, silver, iron, brass, or any other kind of material; that he will literally cast him into the bottomless pit and lock him up, as a culprit is confined in a jail or penitentiary; that during the period of his imprisonment the souls of the martyrs and of those who had not worshiped the Beast and his image, will sit on literal thrones, and literally reign with Christ, while all the rest of the dead will slumber in their graves; and that at the expiration of one thousand years the literal chain will be literally taken off Satan, the doors of his prison opened, and he permitted thus to go out once more to deceive the nations—this we presume is rather too literal for almost any one. The Apocalypse is, by common consent, one of the most highly figurative and symbolical books ever written. The four Living Creatures, the twenty-four Elders, the Lamb in the midst of the throne, the little book in the right hand of Him who sat on it, the opening of the seven seals, the sounding of the seven trumpets, the Two Witnesses in sackcloth, the

Symbolical character of the Apocalypse illustrated.

woman clothed with the Sun, the great red Dragon, the ten-horned Beast that rose out of the sea, the two-horned Beast that rose out of the earth, the False Prophet, the pouring out of the seven vials, and the Harlot on many waters, are all as certainly symbols as were the patterns that were given to Moses in the mount.

What is implied in the binding of Satan.

We have no reason to think that the twentieth chapter is an exception to the general law of symbolic representation which characterizes all other parts of this wonderful book. Indeed, it is very difficult to conceive how Satan, who is a fallen *spirit*, could be bound with a material chain and confined in a material abyss of any kind. But he has always been a proper subject of moral restraints. In the case of Job, for instance, he could not go one hair's breadth beyond the permission of God. And since the coronation of the Messiah, and the new order and arrangement of all the powers of the moral universe under him, the chain of this arch-apostate has been very much contracted. Every Bible since published has served to limit the sphere of his influence. And when the knowledge of the Lord shall cover the whole Earth, as the waters cover the sea, then the *effect* will be as if he were bound with fetters of brass; as if he were cast into the bottomless pit, and as if the world were delivered from the tyranny of his iron scepter.

In what sense the souls of the martyrs will reign with Christ a thousand years.

And then the saints will rise and reign with Christ a thousand years. That is, I presume, the *effect* will be the same as if the spirits of the most pious of the ancient saints should return to the Earth, take possession of it, and reign over it for a thousand years. The resurrection is, I think, the same, *in part*, with that which is described by Paul in the eleventh chapter of the Romans, and which, as we have seen, will be brought about by the evangelical labors of the Jews, resulting in the conversion and spiritual resurrection of the whole Gentile world. The passage does not mean that the bodies of the ancient martyrs will then be raised from the dead, nor does it mean that even their identical spirits will then rise and be promoted to places of honor and distinction in the government of the world, but it means simply that persons of like spirit and character will then have the supremacy, and hold in their hands, under Christ, the reins of universal government.

Illustrations of the use of this figure.

This figure is very common, even in books that are far less symbolical than the Apocalypse. Isaiah, for instance, says, "Upon the land of my people shall come up thorns and briers; yea, upon all the houses of joy in the joyous city: because the palaces shall be forsaken; the multitude of the city shall be left; the forts and towers shall be for dens forever, a joy of wild asses, a pasture of flocks, *until the Spirit be poured upon* US *from on high,* and the wilderness be a fruitful field, and the fruitful field be counted for a forest. Then judgment shall dwell in the wilderness, and righteousness remain in the fruitful field: and the work of righteousness shall be peace; and the effect of righteousness, quietness and assurance forever: and my people shall dwell in a peaceable habitation, and in sure dwellings, and in quiet resting-places." Isaiah xxxii, 13–18. That this has reference to the future restoration of the Jews is evident from the context. And hence the pronoun *us* can include neither the prophet himself nor any of his contemporaries, except by analogy.

In like manner, Paul says to the Thessalonians, "The

Lord himself shall descend from heaven with a shout, with the voice of the archangel, and with the trump of God: and the dead in Christ shall rise first. Then *we* who are alive and remain shall be caught up together with them in the clouds to meet the Lord in the air." 1 Thess. iv, 16, 17. That the Apostle does not refer here to the generation then living is evident from his second letter to the same Church. It seems there were among the Thessalonians certain *literalists* who inferred from the words cited that the second advent of Christ, the resurrection of the dead, and the final judgment were just at hand. And hence they began to walk disorderly, neglecting their own temporal wants and the wants of their families. But in his second letter Paul corrected their mistake. "Let no man," he says, "deceive you by any means: for that day will not come, except there come a falling away first; and that man of sin be revealed the son of perdition." The phrase "*we who are alive*" must, therefore, refer to persons then unborn, but who would be of like character with Paul and his contemporary followers of Christ.

Still more direct and appropriate are the following words of the Lord by Malachi: "Behold I send you Elijah the prophet before the coming of the great and dreadful day of the Lord; and he shall turn the heart of the fathers to the children, and the heart of the children to their fathers, lest I come and smite the Earth with a curse." Mal. iv, 5, 6. From this promise many of the Jews inferred that Elijah himself would come in *propria persona;* but we find that Christ applied these words to John the Baptist, who came in the spirit and power of Elijah. Matthew xvii, 10–13.

From such examples, then, it is evident that by the

words, "*the souls of them that were beheaded for the witness of Jesus and for the word of God*," etc., John may simply mean those who shall bear the image and moral likeness of the ancient martyrs. And, in a book of symbols, this is by far the most rational conclusion. It would be very difficult to show why these words should be made an exception to the general style of the narrative. But it is quite evident, from this and many other passages of Scripture, that during the Millennium nearly all persons then living on Earth will greatly resemble the ancient martyrs in all the elements of their Christian character. Every thing will then be holiness to the Lord. There will be no apostasies from the truth; those who shall have a part in the first resurrection will also rise among the first to meet their Lord in the air, and so shall they ever be with the Lord.*

* It is well known that those who are now technically called *Second Adventists* rely chiefly on this passage in support of their peculiar tenets, the principal of which are as follows:

Tenets of the Second Adventists.

1. That at the beginning of the Millennium Christ will descend from Heaven and reign personally on Earth for a period of one thousand literal years.

2. That he will make Jerusalem the capital of his empire.

3. That the righteous dead will then be raised in immortal bodies, and assist Christ in the government of the world during the Millennium.

4. That at the beginning of this period the world will be subdued, not by the moral power of the Gospel, but by the personal presence and reign of Christ.

5. That at the close of the one thousand years the rest of the dead will be raised, the world judged, and the Kingdom given up to the Father. See Elliott on the Apocalypse, Lord on the Apocalypse, Bickerstith's Divine Warning, A. Bonar's Redemption Drawing Nigh, H. Bonar's Prophetical Landmarks, etc.

Objection to the hypothesis of the Second Adventists.

This hypothesis, though supported by many great and good men, is liable to sundry very grave objections, some of which seem to me to be wholly unanswerable. Of these I will state but one at present. After the most careful examination of this whole subject, I must confess that I am unable, without doing violence to the Scriptures, to separate the second personal coming of Christ

Duration of the Millennium.

With regard to the duration of the period denoted by the phrase "*a thousand years*," there are three, and only three conceivable hypotheses:

1. That these words are to be understood literally. This is the view of most of the Second Adventists.

2. That they denote, according to the year-day theory, a period of three hundred and sixty thousand years.

3. That they denote simply a long, indefinite period. This is most likely their true meaning.

John's account of this apostasy.

IX. *Postmillennial apostasy.* The most particular account given of this apostasy is contained in the following extract from the Apocalypse: "And when the thousand years are expired, Satan shall be loosed out of his prison; and shall go out to deceive the nations which are in the four quarters of the Earth, Gog and Magog, to gather them together to battle: the number of whom is as the sand of the sea. And they went up on the breadth of the Earth, and compassed the camp of the saints about, and the beloved city: and fire came down from God out of Heaven and devoured them. And the Devil that deceived them was cast into the lake of fire and brimstone, where the Beast and the False Prophet are, and shall be tormented day and night forever and ever." Rev. xx, 7–10.

What we may learn from this passage.

All this is, of course, highly symbolical, and care should, therefore, be taken not to press the analogies too far. But, from what is here recorded, it is evident,

from the final renovation of the Earth by fire, and the simultaneous judgment of both the righteous and the wicked. Let the reader consider carefully the following passages in their proper logical connection, and then let him draw his own conclusion from the premises: Matthew xiii, 30, 41–43; xvi, 27; xxv, 31–46; John v, 28, 29; Acts xvii, 31; Romans ii, 5–16; 1 Cor. xv, 51–54; 1 Thess. iv, 15–18; 2 Thess. i, 6–10; 2 Timothy iv, 1; 2 Peter iii, 7–10; and Rev. xx, 11–15

1. That *after* the Millennium there will be a very alarming and wide-spread departure from the truth.

2. That this will be brought about by the agency of Satan, who, having been freed in some measure from his previous restraints, will go out again to deceive the nations.

3. That this conflict between the enemies of the Church and the followers of Christ will be short and decisive.

4. But, nevertheless, that it will continue till God himself interposes, in a very sudden and unexpected manner, for the deliverance of his saints. And this will most likely be at the close of the present dispensation, for, from the following passages, it is evident that wickedness will abound in the Earth, even at the coming of Christ: "As it was in the days of Noah, so shall it be also in the days of the Son of man. They did eat, they drank, they were given in marriage, until the day that Noah entered into the ark, and the flood came and destroyed them all. Likewise also as it was in the days of Lot: they did eat, they drank, they bought, they sold, they planted, they builded; but the same day that Lot went out of Sodom, it rained fire and brimstone from Heaven, and destroyed them all. *Even thus it shall be when the Son of Man shall be revealed.*" Luke xvii, 26–30. See, also, Luke xviii, 8; 1 Thessalonians v, 2, 3; 2 Peter iii, 3, 4, etc.

X. *The second personal coming of Christ, and the events immediately connected therewith.* That Christ will come again in person is clearly proved by such passages as the following: "Ye men of Galilee, why stand ye gazing up into Heaven? This same Jesus, who is taken up from you into Heaven, will

Proof of Christ's second personal coming.

come in the same manner in which ye saw him go into Heaven" Acts i, 11. See, also, Matt. xxv, 31; 1 Thess. v, 16; 2 Thess. i, 6–10; 2 Tim. iv, 1; 2 Peter iii, 3–13; Jude 14, etc.

Other events connected with it.

With this will be associated sundry other events of intense interest, and which will most likely occur in the following order:

1. *The resurrection of the dead saints, and the simultaneous change of the living.* Thus Paul testifies in his first letter to the Thessalonians: "For this we say to you by the word of the Lord, that we who are alive and remain to the coming of the Lord, shall not anticipate them who are asleep. For the Lord himself will descend from Heaven with a shout, with the voice of the archangel, and with the trump of God; and the dead in Christ will rise first. Then we who are alive and remain will be caught up together with them in the clouds, to meet the Lord in the air; and so shall we ever be with the Lord." 1 Thess. iv, 15–17. And, again, the same Apostle says to the Corinthians: "Behold! I show you a mystery. We shall not all sleep; but we shall all be changed in a moment, in the twinkling of an eye, at the last trumpet; for the trumpet shall sound, and the dead shall be raised incorruptible, and we shall be changed. For this corruptible must put on incorruption; and this mortal must put on immortality. And when this corruptible shall have put on incorruption, and this mortal shall have put on immortality, then shall be brought to pass the saying that is written: Death is swallowed up in victory." 1 Cor. xv, 51–54.

2. *The destruction of the wicked, and the renovation of the Earth by fire.* This is very clearly proved by the following passages: "Seeing it is a righteous thing with

God to recompense tribulation to them that trouble you; and to you who are troubled rest with us when the Lord Jesus shall be revealed from Heaven with his mighty angels, in flaming fire, taking vengeance on them that know not God and that obey not the Gospel of our Lord Jesus Christ: who shall be punished with an everlasting destruction from the presence of the Lord and from the glory of his power, on that day when he shall come to be glorified in his saints, and to be admired in all them that believe." 2 Thess. i, 6–10. "The Lord is not slack concerning his promise, as some men count slackness, but is long-suffering toward us; not willing that any should perish, but that all should come to repentance. But the day of the Lord will come as a thief in the night; in which the Heavens shall pass away with a great noise, and the elements shall melt with fervent heat; the Earth also, and the works that are therein, shall be burned up. Seeing, then, that all these things shall be dissolved, what manner of persons ought ye to be in all holy conversation and godliness, looking for and hasting unto the coming of the day of God, wherein the Heavens being on fire, shall be dissolved, and the elements shall melt with fervent heat. Nevertheless we, according to his promise, look for new Heavens and a new Earth, wherein dwelleth righteousness." 2 Peter iii, 9–13.

3. *The resurrection of all the wicked out of the burning and melting Earth.* This is a matter of inference, and not of direct revelation. But from 2 Peter iii, 7, it is evident that one object for which the Earth will be set on fire is "*the perdition of ungodly men.*" And from Matt. xxv, 31–46, etc., it is equally plain that the wicked will all be judged *with* the righteous, according to their works. And hence it seems to follow, of necessity, that they will

all be literally baptized in the final conflagration; and that they will rise out of the lurid flames and appear before the great white throne, to give an account for the deeds done in their bodies.

4. *The final judgment of the whole human race: old and young, rich and poor, bond and free, male and female, saint and sinner.* "And I saw," says John, "a great white throne, and Him that sat on it, from whose face the Earth and the Heaven fled away; and there was found no place for them. And I saw the dead, small and great, stand before God; and the books were opened; and another book was opened, which is the Book of Life; and the dead were judged out of those things which were written in the books, according to their works. And the sea gave up the dead which were in it; and Death and Hades gave up the dead which were in them; and they were judged, every man according to his works." Rev. xx, 11–13.

5. *The final and eternal separation and allotment of the righteous and the wicked.* "These," says Christ, "shall go away into eternal punishment; but the righteous into eternal life." Matt. xxv, 46. God is a God of order. He has a place for every thing. Fish swim in the sea; birds fly in the air, and beasts roam on the Earth. So, when Dives died, he went to his own place; and so did Lazarus; and so will every other man, both at his death and at the judgment. When the great Judge says to the wicked, "Depart from me, ye cursed, into eternal fire, prepared for the Devil and his angels," their destiny will be forever fixed. He that is filthy then must be filthy still. Rev. xxii, 11. Nothing will remain for them but the piercings of that worm that will never die, and the torments of that fire that will never be quenched. And

when he says to the righteous, "Come ye blessed of my Father, inherit the kingdom prepared for you from the foundation of the world," their happiness will be complete; they can die no more, for they will be like the angels. Luke xx, 36. And whether they remain forever in the New Jerusalem, on the newly renovated Earth, or wing their way as messengers of love and mercy to worlds unknown, the same gracious hand that conducted them safely through their earthly pilgrimage will ever lead them to fountains of living waters, and wipe away all tears from their eyes. Rev. xxi, xxii.

Conservative influence of the Scheme of Redemption.

Thus will be consummated the ***work*** of human redemption; but the ***influence*** of the Scheme will be as enduring as the throne of God, and will, in all probability, be forever *felt* throughout his vast dominions as the great attractive and conservative power of the moral universe. Suns may grow dim with age, and the Heavens themselves may pass away as a scroll, but that time will never come when holy angels and the redeemed of Earth will cease to look with wonder and admiration into the history, philosophy, and conservative influence of the Scheme of Redemption, and to exclaim, with the great Apostle, in reference to it, "O! the depth of the riches, and of the wisdom, and of the knowledge of God! how unsearchable are his judgments, and his ways past finding out! For who hath known the mind of the Lord? or who hath been his counselor? or who hath first given to him and it shall be recompensed to him again? For from him, and through him, and to him, are all things. To him be the glory forever. Amen."

THE END.

INDEX.